Mentor of Generations

Reflections on Rabbi Joseph B. Soloveitchik

Mentor of Generations

Reflections on Rabbi Joseph B. Soloveitchik

Edited by
Zev Eleff

KTAV Publishing House, Inc.
Jersey City, NJ

Library of Congress Cataloging-in-Publication Data

Mentor of generations : reflections on Rabbi Joseph B. Soloveitchik / edited
by Zev Eleff.
  p. cm.
 ISBN 978-1-60280-011-3
 1. Soloveitchik, Joseph Dov--Anecdotes. 2. Rabbis--United
States--Anecdotes. 3. Jewish scholars--United States--Anecdotes. I. Eleff,
Zev.
 BM755.S6144M465 2008
 296.8'32092--dc22
 [B]

                                                        2007040217

                        Published by
                KTAV Publishing House, Inc.
                    930 Newark Avenue
                   Jersey City, NJ 07306
                  Email: bernie@ktav.com
                       www.ktav.com
                     (201) 963-9524
                   Fax (201) 963-0102

Table of Contents

The '60s: Mentor of Generations

The '70s: A Legacy of Many Perspectives

The '80s: An Aging Giant

Glossary   347

In memory of my beloved grandfather Jack Moss
My other hero
He began this book with me and now finishes it with me

And to Rabbi Yitzchak Korn
My mentor
As well as a student of the Rav

Z.E.

Preface

"And There Arose A New Generation That Did Not Know Joseph"
(Shemot 1:8)

Zev Eleff

The Torah sages of yesteryear leave behind writings to be cherished generations later. Their books and Talmudic insights become their biographies and the details of their personal lives are considered secondary. Thus, while many might recognize the name of the great Lithuanian scholar Rabbi Israel Meir Kagan, they feel a more intimate connection when referring to him by his work, the *Hafetz Hayyim*. Over the course of Jewish history there arise a few personalities of Maimonidean proportion who shift the culture of our faith community. For these exceptional individuals, Jewish history craves to know every biographical detail of their lives. This volume of essays that ran as a series in *The Commentator*, the official undergraduate newspaper of Yeshiva College, serves as further evidence that Rabbi Joseph B. Soloveitchik is to be considered one of these celebrated figures.

The idea for *The Commentator* series was a natural one. Although the newspaper has taken on different personas since it was founded over seventy-two years ago, *The Commentator* has remained a major factor in Yeshiva University's development and culture. One steady component of the University's character is its inescapable fascination with the versatile persona of the Rav.

To the Yeshiva University community, the Rav is at the same time the champion of the yeshiva and the academy. He is the rabbi most quoted in *shiur* and the philosopher cited most often by secular professors in their attempt to connect with their students. He is the personification of excellence who forces us to redouble our efforts in the *beit midrash,* and the model citizen of modernity who, even in his passing, gives us courage to participate in the outside world.

With this dynamic to serve as motivation, and after months of preparation, we entitled the series "Legacies and Perspectives" and printed three reminiscences of Rabbi Soloveitchik in every issue of the seventy-first volume of *The Commentator.* The popularity of the series in print and online is a testament to the continuing impact of the Rav and to the reputations of the distinguished writers who shared their stories and impressions with our readers. The content and style of these articles vary. We made sure to solicit contributions across the spectrum of the Rav's classroom. In a few cases we expanded our search and petitioned individuals who may not have studied under the Rav but knew him in different contexts, having served on organizational boards or otherwise worked with him. We were reluctant to direct writers on the topics for their contributions. Thus, some writers found comfort in anchoring their essays in the lecture notes they still hold from decades past when they sat in the Rav's *shiur.* Almost universally, our contributors recounted the humanity of the Rav. Many contributors observed that to describe the Rav as an intellectual *rosh yeshiva* or as lonely philosophical man presented only two aspects of this multi-faceted personality. Although a case can be made that the Rav's devotees disagree on many pivotal issues regarding him, it would appear from this collection that at least they agree that the Rav was a polymath, yet full of kindness and charisma. As the reader will quickly find through a perusal of these pages, the Rav even had a keen sense of humor.

The contributors themselves represent the breadth of the Rav's genius. Some writers are *roshei yeshiva,* others are accountants or philosophers or high school principals. Some are Bostonians staking claim as the Rav's original students, and another holds the distinction of contributing the first academic critique of the Rav's immortal essay, *Ish HaHalakhah.* Indeed, several writers remember him as the *Rav* and others prefer to recall him as the *Rov.* Whatever the politics or versions of the Rabbi Soloveitchik recalled through the hundreds of pages of this volume, the nuanced differences among the accounts should be seen as part of a panoramic description of a dazzling giant, rather than a debate over the truest depiction of the Rav.

The same lesson is echoed throughout our tradition but one example will suffice. The description in the Talmud of the demise of

Rabbi Akiva's 12,000 pairs of students is puzzling (*Yevamot* 62b). The tragedy is refocused from the deaths of thousands of Jews to the catastrophic loss of Rabbi Akiva's teachings. Yet, the five students who survived their peers' fate, led by Rabbi Meir, held their own and successfully transmitted their teacher's legacy to the following generation of scholars. Perhaps along a theme developed by Rabbi Levi Yitzhak of Berditchev, the core of R. Akiva's teachings, his *halakhah*, was properly transmitted, but even the brilliant R. Meir was unable to capture the entire personality of his legendary teacher. Alas, without the aid of the thousands of perished students, the full scope of Rabbi Akiva's Torah did not survive. Rabbi Akiva's intellect was too great for even his star pupil to fully contain.

Similarly, though with obvious religious differences one might contend that Socrates was granted a favor in that we know him only through the writings of Plato. Perhaps Socrates had other formidable students, but they did not leave their accounts of their master's thoughts. Plato may not have captured everything, but we rely on him and do not debate what Socrates believed. Indeed, even if Plato had been Socrates' most beloved pupil, whatever different shades of Socrates Plato did not manage to capture were lost with the passing of his other disciples.

In that same vein, another point bears mentioning. Although this collection contains the largest corpus of essays on the Rav to date, readers familiar with the Rav's legacy will notice certain omissions. Over the course of this project, we contacted over a hundred individuals who had ties to the Rav. While the majority of these people contributed essays to this volume, others declined for a variety of reasons. Some had already made their memories public in previously published works, and others felt their relationship with the Rav inadequate for an essay. Certain individuals declined to contribute claiming the Rav himself would have preferred to keep their memories private. We regret that they withhold memories that, due to the Rav's pervasive influence on later generations, we can ill afford to lose.

Like the chain of tradition that began with Moses standing atop the peak of Sinai, the Torah and its history always belong to the current generation, eager to expand upon this tradition before transmitting it to the next one. In the same way that the Rav's most devoted students have assembled pages testifying to the tremendous wealth of Torah learning he produced, everyone who contributed to this volume has done so hoping to preserve the qualities of the Rav; a generation which did not merit to learn with him will be able to appreciate the man whose legacy is for the ages. While a large portion of this volume's readers will be older people already immersed in the life and teachings of the Rav, the target audience is the younger group, my peers, who by virtue of birth-year do not have memories of Rabbi Soloveitchik.

As readers of this volume will notice, formats for transliteration found in various essays vary. In certain instances, the style of transliteration is part of the theme. Some of the essays are longer than others. We asked the thirty or so contributors to the "Legacies" series printed in *The Commentator* to keep their essays under 3,000 words. When final preparations for this volume began the following summer and more writers were sought, we were less exacting. A few authors added to their previously published *Commentator* essays and no word limit was placed on new writers.

Finally, the Rav has posthumously taken on varying ideologies. Undoubtedly, some readers will be uncomfortable with the different Rabbi Soloveitchiks described in this collection. Perhaps in finding contributors we should have excluded everyone but the Rav's closest students. We believe such a strategy would have left this project incomplete. Whether with a neighbor in Boston or a trustee of the Board of Jewish Education of Greater New York, the Rav shared a part of himself with a variety of individuals. We felt that the same should be done in this book; we leave the politics for others to contest on the ideological battlefield.

If we have erred, may God in His goodness forgive us.

Zev Eleff
Yeshiva University
19 Heshvan 5768
October 31, 2007

Acknowledgements

About four years ago my dear friend Daniel Bornstein handed me a copy of *The Lonely Man of Faith*. I spent more time consulting the dictionary than I did with the text itself but once I finished it, that book changed my life forever. I am thankful to Daniel and all my wonderful friends for their love and support since this moment and for all the moments preceding.

My first thank you regarding this volume is reserved for all its contributors. Some of them endured my barrage of phone calls and e-mails for over a year before they acquiesced and found time in their busy schedules to write. These writers were open-minded to be a part of a large work that includes essays with ideas to which they do not necessarily subscribe. Moreover, it should be recognized that many writers in this volume were generous in sharing intimate stories and private memories of their lives. None of these writers received monetary compensation; they contributed without any agenda other than to add to the collective memory of the Rav.

For close to three years I have sat at the feet of my *rebbe*, Rabbi Hershel Schachter, inspired by his genius and humbled by his modesty. Rabbi Schachter has responded to my daily questions on all sorts of topics and areas of *halakhah* with a warm smile and sensitivity. I thank him for his advice and help throughout this project; they are only a sample of his undeserved kindness to me and the impact he has made on me.

I owe a great deal of gratitude to my dear teachers: Rabbis Yosef Blau, Shalom Carmy, Menachem Genack and Jacob J. Schacter. Over the years these distinguished individuals have ensured that Yeshiva University's students, and indeed the broader Jewish community, stay cognizant of the many dimensions of the genius of Rabbi Soloveitchik. They helped recruit several key contributors for this volume and, on a personal note, they have been pivotal to my development at Yeshiva.

In addition, Dr. Rivkah Teitz Blau deserves many thanks for her help and support throughout the production of this volume. Through her devotion to the Rav's memory, Dr. Blau deserves much credit as we saw this work to completion.

Thank you to Rabbi Kenneth Brander, Dean of Yeshiva University's Center for the Jewish Future, for his willingness to work with me to make sure that *The Commentator's* profits from this volume go to educational insitutions in need of works by and about Rabbi Soloveitchik.

Of course, I am indebted to Bernard Sharfstein, Adam Bengal and the Ktav Publishing House staff for their dedication to ensuring that these memories of the Rav and many other memories and teachings are captured within the sacred power of the written word. Their efforts will surely be felt for many generations to come. In addition, Mrs. Shulamith Berger, Curator of Special Collections at Yeshiva University's Mendel Gottesman Library was especially gracious in helping us locate photographs for this volume.

I thank Rabbi Gil Student for his important role in the creation of this volume. His work over the Internet in the past year to inform people of our *Commentator* series was critical in generating unprecedented readership. In the same vein, our readers, too, are owed thanks for their many comments during the production of this *Commentator* series.

I thank Rabbi Aryeh Lieberman and Dr. Arnold Lustiger for devoting countless hours to preserving the Rav's Torah for posterity and for their advice during the early stages of this volume. Thanks also to my friend Menachem Butler whose advice proved instrumental in going about this project professionally and efficiently.

I am greatly appreciative for the help and time offered by my fellow *Commentator* editors and to the Yeshiva University administration for their considerable accommodations during the production of this volume. Specifically, thanks go to Ms. Toby Stone for her legal counsel and help launching this book. Additional thanks go to Rabbi Elly Krimsky, Avi Ashkenazi, Chesky Gewirtz and Solomon Sved for their assistance in composing several essays in the volume.

My love and admiration go out to my extended family of grandparents, aunts, uncles and cousins who serve as a network I have come to rely upon and cherish throughout all my endeavors.

Finally, words come up short to describe my love and appreciation for my parents, Dr. Scott and Susan Eleff. My father's advice and unconditional support in all my endeavors have proven invaluable as I go on to meet the world. My mother has served as my personal editor-in-chief for many years and my love and respect for all she does for our family are boundless. My brothers, David, Ben and Joey, have been my best friends ever since they began arriving in my life some twenty years ago. Each of us is unique and different from the others but this volume should surely be viewed as another accomplishment for us as an unbeatable team.

Z.E.

Introduction

Norman Lamm

"Is not My word like a fire? says the Lord; and like a hammer that breaks the rock into pieces?"

The divine word, says Jeremiah, is layered or multi-dimensional. Like the many splinters of a rock split by a hammer, so the divine message lends itself to manifold situations and interpretations.

Torah, like its Giver, is capable of many explications and applications. The same holds true for teachers of Torah: they are not monochromatic, and their teachings, like Torah itself, are multivalent; they can be understood at many levels, reveal many secret aspects of the Torah, and throw light on the most obscure passages.

Such a person was our great teacher, the Rav, Rabbi Joseph B. Soloveitchik, of blessed memory. The essays in this volume give us a glimpse of the complexity of his personality as well as the universality of his legacy as perceived by his students. His genius, his probing intellect, his unassailable loyalty to the God of Israel, his incredible mastery of *Halakhah* and *Aggadah*, and the broad sweep of his knowledge of so many other disciplines—all made him resistant to easy classifications. He was a man who could never be bored and, equally, could never be boring. He was the Teacher par excellence, and we were honored to be allowed into his class.

His complexity and coruscant creativity were such that he rarely repeated interpretations of a text when he came to it at a later date. Thus, when I was a student of his we learned the tractate *Shabbat*. His *shiurim* were, of course, masterful. Several years later, I heard that he had given *shiurim* on the same tractate. I managed to obtain the notes of some of his very good students—and there was hardly any relation between the interpretations he gave when I was in his class and the new ones! He simply approached the material with a fresh mind, and exercised those areas of his creative brain to yield insights that were new and different from what he had offered previously.

Moreover, the range of his intellectual interest was extremely broad. It was not unusual to sit in a *shiur* or a *yahrzeit* lecture in which he descended into the depths—or perhaps ascended to the heights—of analysis of a Talmudic text and the *Rishonim* on the entire *sugya*, and shortly thereafter segued almost imperceptibly into citations from Augustine or Kant or non-Aristotelian logic.

All this time, he also exercised leadership on behalf of Modern Orthodoxy (via the Rabbinical Council of America) and the entire people of Israel. His personality was enhanced by a sense of humor which was always relevant, always insightful, and always wise.

His major interest, of course, lay in his Torah studies. He was an inexhaustible supply of *shiurim* on a vast variety of topics. This was his life, and from this he drew his life's meaning(s).

Both the catholicity and the variety of his interests are mirrored in the nearly sixty contributions to this volume by a variety of people, mostly his students, all of which are testament to the precious "pieces" or sparks hammered from the rock of his intellect.

The Rav was not a one-issue person. In addition to his immortal Torah contributions, the very variety of his life and legacy include Religious Zionism, advanced academic studies, support for Torah education for women, and more. His greatness will survive even the attempts of those whose adulation would have him confined solely to his role as *Rosh HaYeshiva*, the great teacher in the yeshiva, or his role as a philosopher grappling with the various challenge of modernity and who ignore all else. But the Rav cannot be forced into the *mitat Sodom* [the bed in Sodom where the guest's body was "adjusted" to the dimensions of the frame]. Readers of this volume will appreciate that each contributor knows only one or two or three of the many varied "sparks" of his magisterial mind, and that together they confirm that narrowness was inimical to his personality.

The essays appearing in this volume—some that have already appeared in *The Commentator* and some that are new—testify to his charismatic personality and to the indelible impression it made upon those who were lucky enough to be his students, as well as those who, even though they were not "official" students of the Rav, pored over his *hiddushim* and adored his profound essays—many of which have already appeared in print and many more that await publication.

Finally, I congratulate Zev Eleff and *The Commentator* staff for their initiative in conceiving and executing this project as a tribute to the memory of our illustrious *Rebbe*.

Yehei zikhro barukh

The '30s: A Bostonian with Sights on New York

The Rav in the 1930s. (Photo courtesy Yeshiva University.)

Learning with the Rav: The Early Years at Yeshiva

Henoch (Henry) Cohen

It was the Rav who had initially made me. Others affected me, but he was different. His *shiur* bewildered you, captivated you, and solidified you in every way possible. Moreover, the Rav was the beacon of light to all generations from the thirties until today. All this was because he was a man of truth.

Before I learned with the Rav, I studied in Torah Vodaath where I met Rav Elchanon Wasserman. He said to me: "I don't know why people talk so unfavorably about Rav Yoshe Ber. I was there in Boston and I never saw somebody eat, sleep and dream Torah as he did." Even someone like Rav Elchanon (*Hashem yenakem damo*, may G-d avenge his blood]) was taken aback by the Torah dedication of the Rav. After that conversation, I knew that I had to study under the tutelage of Rabbi Soloveitchik.

I was sixteen when I began to learn by the Rav in Boston in the year that the Second World War broke out. All the other students— for example, Rabbi Michel Feinstein—were much older than I. (My father was a student of Rabbi Hershel Glicksen who was the Rav's uncle—the son-in-law, who was a Ger Chassid, of Rav Chaim).

In Boston the Rav was very much at home. Still, while he enjoyed a certain amount of peace, he was never comfortable with his complete role in Boston. The community gave him the title of Chief Rabbi, but it was always unclear what that truly meant. The rabbis in Boston related very differently to the Rav. Many of them were jealous of him. He broke the barrier however. Being in his thirties, the Rav was like none other. When he went to Israel as a candidate for the chief rabbinate of Tel Aviv, the people there absolutely loved

Rabbi Henoch Cohen received ordination at RIETS in 1944. He served previously as *Rosh Kollel* at Yeshivat Ramat Tamir in Jerusalem.

his Torah. Even Reb Chaim was said to have commented about his grandson that he had never seen a head like that of Rav Yoshe Ber.

There was a lot of debate when Rabbi Moshe Soloveitchik, the Rav's father, passed away about whether or not the Rav would leave Boston to become a *rosh yeshiva* at YU. Not everyone went along with it in Boston and it therefore became a very trying time for the Rav. In the end, of course, the Rav accepted YU's offer, splitting his time between Boston and New York.

One had to go to college at this time. The Conservative movement was becoming very powerful; even daughters of the *rabbanim* of the Agudah married Conservative rabbis. Those who sought to enter the rabbinate required a college education in order to avoid the dynamic power of the Conservative movement. Certainly, at that time, Yeshiva was a strong option for those seeking a college education. RIETS had many *gedolim*, prominent scholars, such as Rabbi Moshe Bick and Rabbi Nosson Zvi Wachtfogel. One of the main reasons for this was that Torah Vodaath was still very young and small. When he arrived in New York, the Rav became a great asset among these Torah giants.

In Boston, there were those who might have followed the Rav to New York, but didn't because of the college. They didn't want to have anything to do with secularism. There were students like myself, though we were more *yeshivish* than the rest, who decided to attend Yeshiva because of the Rav. It was not easy going to YU. In some places, you weren't even allowed to hold a *sefer Torah* if you attended YU. To his credit the Rav avoided these politics as much as possible. He generally ran away from politics and lived in isolation. It took a long time, therefore, before he was recognized for who he was. He was always honest in what he stood for. He was his own man and meant everything he did. Sometimes, students who were grappling with secular studies would drag his name into the mud by saying things that he never said. However, he never wanted to go to war over this. He was a sick man. He shook a lot whenever he gave *shiur* or an address. He didn't have the strength to fight politics all of the time and sacrificed a lot of his own health in order to teach.

The Boston *kollel* was the first time that the Rav had a real opportunity to be a teacher and deliver *shiurim*. Still, his main source of income came from supervising the *kashrut* in Boston. It is well known, of course, that the Rav suffered a great deal from the corruption of the industry in Boston. When the Rav arrived in New York it was the first time that he was a *rosh yeshiva*. It was nothing new to him, though, because of his experiences in the *kollel* in Boston.

I was in the Rav's second *semikhah* class at YU. The Rav's *semikhah* tests were like a four-hour torture chamber. When you were through with it, you *bentched gomel* [said a prayer of gratitude for surviving the ordeal]. I remember after getting *semikhah* my parents wanted me to rest for the summer; they saw that I had been through an exciting but equally grueling experience. Unfortunately, some of my classmates from that *semikhah* class were geniuses who went astray. There was one who graduated from RIETS, went to Berkeley and became a major politician in the Eisenhower administration. When he came once to Yeshiva to see the Rav, nobody wanted to speak with him. The Rav saw this but could not do much to stop it.

The composure of Brisk, the Rav's style of learning, made him very tough at times. Very often my father had to remind me that this was nothing personal. It was just the intense style to which the Rav subscribed. On a number of occasions the Rav asked me to translate the long essays by Reb Chaim into English. After I painstakingly read through the Reb Chaim's *sefer* and translated every word, I would submit the translation to the Rav and he would check it to make sure that I understood Reb Chaim. Many people will tell you that the Rav was a cold individual, but that is not true. You just needed to know how to get a hold of him and then you would realize just how personable he was.

Things didn't always go as the Rav had anticipated, and he therefore became a very anxious person. Still, he raised a tremendous family. How many of the *gedolim* from that time can boast that their grandchildren would become *talmidei hakhamim*? A great part of this achievement is due to the Rav's wife, Tonya, a very independent and strong individual. He needed someone like her in many ways. I remember that when I was learning in the Rav's *kollel* and was sitting at the Rav's *Pesach* table, I was asked to say something. As I stood up to speak, I accidentally knocked over a glass and spilled wine on the tablecloth. I was so embarrassed, but the Rav's wife immediately comforted me and explained that it was not a big deal.

Aside from his personal accomplishments and his familial success, the Rav during his lifetime was well-respected by all of the major American *rabbanim*. One Sunday, when I was in my fifties, I returned to Boston to attend the Rav's special *Tishah B'Av shiur* at the Maimonides School. When I entered the building, I was shocked. There were Satmar *hassidim* waiting to hear the Rav deliver his *shiur*. I knew a few of them and asked what they were doing there. They answered that they simply wanted to hear what the Rav had to say on *Kadshim*. I asked them how they found out about the Rav. They answered that the Satmar Rav himself had sent them to hear the Rav. I didn't hesitate; the next morning I went to see the Satmar Rav to ask about this. He responded: "What's the matter with you! Who in the whole world knows *Kadshim* like Rav Yoshe Ber?"

Such was the great legacy of my teacher, the Rav.

A Lifelong Personal Encounter with the Rav

Bernard Lander

I was in Rabbi Moshe Soloveitchik's *shiur* at Yeshiva in the 1930s. The *shiur* was relatively small, no more than ten students. I recall among them were Rabbi Aaron Soloveichik, Rabbi Chayim Zimmerman, Rabbi Melech Schachter, Rabbi Joseph Weiss, and Rabbi Mayer Kobrin also known as the *Iluy* of Moscow. Rav Moshe gave *shiur* twice a week, each one lasting an hour and a half. The *shiur* invariably focused on the Rambam; he would interpret the Rambam, often resolving a contradiction between the Rambam and the *Gemara*.

Rav Moshe was very close to Rabbi Aharon Yitzchak Zalmanowitz who was a Gerrer *chassid* and a *rosh yeshiva* at Yeshiva. In my mind's eye, I can see them walking the halls talking in Torah and inevitably, Rav Moshe would speak to Rabbi Zalmanowitz as he did with almost anyone, about his prodigious son, Rav Yosef Dov. I never saw a greater love of a father to a son than Rav Moshe's for Rav Yosef Dov.

Despite the stereotypical austere, forbidding image that one conjures when thinking of Brisk, Rav Moshe was a very warm and caring person. He was especially kind to me and concerned with my welfare. He invited me to all his family *simchos* [celebrations]. I remember Rav Aharon Soloveichik's wedding in which Rav Aharon gave a brilliant but extended *dvar Torah* about *kedushas haaretz* [the sanctity of the Land of Israel]. Rav Moshe once came to me saying that he wanted to propose my candidacy for the rabbinate at Boston's Bluehill Avenue synagogue which his son Rav Yosef Dov attended. At the time, I had been accepted at Harvard Law School and was seriously considering the move to Boston. However, I rejected the proposal because I questioned my fluency in delivering sermons in Yiddish to a crowd of several hundred worshippers and

Rabbi Dr. Bernard Lander is President of Touro College

the thought of delivering a sermon in the presence of the *gaon* Rav Yosef Dov was daunting. In the end I became a rabbi in Baltimore, and switched my area of study from law to sociology.

Rav Moshe also helped my close friend, Rabbi Moshe Besdin, who would go on to found the JSS program at Yeshiva College, obtain his position as the rabbi of the Beth Medrash Hagadol in Washington Heights where Rav Moshe himself would often daven.

It was through my association with Rav Moshe that I came to know Rav Yosef Dov. I would often accompany the Rav on long walks in which I was stunned by the erudition of even his casual conversation. The topics he dealt with ranged from discussions in Christian theology to Western Literature, from Rambam and matters of *halakhah* to Kant and Rudolf Otto, from ancient academic texts to current issues in that day's *New York Times*. When the Rav visited my home while I was sitting *shivah* for my late father, he told me that I was the second friend that he had made in the United States.

In 1937 the Rav was the invited guest, with Dr. Revel presiding, at the *chag hasemikhah* [celebration of rabbinic ordination] where I was to receive my official *semikhah*. The Rav delivered a fiery speech decrying the association of Yeshivas Rabbeinu Yitzchak Elchanan and Yeshiva College. Yeshiva College was still new, having graduated its first class in 1932. He stated that a *sefer Torah* written in gold-tinted ink was invalid and that only a *sefer Torah* written with black ink on white parchment was acceptable. Dr. Revel was understandably surprised with this critique, as the Rav himself was a recipient of a PhD in mathematics and philosophy, and he refused to offer the Rav any position at the yeshiva. However, Rav Moshe surreptitiously encouraged me to organize a class in Jewish philosophy, given by the Rav, which met on a weekly basis in the dormitory building. In 1938, I left for Baltimore to accept the role as rabbi of Beth Jacob and the Rav established a yeshiva in Boston.

Our friendship resumed actively when I became dean of the Bernard Revel Graduate School which included Rabbi Soloveitchik amongst its distinguished faculty. As colleagues, we frequently shared our many views on the direction of Yeshiva College. Both of us vocally resisted Dr. Belkin's intended plan to bring Stern College to the larger campus of Yeshiva College in Washington Heights. With the Rav's opposition the idea was dropped.

In 1970 I was present at the *chag hasemikhah* and the luncheon in which the Rav dramatically opposed Dr. Belkin's decision to modify the charter of Yeshiva College to be non-sectarian, thus making the college eligible for government funds. RIETS would remain a religious school affiliated with Yeshiva University. The Rav was concerned that some time in the future the Yeshiva's change of status would ultimately compromise the Yeshiva's missions and standards. Though he had confidence that Dr. Belkin would not permit this to happen, the Rav recalled the ancient syllogism: all men are mortal; Aristotle is a man; therefore, Aristotle is mortal. This issue became a point of great tension between the Rav and Dr. Belkin.

The *chagei hasemikhah* of 1937 and 1970 bracketed the Rav's career at Yeshiva and demonstrated his deep commitment to the pristine nature of the Torah environment of Yeshiva. I do not mean, however, to suggest that the Rav was an obscurantist or opposed to secular knowledge. This was of course not the case. The Rav was a towering intellect; the breadth and depth of his knowledge in all areas was astounding. He believed that we must encounter and engage the general society.

The Torah records (Genesis 21:33) 'Abraham planted an *eshel* tree in Beer Sheva, and there he called upon the name of the LORD, the Eternal God.' The Rav explained that this tree was a metaphor for Abraham's and subsequently the Jewish people's approach to life. A Jew needs roots; he must be deeply rooted in the experience and traditions of the past. The past for the Jew is always alive and relevant. It's that past that animates the present and inspires our future, represented by the branches and foliage of the tree. The Rav personified that Abrahamic *eshel*. While open to the wisdom and culture of the modern world, he remained always anchored in the rich tradition of Brisk. He believed that no Jewish philosophy was valid unless it was shaped by the methodology and spirit of the *halakhah*.

He once commented that the current problem confronting the Christian world was the clash of religion and science. He thought that for the Jew this was an irrelevant and trivial issue. For Judaism the challenge was to maintain the uniqueness and singularity of this relationship. To the uninformed there would seem to be tension between these two worlds of Rabbi Soloveitchik; but the reality was that within the greatness of the Rav's personality, as that of his philosophical antecedent Maimonides, these worlds were integrated and dedicated to the service of *Hashem*.

From Boston to New York

William Millen

Raised in Boston and studying later at Yeshiva, I made sure to take shelter under the influence and care of our late teacher, Rabbi Joseph Dov Soloveitchik. Even today, as I no longer have the luxury of turning to the Rav for a question here or some advice there, I take solace in that I am conducting my life in the way he would have wanted. In fact, when I don't live up to my own expectations, I can see the Rav in my mind chastising me, saying, "I'm not going to tell you what to do, but if I were you ..."

I was fortunate to have a very close relationship with the Rav for two reasons. First, my parents were very involved with the Soloveitchiks. My mother was the second president of the Maimonides School's Women's Auxiliary (the Rav's wife, Tonya Soloveitchik, was the first) and my father was the Rav's personal driver in Boston. Second, I was one of the three original students enrolled in the Maimonides School he founded in Boston in 1937. I attended the school for the first six years of its existence. I was forced to attend public school after the sixth year because the school could not sustain a seventh grade. After a few years at a Boston public school, I asked my parents to allow me to attend Yeshiva University's high school. I recall begging my parents to allow me to go to New York for high school, but they consistently refused. Finally, after my diligent protests, my parents asked the Rav for his opinion on the matter. The Rav did not approve of my request. I found out later that this was because he was under the impression that the high school's dormitory supervision was poor and he was afraid

Rabbi Millen has served as principal of schools in various communities including Dayton, OH; Ottawa, ONT; Silver Spring, MD. He has been in Silver Spring teaching at Melvin J. Berman Hebrew Academy for the past thirty-two years.

that I would be influenced by the New York night life. Shocked after my father reported the Rav's decision to me, I insisted on speaking with the Rav directly. During that conversation with the Rav, he tried to persuade me to wait until college to study in New York but I maintained that Boston was no place for a boy my age. And besides, all of my Boston friends were already there in New York!

"They were all going against my wishes," responded the Rav.

"Can't I go against your wishes, too?" I asked half seriously.

After a brief silence, I exclaimed, "*Rebbe*, what do I have here in Boston?" With that, I thought I had finally worn him down. The Rav placed his head in his hands for about a minute until he finally looked at me and said, "I'll make a class for you." He hired Rabbi Schoenfeld to teach a few of us after school for two hours. The Rav even sent his own daughter Atarah to learn with us in this after-school class. She was the only girl in the class amongst six or seven boys but she always knew the answer before the rest of us!

Even with this class, I was still unhappy at public school. I decided to purposely fail my classes to force my parents and the Rav to send me to Yeshiva. Both the Rav and my parents got the message, and I was off to New York the following year. As I was making final arrangements for the trip, the Rav asked to see me. I promptly walked to his home where he asked me how I planned to travel from Boston to New York. I said that I planned to take the train. The Rav suggested that I avoid arriving at Grand Central Station and instead stop at 125th Street where I could take the Fort Tryon bus to Washington Heights. I did not understand at the time why the Rav was so interested in my travel itinerary but I thanked him and told him the exact time I expected to arrive at the high school dormitory. I rerouted my trip as suggested, and not twenty seconds after I entered my dorm room the Rav appeared at my doorway. "I see you made it!" exclaimed the Rav. Then he ushered me down the stairs and into the office of Yeshiva President Dr. Shmuel Belkin. The Rav introduced me to Dr. Belkin with great pride. To me this indicates the type of care the Rav had for his students in those days. His care for me lasted throughout my eleven years at Yeshiva.

During my last years at Yeshiva, I was completing *semikhah* at RIETS. I remember vividly how murderous the Rav's written examinations were. More than the difficult questions and vast amount of material for which we were responsible, the fear of failing the exam and having to prepare to retake it burdened our thoughts. In his shiurim on *Yoreh Dei'ah*, we were expected to have a command of the *Gemara, Rishonim, Beit Yosef* and the *Shulhan Arukh*. I recall one year when a *shiur* that started with fifty students shrank to thirty-six within a few weeks. Those of us who survived to take the test at the end of the year were seated in a hot room without air-conditioning for hours. After the test we shared with one another the number of pages we used for the test. Each of us used over thirty pages for our answers; we figured that there was no way that Rabbi Yosef Weiss, the Rav's *shiur* assistant, could mark all of the tests. With this hope in mind, we were confident that none of us would have to retake the exam. Rabbi Weiss managed to grade all of the tests and those who failed were forced to repeat the grueling process.

Later, while I was dating my wife, I found out that I nearly failed one of the *semikhah* tests. While on a date at the restaurant near Yeshiva, the Rav confronted me and said, "You didn't do so well on the last test! You must do better on the next one." Apparently, if I did fail, the Rav was willing to give me a break. The tactic worked. I forced my *chavrutot* [study partners] to stay up late nights with me a month before the test out of fear of what the Rav might say if I didn't perform adequately on the next test. I scored a 99 percent.

In 1955 the Rav went through a stressful period. It was clear to his students in Yeshiva that our teacher was burdened and overworked. In the midst of this difficult time, the Rav returned to Boston for an important board meeting for the Maimonides School. My mother, who was also on the school board, reported when she came home that something terrible had happened at the meeting. One of the more prominent and affluent members of the board said something that upset the Rav a great deal. The Rav, whose temper in those days was fierce, shouted at this gentleman. Consequently, the man stormed out of the room, and those remaining at the meeting, including Mrs. Soloveitchik, were left in utter disbelief. My mother was upset because she realized that this gentleman's support was very important to the future of the Maimonides School. She called him on the phone later that night, and after a half hour, he agreed that if the Rav were to call him, he would return to the school. My mother then called the Soloveitchik home and explained the situation to Tonya Soloveitchik. The Rav's wife agreed with the plan but, still aware of the Rav's temper, insisted that my mother be the one to pose it to the Rav. The Rav picked up the phone receiver and my mother pleaded with him to call up the insulted board member. The Rav didn't say a word as my mother poured her heart out; she was sobbing, and tears were streaming down her face. He listened to what she had to say, thanked her, and hung up the phone. My mother wasn't sure what to expect. The next day Mrs. Soloveitchik called my mother and told her that the Rav had called the gentleman exactly as my mother had asked. Mrs. Soloveitchik also confided that she asked the Rav what had changed his mind. "I couldn't stand to listen to Mrs. Millen's tears," he explained.

The reason for the Rav's high expectations for us as students and members of his community was that he was simply on a different level. Very often at the Maimonides School where we would *daven* on *Shabbat*, the Rav would correct the *hazzan* or correct me, as I was often expected to read from the Torah. When the Rav would raise his voice to make a *halakhic* modification, his way of speaking showed that he assumed that the person he was correcting was as learned as he. For example, one year before *Sukkot* my mother called the Rav to ask for instructions on how to build a private *eruv* for our home. The Rav told her to put me—I was 12 or 13 at the time—on the phone. As soon as I picked up the receiver, the Rav shouted a few lines of *Gemara* at me. I reminded him that I was still a young boy and was not on top of that particular area of *halakhah*. Perhaps bemused by my ignorance, the Rav told me to meet him at the school to escort him to my house. Once there, I stood in my back-yard bewildered at the sight of the Rav with a hammer building our family's *eruv*.

Over the years, many have portrayed the Rav as a fierce intellectual who would terrorize his students with impossible expectations. While it is certainly true of the Rav that very often he forgot that not everyone surrounding him was as brilliant as he, it is important that a portrait of the Rav include his unwavering concern for others. One day a man appeared at the door of the Rav's classroom. None of the fifty students could make out what the elderly man was saying, but the boys understood that he had come to collect money. The Rav asked, "What does he want?" One of the boys responded that he is here to collect money. The Rav immediately reached into his wallet, pulled out a dollar bill, and directed his students to give it to the man at the door. The man left the room with at least fifty dollars after all the students were inspired by the kindness of the Rav to in-terrupt *shiur* to give this man *tzedakah*. Similarly, I recall that a group of us travelled on the subway with the Rav after he finished delivering his weekly *shiur* at Moriah Synagogue. As we sat in the crowded subway car, a blind man walked through the aisle trying to collect whatever money he could. Although nobody else seemed to even notice the blind man, the Rav, surrounded by his students and in the midst of intense discussion on some Torah theme, made sure to place some money in this man's hands. Stories of this nature abound in the memories of those who recall the Rav. Personally, there were many occasions when the Rav helped my family, and such gratitude should not escape our recollections.

Rav Soloveitchik and his wife were each attentive to the other's welfare. She freed her husband's time for learning by taking care of all the details of daily life and preventing people with an agenda from bothering him. An example of the relationship between him and his beloved Tonya occurred on a *motza'ei Shabbat*. When the Rav gave *shiurim* in various *shuls*, he wrote out each *shiur* on sheets of paper that he brought to the *shul* before *Shabbat*. After the class ended on one *Shabbat*, we *davened Maariv*, and the Rav motioned me over to him. "Billy," he said, "since I hold by Rabbeinu Tam's position and *Shabbat* is not yet over for me, would you mind carrying my *drashah* home for me?" My father and I agreed to accompany the Rav. During the walk, there was a group of teenagers making noise in front of the local drugstore. As soon as they saw the Rav, they quieted themselves and moved out of the way. At that moment Mrs. Soloveitchik appeared from around the corner and called, "Berel (as he was known to his immediate family), I brought you a coat!" Although it had turned cold after sunset, the Rav said curtly that he didn't need a coat. Mrs. Soloveitchik said, "What do you mean you don't need a coat!" The Rav took the coat from her hands while everyone nearby smiled. Although this story is on the lighter side, it shows the respect the Rav had for his wife and the devotion she had to him.

Current events and secular studies were certainly of great interest to the Rav. When I was engaged to my wife, we traveled to Boston so she could meet my parents. Of course, we paid a visit to the Rav. After he briefly quizzed my wife on what she was studying at Stern College, we began to discuss the space race and the Russians' launching of Sputnik. The Rav's eyes lit up as he explained the incredible nature of this feat. On another occasion, I remember speaking privately with the Rav in his home. During our conversation he excused himself for a moment to take a phone call in another room. I noticed that there was a book lying face down near his chair. When I looked at the title and the table of contents, I realized it was similar to a text I was using in an advanced biology class. Although no one would expect a Talmudic scholar of his caliber to be interested in the technical details of chromosomes and genes, the Rav was up on everything and was interested in all subjects.

A number of years ago when my wife and I were honored at the Young Israel of Silver Spring, I thanked all of the people who shaped me as an educator. The list included my parents, wife, children and, of course, the Rav. I was not going to say anything about the Rav because whatever I could say would be inadequate. Instead, I spoke to the Rav:

> *Rebbe,* I have been involved in Jewish education for over fifty years and each of those years belongs to you. I can see you sitting in front of me during one of your *shiurim* and in your inimitable way saying, "God Himself is a teacher as we say every day, *ha-melamed Torah l-amo Yisrael.*" Whether it was the sincerity or the integrity or a combination of those qualities that made an impression on me, I wanted in these respects to emulate you. Therefore, the last fifty years of my work in *hinukh* are your doing and belong to you.

Personal Glimpses into the Persona of the Rav

Alvin I. Schiff

About the Rav

The Rav was a multifaceted intellectual giant with many personal qualities that inspired and motivated numerous practical insights and actions. This essay describes some of his personal interests and involvements in a variety of communal and educational contexts that are not well known or not known at all in the Orthodox community today.

B'kohl makom she'attah motzei g'dulato shel Ha-Kadosh Barukh Hu shom attah motzei anvanuto (*Megillah* 31a) The Rav personified Rabbi Yohanan's Talmudic statement about *Hashem*. Despite his towering presence as a Torah luminary, a distinguished world-renowned scholar, and extraordinary teacher and orator, who obviously realized his influential role in American society and the Jewish community, there was genuine humility in his personal behavior.

What I describe in this essay is based solely upon personal conversations and meetings with the Rav and observations of him in action in a variety of settings that shed light on his sterling character. I believe that my comments reflect accurately on the true persona of the Rav.

Early Years in Boston

I first saw Rabbi Joseph B. Soloveitchik when he arrived in Boston in 1932 to assume the post of *rav ha-ir* [rabbi of the city] and rav of

Alvin I. Schiff, PhD, founding director of Graduate Jewish Education at Yeshiva University (now the Azrieli Graduate School); Irving I. Stone distinguished professor of Jewish education, AGS; executive vice president emeritus Board of Jewish Education of Greater New York; recipient of the President's Prize in Jewish Education.

the *Chevra Shas* and to become the *rav hamakhshir* [rabbi who super-
vises the kashruth] of the kosher sausage factory, Morrison and
Schiff, founded by my grandfather. Although I was only six years
old, I recall the excitement associated with the arrival of "the big
rabbi."

The Jewish community in Greater Boston, numbering about
100,000 in 1932, was largely concentrated in three contiguous
areas—Dorchester, Mattapan and Roxbury—where there were fifteen large Orthodox synagogues and one large Conservative temple.
In addition, there were twelve Orthodox synagogues in outlying
areas: Chelsea, Lynn, Malden, Quincy, Revere, and Winthrop. As a
youngster, I heard the Jewish community of Boston referred to as
"*Yerushalayim d'America*". In reality, except for those who filled the
synagogues each *Shabbat* and *Yom Tov*, and the members of the *chevra
shas* study groups, most of the Jewish families, particularly the
young adults and youth, were not observant.

Most of the rabbis were older European Yiddish-speaking *rabbanim* with grey beards; they did not relate well to the American-
born young adults and children. In contrast, the Rav was a young,
handsome, twenty-nine-year-old scholar with a well-trimmed black
chin beard who related easily to a wide variety of Jews of all ages.

In 1932 Baltimore and New York were the only cities in the
United States that had yeshivot or day schools. Boston had a well-
developed Talmud Torah system, supervised by the Bureau of Jewish Education, which served most of the community. By and large,
these institutions were intensive, ten-hour per week *Ivrit b'Ivrit* [He-
brew schools where lessons were taught exclusively in Hebrew]
schools, comparable in many ways to the Jewish Studies departments of *Ivrit b'Ivrit* day schools. The Rav visited the Beth El Hebrew School, which I attended, several times a year. I was eight
years old when an excited teacher introduced us to him during one
of these visits. He proceeded to engage us in a long discussion in
clear, understandable English. To the pupils this was a revelation.

One of the reasons the Rav came to the Hebrew schools was to
encourage students in the graduating class to continue their Jewish
education after they completed elementary school. Toward this end,
he organized Hebrew High School classes at Beth El which were in-
corporated eventually into the Prozdor high school program of the
Hebrew Teachers College in Roxbury. The Rav was pained that he
was unable to convince the majority of graduates in the various He-

brew schools (or their parents) to enroll in the Hebrew High School programs.

Even though there were many intensive Hebrew supplementary schools in Boston whose curricula included serious study of *Humash* [Bible], *N'viim Rishonim* [Early Prophets], Hebrew language and literature, Hebrew grammar, Jewish history, *Halakhah* and introduction to *Torah she-b'al peh* [Oral Torah], the Rav felt strongly that elementary school students should be exposed to more intensive study of *Mishnah* and *Gemara* prior to the age of bar mitzvah. Moreover, he wanted them to be immersed in an all-day Jewish environment for both Jewish and general studies.

The Maimonides School

In 1937, after overcoming the apathy and strong antagonism of Jewish lay leaders, including many Orthodox *ba'alei battim*, the Rav succeeded, at the age of thirty-four, in founding the Maimonides Day School. He was proud of the success of the school, whose education committee was chaired conscientiously and energetically by his wife, Dr. Tonya Soloveitchik. He visited the school once or twice a week and established warm relationships with the principal and many teachers. He noted, more than once, that he was not responsible for the effectiveness of Maimonides and gave credit to the dedicated efforts of the principal, Rabbi Moses J. Cohn.

In the 1960s, when I was pedagogic supervisor of the Department of Yeshivot and Jewish Day Schools of the Jewish Education Committee of New York (now the Board of Jewish Education of Greater New York), the Rav invited me to visit Maimonides. It was apparent that he enjoyed being with the pupils and relished engaging them in discussion. And it was obvious that the students admired him.

The Rav was concerned about the instructional methodology in the Jewish Studies classes. He wanted the teachers of Judaic subjects to have better pedagogic training, "like the professional preparation that general studies teachers receive." When I served as director of Graduate Jewish Education at Yeshiva University (now the Azrieli Graduate School of Jewish Education and Administration), he encouraged me to emphasize techniques of teaching for master's degree students in Jewish Elementary and Secondary Education.

Maimonides is a co-ed yeshiva. The question of co-education, for the Rav, was not a *halakhic* issue, but an educational matter depending on the nature of the Jewish community that the school served. While he did not advocate publicly for co-education, he was happy about how it worked in the Maimonides School and believed that girls should receive intensive Jewish schooling, not less than boys. In many cases he was convinced that co-education was the way to achieve this. He was ardently in favor of teaching *Torah she-b'al peh* to girls. His reason for intensive Judaic instruction for female students was clear. It was extremely important for Jewish women in America to have sound training in Judaic studies because, as mothers, they would have as much or more influence than the fathers on the Jewish behavior of their progeny.

The Rav favored an *Ivrit b'Ivrit* approach for the Jewish day school, but he accepted the reality that as European-trained teachers passed away, as the Hebrew Teachers Colleges relaxed their training of Hebrew-speaking teachers and became colleges of Jewish studies, and as American-trained, *haredi* yeshiva graduates became the instructors in day schools, teachers able to communicate in Hebrew became an extinct breed.

The Rav's Yeshiva in Boston

In the late 1930's, the Rav started a yeshiva for a small group of mature yeshiva students who arrived from Eastern Europe. He planned to establish it as a permanent *yeshiva gedolah* and *kollel* for advanced Judaic learning. However, as luck would have it, this plan never materialized. After the death of his father, the *Gaon* Rabbi Moses Soloveitchik, in 1941, the Rav was installed as senior *Rosh HaYeshiva* in his father's place. This happened despite much difficulty and opposition, including negative articles in *The Commentator* Yeshiva College's official newspaper. Most helpful was the vigorous support he received from the Agudath HaRabbanim. I learned from the Rav's sister, Shulamith Meiselman, who lived in Boston after her marriage that the Rav was given, grudgingly, a one-year contract by the Yeshiva College board, but after his inaugural *shiur*, which impressed everyone who heard him, he was granted tenure.

Because of this appointment, which meant so much to the Rav, he had to close his yeshiva in Boston. He was not happy to give up an institution he had founded, one that gave him genuine *sippuk nefesh* [literally, "satisfaction of the soul"]. But he had no alternative. With the closing of the yeshiva, the Maimonides School became even more important to him and to Jewish education in Boston.

Rabbi Soloveitchik as Community Rav

One of the ways Rabbi Soloveitchik served Boston Jewry as community Rav was to give public *shiurim* on special *Shabbatot* at different synagogues two or three hours before *minhah*—on *Shabbat Shuvah, Shabbat Hol Ha-Moed Sukkot* and *Pesah, Shabbat Hanukkah, Shabbat Zakhor, Shabbat Ha-Gadol, Shabbat* before *Shavuot, Shabbat Hazon* and *Shabbat Nahamu*. Given his extraordinary erudition combined with his unmatched ability and dynamism as a speaker and teacher, his *shiurim* were received enthusiastically by the hundreds of people who came to hear him. According to the Rav's father, in a letter to the secretary of the Religious Council of Tel Aviv in 1935, in support of the Rav's candidacy for the Chief Rabbinate of Tel Aviv, "God blessed him with phenomenal speaking talent. His speeches are full of pearls of wisdom, and he can speak fluently in various languages: Hebrew, Yiddish, German, English. He has a vast knowledge of *Hokhmat Yisrael* [literally Jewish wisdom], Jewish history and Hebrew and Yiddish literature. He speaks with authority which comes from competence and the ability to express himself lucidly. He captures his audience and commands their love and respect." The Rav's public lectures in Boston demonstrated the truth of his father's comments.

I was one of the lucky youngsters to be exposed to the Rav's communal presentations when, as a high school student, together with my friends in Hashomer Hadati, I attended all of his *shiurim*. Since we were all from Yiddish-speaking families, we had no problem understanding the Rav. Not always, however, did we comprehend fully his content or message.

Prior to the *shiur*, at the request of the Rav, the *shamash* [sexton] of each *shul* where the Rav spoke would place on a table near the speaker's stand the *seforim* from which the Rav would quote. On *Shabbat Hanukkah* 1941, several months after the mass murder of Jews began in Eastern Europe, the Rav in his *shiur* referred frequently to a pile of newspapers which he had prepared in addition to traditional Judaic texts. He analyzed the news of the previous months and used this occasion to speak dramatically about the world situation vis-à-vis the Jewish people. In his unique animated manner, he spoke emotionally about the Nazi threat to the Jewish people. He forecast the annihilation of European Jewry unless something drastic was done to stop Adolf Hitler from fulfilling his murderous aspirations. I vividly remember how the Rav implored his listeners to communicate with President Roosevelt, senators and representatives to intervene and help stop the slaughter.

Kashrut in Boston

Shortly after the Rav came to Boston, he invited my father, who was known as the "Brezer *ilui*" in his Lithuanian town of Brestovitz, to become a *kashrut* supervisor for the *Va'ad Ha-Ir* [the city council]. I occasionally accompanied my father when he met with the Rav about the status of *kashrut* in the Jewish community. It was obvious that he was a *mahmir* [strict] regarding *kashrut*. He had particular interest in *sh'hitat ofot* [slaughter of fowl] about which other *rabbanim* were more lenient.

I recall the Rav's active involvement in enforcing kashrut rules. When one of the "kosher" butcher shops refused to submit to supervision by the *Va'ad Ha-ir*, he stood on a truck parked in front of the store and pleaded with people not to enter it. Since the store was in the Grove Hall area of Roxbury, a bustling Jewish shopping district, his dynamic appeal drew many listeners.

Broad Hebraic Interests

One of the Rav's intellectual qualities was his interest in every aspect of Hebraic/Judaic knowledge. My father, who was known for his mastery of *Tanakh* [the Bible, Prophets and Writings]and *dikduk* [Hebrew grammar] would often discuss biblical and grammatical matters with him. One *Shabbat* afternoon in the mid 1930s, when I came to *shul* for *minhah*, I found the Rav and my father engrossed in deep discussion. When they finished talking, my father explained that among other things, they considered the *nasog ahor*, the regressive accent in Hebrew grammar. After the discussion, my father exclaimed, "*Azzah ga-onishe kop*," such a brilliant mind of a genius.

The Compassion of the Rav

One of the Rav's personal attributes was compassion, particularly towards students to whom he often showed his sterner side. In 1945 I was the fortunate recipient of his compassion. In my sophomore year in Yeshiva College, I woke up in the dormitory one morning with double vision. My roommate, Asher Kahn, accompanied me to the emergency room of the local Jewish Memorial Hospital, where I was told that it might be due to a brain tumor. Asher told the Rav, who became personally involved. He tried to calm me, phoned my parents, and helped make an appointment for me at Columbia Presbyterian Hospital for a more definitive diagnosis.

My eye problem lasted for nine months. During this time, the Rav inquired frequently about my condition. When my eyesight was restored to normalcy, the Rav expressed his delight with his hearty, broad smile.

Teaching Secular Professional Leaders

The Rav had the unique ability of relating, on an intellectual level, to all types of people. This he demonstrated in the ten-session course he gave at the Jewish Orientation Training Seminar (JOTS) sponsored by the Jewish Education Committee (now the Board of Jewish Education of Greater New York) in the autumn of 1958. JOTS was instituted to enable the secular "left wing" professional leaders of Federation agencies to gain knowledge and insight into Jewish thought and tradition.

Rabbi Leon Feldman, who directed the program, asked if I would contact the Rav about the possibility of his giving a course on a topic of his choosing. When I approached the Rav, his response was surprisingly enthusiastic. It was as if he was waiting for an invitation to teach these people. He told me that he would like to "open the gates of Torah for them and help them enter the sanctuary of Jewish life." He suggested that he give a course on "The Philosophy of Prayer."

The twenty participants—all executives of Federation agencies—were "amazed by the breadth of his knowledge and his unique inspiring approach to teaching." One participant noted, "I have a doctorate in social work and two master's degrees. This is the most exhilarating intellectual experience I've ever had."

To observe the warm, exciting interaction between the Rav and his secular students was to see a master at his craft. In his lectures, the Rav underscored the fact that prayer is a primary religious experience on four levels. In class, he stressed the intellectual and emotional planes of prayer. In this regard, he noted that Torah study was related to religious experience. Torah study is not only a means to achieve religious and ethical behavior, but is itself a mode of worship. Through study of Torah one joins with God who endows man with wisdom and knowledge as we state in the Amidah prayer, *"Attah honen l'adam da-at"* [You endow man with wisdom].

Intellectual contact with God creates a strong awareness of Him. Sharing in Divine knowledge is a manner of communicating with the Almighty. The emotional level—the heart more than the mind— helps us achieve *d'veikut* [literally, "adhesion"; devotion] with God. It creates a real attachment to Him. Passionate engagement with Torah study is a desideratum in Judaism. Prayer devoid of emotion is not an effective way to communicate with the Creator.

Guiding the Distribution of Grants to Jewish Schools

One of my favorite memories of the Rav relates to his concern for the welfare of all Jews. In this case, it was for the well-being of Haredi/Hasidic students in Brooklyn. From 1973 to 1978 the Rav was a member of the Professional Advisory Committee of the Program Development Fund for Jewish Education of New York UJA-Federation (PDF). This committee dealt with funds contributed by Joseph and Caroline Gruss which were matched, in part, by UJA-Federation, solely for the distribution of grants to Jewish schools in Greater New York.

As a member of the PDF Advisory Committee which I chaired, the Rav came every six weeks to my office at the Board of Jewish Education of Greater New York to meet with other committee members, all of them leaders of diverse ideological groups in the larger Jewish community. It is instructive to note who the other members of the committee were: Dr. Eugene Borowitz, leading Reform theologian and professor of Jewish philosophy at the Hebrew Union College—Jewish Institute of Religion; Dr. Gerson Cohen, president of the Jewish Theological Seminary; Mr. Joseph Gruss, philanthropist; Mr. Saul Litt, past president of the Jewish Welfare Board and chairman of the Program Development Fund of UJA-Federation; Dr. Emanuel Rackman, rabbi of the Fifth Avenue Synagogue and co-chair of the Program Development Fund; Mr. Sanford Solender, executive vice president, UJA-Federation; and Dr. Isadore Twersky, Nathan Littauer Professor of Hebrew Literature and Philosophy, Harvard University. Rabbi Seymour Brickman, staff member of the Board of Jewish Education, served as secretary to the committee.

The Professional Advisory Committee was created at the request of Mr. Gruss that a group of leaders help guide distribution of funds to Jewish schools. The Rav's active participation was essential to insure that the funds would be allocated for intensive Jewish education. The esteem with which the Rav was regarded was evident at every meeting and was most helpful in the formulation of the principles and practices of PDF. The allocation formulae guaranteed that the overwhelming portion of the grants would be used to support Jewish day schools and yeshivot.

Prior to the formation of PDF, an important scenario took place which involved the Rav. He agreed to participate in a funding process after my first meeting with Mr. Gruss, in the fall of 1970, regarding direct financial support to Jewish schools in New York—something that Federation did not do heretofore. Mr. Gruss indicated his readiness to contribute substantially and asked me to inform Federation leadership that he would make an initial challenge grant of one hundred thousand dollars for building-renovations for Jewish day schools and yeshivot, provided that Federation would match it. Mr. Gruss was a major donor to Federation and his request could not be taken lightly. His pledge was matched by several Federation leaders at a board meeting at which I presented Mr. Gruss's offer.

Because of the importance of this initial funding step by Federation to Jewish schools in Greater New York, I discussed this development with the Rav. He was never a fan of Federation, but he was happy to help implement the distribution of these monies. According to Mr. Gruss's request, an ad hoc committee including the Rav, Rabbi Rackman and me was formed to develop criteria for the allocation of building-renovation grants. The Rav saw the great potential of such a program to provide much-needed financial support to Jewish day schools and yeshivot and he readily agreed to serve on this committee.

Rabbi Rackman and I met twice with the Rav, once in his apartment at Yeshiva and once in his home in Brookline, Massachusetts, where he was usually more relaxed. His ideas were crucial to the development of criteria and a hierarchy of needs to guide the selection of recipients of building renovation grants. Interestingly, at the suggestion of Mr. Gruss, we considered the problem of the rickety busses used by the Brooklyn yeshivot. Our committee decided to recommend building-renovation allocations for bus repair and the purchase of new vehicles. Even though the Rav knew very well that he was not *persona grata* in the *haredi* and *hasidic* communities, he advocated strongly for bus repair. Accordingly, he rendered a *p'sak* [rabbinic decision] which made busses eligible for building renovations. He noted that not unlike a *sukkah* which is a *deerah ara-it*, a temporary abode during the week of *Sukkot*, a bus can be considered a *deerah ara-it* during the time students were riding to and from school. Based upon this *p'sak*, we recommended funding of busses. When PDF was established after the successful completion of this initial building grants program, which took two years to implement, the PDF Professional Advisory Committee continued to support bus grants for the *haredi/hasidic* community. It was the Rav's deep, abiding concern for the welfare of all Jewish children that led to the implementation of this grant program.

The Rav's relationship to the other committee members who scrutinized the needs of Jewish schools carefully and his comments at our meetings led to the development of a set of guidelines whereby well over ninety percent of all PDF grants were allocated to Jewish day schools and yeshivot. This arrangement has been of supreme importance to intensive Jewish education in Greater New York. Since 1970, via the Caroline and Joseph Gruss Life Monument Fund in cooperation with UJA-Federation, about one half billion dollars has been distributed to yeshivot and Jewish day schools 1) for educator benefits, health insurance, life insurance and pension support; 2) as formula grants based upon size and budget of schools; 3) as grants for Russian immigrant students; 4) for enrichment programs in Jewish and general studies; 5) for special education; 6) for creative programming; and 7) as teacher incentive awards.

In retrospect, in addition to the extraordinary intellectual impact of the Rav on Judaism, on Modern Orthodoxy and the Jewish community, he contributed significantly via his sterling personal qualities to the enhancement and continuity of Jewish education and Jewish life in this country.

The '40s:
The Emergence of Halakhik Man

The Rav in a humorous mood. Seated next to him is his colleague, Rabbi Samuel Gerstenfeld. (Photo courtesy Yeshiva University.)

The Rov: A Memoir

Nathan Epstein

In November of 1982, in a motel in Tewksbury, Massachusetts, three rabbis blew a shofar and snuffed candles in a ceremony meant to excommunicate the American historian, jazz critic and columnist Nat Hentoff. His sin was signing an ad in *The New York Times* protesting the 1982 Israeli invasion of Lebanon. Hentoff tells this tale in his sensitive and moving autobiography, *Boston Boy*. When he found out about the excommunication from a news report in *The Washington Post*, he was outraged. His immediate fantasy, he writes, was to call Rabbi Soloveitchik, who, with his enormous authority, would call for a rehearing, "and then, with his scholarship and soul force, he would smite that tribunal into sawdust."

I was very much taken by his use of the term "soul force" to describe the Rov.

Hentoff saw the Rov up close only once in his life. In 1938, the Rov was in the *shul* where Hentoff celebrated becoming a bar mitzvah. In those days it was the Rov's custom to visit the various *shuls* each *Shabbos*—especially for a bar mitzvah. Hentoff writes that after the *haftorah*, the Rov, as he nodded gravely to Hentoff, had a slight smile on his lips.

Nat Hentoff is not an Orthodox Jew. He did not come into the Rov's ambit. Yet the Rov made an impact on him. Such was the Rov's spiritual presence in Boston.

I have often said that the definitive biography of the Rov can be written only by a Bostonian. Bostonians witnessed the Rov in all his

---

Nathan H. Epstein was born in Boston, Massachusetts, in 1940. He graduated from Maimonides in 1958, from Yeshiva College in 1962, and earned a Master's degree in actuarial science from Northeastern University in 1967. He is a Fellow of The Society of Actuaries and a Member of the American Academy of Actuaries.

facets: as a family man, as their rabbi, as an educator, and as a community leader and spokesman.

In Boston his word was law. A Bostonian Yeshiva student who was a *kohen* asked the Rov if he could become a medical doctor. The Rov said no. The Yeshiva student went into another field. To a Bostonian, the Rov's word was law!

I first became aware of the Rov in September 1949, when I started attending Maimonides in the fourth grade. A year earlier my cousin Selwyn enrolled in Maimonides after his mother decided to go back to work. Because the hours at Maimonides were longer than those at the public school, she would be able to get home from work before Selwyn returned from school. When my mother also decided to go to work, I entered Maimonides.

I said I started in the fourth grade. That was only partially true. I was in the fourth grade for English, but even though I had gone to afternoon Hebrew School after public school, I wasn't up to snuff in Hebrew and had to be in the third grade for Jewish studies. This frosted my father and me!

After a few weeks, my father asked me how I was doing in Hebrew. I said I was doing well, but there was a kid in my class who had an Uncle Berel, and his Uncle Berel was giving him all the answers. I wished I had an Uncle Berel! That kid is my life-long friend Rabbi Moshe Meiselman, and his Uncle Berel, of course, was the Rov.

The Rov founded Maimonides in 1937 together with his wife, Dr. Tonya Soloveitchik, who bore the brunt of the day-to-day operations. In those years there was tremendous opposition in the Jewish community to the founding of an all-day Jewish school in Boston. It was un-American to not attend public school. Day school children, it was feared, wouldn't be able to speak proper English. They wouldn't be able to function in the general society. They wouldn't get jobs or be able to do well in them. Even their physical growth would be stunted! Parents who sent their children to Maimonides were swimming against a strong tide.

I remember the first high school graduation of Maimonides in June 1953. The Rov had gotten the great Rabbi Dr. Joseph Lookstein, Professor of Homiletics at Yeshiva University, to be the commencement speaker. Some of the men asked my father, "*Vos iz dos* homiletics?"

"*Ehr lernt zey vi'azay me macht a droshoh,*" [He teaches them how to give a talk] he answered them.

"Ah! Machen a droshoh," they replied. *"So vhy didn't dey say so?"*

In the middle of his speech, Rabbi Lookstein, pulling himself up to his full height, which was in the five foot area, and with an upraised finger, exclaimed, "And I wouldn't have grown an inch taller if I had gone to public school!" The place exploded with applause.

After Yeshiva, I quickly saw how wrong the arguments against the establishment of Maimonides were—and how right the Rov was.

When I applied for an actuarial job at the John Hancock Life Insurance Company, I was given the Society of Actuaries' Actuarial Aptitude Test, which consisted of 25 math questions and 40 verbal questions. It was quickly graded while I was being interviewed by various Hancock actuaries. When I returned to personnel, the director had my exam results and was looking at me strangely. I immediately thought I had bombed. "Did I do okay?" I asked, nervously.

He said I had gotten 23 out of the 25 math questions right. "Is that bad?" I asked.

"Not at all," he said. "You need only 18 right to get a job here." Then he said, "But you got all 40 of the verbal right. In all the years we've been giving this test, we've never had a job candidate get all the verbal questions correct. In fact, the highest score before you was 31." Shades of C.P. Snow's *The Two Cultures*! There went the argument that I'd never speak English if I went to Maimonides.

At the Hancock, quite a few of my fellow actuarial trainees, some from America's first families, had gone to Phillips Exeter, Phillips Andover, and other exclusive private schools. There went the argument that it was un-American to miss out on public school.

These colleagues were interested in whether I had Latin and Greek at Maimonides. I said we had Latin, but I didn't have Greek until I was in Yeshiva College. The classical languages were evidence of an elite education, which was a prerequisite for assuming a position of importance in the Boston business community. Of course, we had other things in common, such as our math backgrounds and our college degrees. In addition to Boston Brahmins from the Back Bay, many of us were from the ethnic wards of Boston. We all got along fine and had a great collegial spirit. There went the argument that I wouldn't be able to deal with general society if I went to Maimonides.

Early in my career, I was working on a crucial project, and had gotten some important results. My boss said I would have to show them to Henry. Henry Huntington, whose family came over on the *Mayflower*, was the final actuarial word at the company and an imposing figure. Even the chairman of the company, himself an actuary, did not make a move without first getting the okay from Henry. With trepidation, I entered Henry's spacious corner office. He took my worksheets, spread them out over his desk, and studied them for what seemed an eternity. He then sat back in his chair and told me a story of when *he* was a trainee and had to take *his* worksheets to *his* chief actuary—the fearsome Fergus McDarmid. McDarmid was a Fellow of the Faculty of Actuaries of Scotland, considered the *ne plus ultra* of the profession. Needless to say, McDarmid was not easily impressed. Yet he looked at Henry and said, "Huntington, I like the way you think."

"So, Epstein," Henry said to me, "I'm telling you: I like the way you think." From then on, I was in—the Boston Brahmin and the Orthodox Jew. There went the argument that I would never advance professionally if I went to Maimonides.

In sum, attending Maimonides did not affect my English speaking, my job opportunities, or my getting along with peers and superiors. And at 5'10", it didn't stunt my growth either!

The Rov had a special love for the parents who sent their children to Maimonides. It was his school. He would personally recruit children for the school. The main street in our part of Roxbury was Humboldt Avenue. All the stores and shops were there, including my uncle's kosher butcher shop. Next door to my uncle's store was a fine residence set back from the avenue and up a hill. It had about thirty stairs leading from the street to the front door. The Rov climbed those stairs and knocked on the door. He told the lady who answered that he wanted to talk to her about sending her young son to Maimonides.

She slammed the door in his face with such vehemence that the Rov was almost knocked backwards down all those stairs. Twenty years later, the same lady came running to the Rov's home, crying that her son was going to marry a non-Jew. The Rov cried, and she cried.

The Rov assembled a top team of faculty and administration.

Rabbi Cohen, our principal, was the consummate administrator. My father, who was especially taken with Rabbi Cohen's skill and knowledge, said he was a real "Cracker-Jack."

Rabbi Wohlgemuth, the faculty mainstay, could teach any grade from elementary through high school. In my first year at Maimonides, he made my transition from public school seamless and even pleasant. A scion of the famous Jewish-German Wohlgemuth family, he had a complete set, in German, of *Jeshurun*, the classic Torah journal which one of his family members had edited. His son, Shlomoh, was my close friend and classmate throughout my Maimonides and Yeshiva years.

Rabbi Simon, our high school *Gemara* and *Chumash rebbe*, was in a class by himself. One of the younger members of the Mir Yeshiva in Europe, he spent the war years in Shanghai. In addition to his teaching us, he was our mentor. On *Shabbos* we were always at his house, where he would learn with us and talk to us. He would take us to the Rov's *Chevra Shas shiur* and review it with us.

He and his wife Betty were a second family to us students. When I was married, they would frequently come over on Friday nights and were with us through the arrival of our two Boston-born sons. Even after I left Boston, we maintained contact.

The Rov and the Rebbetzin were also the bosses of my wife, Diane, a graduate of Stern College and Columbia's Teachers College, who was hired to teach English at Maimonides.

I remember the first time she met the Rov. A friend of mine was visiting from New York and wanted to see the Rov. We all drove over to the Rov's house. The Rebbetzin, who had previously interviewed and hired my wife, greeted us and told the Rov we had arrived. Introducing Diane, she said to the Rov, "And this is Nathan's wife," to which the Rov replied, "Who else would it be on a Sunday morning?"

The Rov was our *posek* for the million-and-one questions newlyweds have. He always had the time and patience for us.

When our baby needed a delicate neurosurgical operation, the Rov *davened* for him. When I thanked him, he said, "*Hamispallel be'ad chaveiro* [for one who prays for another], no thanks are needed!"

As a youngster in Roxbury I attended Toras Moshe, the *shul* where my maternal grandfather was *gabbai rishon* [first officer of the synagogue]. But in 1956, as the Jews were moving from Roxbury, the Talner Bais Medrash was experiencing difficulty in obtaining a daily *minyan*. The Talner Rebbe was the Rov's *mechutan* [a child's father-in-law]. Because the Talner Bais Midrash was near Maimonides, the Rov sent Maimonides boys to help with the daily *minyan*.

There I met Professor Yitzchak Twersky, the Rebbe's son and the Rov's son-in-law. He became a mentor of mine. Since I lived near him, I often walked home with him from davening.

Years later, when the Rov was considerably weaker, and I didn't want to bother him, I would call Professor Twersky with my *shailos* [halakhic questions]. For one serious *shailah*, he gave me an answer that I didn't like. Hearing the hesitancy in my voice and reading my mind, he said that he had conferred with the Rov. Once he said that, I was satisfied. The Rov's word was law. He then gave me a *brakhah* that all should go well. I always cherished that *brakhah* from a noble scion of the great Chernobyl Dynasty and a major personality and disciple of *Beis Harav*.

The Rov's son, Haym, is a brilliant *talmid chochom* in his own right. When I was in the twelfth grade at Maimonides, my father was worried that I wouldn't be prepared for the *Gemara shiurim* at RIETS. I asked Haym if he would tutor me. He consented, and I learned with him Sunday mornings throughout my senior year. His tutoring enabled me to do very well on my entrance *bechinah* [test] with Rav Mendel Zaks. (It also helped that my Yiddish at that time was first-rate.) Rav Mendel even made a point of telling the Rov how well we had done. The Rov was very proud.

Haym also inherited the Soloveitchik character trait of doing *chesed* [kindness]. He once called me during vacation from Yeshiva to suggest that we get some of the boys together and visit Mr. Ajemian. Mr. Ajemian, an Armenian non-Jew, was the French and Latin teacher at Maimonides. He traveled to school every day by train and trolley from his home in Palmer, Mass., which was quite a distance from Boston. I called some of the other boys, and with Haym in the driver's seat we went to Palmer for an enjoyable hour with an appreciative Mr. Ajemian.

The Rov was also my boss. In the summer between my eleventh and twelfth grade years, I worked as a helper for the *mashgichim* [supervisors of kashrut] and *shochtim* [those who slaughter an animal in accordance with Jewish law] at the kosher slaughter department of Swift's Meat Packing Plant. The Rov was *rav hamakhshir* [the supervisor over all].

Once the *shochtim* came across a tough *shailah* and even though, in addition to being top *shochtim*, most also were learned *rabbonim*, they were stymied in this instance. When they brought the *shailah* to the Rov, he was standing on the slaughterhouse floor. Without hesitation he told one of the *shochtim* to get a certain *sefer*. The Rov took the *sefer*, immediately opened it to the right page and showed them a picture of the exact problem along with the answer to the question. They were all amazed at the Rov's encyclopedic knowledge. The U. S. government veterinarian was also standing there and had looked into the *sefer*. He turned to me and said that he had never seen that particular part in any of the veterinary books. That summer's experience helped me immeasurably when I studied *Yoreh Dei'ah*. I think every *semikhah* student should spend a couple of months in a slaughterhouse.

The Rov's official job in Boston was rabbi of the *Chevra Shas*. His famous *Motzoei Shabbos shiurim* were under the aegis of the *Chevra Shas*. For his entire life in America he gave those *shiurim*. By 1969, when I moved from Boston, there were people who had been attending those *shiurim* for close to forty years.

The highlight of the Orthodox week in Boston was the Rov's *Chevra Shas shiur*. Rabbis and learned laymen would come from the entire Boston area to attend it. I started attending the *shiur* when I was in the tenth grade, in 1956. The Rov was saying *shiurim* in *Chulin*. Why *Chulin*? In Maimonides we learned *Chulin* in the twelfth grade. Herby Millen, who was in the twelfth grade that year, had asked the Rov during the summer if he would learn *Chulin* in the new year starting from *Motzoei Shabbos Bereishis*. The Rov accommodated him. Such was his love for his Maimonides children.

The *shiur* was divided into two parts: the *mesechta* for two or more hours and the *parshah* of the week for an hour-and-a-half plus. Rabbi Simon, our *Gemara rebbe*, would always be available during the week to go over any questions we had. That was a big help. At times when he felt we had a good question, we would go and ask the Rov himself!

It wasn't until after I finished Yeshiva and was back in Boston that I realized that the *Chevra Shas shiur* was on an even higher level than the RIETS *shiur*. I attributed this to the fact that the *Chevra Shas* audience consisted of older, more seasoned and learned *talmidei chachomim*, many of whom were European yeshiva graduates.

In the RIETS *shiur* the Rov had a fearsome reputation for being extremely hard on the boys. His harsh demeanor was in direct contradiction to his usually warm and kind disposition.

I attribute this to the fact that the *shiur* was where the Rov "lived." A *talmid chochom* like the Rov comes along only once every two or three generations. He had no peer in his power of *Gemara* analysis and no equal in his ability to teach. He reminds me of a comment of the Rambam.

In his introduction to his commentary on the *Mishnah*, the Rambam analyzes the *aggadah* that states that *Hashem* has in this world only the four ells of the *halakhah*. He explains that this means the whole world was created for the purpose of developing the perfect man who achieves his perfection only through the four ells of the *halakhah*. The Rambam gives R' Shimon bar Yochai as an example in his time.

So, too, the Rov in our time.

The Rov was also a link in the chain of the *mesorah* through his father, the *gaon* Rabbi Moshe Soloveitchick, *zt"l*, who brought the advanced Brisker *derekh* to America, and his grandfather, the *gaon* Rabbi Chaim Brisker, *zt"l*, who developed the *derekh*.

His perfection and his being in the chain of the *mesorah* render the Rov's "*Da'as Torah*" on inter-faith relations and intra-faith, women's issues, secular studies, and the State of Israel, authoritative.

He therefore took his responsibility in the transmission of Torah to the next generation exceedingly seriously. To the Rov, the phrase "*milchamta shel Torah*" [the battle for Torah], was not an oratorical flourish. He was preparing soldiers to do battle in Torah and for Torah. He was training not merely regular soldiers but elite troops. Those charged with the training of Army Rangers, Navy SEALS, and Marines are not noted for their mollycoddling. How much more so for elite Torah soldiers! He pushed us to be the very best we could be.

Once out of the *shiur*, he loved all his students equally and would just as quickly go out of his way to do a *chesed* [kindness] for the weaker student as for the top student.

The Rov was famous for his *teshuvah droshos* [talks on repentance]. For me the *Aseres Y'mai Teshuvah* aren't the same without his *droshah*. But the biggest impetus to *teshuvah* was just to see him. The Rambam closes *Hilchos Teshuva*, indeed the whole *Sefer Mada*, with a panegyric on the true *Oved Hashem*, the *Oved Hashem mei'ahavah*, one who serves Hashem from love.

The Rov was that *Oved Hashem mei'ahava*. He loved *Hashem* and His Torah, and he loved us, Hashem's people.

Nat Hentoff was right in talking of the Rov's "soul force." I would submit additionally that for me it would be his love.

I am convinced that he is in heaven next to the *Kisei Hakovod* [the seat of Glory], being a *meilitz yosher* [advocate for justice] for us and looking down with love on his family: his biological family; his family of the covenant of Faith; his disciples and followers; and his family of the covenant of Fate—all Jews everywhere.

We are family, and he loves us one and all.

The Rav: Public Giant, Private Mentsch

Norman Lamm

I do not recall exactly when it happened—whether it was at an extra-curricular gathering, or in the course of a *shiur*, or slightly afterwards when he was unwinding—but this is the gist of his brief remark, which was not only wistful but also revealing of a larger pathos than any of us had ever expected. The Rav said, "Why is it that my *talmidim* never think of sending me Rosh Hashanah greetings?"

I was crushed—not at his felt need for friendship rather than admiration alone, but at our sheer indifference to his inner feelings. Why, in our boundless esteem, did we not ever realize that he had a heart, that he was a sensitive human being, that he was oh so very human, that he experienced the need for approbation not as the intellectual giant he was but as a real flesh-and-blood person?

His greatness created a natural distance between him and his disciples, and that gulf was probably the cause of much of his loneliness. But it was inexcusable for us to be so unconcerned for him as a person, to allow our near apotheosis of him to lead us to refrain from extending to him private courtesies, to imagine him as a perpetual motion machine of great ideas, of exciting *shiurim*, of finely balanced distinctions, of profound intellectual creativity—without recognizing him as well as a person, as a sensitive human whose emotional needs were not that different from our own. Perhaps that is the price one pays for fame and genius, but that is not an excuse for the rest of us.

The following year and ever since, until he passed away, I never failed to send him a greeting card for Rosh Hashanah. He always

---

Rabbi Dr. Norman Lamm is Chancellor of Yeshiva University and *Rosh HaYeshiva* of RIETS. He served as President of Yeshiva University from 1976-2003.

answered—always!—with a handwritten letter of blessings for the New Year. I confess in shame that I merely sent him a printed card, with added remarks penned in, while he wrote a whole letter by hand, personally.

I failed to learn the lesson. I shall always feel guilty.

* * *

I came to Yeshiva University from Torah Vodaath for two reasons. First, I wanted an academic education in the same place I would be learning Torah (I had not yet heard the term "Torah Umadda," but effectively I was already committed to it.) Second, the Rav had just begun to achieve great fame. As a Torah Vodaath boy, any praise for YU was muted, at best. But my grandfather, zt"l, who was a Galizianer *Gaon*, encouraged me to enroll in YU because he wanted me to learn under "that young *Gaon* Soloveitchik."

Most high school graduates were placed in the lower grades, and I was fortunate to be accepted by Dr. Belkin zt"l in his own *shiur*, the last one he was to give before the burdens of his ever growing responsibility as the president forced him to withdraw from presenting a *shiur*. (I tried co-teaching a *shiur* during my second year in office, but I quickly albeit regretfully had to give it up for the same reason that Dr. Belkin did.) My next *rebbe*, the Lomzher Rav, Rav Shatzkes zt"l, was a greatly erudite and endearing (and, as well, a most handsome) man. Only then was I permitted to attend the *shiur* of the Rav zt"l.

What an experience that was! The language of discourse then was Yiddish which, in and of itself, didn't frighten me. But the Rav's Yiddish was pure Lithuanian and, while I could get used to his accent, certain idiomatic expressions eluded me. What, for instance, did "*an'oig'n'blik*" mean? I finally found someone who explained that it was *ein oigen blick*—"one blink of the eye"—which meant, as any Litvak would know, "Wait a minute" or "Hold off for a while" or something of the sort.

But language was the least of my problems. Thorough preparation was an absolute requirement. The Rav was totally intolerant of sloppy preparation or sloppy thinking. He could not and would not tolerate superficial answers; he had no patience whatever for fools. I have written elsewhere of my experiences with the Rav which are engraved in my memory. Even when, years later, I became President of Yeshiva, my enormous reverence for him, bordering on fear, was not in the least diminished. I have always been proud of the fact that I received both *semikhah* and my PhD from him.

Psychologists and educators will tell you that you can't get students to think and understand and achieve in a climate of fear. Not true! Or, that may hold true for little children, but not for advanced students. The Rav forced us to think the way he thinks. We had to learn quickly his analytic method, the *"Brisker Derekh,"* and to be original if need be. His greatest passion, as a scholar and a teacher, was Truth. No "brilliant" solutions were permitted in class if they did not truthfully represent what the text intended.

He insisted that each of us think for himself, not just give him back his own interpretations, an activity he considered parrot-like, the sign of a sub-human intellect.

Once, after a public lecture, a rather bold member of the audience challenged him and said, "But Rabbi Soloveitchik, what is your source?" The Rav immediately replied, "A clear and logical mind." Indeed, his mind was uncluttered and profoundly logical.

Some of his students who sat at his feet admiringly imbibing his Torah interpretations were reluctant to accept his ideology. He often said—once to me personally—"Some of my most attentive students who would willingly get up in the middle of the night to hear a *shiur* from me, secretly suspect that I'm an *apikores*..." I clearly remember the Rav using the sobriquet *"Torah Umadda"* as part of a homily, and it was said approvingly. He didn't have to preach it loudly and often; he just lived it.

Example: I was elected President in August of 1976. The following September when school began and the Rav returned to New York to deliver his *shiurim*, I went to his apartment to consult with him, because I was just beginning to realize the enormity of the burden that had been placed on my shoulders. I asked the Rav, *"Rebbe,* what do you think should be the first goal I must set for myself?" He answered at once rather surprisingly, "Improve the college!"

That should put to rest all the doubts that were occasionally raised as to his commitment to *Torah Umadda*...including the startling comment by a former *talmid* that the Rav could not possibly be a supporter of *Torah Umadda*, nor did he in any way relate to secular wisdom, because this student often accompanied the Rav to his apartment after the *shiur*, and he never saw the Rav reading or holding such a volume in his hands. Obviously, such "arguments from silence" are totally inappropriate and hence have no value whatsoever.

The Rav was remarkable for his intellectual honesty. He never pretended to know what he did not know. He was always—always!—ready to admit that he was wrong. When I was involved in setting up the Manhattan *eruv* in the 1960's and I asked him for his opinion, his answer was, "I don't know. I never learned *Eruvin*." (He later did learn *Eruvin* and did not come to the conclusion that I did.)

Interestingly, I had a similar experience with the late *Gaon* Rabbi Aharon Kotler *zt"l*. He attempted to place an *issur* [prohibition] on behalf of the Agudas Harabonim on those who were preparing to announce the *eruv*. He was obviously convinced that an *eruv* in Manhattan was prohibited, and he asked that I come down to the Agudas Harabonim office to hear his *pesak*. Still young and politically naive, I accepted at once ("like a Lamm to the slaughter," as one of their members later told me). Rav Kotler presided over a crowded and unsympathetic (to me) room. He must have been troubled by the arguments I gave in defense of the *eruv*, because he called me early the next morning. The content of that discussion I shall leave for another occasion. For the present, it is in place to record a brief snippet at the end of our dialogue. He said he wanted to rethink his position and asked that both sides postpone any public announcement (in print). I was bold enough to ask him, "Kletzker *Rosh Yeshiva*, why is it necessary to wait? Our people are ready to proceed with an announcement, and you are fully aware of the issues and of your objections."

"I'll tell you," he said, "I really never learned *Eruvin*..."

So, here were two *gedolim* who manifested remarkable intellectual honesty. No wonder that, despite differences of opinion and approach, they regarded each other so highly! One cannot help but admire such gallant and courageous rabbinic giants.

* * *

Intellectually, the Rav operated in the Brisker Talmudic tradition, founded by his eminent grandfather, R. Hayyim Soloveitchik *zt"l*. He made remarkably creative contributions to it, enlarging its scope and ennobling it. This was his mode of Talmudic analysis, his intellectual signature. Of course, I admired the Brisker methodology, and especially the elegant and creative way the Rav used it. But I confess that—subconsciously—I had my doubts. There was something too easy, too "popular" and facile, and almost mechanical about the manner in which some acolytes of the Rav and other *rebbeim* and their *talmidim* spouted "Brisker Torah" and solved all problems by declaring that there were really "*tzvei dinnim*," that every legal precept can be broken down into two other fundamental ideas or categories.

I was therefore genuinely pleased when the Rav, in the course of a *shiur*, casually proposed that there was a method for differentiating between authentic and illegitimate "Brisker Torah." His method: try translating your *chiddush* into English—without resorting to any of the terminology of Brisk. If your idea makes sense in English, it is valuable. If not, it means you were playing with words, and scrap it no matter how attractive you may find it. The pseudo-Brisk manipulation of a wise, honored, and exacting Talmudic method is an instance of intellectual abuse.

I still remain with a tiny dose of skepticism about the Brisker methodology as practiced by some members of that school. Example: a theory is proposed by the *Rishonim* or *Acharonim*. The questioner then presents contradictory evidence. Here the proud Brisker replies, in Yiddish: "*Ut, dos iz doss, takeh!*"—"that's the point"—as if the original and the counter-proposition, question and answer, thesis and antithesis, merely by being set up in opposition to each other, are both equally expressive of the one idea in two different modes; hence no *kasheh* [question, difficulty], all problems solved. Maybe that is occasionally appropriate, but when inappropriate it is no more than a semantic hoax unwittingly perpetrated by an innocent and unsophisticated novice drifting carelessly and irresponsibly in the great Brisker tradition.

* * *

As the years go by and the number of those fortunate enough to have studied under him begins to dwindle, every effort must be made to transmit to the next generation of *talmidim* an honest appraisal of the complex and dialectical character of this giant, without unconsciously but arrogantly "cutting him down to size"—or by excessive hero worship, because that too is a form of distortion.

As a student of the Rav, I congratulate the editors of *The Commentator* on undertaking this series. If not all contributors to this important collection agree or give the same impression, that is at least partly because he was indeed such a complex and dialectical personality. That is hard for students—but wonderful grist for the mills of biographers.

I am fortunate that I had the *zekhut* [privilege] to study under him in my youth, and to communicate often with him in my mature years. I know I shall never meet another like him—certainly not in my lifetime. Once is enough, and for that privilege I will always be thankful to the Almighty.

Yehi zikhro barukh.

The Unique Phenomenon that was the Rav

Bernard Rosensweig

I came to RIETS and to Yeshiva College in September of 1944. The next six years would be the most exciting period of my life, and the almost four years that I spent in the *shiur* of Rav Yosef Dov Halevi Soloveitchik *zt"l*, who was known simply as the Rav, would define my commitment, my *weltanschauung* and the direction that I would take for the rest of my life. In my time, the Rav's *shiur* had no more than twenty-two boys who, I suspect, the Rav hand-picked. Rabbi Dr. Norman Lamm, who was also my roommate, Rabbi Dr. Moshe Tendler and Rabbi Dr. Sol Roth, all familiar names to our students, were part of an illustrious group who went on to make distinguished careers in the Jewish world and to profoundly influence the direction of Torah Judaism. The man who was our life-long guide and whose thinking influenced our own was the Rav.

However, in order to understand the Rav and to appreciate the role he played in the life of his students, we have to understand his background, his persona, as well as his ideological position. The Rav, the outstanding explicator of the Rambam in our time, like the Rambam never attended a Yeshiva; and, again, like the Rambam, his father was his only teacher. When the Rav was a youngster, he was already acknowledged as an *ilui*, a prodigy. The Rav once told me that he had a notebook at home in Boston containing the *chiddushei Torah*, the novellae, which he had written when he was twelve or thirteen years old. His father, R. Moshe, *zt"l*, would regularly send these *chiddushim* to the Rav's grandfather, Rav Chaim of Brisk, for his comments. Rav Chaim, who was amazed at the level of his

---

Rabbi Dr. Bernard Rosensweig is Professor of Jewish History at Yeshiva College and Rabbi Emeritus of the Kew Gardens Adath Jeshurun Synagogue in Queens, NY. He is a past president of the Rabbinical Council of America.

grandson's Torah knowledge and insight, would invariably write back in the notebook that these *chiddushim* were worthy enough to have been developed by the Brisker Rav himself. There can be no doubt that Rav Chaim saw his future in the Rav and considered him to be the appropriate heir to the mantle of Brisker scholarship.

And then, at the age of twenty-three, the Rav, who had spent his formative years immersed in the study of the Torah, decided to go to Berlin and to study philosophy at the University of Berlin. Whatever the motivation, the move into the secular world of Berlin had to be traumatic for him. The Rav once told my dear friend and colleague, Rabbi Dr. Walter Wurzburger *zt"l*, "You have no idea how enormously difficult it was for me to move from the world of Rav Chaim to that of Berlin University." However, while he took his studies seriously at the university, the study of the Torah remained central to him—even in Berlin. The Rav's son, Dr. Haym Soloveitchik, recently published a volume, *Iggrot Ha-Grid Halevi*, which includes at least a dozen *chiddushei Torah* on many difficult *sugyot* in *Shas* which the Rav sent to his father during that time. For the Rav, Berlin and his university studies were not an escape from his background, as they were for some of his contemporaries. He was not looking to abandon his religious roots but, on the contrary, to defend them in the intellectual world which had made such inroads on the finest Jewish minds of the time. The Rav viewed his engagement with the world of the university as a positive element in projecting Traditional Judaism to a new generation of Jews.

Soon after his arrival in the United States in 1932, the Rav was appointed Chief Rabbi of the Orthodox community of Boston, where he would live the rest of his life; and in 1941, after the death of his father Rav Moshe *zt"l*, the Rav was appointed as *Rosh Yeshiva* in RIETS. The Rav's greatest impact and, ultimately, his legacy, emerged from his *shiurim* in our yeshiva where he taught from 1941 to 1985, and where he trained thousands of advanced students. The Rav liked to refer to himself modestly as a *melamed*, "a simple teacher of the Torah"—and then he would add whimsically that this was not so bad because G-d Himself is called a *melamed* in the blessing, *ha-melamed Torah l'amo Yisrael*. In fact, the Rav was the teacher, better, the *Rosh Yeshiva* par excellence. No matter what his other involvements were—and they were multifaceted—he remained primarily and quintessentially the teacher of the Torah and the transmitter of the *mesorah*.

I can say without any reservations that I have never known anyone else who developed a *shiur* with such depth and such clarity and with such novel insights. It was he who made the Brisker method of analysis an integral part of the learning equipment of the American Yeshiva *bachur* [student]. The Brisker method, with its insistence on incisive conceptual analysis, exact classification and its emphasis on the Rambam's *Mishneh Torah,* was tailor-made for the bright, inquiring minds of the students of our yeshiva. The Rav used that method, gave it his own extension, and opened up a new intellectual world for his students.

To be in the Rav's *shiur* was to be involved in an unforgettable experience. He was an unbelievable *maggid shiur* who knew how to make a *sugya* come alive. As I indicated, I was in the Rav's *shiur* in the 40's, when he was at the height of his intellectual power. He was demanding, he was rigorous, he was terrifying, particularly in those early years—and he was awesome. His clarity, charisma and intellectual integrity were exciting. As much as he demanded of his students, he demanded much more from himself. The Rav was thoroughly prepared and expected the same from his students. I remember the Rav coming to class with his notebooks. Woe betide a student who was not equally prepared. The Rav's *shiurim* were models of clarity of thought, precision of expression and the relentless search for conceptual understanding. He would develop his thesis with "Brisker analysis" and, at the end, there emerged the *chiddush,* the new insight which was overpowering in its scope and implication and brought the discussion to a new level of understanding.

The Rav's intellectual honesty was impressive and awe-inspiring. He had been developing a certain line of thought in one of the *sugyot* over a number of days, when one of my friends interrupted him to say that one of the *Rishonim* appeared to contradict his whole thesis. His first reaction, and this was not unusual, was to literally scream at whoever interrupted or contradicted him, and to vigorously defend his position. This time was no exception; then suddenly he fell silent, put his head in his hands and said nothing for twenty minutes. After the twenty minutes, the Rav stood up, closed his *Gemara* and announced to his stunned students that the *shiur* was over. The next day he came to the class, announced that the student had made a valid point and had caused him to rework the concept and the *shiur* to include the objections which had been raised. We were overwhelmed by his remarkable intellectual honesty! The Rav could have fudged it, he could have used his superior mind and knowledge to manipulate the text and, in the process, rescue his theory and his ego. But he did nothing of the sort! Through that incident he showed us in the clearest manner that the primary goal of *Talmud Torah* is truth, and that in the pursuit of intellectual honesty and "truth in learning,"nothing can be an impediment.

The Rav was not only a *gaon* in Torah but, like his grandfather Rav Chaim, a *gaon* in *chesed* as well. There are so many stories of the Rav's acts of kindness that they could fill a volume in their own right—all of which, incidentally, he performed without fuss or fanfare. When I became president of the Rabbinical Council of America, the unforgettable Rabbi Israel Klavan *zt"l*, who was the Vice-President of the RCA, passed away. Rabbi Klavan was a superb executive who made life much easier for his presidents. I went to Boston to discuss with the Rav the situation created by Rabbi Klavan's passing. Without a moment's hesitation, he said to me, "Don't worry! I will be your Klavan." And he was as good as his word. He literally became my guide, my advisor, my confidant—and my friend. The relationship which we had developed over the years, beginning with my student days, deepened and strengthened.

The Rav's relationships and influence moved across a wide spectrum and embraced the greater part of American and world Jewry. The people who related to him and sought his guidance and advice covered the gamut of the Jewish community, including the giants of the previous generation. Any personality of any consequence in the Israeli establishment—political, economic, academic or religious—made a pilgrimage to Boston or to Yeshiva to meet with the Rav and to exchange insights with him on their favorite themes. Practically every Prime Minister from Ben Gurion to Begin sought an opportunity to meet with the Rav and to bask in his scholarship and wisdom. I was present when the Rav met with Menachem Begin, whose father had been the secretary of the *Kehillah* of Brisk—and it was quite an experience. Every Chief Rabbi, Ashkenazic or Sephardic, considered it a privilege to "talk in" Torah with the Rav, to keep him abreast of the activities of the Chief Rabbinate, and to seek his counsel on current problems. The Rav's reaction to these men and their scholarship, as I can testify, was extremely insightful.

All the rabbinic giants of the past generation were involved with him and related to him on the highest level. Rav Moshe Feinstein *zt"l*, was his cousin and his friend. His relationship with Rav Menachem Mendel Shneersohn *zt"l*, the Lubavitcher Rebbe, went back to their days in Berlin, as did his relationship with Rav Yitzchok Hutner *zt"l*. He enjoyed a special camaraderie with Rav Aharon Kotler *zt"l*. I remember accompanying the Rav in 1949 to three meetings about Chinuch Atzmai, the network of religious schools in Israel. Witnessing the mutual respect and the genuine friendship between these two spiritual giants is an experience which remains indelibly imprinted on my mind. It is not at all surprising that Rav Aharon insisted that the Rav should be the guest speaker at the Chinuch Atzmai dinner which honored him in 1956, and the genuine tribute which the Rav paid him was a reflection of his feelings for Rav Aharon.

Thirty years later, in 1979, I accompanied the Rav, to a meeting with the leadership of the JDC, the Joint Distribution Committee. The Vaad Ha-Yeshivot of Israel had asked the Rav and me, in my capacity as president of the Rabbinical Council of America, to intercede on their behalf for a much-needed grant for their institutions. When we came into the conference room, the top leadership of the Joint was present. Not one of them was an Orthodox Jew, but when the Rav walked in, instinctively, they stood up, as a sign of respect for a great man. The Rav spoke to them for thirty minutes, and they were mesmerized. He developed the theme of *hakarat hatov*, of gratitude; he thanked them for what the Joint had done for his family in Europe in the aftermath of the First World War. I can see the wonderful smile which lit up his face as he told them that he could still feel the taste of the chocolate in his mouth. He then proceeded to apply this principle to the need to support Torah and Torah institutions. When he was through, the president of the Joint responded that because the Rav had appeared before them and had spoken to them, the grant would be forthcoming. It is important to understand that the *Roshei Yeshiva* of the Vaad Ha-Yeshivot were not particularly his friends; in fact, a number of them endeavored to undermine his stature and his greatness. But the Rav's love for Torah and the study of Torah was such that it translated itself into his unstinting support of Torah institutions.

The Rav was, as the *New York Times* once put it, "the rabbi's rabbi"—and more particularly, the rabbi of the RCA. As chairman of our Halacha Commission, the Rav fought the battle against mixed pews and emerged as the defender of *shechitah*, kosher slaughter, in the United States and Canada. The Rav also provided the ideological underpinnings for the parameters of our relationship with the Conservative and Reform movements; in his first English article, "Confrontation," which appeared in *Tradition*, he defined the boundaries of our dialogue with the Christian churches. Both as president of the RCA and, at one time, the chairman of our delegation to the Synagogue Council of America, I can vouch for the fact that these rules were rigorously enforced and the RCA never moved in these areas without a full discussion of these issues with the Rav.

The Rav was totally committed to the concept of *Torah U'Madda* and its ideology reflected his *weltanschauung* exactly. However, it is important to understand that even though the Rav was committed to a synthesis between the world of the Torah and the society in which we live, nonetheless, for him always, the priority, the emphasis, was on the Torah and its value system, which alone conditioned his world-view. The Rav's *shiur* was not only the focal point of his all his activities and interests, it was the prism through which he viewed everything else. His philosophy is anchored squarely within the *Halakhah*, which he was convinced mediated man's relationship to G-d, to the world and to himself.

The attempt on the part of some on the left of the Orthodox spectrum to paint the Rav as a modern Orthodox philosopher who re-interpreted Torah Judaism to satisfy the demands of the modern world is an absolute form of revisionism and a distortion of the Rav's persona and his theological commitment. In responding to a series of distortions about the Rav that were uttered at an Edah conference, Rav Aharon Lichtenstein, the Rav's son-in-law, outstanding student and *Rosh Ha-Yeshiva* in Har Etzion, wrote: "It is critical to bear in mind that the Rav's essence was manifested not only in the philosophical writings which he authored, but in the theological principles to which he was committed and, above all, a rigorous halachic discipline, which was both his patrimony and his legacy. These, as the Rav's innermost being were forged in the tradition of Brisk rather than in Berlin; …He was unstintingly tenacious in insisting upon the autonomy of Halacha and the rejection of historicism; in placing lomdut (knowledge), in the realms of theory and practice, both at the epicenter of Jewish life and in predicating the authority of Chazal as its polestar." He them concluded: "Had the Rav been compelled to choose between what some refer to nega-

tively as 'the fervently Orthodox Yeshiva world' and its denigra-
tors, there is not a shadow of doubt what his decision would have
been. The point is that he did not want to make that choice, and he
did not need to make it. He sought, as we should, the best of the
Torah world and the best of modernity."

While the Rav was indeed, in many respects, "the lonely man of
faith," his students will always remember him essentially as the "*Ish
ha-Halacha.*"

The Halakhic Mind of the Halakhic Man: A Perspective on the Rav

Sol Roth

I have been invited often to record in writing my personal impressions of the Rav and I have hesitated to do so. It is difficult if not impossible to describe with accuracy any human being. The portrait always clashes with the reality; a verbal picture suffers from the same flaws as does a painting. It is at best an imperfect reflection of the real person. The task becomes even more difficult when one experiences reverence for the person he tries to depict. I was a student in the Rav's *shiur* for five years. I was stimulated by his discourses, infected by his passion for Torah, and inspired by his charisma. The result was a feeling of reverence for a great intellectual and spiritual personality that restrained me from any effort to describe him for fear of falling short. I was prepared to discuss and even to write about a *halachic* or philosophic insight that I gained from his *shiurim* or his written work but I hesitated to speak about the person.

It was not difficult for me to resist the persuasive power of journal editors or producers of anthologies to undertake a biographical effort, but I find it more difficult to do so when the invitation comes from a student. I will limit myself, however, in this essay, to recording my impressions of that aspect of his personality most familiar to me, namely, his intellectual power. Of course, it was not unrelated to his spiritual energy.

First, let me focus on the purely intellectual. There is a discussion at the end of *Masechet Brachot* as to which of two intellectual virtues

Rabbi Dr. Sol Roth is Samson R. Hirsch Professor of Torah and Derekh Eretz at Yeshiva University. A past president of the RCA, RZA, and NY Board of Rabbis, he is the author of *Halakhah and Politics: The Jewish Idea of the State* among other scholarly works.

is greater: *sinai* or *oker harim*? Rashi explains that *sinai* refers to a scholar who has managed to accumulate vast and accurate knowledge of Torah, a state of affairs clearly dependent on a powerful memory. *Oker harim*, which literally means "one who uproots mountains," is interpreted as a metaphor for an individual who possesses impressive powers of analysis. This discussion does not contemplate the personality who exemplifies both these virtues, and to an extraordinary degree. Such a person was the Rav. His memory was endowed with an immense capacity and his even more impressive analytic power was revealed in his ability to identify subtle distinctions and to discover common elements in a series of apparently disparate Talmudic discussions.

His annual *yahrzeit shiur* was an intellectual marathon. It belonged to the category of the phenomenal. During an uninterrupted period of four hours, he would deliver a Talmudic discussion for two hours followed by a philosophical discourse interspersed with midrashic interpretations for the remaining two. But what was striking about this experience was not so much the sheer physical energy of an essentially spiritual personality who could speak without interruption for so long a period of time and in a standing position, but his spectacular ability to penetrate into the logical core of halachic issues discussed in the Talmud and elaborated by its commentators, to identify common elements in debates that were apparently unrelated and to exhibit them as essentially interdependent. He would begin the Talmudic portion of his discourse with a series of questions—as many as eight or ten—highlighting inherent difficulties in the texts and commentaries on a variety of issues. He would then proceed to the analysis of a concept indicating the ambiguity it contained and resolving it by exhibiting its various aspects or components. He would then answer successfully all the questions he raised on the basis of the distinction he introduced in his conceptual analysis. He dissected a concept and constructed a logical system based on that concept all at once. When he concluded, I had the sense that I heard not only an intellectual but also an artistic masterpiece. It was a thing of beauty.

What made it possible for the Rav to repeat such an astounding performance year after year? It could be argued that the combination of a capacious memory and powerful analytic abilities are not quite sufficient. Something more was needed: the motivation to utilize and apply his extraordinary intellectual talents to a maximum degree. Such motivation derives from a spiritual source; it is akin to dedication. His son, Dr. Haym Soloveitchik, in a eulogy delivered on the occasion of the *shloshim* [the thirtieth day] following his father's passing, declared that his father had the capacity to concentrate eighteen hours a day. This is a dramatic manifestation of exceptional spiritual power.

Then there is his clarity of thought and expression. It is alleged that a halakhic discussion he presented was once challenged with the question, "What is the source for your conclusion; on what is it based?" He replied, "On a clear and logical mind!" Clarity is a virtue that he demanded of his students and himself. He did not however identify clarity with simplicity but with logical rigor. His written works are not easily grasped. He wrote in a literary and a linguistically sophisticated style. In addition, his philosophic publications generally presupposed a familiarity with a vocabulary and an array of concepts alien to the philosophically untutored. But those who possess that background find his arguments compelling.

I believe that his intellectual power was epitomized by one of his former students, an individual of considerable discernment, in the observation, "When the Rav would complete a halakhic discussion on an intricate subject by introducing cogent distinctions, his conclusions seemed so obvious that I wondered, How come I did not think of them myself?"

How the Rav Stayed With Me

Fred Sommers*

I was in the *shiur* of Rabbi Joseph B. Soloveitchik, whom we all called the Rav, for five years ending in 1947. In 1949, I began graduate work in philosophy at Columbia University and found to my astonishment that none of the lights in contemporary philosophy had his intellectual stature and power. This made things more difficult for me, since it was usual for students of philosophy to become disciples of some major figure or to become closely identified with some school of philosophy. The Rav, who never himself preached or encouraged discipleship, had effectively spoiled me for all discipleships and "schools." The Rav always expected his students to criticize his assertions and I was not in a mood to be anyone's "*chasid*." In any case, after having studied with the Rav, there was no one around who could command from me the kind of respect I'd had for him as my mentor.

I had learned from the Rav—more by his example than by any explicit teaching of method—to treat each *sugya* with an independence of mind that was literally "unorthodox." I had come to Yeshiva College from Yeshivat Chaim Berlin where I had studied with Rabbi Isaac Hutner. Rav Hutner was keen but his method was standard. We learned the text with Rashi, Tosephot and other major commentaries, after which we might raise questions about the various

---

Dr. Fred Sommers was Harry Austryn Wolfson Professor of Philosophy at Brandeis University. A prolific writer, Dr. Sommers has published extensively on many topics including medicine and *Halakhah*.

*This essay was originally published in "My Yeshiva College: 75 Years of Memories" and is being reprinted with the permission of the editors.

positions and interpretations that had already thoroughly "cooked" the *sugya* for us in various ways. At no point were we encouraged to look with our own eyes on the *peshat* [plain meaning] of the *Gemara*, unfiltered by the major authorities.

By sharp contrast, the Rav would approach a *sugya* in a notably objective, unencumbered way, without relying on the authoritative traditional interpretations. He did not explicitly tell us to approach the *Gemara* texts in this way but those of us who were alert saw that this is what he did; even to those of us who were not methodologically self-conscious, the Rav's exemplary independence of mind was inspiring, if not contagious. *Shiur* after exhilarating *shiur*, we watched the Rav coolly, objectively and incisively reason to achieve an interpretation of the Talmudic texts that was intellectually elegant and as consistent as possible with other texts. He did turn to the *Rishonim* and *Achronim* as the *shiur* unfolded, but only after we all had a clear understanding of the issues and were in a position to see what was going on and why the various controversies among the *meforshim* [commentaries] had arisen. He gave us the means to understand why the differing authorities said what they said, why they differed and we also had the means to judge which one was more likely to be right. We were never encouraged to rely on the authorities as a substitute for thinking on our own. The Rav thus exemplified an intellectually independent approach and he respected this approach in any of his students who dared to take it. Indeed he encouraged and expected it from us.

Please do not misunderstand me. When it comes to philosophy itself I am no disciple of the Rav. The Rav, who had studied philosophy in Berlin, was much too respectful of continental philosophy in the first half of the 20th century; I never went along with him in his admiration for the existentialists or for philosophers of religion like Rudolph Otto. Where I remain forever in his debt was in his approach to the *Gemara* and *Halakhah*. There he taught me what it means to be incisive, unafraid, and thoroughly honest. He taught me to be intellectually on my own, never to defer to authority in the face of reason, never to approach a text or a problem with a cooked "official" point of view. *Lo Ba-Shamayim Hee* [it is not in the heavens, referring to a famous *aggadah*] and also not in the *meforshim*. He taught his students always to look at the problems without prejudgment and never to turn to authorities without having tried our best to fathom the issues on our own. That approach works wonders in any intellectual endeavor and it was to give me my way in philosophy.

It may sound odd that a teacher of Talmud should be more intellectually independent in his approach than the great secular teachers of philosophy in institutions like Columbia, Harvard and Oxford where intellectuals take special pride in being open minded, objective and uncommitted to anything but reasonable and rational thinking. But the Rav's virtues were not to be found in these academies and as I say, I was not prepared for this. I'm now over eighty years old and I've known only one other person who was the Rav's equal in incisiveness, intellectual honesty and effortless brilliance. He was not a philosopher but the scientist Francis Crick (recently deceased) whose name will ever be remembered as the co-discoverer of the DNA double helix.

The Rav himself had no pretensions; he had no axe to grind; he never gave the impression that he had a personal stake in getting you to agree with him. He was passionately and dispassionately interested in the subject matter at hand. That subject might well be tradition bound and we who studied it were committed to it as a practical ethos of faith. But given that constraint, the Rav's treatment of the subject was a brilliant paradigm of the unprejudiced and unfettered use of reason. He was also never less than professional; the Rav was masterful and we learned from him what it meant to be a master of a subject.

The effect on me of the Rav's example was decisive. It "doomed" me to do independent solitary work on hard and controversial subjects and to work things out very much on my own. I had no desire whatsoever to join any "school" or to commit myself to any particular approach or method, however popular. Independence. The Rav's example had left me with no option; if I was going to do philosophy as he did Talmud, I must be focused on the subject matter and not on the potential reader. Being a student of the Rav also gave me a taste for the most fundamental classical areas in philosophy; in the 20th century this meant logic, the philosophy of language and ontology. My own interests veered to logic and the theory of predication and eventually I succeeded to make some original discoveries in these areas. Early in 2005, MIT University Press will be publishing a book of essays in a "Festschrift" volume honoring my work.

Certainly the Rav could be caustic and uncomplimentary in criticizing you. He wanted us to know the truth of the matter and when we got it wrong, he did not bother to be diplomatic or sparing of our feelings. Always his reprimand was objective, it was never his purpose to put anyone down; he sharply criticized your argument, never your person. We understood that and took no offense. On the other hand if you said something apt and right to the point, he would look at you with great love, appreciation and gratitude. He would smile with delight. That was personal. I treasure the moments that brought him to that kind of reaction, even though it was not his custom to say more than a decisive and thundering "Gerecht!" Once—some two decades later—when I had solved a particularly vexing problem (it happened when I was in Israel on the first day of the Six Day War in June 1967) I too accorded myself the compliment of saying "Gerecht!"

The Rav's example inspired me to do careful systematic work. If I had to put the Rav's influence on me in a few phrases and sentences that express the ideals I strove to emulate, they would be something like the following:

1. Independence of mind and method.
2. Be incisive, be bold but also be meticulous, systematic and careful.
3. The problem you choose may be hard but it must allow for a systematic analytic approach. Don't tackle a problem if you do not have a systematic strategy for solving it. (This meant to me, that I must avoid some deep, clearly important and fascinating problems in philosophy. Some of these were fashionable and popular but if I could see no way to approach them with any prospect of solving them or even to getting close to a solution, I would not work on them. I later realized that not all important problems were ripe for a fruitful approach to solving them. (Sometimes we just need to have more scientific knowledge.) The Rav instinctively understood these limitations and he was always selective in his choices of *sugyot* to be tackled.
4. Keeping (3) in mind, make an effort to make some progress on some fundamental problem.
5. Don't be seduced by metaphors. Keep to a common sense interpretation and a sensible, reasonable line of approach. (The Rav, who loved *Aggadita*, never let it intrude in his formal analysis of Halakhic subject-matter.)

Some of you who read this will be doing intellectual and scientific work in fields outside Judaica. If so you will be applying some of the powerful approaches you are now practicing in your study of the Talmud, especially if you study it in the inspiring and effective way the Rav taught us. The above rules would have been phrased far more elegantly by the Rav himself. But, they are roughly his rules as I learned them from listening to and absorbing him over many years. He was the teacher who influenced me most deeply. What cannot be put into words is the inspiration I got from constantly watching a pure, honest and effortlessly brilliant *Gaon*, always unfailingly clearheaded, never ceasing in his joyful intellectual labors, day after day, week after week, an inspiring example of unpretentious genius who loved learning, loved argument, loved Torah and was the embodiment of the maxim that a true scholar is never envious of his students. He took joy in us and long after we left his presence, we, his students, never ceased taking joy in him.

The '50s:
In and Out of the Classroom

Facing the Rav is Rabbi Shapiro (far left), a benefactor and member of the Board of Trustees of Yeshiva University. (Photo courtesy Yeshiva University.)

The Approach of the Rav to *P'sak* and Public Policy

Saul J. Berman

It was not until I became rabbi at the Young Israel of Brookline, MA, in 1969 that I recognized the disparate ways in which Rav Soloveitchik, *zt"l*, responded to *She'elot* from lay members of the community as opposed to those from his own *musmachim* who were actually serving in the rabbinate.

When responding to a question from a lay person, the Rav was gentle and caring, but usually quite decisive—he had been asked for a *p'sak*, and so he issued one, his best judgment at that moment in time. When asked a question by one of his *musmachim* serving in the rabbinate, his approach was quite different. After hearing the description of the facts and asking whatever factual questions he needed to ask to elicit all of the information necessary, the Rav would say to his student, for example to me, "So Rabbi Berman, what do you think?" His own *musmach* could never approach the Rav without having done his homework in researching the question in a thorough manner.

The Rav would hear out the outline description of the basic *sugya* in *Gemara*, the debate amongst *Rishonim*, the resolution in *Shulchan Aruch* and *Rama* and the dominant positions of *Acharonim*, with only an occasional muttered, "Yes, yes." If nothing major was missing, the Rav would move on to his next question, "How do you want to *pasken*?" At that point the *musmach* would present the position that he wanted to adopt with a very brief explanation of his rationale.

Rabbi Saul J. Berman is Associate Professor of Jewish Studies at Stern College, Adjunct Professor at Columbia University School of Law, and Director of Continuing Rabbinic Education at Yeshivat Chovevei Torah.

The Rav would make one of three responses to the rabbi's proposal. He might say, "No," and then explain why he thought the conclusion was not sound. He might say, "Yes, I agree," meaning that he would arrive at the same conclusion. Or he might say, "Yes, you can *pasken* that way," which meant that he personally might not arrive at the same conclusion but that it was a perfectly legitimate halachic conclusion and that the *musmach* who had asked the question could issue that *p'sak*.

A number of realizations dawned on me as I recognized this pattern in the behavior of the Rav. Firstly, the Rav was intent on supporting the autonomous responsibility of his *musmachim* in the rabbinate to issue *p'sak halachah*. He was not interested in creating clones who could simply call him on the phone and then mouth his positions. He wanted *talmidim* who had learned from him how to analyze an issue properly and arrive at a responsible decision within the context of their own communities. It was to further that sense of responsibility that the Rav would expect that proper research be done before the call to him was made. (On one occasion I was traveling and a serious *she'elah* arose in a location where I had no access to *sefarim*. I called the Rav to ask for his *p'sak*, and before I could even explain the circumstances he chastised me harshly for calling without having learned the *sugya* through carefully.)

Secondly, the Rav was deeply cognizant of the diversity of legitimate halachic conclusions which could be reached on many matters. He himself, in *shiur* and often as well in matters of *p'sak*, would radically alter his analysis of a *sugya* and would emerge with very divergent conclusions from those which he had reached only a short time before. He did not desire to impose uniform positions on his students, particularly not in relation to rabbis who were serving distinctively different communities. Two other occasions made this approach even more clear to me.

When I arrived in Brookline in the summer of 1969, I went to visit the Rav and asked him to outline for me the *minhagei tefillah* [{local} customs of prayer] which he had introduced at his minyan at the Maimonides School. Since he was the *Chacham Hamakom* [the scholar of the city], I told him, I wanted to bring the *minhagei tefillah* of the Young Israel into conformity with his positions. He insisted that I not proceed with that plan, that each synagogue was distinct in regard to *minhagei hamakom*, and that I needed to work with my own synagogue to evolve *minhagim* which were appropriate to that particular context and gathering of persons.

In the early 1980s I spoke to the Rav about how the Lubavitcher Rebbe *zt"l* viewed adoptions. The Rebbe generally opposed adoption within his community because he considered the *Issur Yichud DeOraita* (prohibition for Jews of opposite gender to be in seclusion) to be applicable in the relationship between an adoptive mother and her adopted son of bar mitzvah age. He considered the *Issur Yichud DeRabbanan* to be applicable between an adoptive father and his adopted daughter above age twelve. I knew from many prior conversations with him that the Rav differed on this matter and considered the functional parent child relationship to be sufficient to eliminate the *Issur Yichud*, despite the absence of biological relationship.

As we spoke further of this debate, the Rav asked me, "What do you think the Rebbe does when there is a family in his community whom he himself thinks ought to adopt children?" I had no answer. The Rav broke into a broad smile and said, "Then he sends them to me to *pasken* the *she'elah*!" What an extraordinary picture the Rav provided us with, of two giants, understanding that their opposite positions were both *Divrei Elokim Chayim* [the words of the living God], who were able to use the position they personally rejected to serve the emotional needs of people for whom they cared as a shepherd cares for his flock.

Thus the Rav not only understood well the existence of legitimate diversity in halachic decision making, but was committed to upholding the responsibility of decision making being based in the local rabbi, not in some central institution or person. Even when he personally did not agree, he understood that the decision should be made by the shepherd who loved and cared for his flock.

This is one reason that the Rav is so often quoted as having taken contradictory positions on matters of *Halachah*. Of course, sometimes the Rav had just changed his mind, as was the case in regard to the permissibility on Pesach of the liquid derivatives of *kitniyot* [legumes] as well as on such ideological matters as *Da'as Torah* and Zionism. But in many instances what circulated in the Rav's name was the uncomfortable combination of his personal conclusion, and the position which he recognized as also halachically correct, which he had allowed a *musmach* to adopt within the latter's responsibility as rabbi of a community.

Unfortunately, some writers, ignorant of this pattern in the conduct of the Rav, go so far as to impugn the integrity of rabbis who report that the Rav had told them that it was acceptable to *pasken* in a manner which diverges from what the writer "knows" to be the Rav's position. Some such scribblers not only fail to take account of the possibility that the Rav had changed his mind, but also, in their own prideful narrow-mindedness cannot share the Rav's own validation of divergent positions as all halachically legitimate.

This pattern in the Rav's attitude towards *p'sak halachah* is even more intensely present in situations related to public policy determinations. The Rav was consulted regularly by rabbis, communal leaders and varied Jewish organizations to help them arrive at conclusions as to what constituted appropriate communal policy in matters of social, political and religious concern. The Rav's approach to such questions had two distinct layers. The first layer had to do with a purely halachic evaluation as to whether the actions were permissible or impermissible. If the actions were permissible, the second stage then began, looking at the communal effects of the policy and whether those effects were beneficial in the short and long term. The difference between those two layers was often critical.

In the early 1960s, as the Student Struggle for Soviet Jewry (SSSJ) was being organized, there was much rabbinic opposition to public demonstrations on behalf of Soviet Jewry. There were many *gedolim* who believed that such public action would offend the Soviet government and cause retribution to be taken against the already weak and vulnerable Jewish community of the Soviet Union. Student organizers eventually went to discuss the matter with Rav Soloveitchik in the hope of getting his overt support. They described the debate and the underlying realities of Soviet Jewry to the Rav and he asked for time to deliberate.

Some time later the Rav called the students in and told them that it is his considered opinion that public demonstration would in fact be injurious to Soviet Jews and that he would not recommend engaging in such actions. The students were crestfallen. The Rav then added that this was not his halachic judgment, it was his considered political opinion and that the students should not view themselves as bound by his opinion—that they should simply take it into account as they gather other opinions and move towards a conclusion.

After much more deliberation the students decided to go ahead with their plans for SSSJ, and made history through their eventual impact on the freeing of Soviet Jewry.

In the winter of 1970 I was preparing to go to Brussels to participate in the First World Conference on Soviet Jewry, and decided to speak with the Rav about some of the issues which I expected would arise at the conference. I began by asking the Rav whether he still held the position he had taken many years before against public demonstrations. He said that he did not; and added that he would not forgive the Israeli representative who had misled him on that matter. He explained that he had assumed that Israel, having diplomatic relations with the USSR at that time, would have an unbiased judgment as to the possible effects of public demonstrations in the US on Soviet policy towards Jews. He was informed that it was Israel's opinion that such actions would be deleterious.

Only after the USSR refused to re-establish diplomatic relations with Israel after the 1967 War, did Israel begin to support public demonstrations about Soviet Jewry. He realized then that their earlier communication to him had been misleading—Israel was then concerned with the interests of the State of Israel, not the interests of Soviet Jewry. While he felt that such a stance was a legitimate one for Israel to take, it was not legitimate for them to have misled him as to their underlying motive.

The Rav understood that while he could not be misled about a matter of Halachah, he was vulnerable to error on public policy judgments based on social and political factors. He had, after all, modified his position on *Da'as Torah* after the Holocaust. He told a student that after the Holocaust only a fool could believe that *chachamim* are infallible. Thus, while the Rav understood his binding authority as a *posek*, he also understood and respected the autonomy of the individual and of the community in arriving at public policy judgments, while taking the opinions of *chachamim* seriously into account—but not as binding dicta.

I see these patterns of the Rav's approach to *p'sak halachah* and to public policy issues as reflective of a single personality quality, his humility. While the Rav well understood the grandeur of his own mind, he had the humility to understand that even he was subject to human error, and that his opinion even in Halachah was not the only possible correct position. As, I believe, the most outstanding

teacher of Torah of the past generation, the Rav recognized the centrality of his role as empowering others to arrive at halachic judgments which they see as true and necessary. His role was to train us
and then guide us, not to be the teachers of the Rav's Torah, but to
be the teachers of God's Torah.

The Rav at Revel – The Rav at RIETS

Robert Blau

When *The Commentator* invited me to prepare an article describing my experiences at Revel, I had to confess that I was never registered at the school, but was there by the kindness of the Rav, who allowed me to audit his lectures.

I was nearing the end of my teens and a newcomer to Yeshiva, motivated by my mother's last wish for me to receive *semikhah* and continue her family's tradition, tragically curtailed by the advent of the Shoah, of forty generations of rabbis.

Understandably, I lacked proficiency in Talmudic learning, but acquiring knowledge of other aspects of Judaism I felt was important as well. That is how I discovered the Rav and his Judaic classes at Revel.

This was before the tape-recorder era and taking notes manually was the only way to preserve what one had heard. I soon discovered that I was a reliable note-taker, facilitated by the Rav's unique pedagogical skills that made it incredibly easy.

The Rav would read first from his written text, look up, and in typical Rav fashion, elaborate on the text just read. The transition from his written text to his oral elaboration was always introduced by his frequently used expression, "I mean."

Some prime topics he dealt with during my years at Revel were "The Relationship between *Halakhah, Aggadah* and *Kabbalah*"; "The *Guide to the Perplexed* of Maimonides"; "An Analysis of Genesis"; "*Tefillah*" [prayer]; "*K'riat Sh'ma*"; and many others.

In my *sefer, Efne V'Eshne*, I transcribed into Hebrew the gist of some of these lectures. I had the good fortune of showing the Rav the first of these transcriptions. He read it, smiled, and expressed his satisfaction.

Rabbi Dr. Robert Blau YC `51 and RIETS `54 is the author of *Efne V'Eshne*.

For me, what happened after the lecture was as interesting as the lecture itself. Some attendees would present the Rav with their personal problems, which he, with great ingenuity, would tackle in search of a viable solution. Others would simply come by to greet him. For example, on one occasion, Rabbi Charles B. Chavel—the noted rabbi who published the first scholarly edition of Ramban's biblical commentary—approached the Rav, who greeted him warmly and said: "Rabbi Chavel, we all have you to thank for bringing the Ramban back to life."

On another occasion, a young man, in great distress, told the Rav that he was engaged to be married, but was informed that his was a forbidden union, since he was a *kohen* and she a divorcée.

"That is correct," said the Rav.

"But Rabbi," pleaded the young man, "that is not fair."

The Rav replied sympathetically, "I agree, but much in life is not fair—a fact you already know or will experience during the course of your lifetime."

I once approached the Rav to help me understand a *mishnah* in *Avoth*: "Whoever forgets one word of his study, Scripture accounts as though he had forfeited his life (3:8)."

"*Rebbe*," I protested, "as humans we are all doomed."

"No," countered the Rav. "The *Mishnah* is correct," and resorting to Yiddish said, "What we really want to remember, we will never forget." A lesson I still remember.

If one were to ask, was there a difference between the Rav of Revel and the Rav of RIETS? The answer is yes. The Rav of Revel was Dr. Soloveitchik, preeminent scholar and lecturer. At RIETS he was the Rav—*Rosh Yeshiva* and explicator par excellence. Was there also a difference in his image and demeanor? Again, the answer is yes.

At Revel, the Rav would welcome any remark or question related to the lecture. In fact, he seemed to invite these interruptions as an opportunity for further clarification. His manner at these lectures was always cordial and pleasant. By contrast, across the street at RIETS, a very different mood prevailed. There the Rav was strict and demanding. Clarity and credibility were the order of the day. Mediocrity and shallowness were unacceptable; slothfulness in thinking—deplorable. The Rav would not abide impromptu guesswork. The student had to know what he was trying to say.

This requirement of clarity in halakhic study the Rav formulated in his remarks outlining "The Relationship among *Halakhah, Aggadah* and *Kabbalah.*"

"Without *halakhah,*" the Rav stressed, "the *aggadah* and *kabbalah* would be in a vacuum. The study of *halakhah* is a science and has its own methodology, and one must be trained mentally and intellectually to understand it. The existential movement in philosophy tries to have the philosopher free himself from the fetters of the scientific nature and speak about the ambiguous nature. It is easier to do the latter. It is the same with Jewish thought. It is easy to philosophize about hassidism by telling a few stories, but not about *halakhah, aggadah* and *kabbalah.* That is difficult. All roads lead to *halakhah,* but no attempt has ever been made to create a world formula from the *halakhah.*"

An added bonus for attending these lectures was the occasional appearance of the Rav's teacher and mentor, *Hagaon Ha'amiti* Reb Chaim Heller *zt"l,* who would come to share some of his genius with us. Admittedly, I could not follow all that he said, but being in his presence was sufficiently rewarding.

A final awesome and unforgettable recollection was seeing the Rav seated next to Reb Chaim, endearingly clasping his hand while Reb Chaim was speaking.

Awesome and unforgettable indeed.

The Impact of the Rav's Presence on Yeshiva

Yosef Blau

Over two decades have passed since the last *shiur* was given by Rav Yosef Dov Soloveitchik *zt"l* at Yeshiva. For present students he is a legendary figure from the past. His many students teaching at Yeshiva are transmitting his insights, but these insights are filtered through their recollections and understanding. Posthumous volumes appear each year coupled with reconstructions of his Torah from the notes of his disciples. It is difficult to fully appreciate the impact that his actual presence each week at Yeshiva had on generations of students.

My recollections cover the second half of the fifties and the first half of the sixties when I was a student, and the years from 1977 to 1985 when I returned to Yeshiva as *Mashgiach Ruchani* (including attending the Rav's *shiur* together with my oldest son for the last two and a half years). The annual *yahrzeit shiur* for his father which was in Yiddish and lasted five hours, and the English *shiur* before Purim which he gave after his wife passed away, each brought to the auditorium and the overflow in the *Beit Midrash* more than a thousand people.

Many of his students traveled to the Moriah *shul* on the West Side to hear his Tuesday night *shiur* which was appropriate for both laity and Talmudic scholars. The annual *T'shuvah* (during the Ten Days of Repentance) *shiur* and the Rav's talks at the Mizrachi conventions were also well attended by Yeshiva students. Those who no longer attended the regular *shiur* and those who had never been there

Rabbi Yosef Blau received his BA at Yeshiva College in 1959, MS in Mathematics in 1960, semikhah in 1961. He was a teacher and principal in three schools, became *Mashgiach Ruchani* [director of religious guidance] at Yeshiva in 1977 and has continued in this position until today.

could go to the public lectures and hear the Rav directly. During the early years there were philosophic talks and classes that he gave in Bernard Revel Graduate School as well.

Even those who never were his students were affected by their attending the institution associated with his name. Daniel Kurtzer, who later served as Dean of Yeshiva College and American Ambassador to Israel, told me that he chose to attend Yeshiva over Columbia when he saw the Rav surrounded by students walking back to his apartment after saying *shiur*. Neither the yeshiva world nor the Ivy League colleges could dismiss Yeshiva while the Rav taught.

Each year before *Pesach* students from other yeshivot, whose break started earlier, would come to Yeshiva only to be able to listen to the Rav saying *shiur*. Prominent *Roshei Yeshiva* would ask students for their notes. I had a great-uncle who was a known Hassidic *talmid hakham*; our conversations consisted primarily of my telling him, in response to his requests, some of the Torah that I heard from the Rav.

When the Catholic Church started the ecumenical movement and some Jewish leaders went to Rome to meet the Pope, it was the Rav's position on interfaith dialogue that became the Orthodox Jewish response. The Rav felt the key battleground was the secular college campuses. During that time I had the honor of introducing the Rav to a packed audience of professors and students at Columbia University in Earl Hall where he gave a talk that was essentially the article "Confrontation" that appeared in *Tradition*. The Rav spoke in Greek, Latin and German, as well as in English, overwhelming the listeners with his erudition.

The intellectual tone of Yeshiva was set by the Rav. His openness to ideas allowed subjects to be taught in the college that other *Roshei Yeshiva* might have not have approved. He was obviously knowledgeable in philosophy, literature, science and mathematics. When I was studying mathematical logic in graduate school and attending his *shiur*, I was surprised to hear him comment that the Talmud had a multi-valued logic.

On one level it was inconceivable that any of his students would be smart enough to disagree with the Rav's ideas, yet he encouraged us to think independently. He was extremely demanding of his students, particularly in the early years, but he invited suggestions and questions and modified his views because of the comments of students. Even a minimal exposure to the many prominent rabbis who were his pupils suffices to prove that he did not force them into a single mold. He wanted them to develop independence.

When I returned to Yeshiva in 1977 the atmosphere had changed. Instead of lectures in philosophy, the Talmud *shiur* was supplemented by talks on the *parshah*. These were insightful and filled with original perspectives. The Rav had aged and was not well. Each year he would struggle more and more in the *shiur*. Remarkably he never allowed older students, who still attended, to help him by reminding him of what he had said earlier on the topic. Learning for the Rav always meant a fresh look at the material.

Even during the period of decline, the sense felt by virtually all in Yeshiva that they were somewhat connected with greatness remained. In many ways the Rav was not only an outstanding *talmid hakham* but an extraordinary individual who appears once in a number of generations. Both the continuance of Rav Chaim of Brisk and the exemplar of the philosophy of Yeshiva, in our eyes the Rav was a second Rambam.

The awe remains, but without a physical presence the memories fade. The great strength of producing disciples who differ in their versions of Orthodoxy, in their interest in pursuing his philosophic outlook or being totally removed from philosophy, and in their approaches to learning became a source of confusion. The endless unresolved question of who is a real *talmid*, who the most outstanding one leaves the new generation confused.

Which part of his heritage was the most significant, his Torah or his thought? What would the Rav have said about the situation today in Israel? What was his real attitude on women's issues in Judaism? Was the Rav truly Modern Orthodox? I could add many more questions but can't prove that I know the correct answers.

Many times when I would visit Yeshiva's Gruss Kollel in Israel I would be asked to resolve a contradiction between Rabbi Hershel Schachter in *Nefesh Harav* and Rabbi Rakefet in his class in Gruss on the Rav. Invariably my response was that my memory is clearly not better than theirs, and many times the Rav said things when I was not present. Frankly, their disagreements are far less fundamental than those of others.

We have a legacy filtered through generations of students and their students. It weakens with time. Yet much Torah of the Rav is being taught. There are many books and articles available to be read.

After the Rambam passed away there were arguments about which writings reflect the true Rambam. Scholars still debate the relationship between the *Moreh Nevukhim* and the *Mishneh Torah*.

For over four decades students at Yeshiva had the merit to be in the presence of greatness. Many base their religious lives on what they learned. They in turn influence the next generation. A reflection is not the same as the presence, but it remains of enormous significance.

Memories of the Rav *Zt"l*

Herbert Bomzer

I had the privilege to be a *talmid* of the Rav beginning in 1950 in Yeshiva, and in the ensuing years until the *petirah* [passing away] of the Rav *zt"l* I attended hundreds of *shiurim* and occasions. The Rav was an *ilui* par excellence, a walking *sefer Torah* as he was described by the *gedolim*, a demanding rebbi-teacher, a gentleman, and role model as a mensch-Torah personality.

I herein relate some personal experiences in Yeshiva and in Congregation Moriah in New York City where on Tuesday nights the Rav gave *shiurim* to hundreds of rabbis and *baalei batim* [laypeople]. During the twenty-five years in Moriah, in rain, sleet, snow and blizzards we learned *Masekhtos Berakhos, Megillah, Sukkah, Taanis* and *Sanhedrin*, and of course hundreds of hours of Rambam.

During that period, the Rav also taught in Bernard Revel Graduate School and I remember two experiences. First, the Rav lectured in Hebrew and as was his talent, it was inspiring to hear his excellent language on the topic of *Kibbud Av v'Aim* [honoring parents] and his elucidations of the halakhic and philosophic aspects of that mitzvah. His vocabulary was exemplary and his literary genius was apparent. I was always amazed, as a teacher, to see the extent of his preparation for the lectures.

Second, I witnessed the following incident. The graduate students were invited to a *shiur* by Rav Chaim Heller *zt"l*, one of the *gedolei hador*. R. Chaim, a mentor of the Rav, was famous for his expositions of *Tanakh* [the Written Torah]. We were asked to honor this aged Torah giant by attending his talk on *Nevi'im* [Prophets]. About twenty-five students gathered in the room. R. Chaim entered, escorted and led by the Rav who sat down at R. Chaim's side. A mi-

Rabbi Dr. Herbert Bomzer teaches at Yeshiva University and is Rabbi Emeritus of the Young Israel of Ocean Parkway, Brooklyn, NY.

crophone and speaker were set upon the desk in front of R. Chaim. His voice was so weak and low that we could hardly hear his *hiddush* [novel insight] which he finished about a half hour later. The Rav said, "I will repeat the *hiddush* of the *Rebbe*," which he then did. Although it was a new thought, the Rav repeated it almost verbatim with great clarity.

The Rav's genius did not surprise us, but the way he treated R. Chaim—holding his hand, seating him, escorting him after the lecture—was a lesson in Torah *midos* [qualities] never to be forgotten.

I once told the Rav that a certain rabbi had issued a decision that declared a brother and sister as *mamzerim* [children of an adulterous relationship]. Their mother had been married and then divorced. However, she had not received a *get* [a divorce in accordance with Jewish law]. She then married another man and the two children were both from that second marriage. She had become very religious, and the children were yeshiva students. When I presented this to the Rav, he excitedly proclaimed, "No one has the right to declare Jewish children *mamzerim*! Go to Rav Moshe Feinstein to pose the problem," which is what I did the very next day.

The couple came before a *Beis Din* [court of Jewish law] led by Rav Moshe *zt"l*, who found that the first marriage was performed by a Reform rabbi with witnesses who were invalid. Thus the mother was not married in the first ceremony, did not require a *get*, and the children from the second marriage were kosher. When it was reported to the Rav, his smile indicated his satisfaction.

Another experience with the Rav occurred in Boston at the *yarhei kallah* [a period of Torah study] during the summer of 1976. Many *talmidim* of the Rav came to Boston for an inspiring three-day intellectual and emotional experience. The Rav taught for two hours in the morning. We then broke for lunch and returned at two o'clock for another *shiur*, usually on *Hilkhot Rosh Hashanah* in Rambam. One of our colleagues celebrated a birthday during those days and the Rav was invited to join in the motel room. It was fantastic. He was jovial, happy and humorous. Every word was a Torah lesson. The emotions were very high not only out of respect but actual love for our *rebbe*.

At the end of one of those *yarhei kallah* sessions, the Rav asked three of us to remain behind to be a *Beis Din* for *hataras nedarim* for him. He told us that his practice had always been to stand the entire day on Yom Kippur. But that year he had been cautioned by his doctor that because he had a pinched nerve, he should not strain his back. Since his custom had been to stand, he needed a *heter* [freeing from a vow] in case he could not stand that year. The formula was, "If I had known that, I would not have accepted standing as a neder" [a vow]. We responded *"Mutar lakhem, mutar lakhem, mutar lakhem"* [the vow is annulled]. A rabbi seated on the side asked why the Rav used three *hed-yotos* [simple people] and not one [expert] *mumhe larabbim* (maybe he meant himself). The Rav with a broad smile immediately responded, "Who is a *mumhe larabbim* is questionable. These three rabbis are surely *hed-yotos*." I later asked the Rav for a memorandum addressed to me as an accepted *hed-yot* for a *Beis Din* accepted by the Rav. He answered that I did not need it in writing.

I close with gratitude to *HaShem* that I had the privilege of learning from the Rav.

My Memories of the Rav

Abba Bronspigel

During my ten years studying under our revered teacher, Rav Yasha Be'er Soloveitchik, I developed a close relationship with him. Through his pure and intense attitude toward Torah study, he became my *rebbe muvhok* [distinguished teacher {above all others}] and the source for most of my Torah learning. He was a Talmudic innovationist par excellence, the caliber of which I have not seen since my time spent with him.

The Rav was always a very demanding teacher. However, by the time I entered his *shiur*, the Rav had already mellowed somewhat. Still, if a student was unprepared for *shiur*, the Rav would get very visibly upset. For instance, there were times when the Rav would ask students if they had prepared the commentary of the *Ba'al Meor* in anticipation for *shiur*. Many times, if the student reported that he had not prepared, the Rav would shout "I was up until three in the morning and you cannot have even the decency of looking at the *Ba'al Meor*?" The Rav controlled himself as much as possible, but he could not tolerate or understand students who neglected their learning.

In the late fifties, the Rav switched from giving *shiur* in Yiddish to English. At the beginning, he was very adamant to keep the *shiur* in Yiddish. This was due to the fact that when the Rav first accepted to teach at Yeshiva, he firmly wished to pattern his *shiur* after the way in which his father—whom the Rav effectively replaced as *maggid shiur* at Yeshiva—delivered his. When administrators would approach the Rav to switch the *shiur* to English, he refused by explaining that his father gave *shiur* in Yiddish and he planned to continue in the same style and tradition. Even when some suggested

---

Rabbi Abba Bronspigel is *Rosh HaYeshiva* at Beis Medrash L'Talmud, an affiliate of Lander College.

to him that switching to English would encourage more students to attend his *shiur*, the Rav still declined on the grounds that he was his father's son and would therefore not deviate from the format already established at Yeshiva by his father many years before. Nonetheless, once students began to complain to the Rav that they might be able to gain more if he switched languages, he agreed to deliver *shiur* in English from that point onward.

The Rav spoke an excellent Yiddish and terrible English. To clarify, the Rav spoke a highly advanced English and used words that none of the students could understand. Not even Rabbi Aaron Lichtenstein—who had a PhD from Harvard in English—was completely familiar with the Rav's English vocabulary and therefore was forced to frequently refer to a dictionary. The difficulty in understanding the Rav's English stemmed from the fact that the Rav himself learned English from reading the dictionary and not from common speech. He therefore used fancy words and complex terminologies instead of a more commonly spoken vernacular.

Very often I was tempted to raise my hand and ask the Rav what a particular word meant. On one occasion, the Rav became flustered with a question I had asked during *shiur* and as a result called me a "Mexican jumping bean." I wanted to at least know what that meant and began to raise my hand to ask "*Rebbe*, what does that mean?" but I thought better of it and kept quiet.

Aside from the regular *shiur* which he delivered at Yeshiva, the Rav customarily addressed various institutions with which he had affiliated himself. Specifically, the Rav delivered a number of addresses in front of the Mizrachi audience in support and praise of the State of Israel. Although the Rav was very much in favor of Israel, he was not afraid at times to openly criticize the State in the same way that one might expect the Satmar Rav might have. On one occasion, the Rav told a number of his students "We need Neturei Karta. For if not for them, who knows where we would be—they keep us grounded." Every year the Rav would donate $500 from the charity fund he was appointed to allocate, to the leaders of the Neturei Karta. This is not to say that the Rav agreed with the group's political positions, but he believed that their survival was essential for maintaining his own more central outlook on Zionism. It should also be noted that toward the end of his life the Rav quieted his public praise for Israel after witnessing how drastic the State's shift was toward the left.

A point that should be made regarding the content on which the Rav lectured: he never publicly discussed secular education or *Torah u-Madda* on an ideological level. Privately, the Rav told several students to further their higher education; he advised me to attend Harvard for graduate school where I could study with his son-in-law, Dr. Isadore Twersky. It is true that the Rav promoted the notion of becoming a highly educated person for purposes of reaching a certain occupational plateau, but I never heard him speak specifically about *Torah u-Madda* or secular education.

The other European rabbis in America during the mid-twentieth century respected the Rav but strongly disagreed with him about such things as secular education. These rabbis held the Rav responsible for being the mentor of the Modern Orthodox rabbis—which is true. In later years, he was privately critical of the directions taken by both Yeshiva University and the Modern Orthodox community in general. Furthermore, there was a declaration by eleven *roshei yeshiva* prohibiting official dialogue between Orthodox and non-Orthodox rabbis. The Rav was also asked to sign this document but refused. From that point onward, many of the more influential American rabbis, including Rabbi Aharon Kotler, severed political ties with the Rav. Still, when great rabbis such as Rabbi Shneur Kotler and Rabbi Shlomo Razovsky fell ill, they demonstrated their personal respect for the Rav and sought medical advice exclusively from doctors referred to them by him.

The Rav and Rabbi Moshe Feinstein were very close. Aside from being cousins, the two would meet very often. Rav Moshe understood that the Rav was special and was therefore apolitical about the debates surrounding the Rav and other rabbinical forces. Very often the Rav would refuse to answer halachik questions and would insist that we direct our question to Rav Moshe. In such a case where the Rav was aware of how Rav Moshe determined a particular *halakhah*, very often he would answer our questions based on the position and reasoning of Rav Moshe. This was by no means a general principle the Rav held to in determining halakhik decisions, but it does represent the great respect the Rav had for Rav Moshe's brilliance.

At the present time, the legacy of the Rav has been distorted. The Rav was a very great person, but both the left and the right have unfortunately misrepresented the man that he was and his teachings. The Modern Orthodox presented the Rav as their mentor, who taught them to be exactly as they are. Specifically, they emphasize his abilities as a scholar and his philosophical expertise instead of focusing on his greatness in the realm of Torah. Unfortunately, the more rightwing yeshiva crowd has judged the Rav based on these students. The Rav had a great variety of students. He had students who were tremendous Torah learners as well as others who did not understand his *shiurim* and world outlook. This can be seen as the root of the confusion surrounding the legacy of the Rav today.

As a result, two distinct sets of students were produced among those who attended the Rav's *shiur*: There were those who were "learners," and those who obtained *smikha* but were essentially preachers. My peers and I always assumed that the ones who would tell over the Rav's Torah would be the former, but instead, the other group has published and told over the Rav's so-called philosophies. It is true that there were a few times when the Rav was asked to deliver a *shiur* at a secular university or someplace of the sort and would aim those *shiurim* at college students or irreligious people. It was in this setting that the Rav spoke a different language from the one more familiar to his students. On such occasions, the Rav would put down his Talmudic texts and review philosophies and the sciences he had learned during his training at the University of Berlin.

To be sure, one cannot state that those who claim that he was very knowledgeable in philosophies are truly wrong. Nevertheless, the Rav was essentially a learner whose main philosophical ideas were derived from his studies of the Talmud and Rambam. This is how the Rav's students remember him.

Like any teacher, the Rav would state something that could be interpreted and construed in several ways. This applies in respect to both *halakhah* and *hashkafa* [philosophy]. To this end, the more modern students sitting in the Rav's *shiur* interpreted his words for what they wanted their appointed mentor to say; they used them for their own ideological support.

For instance, the Rav was opposed to reciting *hallel* on *Yom HaAtzma'ut* [Israel Independence Day] and said so publicly in a *yahrzeit shiur* for his father. Nonetheless, the public now remembers the Rav as an advocate for such a practice. I remember being approached many years ago by several of my students at Yeshiva who claimed that the Rav did in fact say *hallel* on *Yom HaAtzma'ut*. I approached the Rav to ask if he had changed his halakhik decision on the matter. He answered that when he davened at Yeshiva on *Yom HaAtz-*

ma'ut, in order to avoid commotion, he would hold his *siddur* to his face and make believe that he too was reciting *hallel* in accordance with the custom of Yeshiva. While this distortion is not as severe as others, it is an example of the way in which current public rabbinical figures have warped the way in which the Orthodox community remembers the Rav. It represents a trend which has continued since the Rav's passing.

It bears mentioning that what the yeshiva world has done to the Rav is equally disturbing. They have stripped him of his Torah genius. While some of these individuals have simply adopted the version of the Rav as presented by the Modern Orthodox community, others who either knew the Rav or were aware of his Torah stature choose to ignore it and diminish his greatness. Still, I cannot argue with this particular group because the development of the Rav's left-wing students hurt any serious attempt to refute their yeshiva world.

The Rav had an uplifting influence on thousands of students. However, owing to the diversity of Yeshiva and the Orthodox community, the essence of the Rav, the study of Torah through the traditional lens of his father and grandfather, has been shattered into varied shapes and sizes.

The Rav and Dr. Belkin

Zevulun Charlop

For those not yet born or too young to remember when Dr. Samuel Belkin *zt"l* served as President of Yeshiva, it would be almost impossible to even imagine his nearly unchallenged role in the governance of Yeshiva and how, almost single handedly, he built a great university. No less significant was his relationship to Rabbi Joseph B. Soloveitchik *zt"l*. Even as the Rav was altogether singular - indeed *sui generis* and *Rabban shel Yisrael*—Dr. Belkin was, in his own way, also one-of-a-kind. For many years the Rav and Dr. Belkin were alone in the reverence in which students and the larger community held them. No one today could doubt this about the Rav; but I have the sense that hardly anyone who didn't live through that period could envisage Dr. Belkin in that same light as well. This, of course, is a tragedy I pray history will rectify.

In my dealings with both the Rav and Dr. Belkin, and, in specific circumstances, I had to relate to them apart and together at the same time, it became clear to me that even as Dr. Belkin sought and coveted the approbation of the Rav above all other people the Rav no less sought the approval and appreciation of Dr. Belkin. They both sensed—paradoxically with a genuine humility that can only be grasped by those who worked with them and on a continual basis— that they were, each of them, very special and also that the other was no less special even as they were indubitably different.

Dr. Belkin was hardly eighteen when he alighted upon the American continent for the first time. Among the things he brought with him was the *Semikha* he received from the sainted *Chofetz Chaim* of *Radun*. He was purported to have been the youngest *talmid* ever to

Rabbi Zevulun Charlop is the Max and Marion Grill Dean of the Rabbi Elchanan Theological Seminary and the spiritual leader of the Young Israel of Mosholu Parkway in The Bronx, NY.

have been accorded this recognition. In an incredible series of events and, in quick order, he was accepted into a doctoral program at Brown University, an Ivy League institution, without ever having received a formal elementary, high school or college education as we know it. It was about this time that the Rav and Dr. Tonya Soloveitchik came to Boston and it wasn't long before word of this rare *illui* of the *Litvishe yeshivos* now studying at Brown for his PhD reached them. He became a frequent Sabbath guest at their home.

It was also about this time that Dr. Belkin, for a semester or two, served as a *magid shiur* in the New Haven Yeshiva founded by Rabbi Yehudah Levenberg. This was remarkable in light of the fact that this yeshiva was the first attempt to emulate the *mussar yeshivot* of Eastern Europe, whose chief model was the Yeshiva of Slobodka which was not necessarily hospitable to general and secular studies. Nonetheless, they turned to the young Rabbi Belkin to deliver one of the two principal *shiurim* even as he was pursuing his doctorate at Brown.

And, it was during this period as well that the long awaited and very much anticipated *Chiddushei Rabbeinu Chayim Halevi* on Maimonides's monumental *Yad HaChazaka* was printed and posthumously published by the Rav's father Reb Moshe *zt"l*, and his younger brother the Brisker Rav *zt"l*. The Rav received one of the first copies to reach America. When Dr. Belkin, on one of his Sabbath visits to the Rav, saw the *sefer* for the first time, he asked the Rav to let him borrow it, for a short while. One can hardly imagine the excitement that built up over the years awaiting the publication of *Reb Chaim's sefer*. After all, *Reb Chaim* revolutionized *Halakhik* thought and analysis through his *shiurim* years before the book was published. The Rav acquiesced to Dr. Belkin's request on condition that he return it on his next visit two weeks later.

I recall how Dr Belkin, who was the main speaker at a special reception honoring the Rav which was tendered by the Yeshiva Rabbinic Alumni, in the presence of the Rav, recounted this story to illustrate what he felt was one of the Rav's supreme qualities that set him apart, and, at the same time willy-nilly, profiled Dr. Belkin's own qualities as well. Matter of factly, he told us that in those two weeks he reviewed the entire *Rabbeinu Chaim*, from beginning to end and put down in writing close to 60 questions provoked by the *sefer*. It was an absolutely mind-boggling assertion. And, when he returned the *sefer*, he shared his questions with the Rav in the hope that the Rav would help to shed light on these difficulties. But, instead, the Rav looked them over, one by one, and unabashedly said *"eneni yode'ah"*—I don't know to every question. "The Rav was unafraid to admit that he didn't know," Dr. Belkin continued. "This was one of the signal hallmarks of Rashi, the prince of all Torah commentaries on the written and oral Law who time and again in his commentaries on Chumash and Gamara acknowledges *eneni yode'ah*. That humility and integrity bespeak the Rav," Dr. Belkin proclaimed. "Only a *gaon*, a scholar of his matchless stature could have mustered the courage and intellectual honesty to give this kind of sweeping acknowledgment, even when it touched his own grandfather, the sainted and incomparable, *Reb Chaim*." One the face of it, the story strikes one as highly implausible. The Rav, himself, learned *Toras Reb Chaim* directly from his father's mouth and very likely, for some time in his early teens from *Reb Chaim* himself when the Rav's family came to Warsaw during World War I, where *Reb Chaim* was staying during that period and indeed where he died and was buried in 1918.

How could it be that the Rav, recognized as a peerless, incisive and accurate interpreter of *Reb Chaim's* Torah and *derekh*, only respond *eneni yode'ah*? Who understood *Reb Chaim* better and more authentically than him? I think the answer was suggested by the Rav himself. I recall on several occasions when *talmidim* had difficulties in understanding *Reb Chaim* in the *sefer* the Rav would tell them, or words to the effect, "I knew *Reb Chaim's chiddushim* before they were published. But the *sefer* cast them in a austerity of language that rendered them more difficult than the way I received them. *Reb Chaim* until his last day kept coming back to his draft; editing, refining and compressing until he was sure there wasn't an unnecessary word or tittle. He wanted the book to be as spare and as lean as possible—in the words of the preface to the *sefer* written by his sons, he "sifted the text seven times over and winnowed it a hundred times more." Whatever enhancements of precision and accuracy of expression *Reb Chaim* may have been seeking and may have indeed achieved, the *sefer* itself may have lost in the exchange some of the strengths of the more fulsome and expansive oral tradition of *Reb Chaim's* Torah. And this could explain Dr. Belkin's questions and the Rav's response of *eneni yode'ah*.

Dr. Belkin became a RIETS Rosh Yeshiva in his late twenties, after having been appointed by Dr. Revel *zt"l* as an instructor and then professor of Greek at Yeshiva College. He was assigned the *shiur* considered then directly below Reb Moshe Soloveitchik's *shiur* which in itself reflects the special regard in which he was held. In 1940, at the height of his power, Dr. Revel, first president of Yeshiva and founder of Yeshiva College suddenly passed away at the age of 55. Incredibly, just four months later, Reb Moshe Soloveitchik, who became Rosh HaYeshiva upon Dr. Revel's death, was also snatched from Yeshiva's midst at age 62.

Not long afterward, Dr. Belkin was appointed Dean of Yeshiva and Rabbi Soloveitchik was asked to take over his father, Reb Moshe's *shiur*. In 1942, Dr. Belkin was chosen Yeshiva's second president.

From then on, Dr. Belkin became the single uncontested voice – save on the rarest occasions, in the guidance and progress of Yeshiva. The first crack in this near monolithic control came near the end of the 60s when Dr. Belkin was persuaded, because of the increasingly desperate financial plight in which Yeshiva found itself, that there must be, for church-state reasons, a separation between RIETS and the Unviersity in order for the University to continue to qualify for governmental aid. It was then that the Rav made his famous "I See Ghosts" speech, which he delivered at a special luncheon appended to that year's *Chag Hasemikhah* celebration. He conjured all the inevitable dangers that lurked in the future. Harvard, Yale, Princeton, all began as divinity schools and Yeshiva, Heaven forbid, could also go the way of all these great and early citadels of American higher education. Today, those erstwhile schools of religion and divinity are hardly noticed specks in the large expansive contours of America's educational campus.

Dr. Belkin could hardly restrain himself against the Rav's peroration and hold his peace. He began audibly crying out "Stop! Stop!" to the startled gasps of the audience. The speech caused an almost unbridgeable divide between them. Dr. Belkin was convinced that he could maintain the integrity of RIETS unto itself and yet have it remain the foundation-stone and moral compass of the entire University. Even while legally, RIETS and the University would be separate entities, in the most critical ways, they would nonetheless remain together as inseparable parts of the whole. By and large, I believe, this has proven to be the case until now and in some very definable ways, more so than before. The advanced *kollelim*, the packed *batei midrash* at night, the deepening and unyielding *yirat shamayim* of our *bnei Torah* all happened after the separation. To my knowledge, since 1971, there has not been one student who upon graduation from Yeshiva College defected to a non-Orthodox rabbinic seminary, where years before, such departures were not altogether uncommon and a source of much dismay. One can also attribute these advances to other causes as well, most notably the almost universal acceptance of a year or two of intensive Torah study in Israel after completing high school. But, in the end, I also believe, that these advances would not have been realized and Yeshiva would not have been able to keep at bay the real and undeniable dangers that the REITS-YU separation portended, were it not for the original and uncropped protests of the Rav. Beyond this, and most importantly, the Rav continued to give *shiurim* for more than 15 years after the separation, and, indeed, became the *Rebbe* of the Yeshiva, even more so than before. One could not imagine the quickening role of learning and *Torah Lishma* at our Yeshiva without the Rav.

On one of his visits to Yeshiva, Rabbi Shlomo Goren, the late chief rabbi of Israel, whose name, from his earliest years, reverberated throughout the Torah world as an uncommon Talmudic *ilui* and was probably most remembered for sounding the *shofar* at the gate of the Old City of Jerusalem when for the first time in two millennia since the destruction of the Temple, Jerusalem was again in Jewish hands—was invited to come to Yeshiva to deliver a public *shiur* on salient *halakhic* aspects of *Eretz Yisrael*. The Rav and Dr. Belkin and most of our complement of Roshei Yeshiva were in attendance. After the *shiur*, the Rav, Rabbi Israel Miller *zt"l* and I assembled in Dr. Belkin's office. Dr. Belkin sat behind his desk and the rest of our party was gathered in an opposite corner. Rabbi Goren, turning his face away from Dr. Belkin and speaking directly to the Rav, asked him what he thought of the *shiur*. The Rav seemed to eschew the usual amenities expressed on such occasions, and instead candidly engaged Rabbi Goren in what is described in diplomatic parlance as an "honest exchange." From across the room, Dr. Belkin, caught up in the discussion, softly noted the point of view of an eminent commentary of centuries before who seemed to be at odds with the premise and conclusion advanced by Rabbi Goren. Rabbi Goren did not seem to care what Dr. Belkin said and hardly deigned to turn to him and listen to what he had to say. The Rav did not let this somewhat untoward moment pass, and pointing to Dr. Belkin, said to the

Chief Rabbi, "He knows what he's talking about. When Dr. Belkin speaks you have to listen." Dr. Belkin again repeated his comment, albeit more loudly, and insistently, but Rabbi Goren continued to ignore him even after the admonition of the Rav. The Rav again made his point about Dr. Belkin. Finally, not a a little bit exasperated, Dr. Belkin ran over to his *seforim* bookcase which was behind us, and to the surprise of all of us, found the source and showed the *sefer* to Rabbi Goren. Rabbi Goren, not expecting Dr. Belkin to be so conversant in *Rishonim*, and a somewhat "exotic" one at that, and on target to boot, was altogether taken by surprise. The Rav, knowingly with a smile, repeated his statement, "I told you Rabbi Goren—when Dr. Belkin speaks, you have to listen."

During those first years when I served as *Menahel* of Yeshiva, some of my *haverim* and colleagues likened my work to that of a lonely circus tightrope walker in the lofty regions of the vaulted ceilings of Madison Square Garden without a safety net— frantically oscillating between Dr. Belkin and the Rav. From the outside it may have appeared that way. However, truth to tell, although it was not always easy, I never really felt absolutely lost or unable to move as I willed to help keep Yeshiva on even keel and indeed to help it dramatically push forward. And that I believe was entirely owing to the conscious sense on the part of both the Rav and Dr. Belkin that they would not allow differences between them to interfere with the Yeshiva's ultimate purpose of teaching Torah and engendering true *yirat shamayim* and continuing to be the fertile breeding ground of *lamdus* and authentic Jewish leadership.

In all my dealings with the Rav and Dr. Belkin, as I've intimated before, I never felt the need to choose between them. The only time I was really put to the test was in the following and somewhat amazing episode. I received a call from the Rav one afternoon telling me that he had just spoken to Mr. Joseph Gruss and made an appointment to see him later that afternoon at his Fifth Avenue apartment. The Rav wanted me to accompany him. Although the Rav didn't exactly tell me the nature of this visit, nor the reason for his unusual and preemptory request that I go with him, I had an inkling about what must have been driving this initiative for a meeting. Mr. Gruss catapulted almost out of nowhere onto center stage of Jewish philanthropy and who became one of the outsized personalities in modern Jewish history who changed the focus and scope of Jewish giving. He understood early on that the quintessential priority for

Jewish survival was Jewish education and he was prepared to give mightily for this purpose, on a massive and altogether unprecedented scale. In great part, his heroic and unparalleled effort, which certainly was to include Yeshiva as well, was ignited by the Rav and possibly even more so, by Rebbetzin Tonya Soloveitchik *zt"l*, whose cherished acquaintanceship he made during her valiant struggle against malignancy.

In those early years, Mr. Gruss made three major contributions to our Yeshiva. As the Rebbetzin's insistent behest, he set up a fund to augment every *rebbe's* salary with a significant additional annual stipend. Another benefaction of his enabled the coming into being of Yeshiva's first Kollel Elyon which over the years has raised the level of Torah learning and dedication beyond our most optimistic expectations. And finally, moved by a vision to link Yeshiva's destiny to a resurgent Israel, he built what has become known as the Carolyn and Joseph Gruss Campus of Yeshiva University in Jerusalem. His ultimate dream was to have Rabbi Soloveitchik come to his Gruss Center and deliver *shiurim* there, on a regular basis which he knew could have incalculable impact upon Israel and upon Torah learning everywhere. He felt he had the received the Rav's promise on that score and went full speed ahead building his Center in the newly developing hills of *Givat Mordechai*, in Jerusalem. Indeed, a special apartment was built for the Rav. As the building was nearing completion and the first handful of *semikha* students who would be inaugurating the Center had already been selected, the Rav found that for overwhelmingly private reasons including health, he could not move to Jerusalem. Mr. Gruss found it difficult to accept the Rav's turnabout. Apparently, hoping to repair this rift, the Rav made the telephone call to see Mr. Gruss.

I could not imagine going on this visit without first informing Dr. Belkin. After all, I reported to him on all matters and our bond was yet deeper than that. I remained indebted to him for having shown confidence in me beyond what I felt I merited myself and for which I could never thank him enough. To my surprise, Dr. Belkin said, "Rabbi Charlop, I don't want you to go with the Rav to see Mr. Gruss. Do you hear me?" As full of consternation as I was at the abruptness of Dr. Belkin's insistence, it seemed to me I had no alterative but to comply. I went to the Rav only moments before our scheduled departure for the meeting with Mr. Gruss and told him of Dr. Belkin's feelings. He looked at me unbelieving. I don't ever recall having seen him in this state of pained disappointment. "Rabbi Charlop, you told me you were going to go with me. And I am insisting that you go with me irrespective of what Dr. Belkin may have said to you." It was the first and only time for me when duty and loyalty, unflinching until then, were tried. In the end and as things evolved, I felt that I had no choice but to go with the Rav. You have to understand that I looked upon the Rav and Dr. Belkin each in a different way, as *rabbeim muvhakim* of mine. Of course the Rav, in addition to my father *zt"l*, was my *rebbe muvhak* in learning and Dr. Belkin was my *rebbe muvhak* by virtue of the trust and confidence he invested in me and the great truths of life I learned from him which I hope to share on another occasion.

The Rav and I arrived for our appointment on time and rang the doorbell. To our amazement, Mr. Gruss opened the door only a few inches and said, "I am not letting you in, Rabbi Soloveitchik, because you did not keep your word about coming to Israel." The Rav was so taken aback that his only reaction was bemused tolerance and concern for at bottom he had great respect and even adoration for Mr. Gruss. "Dear friend, I came here to explain to you why I can't go," said the Rav. Nonetheless, Mr. Gruss held the door firmly. He inched his way out of the apartment, all the while holding the door, only slightly ajar. Before we knew it, the door closed behind him and he managed to make his way into the small foyer facing the elevator where we were standing. He continued to vent his disappointment in the Rav's change of mind. The Rav tried to explain to him and give him a sense of why he could not go. The whole thing took about 20 minutes and we finally left, returning to Yeshiva. I didn't know whether or not I still had a job. The following morning, I called Dr. Belkin, briefly reviewing what had transpired in our meeting with Mr. Gruss. Under the circumstances, I told Dr. Belkin, I had no reasonable or honorable option but to accompany the Rav. The matter was never again brought up.

An appropriate postscript is in order. Several years later, Mr. Gruss had undertaken a major renovation of the Harry Fischel *Beis Medrish*, the chief study hall of our Yeshiva. The Rav was the dedicatory speaker. In the presence of Mrs. Gruss and their children, and to a packed-standing-room-only *beis medrish*, he compared Mr. Gruss to the Rothschilds and said "I believe that Mr. Gruss has given more money in shorter time to raise the banner of Jewish learning." To which Mr. Gruss rose and offered the following acknowledgement: "Winston Churchill had a short speech and a long speech—the short speech was 'Thank you.' Mr. Gruss turned to the Rav and, looking directly at him, gave the long speech, 'Thank you very much.'"

When news of Dr. Belkin's mortal illness reached the Rav, it affected him profoundly and personally as if he were a member of his own family, their disagreement of the past notwithstanding. The old and shared bonds of learning and outlook and experience which linked them together in camaraderie and competition, deep down hardly loosened even when events seemed to pull them apart. Dr. Belkin's health, regretfully, deteriorated quickly. At first he was at the Mt. Sinai Hospital. But, as his condition worsened, apparently irreversibly, he was transferred to the Hospital of the Albert Einstein College of Medicine which he himself founded and built. I knew that there was not much time and instinctively called the Rav in Boston to tell him the somber news. "I think you should come and see Dr. Belkin now," I told him. The Rav immediately booked a flight. He arrived the following morning, bringing with him his son-in-law Dr. Isadore Twersky *zt"l*, Professor and Chairman of Jewish Studies at Harvard, for whom I knew Dr. Belkin had special affection. I met them at the Hospital's parking lot. Without conversation, we went directly to Dr. Belkin's hospital room. I remained at the open door while the Rav and Dr. Twersky walked to the bed. It's hard to say who burst into tears first, but both the Rav and Dr. Belkin were sobbing quietly and uncontrollably. After the Rav stayed in the room for about 10-15 minutes, he and Dr. Twersky walked out. From where I was standing I couldn't catch the few words they said to each other amid the tears. We left quietly, again without a word spoken among us, and the Rav and Dr. Twersky got into their car and returned to the airport. About two or three weeks later, during *Chol Hamoed Pesach*, Dr. Belkin passed away. It was the Rav who delivered the single and most memorable eulogy over his friend. He was the only one giant enough to do it!

Ultimately, and incredibly, but not inappropriately, the two *gedolim* shared the same *yahrtzeit*, 17 years apart.

Reflections on the Rav:
Life at RIETS Some 50 Years Ago

Samuel Danishefsky

Decisions made at various forks in the road can bring with them considerable consequences. So it was for me, when it was decided in a family gathering that I would go to high school at MTA. The year was 1948. Until then, I had attended public school in Bayonne, New Jersey where my father *zt"l* was a Rav. The decision to enroll at RIETS-MTA was not a simple one, since there were excellent alternative Yeshivas in New York. My RIETS-MTA-YU experience was transforming. The central event was the high *zechus* [privilege] of being in the Rav's *shiur* for three years. In this paper, I hope to share my recollections of that *zechus* in the setting of the RIETS of those days, which was a very special place and time.

For instance, before gaining admission to RIETS-MTA I was examined (*farherred*) by Rav Mendel Zaks *zt"l*, who was the *bochen* [examiner] of the Yeshiva. In addition to being a highly analytic Torah giant on his own, Rav Zaks was the son-in-law (*eidem*) of the Chofetz Chaim *zt"l*. Rav Zaks had the capacity to ask piercing questions which interrogated not only the *bochur*'s [young man's] grasp of the particulars of the *inyan* [topic] at hand, but also his general poise in learning. When Rav Mendel heard an answer which he liked, an unmistakable sense of satisfaction permeated his face. If an answer came back which he did not like, there was a hint of a frown; without Rav Mendel ever raising his voice the damage was

Dr. Samuel J. Danishefsky is Professor of Chemistry at Columbia University and Director of the Laboratory for Bioorganic Chemistry at Memorial Sloan-Kettering Cancer Center. Previously, Dr. Danishefsky held faculty positions at the University of Pittsburgh and Yale University.

done. I have always treasured my memories of "speaking in learning" with Rav Zaks. His was the capacity to express great ideas in few words. Rav Zaks granted me quite advanced standing, permitting me to enter a senior *shiur*. This "jump start" reflected, no doubt, the advantages of learning privately with my father *zt"l*, who cared deeply that his children be *lomdei Torah* and *ohavei Torah* [learners and lovers of Torah].

In my days at RIETS-MTA I had the *zechus* to study under three wonderful *rebbeim*: Rav Noach Borenstein *zt"l* (Mir), Rav Yeruchum Gorelick *zt"l* (Brisk), and Rav Shmuel Eliezer Volk *zt"l* (Telshe), all of whom benefited me greatly. Rav Noach *zt"l* attempted to inculcate the capacity to plumb the fundamentals of a *sugya*. He also had the gift of terseness and presented his ideas in a highly analytic style, with surgical precision. By contrast, Rav Yeruchum *zt"l* gave a dramatic *shiur* full of passion and exuberance. His highly evocative style elevated the *bochur* to a level of excitement and *tshuka* [endearment] for learning that I shall always cherish. Rav Volk encouraged a somewhat more speculative but always well-reasoned style. He particularly enjoyed showing how the two sides of a *hakira* [analytical inquiry] could explicate the differing views of a *Ktsos Hahoshen* versus a *Nesivos*.

Though different from one another in style and pedagogic strategy, these three *rebbeim* were clearly highly accomplished Torah scholars. All had been torn by the war from the great nurturing Litvishe Yeshivas and cast ashore into the America of the 1940s, in some cases after a harrowing stay in Shanghai or Siberia. The Litvishe-trained *rebbeim* in those days were most comfortable giving their *shiurim* in Yiddish, notwithstanding the fact that most of their students had, at best, a scant "command" of this language. (In my case, Yiddish was not a problem, since it was my mother language). Though the *shiurim* were in Yiddish, the *rebbeim* learned enough English such that, in the end, discourse was possible. Actually, at that time, there began to emerge younger *rebbeim* who would teach in English, but this phenomenon was still rather rare. I felt a great admiration for these and other Litvishe-trained *rebbeim* at RIETS for their Torah eminence, for their forcefully stated *hashkofos* [religious/philosophical points of view], for their wit and for their courage in re-acclimating as best as possible after the nightmare of the *Churban Lita* [the destruction of Lithuanian Jewry].

Correspondingly, RIETS and particularly YU President Rabbi Dr. Samuel Belkin *zt"l* (Radin; followed by a Ph.D. from Brown) deserve tremendous credit for providing a *bekov'dikh* [dignified] home for those Litvishe-trained *lamdonim* [scholars]. Dr. Belkin knew full well that their deeply held views were at considerable variance with his own and with those of RIETS-YU, particularly on matters of *Madda* and on the intrinsic value of secular studies. However, he was determined that the *talmidim* of RIETS learn from highly accomplished *Bnei Torah* [Torah scholars]. Dr. Belkin did not attempt to suppress their *hashkofos*. That the *rebbeim* were often not "on board" with the *hashkofos* of YU mattered less to Dr. Belkin than that RIETS *talmidim* be exposed to the authentic *pleitat sofrim* [the remnant of scholars] from the pre-WWII Yeshiva world. Parenthetically, one can't help but contrast the openness of RIETS to a cross-current of thought within the *Bnei Torah* family, with the rather strict, unforgiving requirements of hashkafic homogeneity operative these days in other great Torah *mosdos* [institutions].

It is interesting and encouraging to note that alumni from RIETS in the 1950s went on to build not only *Hesder* Yeshivas and day schools but also to found a *Kollel* in Israel and lead a quite traditional type of Yeshiva in the Midwest USA. As I recall, several alumni moved to Lakewood for extended and productive stays in learning. Still others went on to be *marbitzei Torah* [disseminators of Torah] at YU, to found various departments at Bar Ilan University or to lead synagogues and build virtually *yesh meayin* [out of nothing], frum communities (cf. *inter alia* Hamilton, Ontario; Bangor, Maine; and Teaneck, New Jersey). Also from the RIETS of those days came a major lawyer who brought landmark cases to the Supreme Court on behalf of critical "*frum*" causes, and a Ph.D. physicist from M.I.T. who was very helpful to the Israeli defense establishment. Thus, the diversity of *hashkofos* gave rise to a diversity of callings of RIETS alumni to be *mekhabeid shem shamayim*.

Thus far, I have confined myself to *rebbeim* to whose *shiur* I was assigned by Rav Mendel Zaks *zt"l*. I would be remiss in not recalling two other critical RIETS luminaries of those days with whom I had important relationships: Rav Dovid Lifshitz (Breinsk) *zt"l* and Rav Yaakov Lessin *zt"l* (Slobodka). While Rav Dovid gave his own *blat shiur* and a special *shiur* in *Chullin*, he also felt a sense of *achrayos* [responsibility] and closeness to many *talmidim* not in his *shiur*. Referred to by many as the "Suvalker" (recalling his rabbinate in Suvalk), Rav Dovid was central to the coherence of RIETS. He understood the range of mindsets of the *talmidim*. His warmth and *ahavas habriyos* rendered him a critical role model in RIETS.

Rav Lessin, a striking figure, was in charge of *mussar* [study of ethics] at RIETS. While time spent on *mussar* was essentially voluntary and there were no formal *sdorim* [scheduled learning periods] in *mussar*, Rav Lessin would visit the individual *shiurim*. Those who remained to hear a Rav Lessin *schmuess* [conversation, chat] were led back to the bygone days of the "*Alter* of Slobodka" under whom Rav Lessin had served and had grown as a *nosei keilim* [literally, an "orderly," but an assistant in yeshiva terms] for many years. In short, Rav Lessin provided a critical link connecting the golden era of Slobodka to a RIETS still struggling to define its identity in the U.S. Interestingly, Rav Soloveitchik was particularly supportive of Rav Lessin. The Rav *zt"l* remained in the shiur room to hear Rav Lessin's *schmuess*, listening to his *divrei hisorrerus* [inspirational words] with rapt concentration and bestowing upon him great deference and *kavod*.

In my first year of college, I had the great privilege to hear *shiurim* on *Mesechta Kiddushin* given by the Lomzer Rov, Rav Moshe Shatzkes *zt"l*. Though precious few could follow, in detail, the Lomzer Rav in his breathtaking and mind-expanding orchestrations of *Shas* (*Yerushalmi* as well as *Bavli*), *rishonim*, *poskim* and later *achronim*) one had the clear sense of being in the presence of an authentic Torah giant. Aside from the *shiur* itself, the opportunity to behold the regal aura of the "Lomzer" and to perceive his kaleidoscopic breadth was truly ennobling (*"achorei d'Rab Meir"*). The Lomzer, by his very presence, encouraged *kavod haTorah*.

I well remember occasions when the Lomzer Rov was driven from the Lower East Side by a car to RIETS, there to be greeted by the President, Dr. Belkin, with reverence. Dr. Belkin *zt"l* was indeed an extraordinary leader for YU. For instance, his vision resulted in the launching of the Albert Einstein College of Medicine. However, it should not be forgotten that Dr. Belkin also laid the basis for the current RIETS associated *kollelim* to encourage serious, sustained learning of Torah. While his agenda was varied and complex, his essence was best seen in the endearment with which he greeted the Lomzer Rov as he entered the Yeshiva.

I then moved on to the Shiur of Rav Yosef Dov Halevi Soloveitchik *zt"l* (the Rav) for three of the most memorable years of my life. It would be an exaggeration to represent myself as a *talmid* of the Rav in the sense that I have the credentials to hold forth on his points of view in matters of *lomdus, psak* or *hashkafah*. In my judgment, this high privilege should only be assumed by those who spent many years studying Torah under the Rav and then used that experience to define the central calling of their earthly missions. Indeed, I often worry about some who, with the best of intentions, quote the Rav with apparent authority on matters of *halachah* and *hashkafah*, though they may not necessarily have met his exacting standards in learning. Accordingly, the rest of this paper should not be read as a statement of reflections of the Rav. Rather, it summarizes my personal reflections on the high privilege of studying in his environs.

I'll start by noting that after leaving YU I've had the good fortune to study and in time to teach at some of the finest universities and research institutes in the world. It may come as a surprise to some of the more yeshivish readers, but there are some incredibly bright, fascinating, and gifted people "out there" from whom there is much to learn. Indeed, the Talmud relates several telling instances where *manhigei yisroel* sought opportunities to learn from external cultures. I have, in my meanderings, been privileged to meet many extraordinary scientists whose research accomplishments were awesome. Yet, I believe that in terms of originality, scholarly depth, range of expertise, and elegance of communication skills, the Rav was *oleh al kulam* [above all of them].

Back to the RIETS *shiurim* of the Rav—they were so deep and elegant as to defy close description. The Rav *zt"l* had a unique capacity to convey grandeur in the struggle to understand a *shtikel Gemara* [a "piece" of Gemara] or a troubling *Tosefot*, not to speak of a *shverer Rambam* [difficult Rambam]. The *shiur* started with recitation of the *sugya* and its nuances. The theories flowed in an organic way from the text of the *sugya*, not the reverse. The Rav would proudly describe himself as a *"melamed"* [teacher] struggling with the texts. To the Rav, all learning of Torah was really a work in progress. I suspect that he entered the *shiur* with general but flexible notions of its overall direction. After reading the text itself with great care to proper cadence, the discussion went on to explicating, if possible, the underlying concepts which governed the overall *sugya* as found in the *blat* [page]. From there, various possibilities were evaluated to rationalize the motifs of the *Rishonim* and to explore, in a methodical fashion, the consistency of the proposed formulation with related *sugyos*. Of course, much was to be learned from the way in which the Rambam's summary halakhic statement is phrased, and even from where the *p'sak* was situated in the *Yad*. For the Rav, the *shiur* was a labor of true love. Another highlight was the care given to how an idea is best expressed. One had the sense that having struggled with the concepts at such a rarefied level, the Rav felt beholden to express his central thoughts in clear, exact language with laser-like surgical precision.

Let me address what are to me troubling, if well-intentioned, exaggerations of some who would portray an occasional stern remark of the Rav as, *lehavdil* [to make a distinction], some form of personal *ragzonus* [hot temper]. I never detected anything remotely personal about these occasional apparent flare-ups. The Rav zt"l did feel that every *talmid* in the class had a responsibility to come in prepared so that the *shiur* would not waste time. The admonitions were really expressions of his very high standards and expectations. His work ethic in Torah learning was so awesome that he couldn't imagine why anyone would squander such magnificent opportunities. I always read his occasional irritations as a defense of the standards of Torah rather than as a personal putdown. What he was opposing was laziness and sloppiness in learning, not anyone in particular.

The Rav had global interests and extraordinary intellectual curiosity. One perceived an inner confidence in the Rav that, in principle, Torah concepts and values are universal and can illuminate many seemingly disparate issues. No one who experienced the Rav could ever doubt that Torah and *Yahadus* [Judaism] were the central passions of his life. As with his biblical namesake, the range of the Rav's interests and the scope of his capacities puzzled and even troubled some of a more classical orientation, dedicated as they were to the rebuilding of Torah life in the difficult terrain of America. Unfortunately, the puzzlement among these surely well-intentioned "*shomrei hasaf*" [guardians of the threshold] led, in some instances, to indications of disapproval and even hostility to the Rav by some in the non-RIETS yeshivish world. One had to marvel at the capacity of the Rav—a very sensitive man—to absorb slights and even worse. The Rav never answered the *mevakrei mumim* [inspectors of defects]. He was, one suspects, deeply apprehensive of the consequences of *machlokes* [controversy] within the ranks of the Torah-centered world. He also had an absolute revulsion to *lashon hara* [gossip]. While the Rav *zt"l* asserted in strong, bold terms the dangers of the abrogating or even chipping away at *halachah*, he never responded to his detractors from within the ranks of the Torah universe. The Rav was, of course, the paradigm of *nimukei immo* [kept his arguments to himself]. He had no shortage of arguments he could posit. His silence was really the ultimate manifestation of *maavir al midosov* [overlooking slights].

One would be remiss in reflecting on the Rav without emphasizing the role of the *yahrzeit shiurim* given to honor the legacy of his father, HaRav Moshe Soloveitchik *zt"l*, who preceded the Rav as the *de facto* head of RIETS. No one who attended these *shiurim* can ever forget the impact which they had on the Torah world. The main *Bais Hamedrash* was packed with lovers of Torah and, in fact, people would be standing in the outer hallway and its adjoining classrooms transfixed by the *Divrei Halachah* and *Milso D'Aggadatoh* which the Rav offered over time-frames of three to four hours. The audiences were packed with *shochrei Torah, rabbonim, mechanchim* and *parnessim*, all joining together to hear the Rav's original correlative insights in *halachah* and beautifully framed *drush*. Some in the *olam* were perhaps not so comfortable about coming to the YU main campus, and about being seen there. But in the magic atmosphere of those *shiurim*, distinctions as to age, details of persuasion, dress and political beliefs (*chareidi* or *tzionni*) all seemed to fade into irrelevance in the face of the Rav's expositions. For the Rav, it was enormously hard work but clearly a labor of love. The *shiurim* given to honor his father *zt"l* had an additional consequence. They showed the deep longing for Torah here in America and energized the Torah word to believe that the grandeur of Torah could indeed be restored, even on these foreign shores. Happily, owing to the diligence of his true *talmidim*, the Rav's Torah insights are now becoming available to the *klal* of *lomdei Torah* [community of those who study Torah]. There are now growing opportunities for later generations to enjoy his Torah.

People of the Rav's intellect, vision and *"hasogos"* [reach] appear rarely and only fleetingly. When they do, they may not be universally accepted here in the *"olam hachumrey"* [material sphere]. Remarkably, given his relentlessly logical style of learning, when it came to the realms of *drush* [interpretations of the deeper meaning of texts] and *machshova* [frameworks of thought], the Rav would, on occasion, provide quantum jumps which transcended strictly linear advances. As with his biblical namesake, the Rav's *"chalomos"* were not always fully appreciated by those who think in rather incremental terms. This is sad because, in the longer sweep of history, it is the *"baaley hachalomos"* who are apt to provide the pivotal mental leaps.

The influence and *maasim tovim* [good deeds] of the Rav were not confined to his generation. The Rav *zt"l*, who carried the burden of living in a particular generation, was really a gift to history, and is undoubtedly now ensconced in the hallowed *mesivta d'rokeah* [yeshiva in the heavens above]. Personally, there isn't a day in my life when I fail to think about the Rav, about the privilege of seeing and hearing him, about his *hesed*, about his *yashrus* [straightforwardness] and about the missed opportunities on my part to take proper advantage of his fleeting presence. It remains for us, for the moment among the living, to attempt to structure our time here, as he did, with the central goal of enhancing *kvod shamayim* [the honor of Heaven], struggling as he did to meet the concisely stated, but challenging goal of the holy prophet, Habakuk: *"tzaddik be'emunoso yichyeh"* [the just shall live by his faith].

The Lonely Man

William Herskowitz

The Rav *zt"l* was indeed "The Lonely Man of Faith." Despite the myriad students who fought to get into his classes, the thousands who attended his *yarhzeit derashot*, and the thousands of people who crowded his public *shiurim*, he was lonely. The Rav was a unique *gadol hador* because of his brilliant intellect, his encyclopedic knowledge of *halakhah*, his *lomdus*, and his broad knowledge of secular subjects. In addition he was a skillful teacher and powerful speaker. He was what we would call today a "superstar" and, as is common with superstars, he was besieged by people who wanted a piece of him. Whether they wanted a favor, to be associated with him, to be able to quote him or to show off their learning by arguing with him, he had to be constantly aware of people's motivations and be suspicious of those who tried to get close to him.

In addition, his weekly schedule was a trying one. He spent half a week in his apartment in New York away from his wife and children. In the early days, his mother and brother were nearby, but then his mother passed away and his brother moved away. In later years, his son, grandsons and some select *talmidim* spent a good deal of time with him, but it was not the same as being at home in Boston. The Rav confided to me that he felt alone and cooped up. I offered to take him for a drive or to some public event, but he demurred. What he wanted was companionship with someone he knew he could trust.

After receiving my MSW from Wurzweiler in 1950 and working in the field, I served in Boston as executive director of the New Eng-

Rabbi Dr. William Herskowitz received his BA from YC, MS from Wurzeiler, PhD from Revel and *semikhah* from RIETS. A former editor of *The Commentator*, he held pulpits in Toronto, Boston and Yonkers. He is the Rabbinic Administrator of the Westchester Vaad Hakashruth and Chairman of the RCA Pension Plan.

land Region of the UOJCA. During that year I was frequently in touch with the Rav on issues with the area synagogues and policy questions. As a single fellow, I was befriended by the Rav's sisters, Ann Gerber and Shulamit Meiselman, and their husbands. At that time Abe Wintman *zt"l* was the Rav's driver in Boston, but when he was unavailable, and for trips to New York, I became the chauffeur.

Toward the end of the year, the Rav asked why I went into social work and I replied that I wanted to help build up the Jewish community. He said that I would be more influential as a rabbi than a social worker and suggested I go back for *semikhah*. That fall, I re-entered Yeshiva, and although I couldn't get into the Rav's *shiur* because I had been away from full-time learning during my years in graduate school and work, I still kept in contact with the Rav. I was married now and worked downtown after *shiur*. I would drive the Rav to the train for his return trip to Boston; at that time (the 1950s) he didn't trust planes.

Friendship or not, the Rav was a force to be reckoned with when it came to the *semikhah bechinah* [test]. In those days it was an oral exam on two *mesekhtot*, *Chulin* and *Yoreh Deiah*. I was expected to cover seven *perakim* [plural of *perek*, chapter] of *Sanhedrin*, even though we had not progressed that far in class. I didn't manage to get to the last part of the last *perek* I was supposed to have mastered. The Rav started off with a question from one of these last pages and it was obvious that I didn't know that material well enough. He began honing in on that area and wouldn't ask on anything else until Dr. Belkin *zt"l* steered him to another *inyan* [topic] and I was saved.

After *semkhah* I spent five years as a rabbi in Toronto, when I regularly called the Rav on *shailos* and policy matters. I then returned to a pulpit in the Boston area and resumed my relationship with him.

The Rav was fond of saying that he didn't have to visit his father's grave because his father, grandfather, and the Rambam were with him at all times. However, with his wife it was different. He was very devoted to her. After her death, he went to the cemetery every Friday.

She was a very special woman who was her own person—you could call her Dr. Soloveitchik or Mrs. Soloveitchik, but never Rebbetzin Soloveitchik. The Rav was deeply attached to her, but that didn't mean that he would always listen to what she said.

The Rav, on the basis of his *lomdus* [learning, vast knowledge], was *meikil* [lenient] on certain things. People were always asking him about these matters. He often would refuse to answer unless he felt the individual had a personal problem or it was a serious student who wanted to learn about the method for answering *shailos*. I remember the Rav saying, "If people want to follow my *kulos*, they have to follow my *chumros* [strict interpretations] as well."

At my *Chag Hasemikhah* the Rav said, "You don't have to be a rav to be *machmir*, but you have to be a rav to be *meikil*." In later years, there was a shift to the right among the *talmidim*. I once was sitting in his *shiur* when a student who was about to get *semikhah* that June raised a kashruth issue with me. I explained the relevant *halakhos* to him and he said he agreed with my exposition, but couldn't go along with me because he was *"machmir."* I was upset because the Rav was training students to examine issues and discover what the *halakhah* was. Here was someone who was going out to lead a community and his judgments would not be based on what the law allowed but on an illogical *chumrah*. I mentioned this to the Rav who said that some of his students had moved so much to the right that he sometimes would hesitate to present to them a conclusion he had reached.

One of the issues on which the Rav had certain *chumros* was the sale of *chometz* [leavened foods and other articles that cannot be in a Jew's possession on Passover]. He wanted to make sure that the contract was a valid one and not a pro forma observance. His *shtar mechirah* [document of sale] had so many extra clauses in it that we were hard put to get them all on the page. I dutifully copied them and made them a part of every *mechiras chametz* I did on my own.

When I moved to Yonkers in 1960 to take a pulpit there, I made it my business to attend the Rav's *shiur* at Yeshiva. By then, he had evidently mellowed. Those who were in his early classes tell how he was intolerant of students who didn't prepare properly or listen attentively. Many *talmidim* were in dread of being singled out, dressed down and embarrassed. It still happened occasionally during these later years, especially if he thought the person gave a stupid answer when he was addressed, but now the Rav, before the class was over, would publicly apologize for denigrating the student.

The Rav was intellectually honest. I recall his building a beautiful structure on a statement in the *Gemara* and a quote from a commentator. We all marveled at how he had been able to interpret the text and derive such inspired principles from it. One of the students asked a question which he managed to answer and, seemingly, the matter ended there. The next day he came into *shiur* and said the *talmid* was right, there was a flaw in the argument, and he proceeded to build a new and more inspiring structure which was flawless.

Shortly after my return to New York, I became the Rav's driver for his weekly *shiurim* at Moriah. He did not want to come early, so our trip was timed to get there at the scheduled start. I would drop him off and then find a place to park. Since I was given the trusted job of taping the *shiur*, I would give one of the other passengers the tape recorder to take upstairs. Although there were people in the crowd who could operate tape recorders, they always left it to me to turn it on. When we got back in the car, the first thing the Rav asked for was the tape. I was told that later on when he checked on the tapes, he was shocked to find out that the first few minutes of each *shiur* were missing.

Although every *shiur* was recorded and speeches written out, the Rav rarely published his material except for a few essays in journals. The tapes were kept in a famous closet in his apartment. I remember when the Rav heard that magnetism could erase the tapes and panicked that his life's work could be obliterated.

In the late '40s and early '50s, I was the editor of *Horizon*, a literature magazine put out by the Hapoel Hamizrachi, the religious Zionist party. I somehow got my hands on a copy of the speech the Rav had given to the Hapoel Hamizrachi conference. It was in Yiddish and I asked my wife, who spoke Yiddish fluently, to translate it. After I had the translation checked, I told people that I was going to publish it. The Rav asked to see it to make sure it was accurate. Despite several requests to get back a corrected copy, I never saw it again.

When Dr. Belkin *zt"l* passed away, as President of the Rabbinic Alumni I was appointed to the committee to select his successor. There were reports that the *roshei yeshiva* were opposed to one of the candidates. I went to the Rav to ask him how he felt and who I should vote for. He refused to voice his preference. He said, "You were put on the committee because they felt you would make an intelligent choice. Vote for whomever you feel is best qualified."

While I, of course, looked up to the Rav as the *gadol* that he was, and as my *posek*, I felt privileged to have a more personal relationship with him. I felt close to him and was devastated when he became ill. I loved him as a person and miss him terribly. To this day I find it hard to say "the Rav *zt"l*" because he lives with me in my heart and mind.

The Rav: His Impact on My Life

Haskel Lookstein

It was March of 1956. I was nearing the completion of my first year in the Rav's *shiur.* According to the rules, I was eligible to study *Chulin* the next year and *Yoreh Dei'ah* the following year and present myself for my *semikhah bechinah.* However, it was exactly at that time that the Rav announced the three-year plan by which he expected to teach the senior students for three years: *Gittin* and its counterpart in the *Shulchan Arukh, Hilkhot Geirushin; Kiddushin* and *Hilkhot Kiddushin;* and then *Yoreh Dei'ah* along with *Chulin.* I was a little older than most of the students because I had gone to Columbia College and begun my rabbinic studies later than they did. Could—or should—I afford the extra year? I went to consult with Dean Samuel Sar, of blessed memory, who gave me the best advice I could possibly have received. He told me that I had had only one year with the Rav at that point and that Providence had given me an opportunity to have three more years. It was certainly worth the extra year I would have to spend in the Yeshiva. To this day I am grateful to Dean Sar. My whole life has been different because of his advice.

As a personality, the Rav affected me more than any other human being except for my father. They both modeled for me what it was to be a learned Jew, devoted to God and committed to the Jewish people. To have been brought up by one and taught by the other was a double blessing that has profoundly influenced me.

I remember the Rav very well as a teacher. How could it be otherwise? Four years, and then many *shiurim* and lectures and listening to tapes and reading the Rav's written works; all of this was entirely transformative for me. I remember vividly when I managed to struggle through *Ish Ha-Halakhah* in the original. It was extremely

---

Rabbi Dr. Haskel Lookstein is Rabbi of Congregation Kehilath Jeshurun, NY and Principal of Ramaz School.

hard work but it was also thrilling. I found myself marveling at how closely his thought, his perceptions, and his conclusions paralleled my own thinking. Then I remember laughing at myself. It wasn't he who was agreeing with my weltanschauung; it was I whose whole thought process had been molded by him over the years so that I actually thought that these ideas were mine when I read them in *Ish Ha-Halakhah*. That's how powerful his influence was as a *rebbe*.

I learned many things from him as a teacher. Among them were his striking integrity and his impeccable honesty. During my four years in his *shiur* I recall three occasions when a student—it happened to be me in one case—respectfully pointed out to the Rav that a whole analysis of his (sometimes two hours long) was at variance with something that we had learned some time before. Think of it: a young student challenging the greatest mind of our generation. He could have destroyed the student with a look or with a word and easily defended his position. But he didn't. I can still hear him saying: "Lookstein is correct; I am incorrect. Do you hear this class? He is correct, I am incorrect. I have to go home and relearn the whole *sugya* and present it again." I have no difficulty, when teaching a class, to be able to say to a student "What a great point! You are absolutely right. I made a mistake." Three times I saw the greatest teacher of our generation do exactly that.

I was fortunate to have had a number of close encounters with the Rav which left me with indelible memories and, in a way, a world view. Let me cite three of them.

On one occasion, in the early 1980s, I went to him with a list of questions that had been bothering me. The first on the list was the use of an elevator, operated by a non-Jew, on *Shabbat*. When I asked him the question he looked at me and said: "What did your father do?" I said that my father lived on the 11th floor and when he came into his apartment house on *Shabbat* the doorman knew to operate the elevator for him. He looked at me again and said: "So why do you have to be more religious than your father?" I was stunned and somewhat embarrassed. I told him that I certainly used the elevator in my father's house and I was not trying to be impudent by asking the question. I reminded him that in the year after I received *semikhah* I used to attend his *shiurim* on *Masekhet Shabbat* and I had actually heard his *heter* [rabbinic permission] for the use of an elevator when it's not possible otherwise (he said above the fifth floor) and it was for a *d'var mitzvah*. Under those circumstances, since he *paskened* that the operation of an elevator was only a rabbinic viola-tion, it was permissible to ask a non-Jew to operate it for a Jew. I ex-plained that, in view of the fact that most of the religious world doesn't use an elevator, I was just trying to find out whether he still felt the same way, especially since elevators in the days of the *shiur* (the 1950s) were manually operated while by 1980 most of them were automatic. He said his views had not changed and that the *p'sak* remained the same. But in his initial response to me—"Why do you have to be more religious than your father?"—I heard in one question the essence of Dr. Haym Soloveitchik's article on the mimetic tradition. That's exactly what he was saying to me. He knew that I grew up in a religious home and he didn't feel that I had to be more *frum* [careful in observance] than my parents.

On another occasion, in the late '70s, I also went to him with a se-ries of questions. After listening attentively and answering them, the Rav asked me: "Tell me, Chatzkel, how is Ramaz?" I understood the question was motivated by his being the founder of the Mai-monides School in Boston. I told him that Ramaz was doing very nicely. He asked me: "How is your enrollment?" I replied: "Fine, thank God." He pressed further and asked: "Do you have more ap-plicants than you have spaces?" I replied that "Yes, thank God, we have more applicants than we have places." He then said to me, "That's because you haven't changed." I was perplexed and asked him, "*Rebbe*, what do you mean we haven't changed?" He looked at me and said: "You haven't moved to the right; don't let them pull you to the right." Ramaz was always a centrist, Modern Orthodox institution. That's the way my father founded it and that's the way it has continued. But those words from the Rav gave me further con-firmation that we were on the right track. I have had occasion to quote them many times in my talks to Ramaz parents.

A particularly poignant exchange between us occurred after I had attended a Rabbinic Alumni convention and heard a prominent rab-binic scholar discuss the issue of Tay-Sachs testing. That scholar ad-vised against any kind of testing for reasons which he explained. Furthermore, he said, once a woman was pregnant there is certainly no reason to test because even if the fetus were found to have Tay-Sachs disease there is nothing that can be done about it. One may not abort. I was concerned about that approach and, as luck had it, I had been invited to have dinner that evening at the home of a member of the Rav's family; the Rav was going to be present. He was scarcely in the door when I described to him the view that had been expressed earlier that day and I asked him what his opinion was. He said very firmly, "You can abort a Tay-Sachs fetus through the sixth month." I said nothing but he must have noticed a quizzical look on my face as if to say—which, of course, I would not— what was the basis for the *p'sak*? I will never forget what he told me. He said, "Chatzkel, did you ever see a Tay-Sachs baby?" I replied that I had not. He said, "We had a Tay-Sachs baby in Boston. I tell you that you can abort a Tay-Sachs fetus through the sixth month." I saw at that moment a *gadol* in action, deciding a difficult question of Jewish law with absolute confidence and courage, based upon his scholarship and experience.

A final recollection: On the occasion of the 100th anniversary of the establishment of Congregation Kehilath Jeshurun, my father invited the Rav to give a public lecture in our main synagogue. Over one thousand people sat in rapt attention for more than an hour listening to the Rav expound on his theory of community—*knesset Yisrael*. My father and I were sitting in the front row. I was busy, as usual, stenographically transcribing every word of the Rav so that I would have his thoughts permanently available to me. When he finished his lecture, he said, "Now I would like to say a few words about my friend, Rabbi Lookstein," referring, of course, to my father. He proceeded to praise my father for his pioneering efforts in Jewish education, in religious Zionism, in homiletics, and in a number of other important areas. When he had finished his beautiful tribute he looked at me and said, "Chatzkel, you want me to say something about you too?" I lowered my head in embarrassment and wished there had been a trap door through which I could disappear. But I will never forget his next words. "Chatzkel, your father I respect; you I love." I knew what he meant and I will forever be grateful to him and to God for those feelings.

Rabbi Joseph B. Soloveitchik: A Guide to Life

David J. Radinsky

The life, breadth of vision and halakhic decisions of Rabbi Joseph B. Soloveitchik *zt"l* exerted the greatest influence, besides that of my family, on my religious and spiritual life during my student years at Yeshiva University and in the more than 41 years I have been in the rabbinate. The Rav influenced me on many levels: as one of his students, as a chaplain in the United States Army, as a Jewish educator and as a pulpit rabbi.

In addition, my wife's family in Boston was closely involved with the Rav and greatly influenced by him from December 1932, when the Rav came to Boston, until 1993 when he passed away. Even today our involvement with the Rav continues since many of my wife's relatives, including her father, Mr. Herman Cooper *a"h* and her uncle Rabbi Alter Aryeh Leib (Leo) Abelow *a"h*, the Rav's *chavruta* [study partner] and probably his closest friend in Boston for over 45 years, are buried not far from the Rav's grave in the Beth El Cemetery in West Roxbury, MA. Whenever we visit my father-in-law's grave we also visit the Rav's grave. Of course, much more importantly the Rav's spiritual legacy continues to influence and inspire us.

As a young student in Seattle, Washington, where I was born in 1940 and raised, I had heard the Rav quoted by Rabbi Gersion Appel, rabbi of our *shul*, Congregation Bikur Cholim. One of my teachers at Yeshivas Rabbeinu Chaim Ozer in Seattle, Rabbi Baruch Katzman, who was a *musmakh* of Yeshivas Rabbeinu Yitzchak Elchanan and had studied with the Rav, quoted him frequently. But it wasn't until the fall of 1958 when I entered Yeshiva College and

Rabbi David J. Radinsky is Rabbi Emeritus of Brith Sholom Beth Israel Congregation, Charleston, SC, and a former executive board member of the Rabbinical Council of America.

the *shiur* of Rabbi Aharon Shatzkes *zt"l* that I was able to comprehend some of the grandeur of the Rav. From 1958 until 1966, when
I received *semikhah*, with the exception of 1961—1962 which I spent
learning in Israel, I attended almost all of the Rav's public *shiurim*
given at Yeshiva University. When I came back from Israel in 1962,
I had the honor of being placed in the Rav's regular *Gemara shiur*,
which was given three times per week. Being in the Rav's *shiur* was
both challenging and intimidating. It was challenging to try to grasp
the Rav's analysis of a *sugya* using the Brisker *derekh*. It was exciting
when one understood the Rav's analysis and the logic behind the
sugya became clear and focused. However, the *shiur* was also intimidating because the Rav expected his students to be one hundred
percent prepared and in tune with his line of reasoning. If the Rav
felt that the student he called on to explain the *Gemara* did not meet
his standards, the Rav would harshly rebuke that student. As a result, students did not want to be called on to read the *Gemara*. In
spite of this fear, the experience of being in the Rav's *shiur* was one
of the most edifying of my life.

After learning with the Rav, I spent two years in Rav Dovid Lifschitz's *shiur*. This was a different experience with emphasis placed
upon understanding how the *Rishonim* explained the *Gemara*. I enjoyed learning with Rav Dovid Lifschitz *zt"l* and felt very close to
him. However, it is the Rav's analytical methodology that made the
greatest impression upon me and I have endeavored to employ the
Rav's *derekh* in my study of Gemara and in all aspects of Torah. After
learning *Yoreh Dei'ah* with Rav Yosef Weiss, I received *Semikhas
Chakhomim* on 12 Tammuz 5726. I feel honored that Rabbi Yosef Dov
Halevi Soloveitchik and Rabbi Samuel Belkin signed my *semikhah*. I
continued learning with the Rav from afar, hearing his *shiurim* at
RCA and Rabbinic Alumni conventions. When I visited my in-laws
in Brookline, MA, I would go with my uncle Rabbi Alter Abelow to
the Rav's Saturday night *shiur* at Maimonides School and the Sunday morning *Gemara shiur*. I studied the Rav's published articles and
shiurim. It is wonderful to see so much of the Rav's Torah being published today. Even after death the Rav continues to be a *ma'ayan
hamisgaber* (a constantly producing source of new Torah knowledge.)

During my last year (1965—1966) in the *semikhah* program, the
administration asked 25 of the 26 members (one was a Canadian) to
participate in a lottery to select four rabbis (our Orthodox quota) to

enter the chaplaincy of the United States Armed Forces. At first most members of the *semikhah* class refused to participate. Rabbi Samuel Belkin, the President of Yeshiva University, convened a meeting of the class and stated that neither he nor Rabbi Soloveitchik would sign the *semikhah* of anyone who refused to participate in the chaplain selection process. Once that ultimatum was given by Rabbi Belkin, everyone participated.

I had understood when I entered the *semikhah* program that I might be called on to serve as a chaplain. My feeling of responsibility to do so was buttressed by a responsum which the Rav wrote to Rabbi Samuel Belkin on April 26, 1951. Rabbi Abraham Avrech, who was Yeshiva's coordinator for the chaplain program, showed it to me in 1965. The Rav states in this responsum:

> In summing up the aforementioned facts, we cannot help but state that by ignoring political realities we might cause great harm to the prestige of the Jewish tradition and thus defeat the very objective to which we are all dedicated. All this leads to one conclusion: it is our duty to meet the challenge of the hour and see to provide the armed forces with as many chaplains as our quota requires.
>
> We must note that our decision is not primarily an expression of a pragmatic-utilitarian approach but reflects a halakhic-historic tradition which has always wanted to see the Jew committed to all social and national institutions of the land of his birth or choice which affords to him all the privileges and prerogatives of citizenship. Particularly, the Halakhah emphasizes the duty of the Jew to share in the defense of his homeland in the way in which he is best fitted.

(*Community, Covenant and Commitment*, ed. N. Helfgot, 2005, p. 57)

These words helped me to understand why the Rav was so vehement about our participation in the chaplain selection process; they also gave me the courage to serve as a chaplain. At the end of June 1966 I "volunteered." I received my commission and began my military training at the army's chaplain school at Fort Hamilton, Brooklyn, N.Y. and at Fort Dix, N.J. I was then assigned to Fort Leonard Wood, MO, where I was the Jewish chaplain for one of the largest basic training posts in the country; I was also the rabbi for central Missouri. My wife and our daughter were able to live there with me and our ten month stay at Fort Leonard Wood was productive.

In June 1967, right after the Six Day War, I was sent to Camp Red Cloud, Uijongbu, South Korea, where I worked for thirteen months. It was not an easy time for many reasons, foremost among them that I couldn't take my family with me to Korea. But on the whole my military experience was invaluable, and I believe that I made a difference in the lives of many Jewish and non-Jewish soldiers. Thank God, I came home safely. All told I served as a chaplain in the U.S. Army with the rank of captain on active duty for two years and in the reserves for another five years until 1973 when I was honorably discharged.

The chaplaincy issue exemplifies how the Rav's broad vision and awareness of the dynamics of the American Jewish scene had an impact on me and many others like me. He recognized that America was different from Europe and the halakhic response to this new environment should reflect this new reality.

In his approach to the State of Israel and religious Zionism the Rav demonstrated that he recognized the changed circumstances of world Jewry in the twentieth century. In *Kol Dodi Dofek*, the address which he delivered on Israel's eighth Independence Day in 1956, the Rav stated why the existence of the State of Israel is a miracle and a manifestation of Divine Providence. Among his many insights, the Jewish pride that the State of Israel has restored to every Jew is the one that resonates for me:

> The honor of every community, like the honor of every individual, resides in the ability to defend its existence and honor. A people that cannot ensure its own freedom and security is not truly independent. The third phrase in God's promise of redemption is: 'And I will redeem you with and outstretched arm and with great judgments.' (Exodus 6:7) Blessed be He Who has granted us life and brought us to this era when Jews have the power, with the help of God, to defend themselves!

(*Fate and Destiny*, Ktav, 1992, pp. 33f.).

The American military establishment took little notice of Israel's miraculous victory in the War of Independence in 1948, but Israel's victory in the Six Day War in 1967 made a great impression. When I first entered the army I heard derogatory remarks about Jews, referring to us as cowards with no military capability. After the Six Day War we were complimented for our military prowess and for

Israel's amazing victory. As the Rav said, "What happens to one Jew happens to all of us!" We Jews in the American army were deriving benefit from Israel's military might.

The Rav knew that the only way to combat assimilation in America was through intensive Jewish education. Therefore, he and his wife founded the Maimonides School in Boston in1937, the first Jewish Day School in New England. Maimonides, 70 years later, is a flourishing co-educational yeshiva day school with more than 600 students from pre-school through high school. On November 15, 1971, in an address to parents at Maimonides, the Rav outlined his educational philosophy and his attitude towards secular and religious knowledge:

> What do we at Maimonides believe? …. We believe that the Jewish child is capable of carrying a double load, the universal secular and the specific Judaic. We believe…that the child is able to study and comprehend two systems of knowledge and to excel in both…We also believe that the Jewish child is capable of mastering both scientific and Biblico-Talmudic knowledge not only from an educational, technical viewpoint but also from an axiological viewpoint. In other words, secular scientific training does not have to undermine the child's commitment to Torah values and commandments…The philosophical reasoning responsible for this optimism concerning the compatibility of the sacred with the mundane, the religious with the secular, is rooted in the thought that Judaism has never distinguished between these allegedly two areas of being. Judaism believes there is no duality in nature…Either everything is profane or everything is sacred. It is up to man either to extend Kedushah to every niche and corner of the universe or to desecrate even the Holy of Holies, the last cubit in the Sanctuary…One may serve God by building a house, or by healing the sick provided that he is aware that he can accomplish nothing without Divine help…We also believe that Judaism…has a great message for modern man…We believe that the modern, successful, sophisticated, cynical and skeptical Jew, knowingly or unknowingly, is yearning for God.
>
> ("Credo Which Guides Maimonides School,"*Legacy*, a special edition of *Kol Rambam*, the Maimonides newsletter, Oct. 1993, p. 2)

Here you have the Rav's attitude toward secular knowledge. In effect there is no Torah and *Mada* (Torah and Science). There is only Torah. There is no secular world. The whole world, everything that is in it and the knowledge of it, are all part of Torah. Man can extend *kedushah* (sanctity) to every corner of the universe. Whatever occupation or aspect of knowledge man is involved with can become Torah if he dedicates his actions and thoughts to Heaven. This concept is the Rav's great innovation and it has opened up new vistas for me as I relate to the world in general and to education in particular.

Another innovation in Jewish education, which the Rav conceived and taught, was his emphasis on equal Jewish education for girls and women in those areas of learning that apply to them:

> Not only is the teaching of *Torah she-be-al peh* [the Oral Tradition of Judaism] to girls permissible but it is nowadays an absolute imperative. This policy of discrimination between the sexes as to subject matter and method of instruction which is still advocated by certain groups within our Orthodox community has contributed greatly to the deterioration and downfall of traditional Judaism. Boys and girls alike should be introduced into the inner halls of *Torah she-be-al peh*.

(*Community, Covenant and Commitment*, p. 83)

I have been guided by the Rav's ruling to teach Talmud to all my students, boys and girls.

The Rav thought that we should not indoctrinate our students. He said, "Of course we teach observance in school. We do teach; we do not preach or indoctrinate…We believe that indoctrinated religiosity does not last long." (*Legacy*, p. 3) This has been one of my guiding principles in Jewish education.

Even though we don't indoctrinate our students, we will be successful educators only if we approach the performance of *mitzvot* with passion, enthusiasm and the joy we feel at acting according to God's will. I remember hearing the Rav say in a *shiur* shortly before *Sukkot* in 1962 that one can perform the *mitzvah* of *lulav* and *etrog* properly only if he approaches the *mitzvah* with passion and enthusiasm, so that the *mitzvah* is not performed in a dry fashion but is saturated in *lachliut* (moisture). He stated in his Maimonides School Credo that "Yahadut is…an experience of intoxicating beauty, enriching man's life, inspiring his heart. It is a rousing experience, cleansing and ennobling the human personality. Judaism is not too happy with the mechanical performance (of *mitzvot*) alone. It demands sensitivity and inner responsiveness on the part of man."

As one who served in the pulpit rabbinate for thirty-eight years, I have been guided by the Rav's rulings. I asked the placement office of Yeshiva to recommend me only to shuls which had a *mechitzah* [partition between men's and women's sections]. My request was based on the Rav's ruling in this matter. My relationship with non-Orthodox Jewish groups was also based on the rulings of the Rav which encourage cooperation in all shared communal concerns, but consider religious debates to be fruitless. I heard from the Rav many times that the primary role of the rabbi is to be an *ish chessed* (a man of kindness) and to defend the defenseless. Following the Rav's example, I have endeavored to fulfill this rabbinic responsibility as well.

The Rav's approach to relationships with non-Jewish religious organizations has been my guide. The Rav stated that the Jew "shares in the travail of man in general and of his people. The Jew is a responsible being, he is responsible for society. Abraham's prayer to God was related to total strangers—the people of Sodom. The Jew must share in the destiny of his people and be concerned with the destiny of mankind." (*Community, Covenant and Commitment*, p. 3. The quotations that follow are from this collection of his writings.) The Rav was courteous and kind to everyone, Jew and non-Jew alike. He related to all human beings as creatures made in the image of God. The Rav was not an isolationist. "The Jewish religious tradition expresses itself in a fusion of universalism and singularism. On the one hand, Jews are vitally concerned with the problems affecting the common destiny of man. We consider ourselves members of the universal community charged with the responsibility of promoting progress in all fields, economic, social, scientific and ethical. As such, we are opposed to a philosophy of isolationism or esotericism which would see the Jews living in a culturally closed society" (p. 259).

The Rav loved America and was grateful for the blessings of religious liberty it afforded the Jews. He even celebrated the American holiday of Thanksgiving. He wrote that "There should be no retreat on the part of the Jew from the full participation in all phases of national life and we are committed to all American institutions" (pp. 8f.). "We are loyal citizens of our great country and committed to all its institutions, political, economic and educational, without any reservation or qualification, as are all other Americans. Hence, joint action and common effort are commendable in all areas of mundane endeavor" (p.114). "We reassert that, as loyal citizens of our great country, we are all, Jew and non-Jew alike, interested in the welfare of our people and in their material as well their spiritual and moral advancement" (p. 267). However, as much as the Rav supported co-operation with non-Jews on social and political issues, he opposed any inter-faith dialogue.

The Rav was completely aware of the complexities of the world and knew that for many problems there were no easy answers. "I once said that there exist problems for which one cannot find a clear-cut decision in the *Shulchan Aruch*; one has to decide intuitively. Sometimes one cannot even know whether a decision was correct. It is very easy for zealots and negativists to solve all problems—they see the world colored black and white. For us, however, many cases are difficult to decide" (*Five Addresses*, pp. 49f.). This attitude reflects the Rav's view of the limitations of the halakhic process and his basic humility. He never forced his opinion on anyone.

My wife, Barbara Cooper Radinsky, was born and raised in Boston-Brookline, MA. Her uncle, Rabbi Alter Aryeh Leib (Leo) Abelow, was on the committee of the Boston *Chevra Shas* which brought the Rav to Boston in December 1932. Rabbi Abelow (the Rav always referred to him as "Rabbi Abelow" when he called on him at public lectures) quickly became one of the Rav's closest friends and staunchest ally in the Boston Jewish community. He was the Rav's *chavruta*. According to Rabbi Nathan Greenblatt of Memphis, TN, who had studied in the Rav's *kibbutz* (*kollel*) in Boston in 1941–1942, the Rav said that were it not for Rabbi Alter Abelow he would not have stayed in Boston.

Rabbi Abelow, who was born in Vashilishag, Lithuania-Poland in the early 1890s, had learned with the *Chafetz Chaim* in Radin and had come to the United States in 1921 with his wife, mother, and many of his siblings, including my future mother-in-law, Frieda Abelow Cooper. His father and a sister had come to America eight years earlier. At first the Chafetz Chaim had not wanted his student Reb Alter to go to America, fearing that he might become spiritually corrupted here. But after seeing the suffering the family endured during World War I, the Chafetz Chaim permitted Reb Alter to leave with his family for America provided he would do three things: set aside a period of time to study Torah daily; help to establish Jewish education in America; raise funds for the Chafetz Chaim's yeshiva in Radin. These three tasks Reb Alter Abelow carried out his whole life; helping the Rav come to Boston and supporting all of the Rav's educational projects certainly fulfilled the Chafetz Chaim's second condition. But even more important, he became the confidant of the Rav in Boston. On November 19, 1933, the Rav performed the wedding ceremony for my in-laws, Herman Cooper and Frieda Abelow. From that time on he participated in the family's happy occasions and, unfortunately, sad ones, too. In 1977 the Rav delivered the eulogy for Rabbi Alter Aryeh Leib Abelow, in which he described the special relationship he had with his friend of over 45 years. A tape of the eulogy is available from (Rabbi) Joseph Abelow, a son of Reb Alter who maintained the friendship with the Rav which his father had developed. Joseph Abelow was one of the few people allowed to visit the Rav, who was incapacitated from 1986 until he passed away on *Chol Hamo'ed Pesach* in 1993. He was one of the pall bearers at the Rav's funeral.

Because of the influence of the Rav and Rabbi Alter Abelow, my wife's parents enrolled her in Maimonides School when she was four years old. She spent thirteen years studying in Maimonides. She is grateful to Rabbi and Mrs. Soloveitchik for creating a school where she was able to grow as a Jewish woman and as an academic student. What the Rav and his wife created continues to be a major factor in my wife's spiritual and religious life and, therefore, in the spiritual and religious life of our family, including our seven children, grandchildren and me.

That is why I can say that, outside of our families, the Rav has directly and indirectly exerted the greatest religious and spiritual influence on my wife and me. For this we are appreciative. May his memory continue to be a blessing for us all.

The Rav: In and Out of the Classroom

Aaron Rakeffett-Rothkoff

The message I derived from acquaintance with the Rav was one of harmonious co-existence. He remained enthusiastically grounded in the Brisk and Volozhin traditions of his family. In addition, the Rav embraced Western culture with both arms. He was totally at home in its milieu and a Brahmin in a positive sense in his relationship to Boston and New England.

While yet a student, I observed the Rav's approach to the ideals of Yeshiva University. Chaim Gold transferred to Yeshiva after studying at Mesivta Chaim Berlin. Previously, he had studied in Israel where his prominent grandfather Rabbi Zev Gold resided. The latter, formerly the president of the American Mizrachi, settled in Eretz Israel in 1935. Shortly after his grandfather's death, Chaim also lost his father, Rabbi Moshe Gold, the Orthodox rabbi of Englewood, New Jersey. Chaim then returned to the States to be with his family. We became good friends. It was a special privilege for me to know someone who had walked the streets of Jerusalem on a daily basis. During his first year at Yeshiva, Chaim attended college in addition to the Rav's lectures. The Rav and Chaim were particularly close since the Rav had known both his father and grandfather. I noticed, as the next academic year began, that Chaim did not go upstairs to Yeshiva College after the Rav's classes. I asked Chaim why he was still in the *beit midrash* at that time. He explained that he decided to delay his college education; he wanted to devote all his efforts to Talmudic study; in a few years he would make a decision about continuing his college studies. I was taken aback by his attitude, and felt that I had to inform the Rav. The Rav asked me to

Rabbi Dr. Aaron Rakeffet-Rothkoff, YC '59, RIETS '61, BRGS '67, is a *RoshYeshiva* and professor of Rabbinic Literature at Yeshiva University's Caroline and Joseph S. Gruss Institute in Jerusalem.

bring Chaim to him. I quickly returned to the *beit midrash* and escorted Chaim back to Room 102, where the Rav was still sitting at his desk after the completion of his *shiur*.

Rav Soloveitchik said [these will not be the exact words, but as clear a remembrance as I can provide], "Chaim, I am responsible for you. Your father has passed away. Our sages declare that the '*beit din* [the members of the rabbinic court] are the parents of orphans' (Gittin 37a). Since you have no father, I am responsible for you. I was told that you do not wish to continue your college education. Let me tell you something: our sages stated that 'it is good to combine Torah study with *derekh eretz*.' I am not certain what the exact translation of *derekh eretz* should be. However, I am positive that nowadays it means that one has to go to college. Listen to me, go upstairs and register for the new semester."

Chaim protested that the term was well underway and it was probably too late to register. The Rav insisted and Chaim had no choice. Right after he headed upstairs, the Rav asked me who was in charge of registration. I responded that Professor Morris Silverman was the registrar. The Rav and I quickly walked down the hall to Dr. Belkin's office. Mrs. Helen Atlas, the president's secretary, greeted the Rav. He asked her to telephone Professor Silverman's extension. Within moments, the Rav was speaking to the registrar and explaining Chaim's situation. I parted from the Rav and returned to the *beit midrash*. About a half hour later, Chaim returned all smiles. He told me that Professor Silverman treated him like a prince. He was able to register for all the classes he wanted. Above all, the late fees were waived. As an afterthought Chaim mentioned that it was strange that Professor Silverman asked him to inform Rabbi Soloveitchik about all the help that was extended to him!

A trivial but revealing incident occurred in which the Rav influenced me. As I advanced in my Torah studies I negated the celebration of Thanksgiving Day; I feared its observance was suggestive of non-Jewish ritual. There were some rabbis who held this opinion and I followed their lead. One week, the Rav had to be in Boston for a wedding on Tuesday night. Our lectures were therefore rescheduled for Wednesday and Thursday. Following Wednesday's class, the Rav studied his watch for a few seconds and announced that Thursday's class would meet promptly at 9 a.m. The Rav evidently understood that this was an early hour for a formal lecture in the yeshiva. He quickly asked, "Will you be here on time?" I immediately responded, "*Rebbe*, if you say so, we will be here." A second later, I blurted out: "But why so early?"

The Rav gazed at me, broke into his infectious smile, and declared, "Arnold, don't you know what tomorrow is? Thursday is Thanksgiving Day. I promised my wife that we will be on the 12 noon plane. We must be at my sister's home at 2 p.m. for Thanksgiving Day dinner."

For years I had annoyed my mother by refusing to partake in the traditional Thanksgiving Day repast. There were always relatives present and I insisted on eating alone after the festivities. This Wednesday, when I returned home from Yeshiva, I asked my mother to place a chair for me at the table for the next day; I would join with the other guests. My mother probed as to what had transpired. I responded that I now learned that Rabbi Soloveitchik observed Thanksgiving Day.

She said, "Arnold, Arnold, why must you be so extreme in your observances? Why can't you be modern like Rabbi Soloveitchik?"

Indeed, the Rav had become my *rebbe muvhak* or my master teacher. I not only gained an immeasurable amount of knowledge from him, but also acquired a more refined Torah approach to life.

The presence of the Rav was constantly inspiring. He was always surrounded by students who utilized every moment to put questions to the master. Whether crossing the streets near the yeshiva or walking through the school's corridors, the Rav was surrounded by a semicircle of his disciples. I believe that this was best expressed by Rabbi Jacob Radin, a 1929 graduate of the Jewish Theological Seminary. He was the spiritual leader of the Inwood Hebrew Congregation, located in an area adjacent to Washington Heights. Radin attended the Rav's classes at the yeshiva during the period when I was a student. Once after class, Radin was caught up in discussion with a number of students about the lecture we had just heard. He suddenly asked whether we would like to hear about the difference between the Rav and Professor Saul Lieberman. We leaned forward to catch every word. While we considered Rabbi Soloveitchik the greatest living Talmudist, we also knew that Professor Lieberman was viewed as the foremost scientific Talmudic scholar. The latter was a graduate of the Slobodka Yeshiva and the Hebrew University. In 1940 he was invited to join the Seminary's faculty following his widely acclaimed publications on the Jerusalem Talmud and the

Tosefta. Lieberman and the Rav were also related by marriage since Professor Lieberman was wed to Judith Berlin, daughter of Rabbi Meyer Berlin, the son of the Rav's forebear, the Netziv of Volozhin. I do not believe that Rabbi Radin could have come up with a better question to arouse our interest.

He told us [again, a memory, not a transcript], "You know that I have attended classes in both the Seminary and the Yeshiva. I have studied with Professor Saul Lieberman and the Rav. The Professor lectures a few times a week. He hurriedly finishes and rushes back to his research. Outside of his formal lectures he is barely available to the students. On the other hand, the Rav is never alone. He has never finished a lecture on time. He always goes overtime. He remains in the classroom afterwards to carry on the Talmudic give and take with the students who cannot part from him. Even when he rises to leave, his disciples surround him and the discussion continues. They do not depart until he reaches his next destination. This scene repeats itself week in and week out at the Yeshiva and its vicinity. This is the basic manifest difference between these two prodigious scholars."

Rabbi Radin's insight left a lasting impression on me. During the subsequent decades, I always valued the students who hesitated before leaving the classroom when I finished my formal lecture. I viewed this as the heart of the relationship between the teacher and his disciples in transmitting the Oral Torah from one generation to the following one. "Each generation will praise your deeds to the next" (Psalms 145.3).

Our Rebbe

Israel Rivkin*

First Impressions

When I arrived at the Yeshiva University *Beis Midrash* for the first time in the late summer of 1955, I was immediately aware that I was in the presence of greatness. I had heard the Rav described as an intellectual giant towering above all the great Torah sages of today and yesteryear. He was known to be demanding of his students, intolerant of laziness, and unwilling to accept anything less than his high standards of scholarship. But from the first time I saw Rabbi Joseph B. Soloveitchik *zt"l* walking on Amsterdam Avenue, I knew this giant would become my *Rebbe*. He inspired me to feel like *Moshe Rabbeinu* when he first encountered the burning bush—"*asura na va'ereh*"—a need to get close to and "know" the Rav, but at the same time a heavenly voice warning all who encountered him "*al tikrav halom*," to be careful not to come too close.

By the time I entered his *shiur* as a junior, I had already come to realize that there was much more to the Rav than just his public image as a great Jewish thinker too brilliant to be approached by a common man. The depth of his *shiurim* was but the tip of the iceberg that lay beneath this special and unique man. In a *shiur* delivered to the Rabbinical Council of America in 1974 discussing the sins of Miriam and the spies, the Rav suggested that it was not that *Moshe* or *Eretz Yisroel* was necessarily better but that each was

Rabbi Dr. Israel Rivkin, RIETS '61, earned a PhD from the University of Connecticut in Basic Medical Science/Immunology and serves currently as consultant to medical laboratories.

*The author expresses appreciation to his daughter Dr. Shira Markowitz and sons-in-law, Sam Markowitz and David Kestenbaum, for editing this article.

unique—not comparable to anything else. That was how I perceived the Rav: unique and in a class all his own.

As I continued to attend *shiurim* and speak with the Rav, I also came to know him as a humble, sensitive, and understanding human being. True, he could be demanding and forever seeking perfection, but his remarkable personality was what made him so special to me. I would like to present some anecdotes of my personal encounters with the Rav to highlight some aspects of this personality that made me and so many others choose this great man as our *Rebbe*.

Personal Encounters

When I entered the *Semikhah* program in 1959, I was one of the few students with a car, providing me with personal quality time as I was often chosen to drive the Rav to and from the airport for his trips to Boston. Upon entering the car he would always greet me with a warm welcome and embark on a lively discussion about the flight: how the pilot coped with turbulence and how he might have handled the situation. I remember that tense evening in 1959 when the Rav returned to Boston for gastric surgery to remove what turned out to be a malignancy. As I escorted him to the door he tearfully turned to me and remarked, "I hope this is not my last passage through these doors." We parted speechless, and I nodded as he disappeared through the doors. As I returned to the Yeshiva that night I realized that after two and a half years in the Rav's *shiur* I had developed an inseparable bond with one of the great men of our generation.

Once again, the Rav's own words express this feeling best. In many *divrei Torah*, he mentioned that we encounter *Bnei Yisroel* upset with Moshe and Aharon and on the verge of stoning them, and the atmosphere in the camp charged with strong emotion. Suddenly the Torah reports "*va'yeira aleihem kvod Hashem*," ["And the glory of God appeared before you"] and all became quiet and calm. The Rav explained that when there is *hashra'as haShekhinah* [appearance of God's glory] it is palpable and on some level physically manifested; when confronted with the Divine presence it is real and engenders an immediate response. This was how it felt in the presence of the Rav. His humble demeanor reflected the *Shekhinah*. He would often say when he gave *shiur* he was not alone; he was simply the mouthpiece for a chain of sages reaching back through the generations from his father, Rav Moshe *zt"l*, his grandfather Rav Chaim *zt"l* and through the ages to Tosfos, Rashi, and the *chakhmei haTalmud*.

Human Insight

Part of the Rav's uniqueness was his ability to portray the human situation in a way that captured its essence and its relationship to Western secular man. His approach was not so much to give *mussar* or some dramatic call to *teshuvah*, but rather to paint a picture in such a way that it immediately drew your entire being into his vision of *darkhei Hashem*. This was especially true at the *kinusei teshuvah*. The way he discussed the Rambam's *hilkhos teshuvah* and other pertinent texts raised the students' spirituality to a higher level through his insightful portrayal of the laws of *teshuvah* and the sanctity of the *Yamim Nora'im*. His lectures on the meaning of prayer would provide insight into one's own psyche and strike a sensitive chord in the hearts of all present. Following his *shiurim* each *yom tov* took on a different *kedushah* and each *talmid* would gain a greater appreciation of the meaning of his prayers. His explanations of *Eichah* and *kinnos* on *Tisha B'av* made us consider our nation's long and tumultuous history and ignited in us a renewed yearning for the redemption.

A Master's Pride

The Rav took great pride in his *shiurim*. If a prominent rabbi was present in the audience on a given evening he would ensure that the *shiur* had a little something extra. The *shiur* did not have a sense of haughtiness, but rather the satisfaction that a great scholar had done his best to prepare and in the process has managed to shed new light on the subject at hand. At the *Yarchei Kallah* held annually in Boston at the end of August, the Rav discussed the Rambam's approach to the *avodah* [service] performed by the *Kohen Gadol* [High Priest] on *Yom Kippur*. The *Mishnah* in *Yoma* mentions that on *Yom Kippur* the *Kohen Gadol* was always accompanied by the *S'gan* [assistant]. The Rav defined the *S'gan* as the official *posek* [decisor] of the sanctuary who was there on the spot to answer any questions concerning the intricate service of this most holy day. The Rav added matter-of-factly, "If I was there I would have had the job." The audience was somewhat startled by the comment and looked at each other in amazement. The Rav picked up on this and tried to reiterate that he had meant that he would be the *S'gan*. Still noting our surprise, he explained, "I am not bragging or boasting; I am just stating a fact. Until I came to this country I never slept on *Yom Kippur* night. Each *Yom Kippur* I spent the entire night studying the laws of the *avodah* service with my father *zt"l*. I know it cold."

One year when *erev Pesach* fell on *Shabbos* the Rav delivered two *shiurim* on the special *halakhos* associated with this phenomenon. He prefaced the first *shiur* by saying much has been recently written about what to do on this particular *Shabbos* with respect to *biur chametz* [burning the leavened foods] and preparing the proper *seudas Shabbos* [Sabbath meal]. However, said the Rav, they were all "searching for the mosquito and missed the elephant staring them in the face." He then defined the unique *halakhic* challenges presented by this day and the various opinions on how to deal with them. The entire topic took on a new and deeper meaning.

The following week the *shiur* reviewed a detailed analysis of baking *matzah* on *erev Pesach* after *chatzot* and how to deal with that on an *erev Pesach shechal b'Shabbos*. It was a long and complex *shiur* demanding our full and complete attention. After the *shiur* the Rav, with a big smile on his face, and obviously exhausted from his lengthy discourse, commented, *"Far dem shiur kumt mir a schnapps."* ["For this I deserve a *schnapps*"] He was like an accomplished painter or composer looking back at his work with great satisfaction and joy.

Search for Perfection

The Rav also lived his life in an unending search for self-perfection. During the '50s and '60s when the Conservative movement was attempting to make inroads in American Jewish life and many came out strongly against the movement, the Rav, who opposed this movement, would advise his *talmidim* to be less critical of others and to work on ourselves. Focus on ensuring that you are doing the right thing and that you set an example that others would be proud to follow. This advice always remained with me and was similar to the way my father *a"h* told me to live my life. Keep working to perfect yourself and always do what is right.

When I would present a complex question to the Rav I was always in awe of the time and thought the Rav invested in reviewing all aspects of the query before responding. While still at YU, the president of a *shul* in my home town of Rochester asked me a question concerning the purchase of a church building for use as a synagogue. I posed the question to the Rav and he requested a copy of the layout of the building. Upon receiving the plans he understood that he would need a more in-depth review before he could answer the question. A week later he invited me to his apartment and laid the building diagram on the table. He then showed me that the building was designed in the shape of a cross and therefore was unsuitable for a *shul* in its current state. He suggested what changes would need to be made to meet the *halakhic* requirements if they still wanted to proceed with the purchase of the building. He did not let me leave until he pulled out a *Shulchan Arukh* and showed me why he does not generally recommend purchasing a church for a synagogue.

Caring for People

The Rav also had a personal side in which he took an interest in people and many aspects of their lives. During my year as a chaplain in Fort Bragg, NC, I was involved in the conversion of an eighteen year-old girl. With the help and guidance of the Rav she was brought into the fold and enrolled in Stern College. For years after that, every time I met the Rav his first question was, "How is the girl?"

The Rav also demonstrated this personal side at the annual *Yarchei Kallah*. Many of us stayed at the Terrace Motel and were invited to a party hosted by one of the attendees in honor of his wife's birthday. The Rav would sit and relax with us and our wives and children and chat casually. I still have the picture of my son, about four years old at the time, sitting on my lap next to the Rav and eating birthday cake.

Conclusion

The Rav embodied the words he used in his own *hesped* [eulogy] for the Lomzer Rav, Rav Aaron Shatzkes *zt"l*. He explained that *gedolei Yisrael* have *tzvei keshenes* [two pockets]; a *gadol* is in one respect *mekayem haolam* [sustaining the world] and at the same time *mevatel haolam* [dismissing the world]. The *gedolim* know how to come down to earth, yet remain at a level of *kedushah* [holiness] which is elusive to the common man. This was my *Rebbe*. He had the *tzvei keshenes*. At once demanding perfection of himself and others, serious about his learning and dealing with life's challenges, he was at the same time a humble and caring human being who related to others each on his own level. His legacy lives on in the hearts and minds of his *talmidim* and all those he touched.

Yehi Zikhro Barukh.

My Rebbe, Rabbi Soloveitchik?

Fabian Schonfeld

Much has been written about Rav Soloveitchik *zt"l* and much more will yet be written about his great wisdom, philosophy, *hiddushei Torah*, and about the limitless influence which he had and will continue to have upon thousands of Jews and even non-Jews. There will continue to be discussions about the meanings of what he said and wrote throughout his life. Those who will discuss or read his writings and remember his many lectures and his *drashot* [talks] will continue to argue as to what he had said and meant.

What has not yet been done sufficiently is to define what is really meant by the word *talmid* and who can be considered a true *talmid* of the Rav.

I remember an incident in the Rav's office at the yeshiva. As I was discussing a particular situation with him, there was a knock at the door and a rabbi, well known in the community, came in and told him of the sad passing of Rabbi Poleyeff. The Rav was very upset and asked this rabbi whether there was something else he wanted to ask. The rabbi said he would like to know if he is supposed to do *keriah* [tearing clothing as a sign of mourning] since he considered Rabbi Poleyeff to have been his *rebbe muvhak*. The Rav responded that the question is not whether the rabbi considered Rabbi Poleyeff to have been his *rebbe muvhak*, but whether Rabbi Poleyeff had considered him to be his *talmid muvhak*.

There are many rabbis and others who used to quote the Rav by saying "I asked my *rebbe*, Rav Soloveitchik, and he told me...." I have heard and so have many others this kind of statement numerous times and always wondered if such a statement was proper and whether whoever made it was relating an accurate account of a par-

Rabbi Fabian Schonfeld is the Rabbi of Young Israel of Kew Garden Hills, NY.

ticular conversation or whether, perhaps, such a claim was made intentionally or otherwise in order to support a particular position in *halakhah* and Jewish communal affairs.

What indeed permits someone to say "My *rebbe*, Rabbi Soloveitchik?" Was the Rav really in this particular instance the traditional *rebbe* whose opinion would make the difference in one decision or another?

There is a story told in *Chagigah* (3b) about two *talmidim*, Rabbi Yochanan ben Broka and Rabbi Elozor ben Chisma, who visited Rabbi Yehoshua in Pekiin. Rabbi Yehoshua asked them what *chidush* was said in the *beth hamidrash*. They responded, "*talmidecho anu*," we are your *talmidim*; we drink from your waters and live by your mouth—meaning, we depend upon you to teach us and we cannot teach you. Rabbi Yochanan reacted by pointing out that, nevertheless, there cannot be any day in the yeshiva without new ideas.

The same story is related in the *Yerushalmi* with one change: instead of saying to their *rebbe* "*talmidecho anu*," they said: "*hakol talmidecho*," all are your *talmidim*, everyone is your student. To understand the difference we have to be aware of two kinds of *talmidim*. There are those who go to a *shiur*, learn something new and audit many of the lectures of a particular sage. Among them there are some who never laid eyes on the image of a particular *gaon* and who never even spoke to him. These are the general *talmidim* who claim to understand a particular idea made by an *adam gadol* [a great person]. They are a part of a vast number of people who claim to be students of a certain great personality. These are the ones who are included in the statement made in the *Yerushalmi*, "*hakol talmidecho*."

Then there are those who not only delve into the meaning of a *shiur* or lecture but delve into the persona of the *gaon* and *rebbe*. They try to understand the pain or problems which a *rebbe* may feel from time to time. They deeply care for the feelings and profound Torah messages of their *rebbe*. They are the ones who are quoted in the *Bavli* text of the story. They are the ones who are not part of the general public but part of the small group of students who fuse their own life with that of the *rebbe*. They try to sense what he wishes them to do and they are sensitive to his needs and concerns. They worry about him and have a kind of umbilical cord that ties them to him. They are the ones who are mentioned in the *Bavli* who say *talmidecho anu*.

There is a *Mishnah* in *Pirkei Avot* which tells us that Rabbi Yochanan ben Zakkai had five students. The question is: after all it was Rabbi Yochanan ben Zakkai who saved the Jewish people during the Roman occupation and rescued the entire structure of *Torah she- b'al Peh* [Oral Torah]; it is because of his request that the Roman emperor allowed him to preserve the yeshiva at Yavneh where hundreds of students perpetuated the study of Torah; in each generation there were hundreds more *chachmei Yavneh*; why does the *Mishnah* speak of only five? The answer is obvious when you read the exact words in the *Mishnah*—"*chamishah talmidim ho-yu lo.*" The word "*lo*" means that these five were the ones who were part of Rabbi Yochanan and lived their lives through him and for him. They were the ones who gathered around him hour by hour, day by day.

The Rav used to spend much of his teaching in defining and describing the *rebbe-talmid* relationship. A statement of *Chazal* [our sages] that he was fond of discussing was the meaning of "*gedolah shimusha shel Torah yoter milimudah,*" serving the Torah is greater than teaching. The Talmud in *Brachoth* finds the source of this idea through the case of Elisha who poured water on the hands of Elijah. The rabbis deduce from that fact that it was not just the study of Torah, but rather the personal service which Elisha rendered to Elijah that led to his being appointed to succeed Elijah. That is why the Rav explained that raising the *Sefer Torah* [Torah scroll] and putting the *gartel* [belt] and mantle on it are considered to be more important than receiving an *aliyah* [calling one to read the Torah].

Before one can say that a particular *gadol* is one's *rebbe*, one must be sure that like Elijah one is part of the inner life of the *rebbe*.

"My *rebbe*, Rabbi Soloveitchik" is a phrase one has to be careful in using, and one has to be worthy of it.

Those who use that expression should be asked how often they visited him when his health was failing, how often they drove him from the airport to the yeshiva and from the yeshiva to any other place he needed to be. The Rav's family knew how easily some used the expression "My *rebbe*, Rabbi Soloveitchik" without truly being entitled to use the term.

I was once with the Rav when he seemed very sorrowful; I summoned up enough courage to inquire what made him so sad. He told me that he had helped a number of organizations and individuals to achieve prominence, but they did not respond to his personal needs during the time after he lost his wife. Not once, he pointed out to me, did they feel the need to reach for the telephone and inquire how he felt. Not once did they make the effort to be in personal touch with him when he was enveloped in sorrow for the great loss he had suffered.

There are many instances I could quote where the Rav gave expression to his feelings of disappointment. I do not mention names in this article for obvious reasons, but I do make an exception for one gracious and noble lady, Mrs. Shirley Feuerstein from Boston. She called me during the period of sorrow which the Rav felt after the passing of his wife and asked me to see that the RCA [Rabbinical Council of America], to whom the Rav had given so much of his life and energy, should arrange for *shiurim* in the summer in order to lift his spirits. We seized upon the idea and suggested to the Rav that we would come to Boston at the end of the summer to spend three days with him studying Torah. At first, he was quite negative, and said, "I am not hopeful that busy rabbis will come to Boston for that purpose." His reaction was due to his disappointment in some of his *talmidim* who had shown little concern for him. We were able to convince him that this was not so. I had the great merit to make arrangements for the event. The first year we started with a group of fifteen rabbis and the number grew to the point where after thirteen years of yearly pilgrimages to him, well over a hundred rabbis came. To sit with him, to study with him and even to dine with him was an unusual and gratifying experience. It was said of a particular *chassid* of the Maggid of Mezritch that he went to him not to study Torah but to see how he tied his shoelaces.

It is obviously only *talmidim* who felt this way who had a moral right to speak of him as "My *rebbe*, Rav Soloveitchik."

Thus we have to continue to follow in his footsteps when we discuss halakhic and communal problems. Let me just mention a few examples. His opposition to engaging in theological discussions with non-Jewish clergy is as valid and relevant today as it was when he gave us his guidelines in the well-known article "Confrontation," published in *Tradition*. There are those who claim that it is time to change and allow such debates to take place. The answer is absolutely not. It is a principle of *Yahadut* [Judaism] which is immutable and part of the very structure of Torah-true Judaism. Another point is the Rav's ruling regarding the method of *shechitah* [kosher slaughter] which must be well understood before any change can be considered. Yet another point was the Rav's adamant though polite attitude toward deviation from the structure of the synagogue and the conduct of prayer. He said and wrote that one must forego even the blowing of the *shofar* and not worship in a deviationist house of worship. Finally, the Rav's attitude to worldly and secular knowledge was not based upon "combining" Torah and secular knowledge. The Rav did not tolerate speaking of a combination of the two.

To him, Torah was rooted in its own principles and did not need and permit a partnership with any other field of science.

Shortly before the last stages of the illness which took him from us, his daughter Atarah Twersky, about whom volumes can be written regarding her practice of the *mitzvah* of *kibbud av* [honoring a parent] with assistance from her late husband, Rabbi Dr. Yitzchak Twersky, took me to visit him at the hospital.

Upon entering the room, I noticed how agitated the Rav was. Atarah tried to tell him that I came to visit hoping it would make him somewhat calmer, but to no avail. When she said, "Your *talmid* Fabian Schonfeld came to ask you a *shailah*," he became calm, his features relaxed and he began to quote the first *halakhah* of the Rambam in the fifth chapter of *Hilchot Yesode Hatorah* which speaks about the *mitzvah* of *Kiddush Hashem*.

Finally, we are reminded of the statement in the Talmud that Rabbi Eliezer never spoke or said anything "*shelo shoma mepi rabbo*" [that he did not hear from the mouth of his teacher]. It seems to me that unless one heard something from his *rebbe*, he would not speak about it or say it. Rav Moshe Feinstein *zt"l* (a cousin of the Rav) explained this to mean that Rabbi Eliezer would never say anything that was not in the spirit of his *rebbe*.

We may refer to "My *rebbe*, Rav Soloveitchik" only if we instinctively understood the real depth of what he said and who he was. Only if we were present "to tie his shoelaces" can we dare to say "we are *talmidim* of the Rav."

Today's generation, which includes a wonderful group of *talmidei chachamim* who study Torah with those who had the merit to learn from the Rav directly, also may refer to "My *rebbe*, Rav Soloveitchik."

The '60s:
Mentor of Generations

The Rav lecturing at Stern College where Rabbi Soloveitchik helped foster women's Torah education. (Photo courtesy Yeshiva University.)

The Rav – How He Developed *P'sak* and His Views of *Da'at Torah*

Julius Berman

As might have been expected, since the Rav's *p'tirah*, much has been written about various aspects of his multi-faceted personality. This essay will be devoted to a description of the Rav's approach to *p'sak*, and then, what I believe is a related subject, the Rav's attitude to *Da'at Torah*.

To best appreciate the manner in which the Rav arrived at a *p'sak*, I decided that I would take one *p'sak* as an example and set forth the manner in which the Rav tackled the subject and, as it were, escort him as he goes, step by step, from the inquiry to the ultimate resolution. The individual *p'sak* I've chosen for this exercise is <u>The Use of the Elevator on Shabbat</u>. I use as my source the notes taken contemporaneously during the Rav's *shiur* and my memory as refreshed by the notes.

The Development of the *P'sak*

It goes without saying that no *posek*, including the Rav, can embark upon developing a halakhic ruling without first going back to the basics, *i.e.*, the potential *issur* (the prohibition) with which we are dealing. In this case, the Rav pointed out that there were two potential *issurim*, albeit somewhat interrelated.

The *Issur*

The first and most obvious *issur* is *amira l'akum shvut*, *i.e.*, a Jew is prohibited to request a non-Jew to act on behalf of a Jew in a man-

Rabbi Julius Berman is Chairman of the Rabbi Isaac Elchanan Theological Seminary Board of Trustees and a past president of the Rabbinical Council of America and the Religious Zionists of America.

ner in which the Jew was not allowed to act himself. While the act of the non-Jew will take place on *Shabbat*, the prohibited instruction by the Jew may have taken place at any time during the week (or on *Shabbat* itself). Thus, in our example, unless a *heter* (permissive ruling) is identified, one cannot make a request—even on a weekday—to have the non-Jewish doorman, elevator operator or fellow passenger act in a manner which is prohibited to the Jew.

Second, independent of the first prohibition and even if no request by the Jew has been made of the non-Jew, if the non-Jew, totally on his own, acts for the benefit of a Jew, the Jew may not receive the benefit of the act.

Thus, returning to our subject, that would mean that even if no instruction at any time were given to the non-Jew, if he acts in a manner that the Jew could not act himself, the latter would not be allowed to receive the benefit of the act by riding on the elevator.

Of course, all this is predicated on the absence of a *heter* that would allow what would be otherwise prohibited by these *issurim*. And, thus, we come to that portion of the development of the *p'sak* that focuses on the possible *heter*.

The Halakhic Analysis

The Rav pointed out that there is one particularly pertinent Talmudic passage, (in *Mesechet Eruvin* (68B)) involving a *milah* [circumcision] on *Shabbat*, when the warm water necessary for the procedure had spilled or was not available in the *reshut* or area in which the baby was located and the question is posed as to what preparatory steps (other than the *milah* itself) can be done via a non-Jew. To use the halakhic terminology, can one request a non-Jew to handle the *makhshirei* [instruments of] *milah*. While the Talmud has a permissive ruling in this regard, the *Rishonim* have differing views as far as the breadth of such ruling.

Rabbeinu Tam's view is most restrictive. He limits the Talmudic passage allowing the act of the non-Jew to those situations in which if the Jew did the act himself, it would violate a rabbinic prohibition, but not a Biblical one. Moreover, even then, it only applies to *milah*, which itself overrides the *Shabbat* restrictions, but not to other *mitzvot*.

Rambam and *Rif* agree with *Rabbeinu Tam* in limiting the *heter* to the acts of a non-Jew for *milah*—preparatory acts that if done by a Jew would constitute a rabbinic violation—but believe that *milah* is merely an example of a *mitzvah* and, consequently, the *heter* applies to all *mitzvot*. Moreover, the *Rambam* considers *mitzvot* as representative of a broader category reflecting significant human needs.

BeHag rules that instruction to a non-Jew is permitted even for an act that if done by a Jew would constitute a Biblical violation, but limits it to the *mitzvah* of *milah*. As to all other *mitzvot*, the *heter* is limited to overrule rabbinic violations only.

Ba'al Ha-Itur has the most lenient position. He accepts the *BeHag's* interpretation of the Talmudic passages to allow use of a non-Jew even to overcome a Biblical violation but agrees with *Rambam* that *milah* is merely an example of a *mitzvah*, and, therefore, the *heter* applies to all *mitzvot*.

The *P'sak* of the Shulchan Arukh

The *Mechaber*, in *Orekh Chaim* (Siman 307) rules in accordance with the *Rambam* and *Rif* that one can instruct a non-Jew to do an act that, if done by a non-Jew would violate a rabbinic prohibition (but not a Biblical prohibition), for <u>any</u> *mitzvah* where there is a need.

However, the *Rama* (Siman 276) comments that if someone instructs a non-Jew to kindle a light (which obviously would be a Biblical violation if done by a Jew) so that the Jew can eat the *seudat Shabbat* [Sabbath meal] in a lit room (which itself is a requirement of *Shabbat, Rashi, Mes. Shabbat* 25B), he should not be criticized since he is relying on the view of the *Ba'al Ha'Itur*.

The Rav's *P'sak*

We have now come full circle. Having referred to the underlying Talmudic passage, the differing interpretations of the *Rishonim* and the rulings in the *Shulchan Arukh*, the Rav concluded that if one were to wish to rely on a *heter* to ride the elevator on *Shabbat*, it would necessarily be predicated on the view of the *Ba'al Ha-itur*, keeping in mind that the latter's position contains <u>three</u> indispensable conditions:

Requirement #1: *amirah l'akum*—having a non-Jew do the act; and
Requirement #2: *mitzvah*—for purposes of fulfilling a *mitzvah*; and
Requirement #3: *l'tzorekh*—The act is necessary for the purpose of fulfilling the *mitzvah* indicated.

Applying the *heter* to the elevator on *Shabbat*, the Rav concluded that one could rely on the *Baal Ha'Itur* to ride the elevator to the upper floors of an apartment house (*l'tzorekh*) via intervention of a non-Jew (*amirah l'akum*), to participate in the *seudat Shabbat* (*mitzvah*).

(At that point, the Rav mentioned that one of the reasons for his reluctance to move to New York was the elevator problem on *Shabbat*. However, when we promptly assured him that we would obtain for him a low floor apartment and eliminate the impediment, he smilingly acknowledged that there were also other reasons for not moving to New York.)

Since the presence of all three requirements is indispensable to application of the *heter*, close analysis of each is important when attempting to apply it in other situations involving the elevator on *Shabbat*. To illustrate:

Requirement #1 mandates the presence of a non-Jew, as elevator operator or, in the event the elevator has been modernized to dispense with the need for manual service, the presence of a non-Jew to push the button to bring the elevator to the floor the Jew is on <u>and</u> to send the elevator to the floor desired. Thus, the *heter* is inapplicable if it is necessary for the Jew either to "call" or "send" the elevator. (This condition may frequently be a complete bar to use of the elevator when one is on an upper floor and wishes to leave the building but has no way of "calling" the elevator without pressing the button himself.)

If, in fact, Requirement #1 has been met, one is then faced with the next condition—*mitzvah* (Requirement #2). While, according to the *Rama*, to ride to an upper floor for *seudat Shabbat* may be a *mitzvah*, there are numerous other scenarios that come to mind. What about leaving to take a walk; to return home for a nap; to visit someone to socialize?—to name a few. Are these *mitzvah* purposes?

By the same token, Requirement #3—*l'tzorekh*—must be present. Can using an elevator to go down to the lobby rather than walking down the steps ever constitute a *tzorekh*? Does it depend on how high a floor one is starting from? Does it turn on the age or strength of the individual? Even on the way up, how many floors up convert the use of the elevator into a *tzorekh*?

In sum, what I attempted to demonstrate is that only when one understands the development of the Rav's *p'sak*, including all the nuances and conditions upon which it is based, can one safely and securely apply it to the factual situation posed. Unfortunately, many times, it militates against a simple "yea" or "nay," but who says that the life of a halakhic Jew should be simple.

* * *

Much has been written—particularly of late—concerning the Rav's attitude toward the concept of *Da'at Torah*. The primary effort seems to have been to infer the Rav's views on this subject through analysis of his published writings. On the one hand, we can use as the springboard the Rav's eulogy for Rav Chaim Ozer Grodzinski of Vilna, the venerable *posek ha-dor* [decisor of *halakhah* for the generation] during the period immediately preceding the outbreak of World War II (*Divrei Hagot ve-Ha'arakha* [Jerusalem, 1981, 187-194]), in which the Rav elaborated on the *kohen gadol's tzitz* [the High Priest's diadem] as symbolizing the purely intellectual, halakhic aspect of Torah leadership, while the *hoshen* [breastplate] represented the guidance provided by Torah leadership on public questions. In the view of the Rav, Rav Chaim Ozer's outstanding virtue was the manner in which he united the two roles.

On the other hand, as Rabbi Aharon Lichtenstein has noted (*Leaves of Faith: The World of Jewish Learning*, pp. 227–228), there are those who focus on the Rav's subsequent statements over the decades in which he accepted and sharpened the distinction between *divrei mitzvah* which are to be decided by halakhic decision makers and *divrei r'shut* ["permissible" matters; in whose domain do these fall?] for which significant weight is attached to the opinion of other leaders. My purpose in this article is not to add to that discussion of the Rav's writings, but, rather, to derive the Rav's views as to the scope of *Da'at Torah* and its limitations, from the relatively few occasions in which he publicly expressed his views on major matters of public policy. Close review of these instances leads me to the following three-fold conclusion, as to the Rav's views on *Da'at Torah*.

1. With total self-discipline, he limited the public statement of his views on matters of public policy to those instances—quite rare—which he felt were of critical importance to the future of the Jewish people, whether due to the danger of *sh'mad* [conversion; apostacy], the abandonment of *halakhah*, or something of equally great moment.

2. When he decided to speak out on a subject, he did not distinguish between the reflection of pure *halakhah* or of public policy or, for that matter, the interlacing of the two disciplines. Indeed, as Rav Aharon Lichtenstein, *sh"lita*, once pointed out, what characterized the Rav and, to some extent his greatness, was not only his stature in a particular area, but the complexity and totality of his personality.
3. Reflecting modesty, even as to matters of great public import, the Rav would emphasize the need to consult with experts in the field in question, which, in and of itself, was a reflection of *halakhah*.

Now to the specifics:

<u>Case</u>: Most would agree that the decision to publish the article "Confrontation" (*Tradition* 6:2 [1964]) is a classic reflection of the Rav's view of *Da'at Torah*. In that article he develops the rationale for, and lays down the strictures surrounding, interreligious dialogue—sanctioning dialogue involving social issues common to many religions and prohibiting those involving religious themes.

It is clear that the Rav felt that it was necessary to lay down such rules. He perceived that interreligious dialogue (in which the Jewish people were involved) had mushroomed throughout the world, on the local, national and international scene. He also was fully aware that interreligious dialogue had theological implications and that it had always been a fertile area in which purveyors of *sh'mad* feasted. Thus, recognizing the grave threat that unlimited, totally undisciplined, interreligious dialogue presented to the future of the Jewish people, the Rav felt impelled to publicly set down the ground rules for such dialogue, what was permitted and, of even greater significance—what was not.

These rules, in effect, became the bible of interreligious dialogue.

<u>Case</u>: Shortly after the conclusion of the Seven-Day War in 1967, when many were issuing public statements that it was halakhically forbidden to "return" any of the territories taken by the Israeli forces in Judea and Samaria <u>even if</u> such a gesture would bring long-sought peace to Israel, the Rav decided it was imperative for him to issue a two-fold public statement—first, that *halakhah* does <u>not</u> forbid the "return" of territory for the sake of true peace, and, second, the decision whether or not such "return" will, in fact, bring peace

is not one that *poskim* are equipped to make, for they must look to the experts, in this case, the military leadership, to determine the advisability of the "exchange," (analogous to the input of doctors into the ruling as to whether one should eat on *Yom Kippur*).

Case: In June of 1982, Israeli Defense Minister Sharon launched the Operation Shalom La'Galil into Lebanon. That fall, an incident occurred in Lebanon at the Lebanese refugee camps of Sabra and Shatila that involved what many considered a massacre by Lebanese Christian troops of Muslim residents in those camps. Unfortunately, the word spread that Israel connived with the Lebanese Christians in connection with that escapade and it didn't take long for the word to spread throughout the world press concerning Israel's alleged culpability, which Prime Minister Begin strongly denied. I was Chairman of the Presidents' Conference at the time and I recall the prime minister saying in the course of a conversation that this charge was but a reflection of the age-old blood libel charge against the Jews; as he put it (in Yiddish), Gentiles are killing Gentiles, and as usual, the Jews are to blame.

The Rav, however, felt very strongly that the failure to conduct an appropriate investigation would leave an immutable moral stain upon the Jewish people. Consequently, he reached out to the prime minister with the plea to convene a judicial commission and, in fact, such a commission, led by retired Supreme Court Justice Yitzhak Kahan, was appointed and, after a full investigation concluded that the Israeli Army leadership did not connive with the Lebanese Christians, but that not enough effort was made to prevent the activity, which ultimately led to Minister Sharon's resignation.

Case: When the movement developed to pressure the Kremlin to allow emigration of those Soviet Jews who wished to leave for the West, and permit those who stayed to practice their religion, a disagreement broke out among the activists as to whether we ought to engage in public protests or revert to the age-old policy of private *shtadlanut* [diplomatic intercession], with many of the *gedolim* opting for the latter and decrying public protests. When the matter was posed to the Rav, he first reviewed and explained the historical approach and then concluded that the ultimate determinant must be the effectiveness of the approach; as to that, one should seek the advice of the Kremlinologists—the resident experts—on the subject.

Case: During the post-WWII period, Orthodoxy in America was in crisis. There was a mass exodus from the cities to the fertile green plains of the suburbs. The Jews were no exception and they too fled the cities. In the case of Orthodox Jews, this meant that they were leaving in place well-established religious institutions, such as *shuls*, and ending up in towns totally bereft of Orthodox houses of prayer. So, the Orthodox Jews that moved to the suburbs were faced with a choice. Does one attend a Conservative or Reform synagogue or stay home? It is understandable that confronted with such a choice, many opted to go to *shul*—any *shul*. Moreover, when it came to the High Holidays, the *mitzvah* of hearing the *shofar* came into play. It was in that climate that the Rav published his famous ruling that one should not attend a synagogue with mixed pews even if he had no other synagogue available, and even if it was *Rosh Hashanah* and, by not attending such a synagogue, he would miss hearing the *shofar*.

* * *

Indeed, even with respect to full-blown *p'sak*, there were occasions when the Rav made a conscious decision to refrain from getting involved.

Case: The Rav was informed that a controversy had erupted within the Jewish community of the British Commonwealth concerning the use of a microphone in Orthodox *shuls* on *Shabbat* and *Yom Tov*. Chief Rabbi Emanuel Jacobowitz had prohibited it, but, subsequently, the Chief Rabbi of Israel, Yehuda Unterman, had ruled that a newly developed microphone that had been installed in the Johannesburg, South Africa *shul* of the local chief rabbi could be used. Moreover, Rav Unterman's son, who was then the rabbi of the Marble Arch Synagogue in London, had publicly stated that in light of his father's recent permissive ruling, he is confident that Chief Rabbi Jacobowitz would re-visit the issue. The Rav was contacted with the request to publicly state his views on the controversy. He refused, explaining that he, sitting in the United States, had no right to issue a ruling in connection with a controversy in another country that was under the spiritual tutelage of its own *morah d'atra* [chief rabbi; literally, rabbi of the place].

Case: A short time after my marriage, my father-in-law asked me to inquire of the Rav concerning the halakhic propriety of a practice that my father-in-law believed the rabbi of the *shul* he attended was going to implement. When I raised the issue to the Rav, he refused

to opine, explaining that he had no right to discuss with a congre-
gant of a *shul* with its own *morah d'atra* the propriety of that rabbi's
ruling. (The Rav then said that if my father-in-law, somehow, can
get the rabbi in question over to the phone to discuss the issue with
the Rav, adding [with an obvious glint in his eye]—"even if he puts
a gun to his head"—he, the Rav, will instruct the rabbi, in no uncertain terms, as to the applicable *halakhah*.)

If one had to sum up in one sentence the Rav's views on *Da'at
Torah*, I would repeat what he told me in 1982 when I, as Chairman
of the Presidents' Conference, consulted with him concerning a position I ought to take on an issue that I faced. He told me, in effect:
"Listen, there is no need to have a position on every issue, and even
if you have one, you must still decide whether to state it publicly,
and if so, when, where and how."

Rav Yosef Dov HaLevi Soloveitchik (The Rov) *ZT"L* Role Model Par Excellence

Heshie Billet

In this article, I would like to paint a portrait of the Rov as I saw him when I was a student from 1969 until 1975. The Rov was a polychromatic personality. He was an exciting master teacher, a wise mentor about life, a dynamic speaker, an insightful adviser with a charismatic yet humble personality. What follows are events which bring these attributes to life. This collection of anecdotes represents moments which I witnessed first-hand between the ages of nineteen and twenty-five, but they remain fresh in my mind to this day as an adult of fifty-seven years.

Pride in Family

The Rov was very proud of the distinguished line of Torah scholars from which he descended. His father, Rav Moshe, was his *rebbe* and the Rov spoke of him with the utmost reverence. He often spoke of his grandfathers, Rav Eliyahu and Rav Chaim, and his great grandfather and namesake, Rav Yosef Dov. Of Rav Chaim he used to say, in many different contexts, "Before Rav Chaim, the world was in the dark ages." I recall the Rov once bringing to class the hand-written notebook of Rav Chaim on *Bava Metzia*. He showed it off with great pride.

The *Melamed*

The Rov often used to say, "I am just a *melamed*," a simple teacher. But what a *melamed* he was! He gave *shiur* at Yeshiva University

Rabbi Heshie Billet has served as the Rabbi of Young Israel of Woodmere since 1980. He served as president of the Rabbinical Council of America from 2001–2003 and Chairman of the Yeshiva University Medical Ethics Hotline in the early '80s.

three times a week, for a minimum of two hours. During the summers of '69 and '70, he gave *shiur* in Boston six times a week at minimum, and on occasion, seven times!

Total Commitment to Truth

The Rov's students had to be impressed with his absolute dedication to the pursuit of truth. I recall learning *Nazir* and *Sotah* one summer in Boston. The last week of *shiur* in August began on Sunday with a difficult *Tosafot* on the subject of *"miktzat hayom kekulo."* At the end of the *shiur*, the Rov was not satisfied that he had come to the correct understanding of *Tosafot*. I left that Sunday night (for a week-long NCSY Conclave in St. Louis), planning to return to Boston on Thursday evening to collect my belongings for an expected return to New York on Friday morning. When I arrived on Thursday, my friends told me that I had not missed anything. The Rov was still not satisfied that he had mastered the *Tosafot*. He decided to invite all of us to his home on Friday morning for one last shot at the difficult text. But Friday's learning failed to shed any new clarifying light. The Rov sheepishly asked us if our parents would mind if we stayed in Boston for *Shabbos*.

On *Shabbos*, we had *shiur* at our regular place, the Maimonides School. The Rov began by telling us that he had a new explanation of *Tosafot*. He then mused, "I wonder what Father would have said about it. He probably would have slapped me across the face!" Incredibly, the Rov still held himself to his late father's high standards of learning! He then proceeded to suggest the interpretation and repeat it several times with growing conviction. Finally he said, "This is the absolute truth. You can go home tonight, boys."

The Bald *Nazir*

One of the funniest episodes I recall from the Rov's *shiur* occurred when we were learning *masechet Nazir*. In the *sugya* about the requirement that the *nazir* cut his hair at the conclusion of the term of his pledge, the Talmud discusses the various laws associated with this haircut. One of the students was curious to know what the law would be in the event that the *nazir* was bald. The Rov, for some reason, ignored the question. But the student was not to be put off, and he persistently repeated the question day after day, but still there was no response. Finally, the Rov said to him, "Will you stop already with the bald-headed *nazir*?!!"

B'li Neder [without pledging oneself]

One year at YU we were learning *masechet Eruvin*. The Rov had decided in the late '60s to learn either the latter sections of traditionally studied *masechtot* which were never reached by the end of a *zeman* [term] in the yeshivot, or to study *masechtot*, such as *Eruvin*, which were not customarily taught. He once remarked, "Which *rosh yeshiva* is crazy enough like me to teach the excruciatingly complex *sugyot* of *Eruvin*?"

One Tuesday the Rov came to *shiur* and announced, "This week we will finish the third chapter of *Eruvin*." On Thursday at 9 AM, he began his *shiur* in front of more than sixty students. He was still lecturing at 4 PM, now to approximately twenty students. Suddenly, he looked up and said, "Boys, why are you so fidgety?" We said, "*Rebbe*, you have been teaching seven hours straight. *Shiur* was supposed to end four hours ago." He replied, "At the beginning of the week I said we will finish the chapter this week, which constitutes a vow accepted by the class. No one said '*b'li neder,*' so we must finish." Soon, in an act of compassion, he asked that we find three rabbis who were not present when the vow was made in order to do *hatarat nedarim* [dissolution of a vow]. Only then did he dismiss us. From then on, whenever the Rov came into class and made a commitment about the week's study, someone would call out "*b'li neder.*"

Rochlin

We were once studying the third chapter of *Baba Batra*, which deals with the subjects of *chezkat raayah* and squatters' rights. Rabbenu Tam, in *Tosafot*, raised an issue about "*rochlin,*" traveling peddlers. For five consecutive lessons, the Rov filled our notebooks with his struggle to understand Rabbenu Tam. This included every extant version of Rabbenu Tam including the *Sefer Hayashar* version. When he finally finished, many of us were grateful to move on. Two months later on a Tuesday, he came into class and announced, "Boys, I have a new *p'shat* [plain meaning] on Rabbenu Tam on *rochlin.*" We had been only too happy to be finished with Rabbenu Tam on *rochlin*, but the Rov was so dedicated to the truth that the issue continued to disturb him until he arrived at a satisfactory explanation.

Bothers My Mind and *G'mar Tov*

One of the Rov's favorite expressions was, "This bothers my mind." Most of us are bothered by external annoyances, but the Rov was bothered by ideas.

One year, in the final moments of the last *shiur* before *Yom Kippur*, the Rov apologized to the class for at times berating us, both for our deficiencies in pursuing ideas completely and for our occasional incomplete preparation for shiur. After all, he explained, it was before *Yom Kippur* and thus a time when one must ask others for forgiveness. He then concluded, "But never in my life have I seen a group of people less dedicated and less committed to the pursuit of truth than my *talmidim*. You sleep well at night when you do not understand Rashi. But I cannot sleep because it bothers my mind. *G'mar Chasimah Tovah* [a wish for a good inscription for the new year]."

The Lubavitcher *Melamed*

In his determination to learn the traditionally untaught later chapters of *masechtot*, the Rov once chose *Perek Hasho'el* near the end of *Baba Metzia*. He told us that he did not know that *perek* [chapter] well because he had last learned it as a child with the Lubavitcher *melamed* whom his father had hired to teach him. But the teacher chose to study *Tanya* instead and opened the *gemara* only when he heard Rav Moshe's footsteps approaching.

The Rov was actually very proficient in *Tanya,* a text which he often quoted. One *chodesh Elul* in Boston, the Rov taught us sections from *Likutei Torah*—written by the *Baal ha-Tanya*—each day. A few of my peers traveled to Russia in the late '60s and actually met the elderly man who in his youth was the Rov's Lubavitcher *melamed.*

This Should Be My Biggest *Aveirah* [lapse; offense]

The Rov's great commitment to teaching and learning was manifest particularly on *Tisha B'Av* and when he had *yahrzeit*. When he observed *yahrzeit*, the Rov would fast the entire day, in addition to teaching *mishnayos* in the third floor *Bais Medrash* of Furst Hall for the day's duration. On *Tisha B'Av*, the Rov would explain *Kinos* for a solid six hours or more. After a visit to the cemetery he would learn the laws of *Tisha B'Av* with us from the *Shulchan Arukh*. The level and style of *shiur* were hardly different from the Rov's usual analytical classes. One year, when we arrived at the section in

Shulchan Arukh which suggests that even if one learns the laws of *Tisha B'Av* on that day, it should be on a very simple level, the Rov said, "So the question is—this *shiur*? The answer is—this should be my biggest *aveirah*." I do not believe that the Rov's mind was capable of learning something without automatically going into an analysis mode in order to understand the underlying principle behind the text that was being studied.

The Rov's *Mentschlichkeit* [humaneness]

There was an outstanding student in the *shiur* who never missed a class taught by the Rov, both in New York City during the school year and in Boston during the summer. Some time before the summer of 1970 this student got married. He showed up for *shiur* on the very first day of class in Boston that summer. When the Rov saw him, he asked where the young man's wife was. He responded that she was in New York and that he would be joining her for *Shabbos*. That Friday morning, before beginning *shiur*, the Rov called the student's name and said, "Go home to your wife now." As the young man reached the door, the Rov added, "Don't come back next week without her." On Sunday, the student was back in Boston with his wife. He remarked to some of us, "I don't know why the Rov was so adamant. Before we got married, I told my wife that next to the Rov, she was the most important person in my life."

Who Said the Torah Wants Us to Shave?

The late '60s and early '70s were turbulent times on US college campuses. After President Nixon ordered the bombing of Cambodia and following the Kent State massacre of four student protestors by the National Guard, college campuses erupted. YU was not exempt from the anti-Vietnam War protest movement. One of the activists was a young man from Boston who had graduated from Maimonides.

At YU, this Boston boy was one of the organizers of a big protest. Flyers went up all over campus. The flyers included some comments about Israel. The Rov was strongly opposed to mixing Israel with Vietnam. At the beginning of *shiur* one day, he had that boy summoned into his classroom on the fourth floor of Furst Hall. The boy came in wearing jeans and sandals, sporting long hair and a scraggly beard. The Rov told him that he had until the end of *shiur* to change the flyers by deleting Israel from them. The boy dutifully complied. Toward the end of the day's *shiur*, he returned to show the Rov the new flyer. Satisfied, the Rov complimented the young man and told him he had acted like a real *ben Torah* [literally, "child of the Torah'; a learned person]. The class erupted in laughter.

Later the Rov mentioned to me that he was quite upset with the students in the *shiur* for laughing. "I know why they laughed," he said. "But who says that short hair and a clean-shaven face are what the Torah wanted?"

Student Fear

There was a whispered tradition in YU that the Rov was a very intimidating teacher. I mean this in the sense that he expected his *talmidim* to be prepared for class. Woe to the student who came unprepared and got caught. By the late '60s and early '70s, the reality did not accord with these hallway tales. The Rov was much gentler with us than he had been with the students of his younger years. Nevertheless, there were days…

One of the most popular seats was behind the pole in Room 401F. It was thought by some to be a kind of *ir miklat*, a safe zone where one could sit unnoticed for the entire class. The Rov used to call names and take attendance the first few days of the semester. If you were absent three times, your name would be crossed off the list. There was no consequence to being crossed off the list because grading for the *shiur* was not done by the Rov but by his assistant who marked the exams. However, there was an advantage to being crossed off the list….that is, if you did not want to get called on in *shiur*. The Rov would often consult the list before randomly calling out a name in class.

One of the boys figured this out and did not respond when the Rov took attendance at the beginning of the semester. It worked; he was crossed off the list and home free for the year. No fear of being called on…. Wrong! One day the Rov walked into class, pointed to that boy, and said, "You, over there, what is your name? I see you come to my class every day and you are not on my list." But the boy was a quick thinker. He gave the Rov a pseudonym. Alas, the Rov wrote the pseudonym on his list. From then on, he regularly called on the young man by his pseudonym to read or answer questions.

The Kinder and Gentler Rov

There was a young man who attended the Rov's *shiur* who clearly had less background than the average student in the class. He was not a shy person, and used to pepper the Rov with elementary questions that were not usually asked in the Rov's class. We once read an anecdote in the *Gemara* about a rabbi from a certain town. This student raised his hand and asked the Rov where that town was located. Now, this was not a question one asked the Rov, we thought. In fact, some expected a nuclear reaction. Instead, the Rov stroked his beard, thought for a moment, and then said, "Somewhere in Babylonia, I think." Clearly, the Rov understood who had asked the question and wanted to encourage the student in his study of Talmud.

Sometimes the Rov would ask a student a question, and the student would give a short response. The Rov would then react with a long discourse covering numerous cross references in the Talmud and *Rishonim*. When he would conclude, he would turn to the student who had given the initial answer and ask him, "Is that what you meant?"

Man of Principle

The Rov was a man with a definitive world view. He was a real leader and took some difficult stands in his life. What follows are three examples of positions he took that I witnessed as a student.

A Torah Institution

In 1970, YU changed its catalogues and removed any reference to itself as a religious institution. The change was dramatic and deliberate and very obvious to anyone familiar with the old catalogues. On paper, students in Yeshiva College were no longer required to attend one of the three religious programs, RIETS, EMC, or JSS. The purpose of the change was to facilitate the appearance of YU as a non-sectarian institution which would be eligible for New York State funding called "Bundy money."

The students, under the guidance of the Rov, Rav Aharon Lichtenstein and Rav Haym Soloveitchik, challenged this change for many reasons. There were *geneivas da'as* [deception] issues. But most significantly, the whole character of Yeshiva College as a religious institution was undermined. We called a student protest demonstration for the day of the upcoming *Chag HaSemikhah*. Both YU and

Stern College students were going to demonstrate in separate areas on campus. All the signs had been prepared by the Concerned Students Coalition to be both respectful and to the point.

The night before the demonstration, the Rov yielded to the tremendous pressure that he was under and told the student leaders to trust him and to call off the strike. But it was too late. Things had gone too far and there was no way to call off the strike.

The *talmidim* in the Rav's *shiur* did not join the picket lines out of deference to the Rov. We went, instead, to hear his speech on the fifth floor of Furst Hall. It was a great speech. The Rov said that unless the Yeshiva officially and definitively owned up to what it was, a place of Torah, and withdrew the false catalogues, he would resign. He then said, "There was supposed to be a demonstration about this today, but I called it off." Someone in the room shouted out, "*Rebbe*, there are 1200 students picketing outside!"

The Rov's response was incredible. "I do not care. These are the finest boys and girls I ever met. This is not a demonstration like they have at Columbia University. This is a demonstration for Torah. I identify with them one hundred percent." I, for one, will never forget that moment. The point was made and *Barukh Hashem* [thank G-d] the character of our Yeshiva was preserved.

Lord Caradon

In 1969 there was a war of attrition between Israel and Egypt across the Suez Canal. David of 1967 was now cast as Goliath by the world, and Israel was being roundly condemned all over. One of the sanctuaries of condemnation was the UN, and one of the most eloquent anti-Israel spokesmen was the British Ambassador to the UN, Lord Caradon.

The YU Political Science Club invited Lord Caradon to speak one Thursday during club hour. An uproar broke out on campus. There were calls for demonstration and tossing spoiled tomatoes at the speaker. The Rov noticed all of the commotion and called for an ad hoc meeting of the student body in the Rubin Hall *shul* on the night before the event. He wanted to address the entire student body. Needless to say, the *shul* was packed with students with standing room only. It was an incredible speech. The Rov began by citing a principle in Greek logic which did not allow one to live within the framework of two contradictory ideas. Hence, for example, man was either a lowly creature or an exalted being, but not both. Thus faced with a choice, the Greeks had chosen to deify man. In Judaism, however, we live with a dialectic of delicately balanced contrary ideas. On the one hand, man is created in G-d's image, and on the other hand, we say *"motar ha'a dam min ha-b'haimah ayin"* [the superiority of man over animal is nil]. We believe in capitalism *a la* the three Bavas, and we believe in the socialism of *shemittah*. We believe that Hashem is both transcendent—*"mimkomo,"* and immanent—*"melo kol ha'aretz kvodo."* We encourage husband and wife to fulfill the mitzvah of *"onah"* and *"peru u'revu"* on the one hand, and we observe the rules of *"taharat hamishpacha"* on the other.

Similarly, the Rov said, we are *Yisrael* and must advocate for our nation. On the other hand, we are *"bain ha'amim,"* a nation among nations, and must behave in a civil manner to the British Representative to the UN.

Lord Caradon cancelled his appearance at the YU Poli Sci Club the next day. But the invitation was well worth it nonetheless, because we learned a fantastic lesson from the Rov as a result.

Man on the Moon

After man landed on the moon there were important theological issues to confront. Neil Armstrong's "one small step for man, one giant leap for mankind" occurred in the summer of '69. We were learning with the Rov in Boston at this historic moment.

The Rov told us that he had received an inquiry from a rabbi whose community saw in this event a challenge to Jewish beliefs. Do we not say that the heavens belong to *Hashem (ha shamayim shamayim laHashem)* and only earth is man's domain? Yet now we find man landing on the moon in the heavens, *Hashem*'s domain? The Rov responded that *shamayim*, heaven, had two connotations. There is physical heaven which is potentially everyone's domain and metaphysical heaven which is the sole province of *Hashem*.

The Rov saw the landing on the moon as a great achievement for man but with one caveat. He was concerned about excess hubris and false illusions of invincibility. He cautioned, "The great sin of modern man is his arrogance." He taught us to feel humbled in the face of the omnipotence of the *Ribbono Shel Olam*.

There was a well-known rabbi who often sought headlines for himself. After the moon landing, he declared that when we say *kiddush levanah* [prayer said on the appearance of the new moon] we should no longer say about the moon *"ve-aini yachol lingoa bakh,"* I cannot touch you. Instead we should say, "As I stand saying this prayer, *aini nogea bakh*," I am not touching you. This was reported in the Boston Jewish Advocate. The Rov bristled, "Doesn't he know that it means that when I say *kididush levanah* on earth I am not able to touch the moon?" Even though the rabbi's amended text is a variant reading in *Masechet Sofrim*, the Rov resented the suggestion to change an old Jewish prayer text just for a sound byte and some publicity.

Sense of Humor

The Rov had a great sense of humor. When we were studying *Eiruvin*, we learned about the possibility of building an *eruv* in "*reshut harabim*," a public domain. There is a dispute about it among the *poskim* which impacts upon the possibility of an *eruv* in New York City. The Rov remarked, "No matter what, today an *eruv* is impossible in New York City, even according to those who allow an *eruv* in a public domain because with Mayor Lindsay, the city has the status of *parutz merubah al ha'omed,* of a city with no barriers."

The 1971 Yeshiva College yearbook had an article on eating at Yeshiva. The editors wrote that one of the local restaurants used so much oil that all the food tasted the same, and that the potato pirogen tasted like they had a lube job at the nearby garage. Once, after a late *shiur*, the Rov went to eat lunch in that restaurant. The owner was livid. He was yelling about the defamation of his eatery, a place in which the authors of the article ate daily! He was going to sue them, he told the Rov. The Rov calmed him by telling him that no one actually reads the yearbook. Once outside, he said to us, "Boys, I do not know what he was so upset about. A matter known to all is not *lashon harah* [slander]."

On a Personal Note

I, along with my peers, adored the Rov. To me he was a teacher, an adviser, a wise grandfather.

I was grateful that he agreed to be my *mesader kiddushin* [in charge of performing the wedding]. At weddings, the Rov used to put ashes on the groom's head in compliance with the Talmud in *Bava Batra* 60b. He asked the caterer for a few ashes. The caterer gave the Rov an entire cup of ashes which he put on my head under my hat at the *chuppah*. I left my hat in the *yichud* room. Afterward, my mother found it and told me that someone had used my hat as an ash tray.

Unbeknownst to the bride and groom, the chazzan at our wedding chose not to sing *"mi bon si'ach"* and instead surprised us with a rendition of *"chiko mamtakim v'khulo machmadim"* as the bride walked around the groom. The Rov was not happy. This, after all, was a *passuk* [verse] in *Shir Hashirim* which he felt should not be applied to a man and woman in a literal sense.

There was no more selfless teacher than the Rov. The Rov encouraged his students to likewise be generous with their time and especially to be unselfish with respect to teaching Torah. When the women at Stern College sought more Torah learning, the Rov told his students to respond by organizing extra classes at Stern and volunteering to teach. I guess it was not hard to find young men to volunteer. The classes were very well attended; in fact, several *shiddukhim* [matches] came out of them. I have always wondered if the Rov had this as a motive as well.

The Rov always gave charity to the beggars at YU, and he always insisted on paying for services rendered to him. I once brought him lunch and he insisted on paying me. He gave me a check which he signed "Joe Solo." I have never cashed the check and have kept it as a memento. I will not sell it on eBay.

In summary, this essay is an account based entirely on things I heard and witnessed myself. I attended every *yahrzeit* and *teshuvah shiur* since ninth grade. In high school, we used to travel on the subway every Tuesday night for the Rov's public *shiur* in Moriah Congregation in Manhattan. I attended *shiur* at YU for six years and for two summers in Boston. I learned much Torah from the Rov. He was a master *rebbe*. But I learned so much more from him about life as a committed Jew, with his words "the primacy of Torah" eternally echoing in my soul.

Memories of Kindness

Rivkah Teitz Blau

The editors of *The Commentator* invited me to recall "non-mythic" events from the daily life of Rav Yosef Dov Soloveitchik in Brookline, Massachusetts, where my husband was assistant principal at the Maimonides School from 1965–67. The first account is of kindness, an immediate response of helping the other. The next two examples demonstrate sensitivity to the feelings of others. I am adding a conversation in New York in 1981 in which Rav Soloveitchik approached a dilemma with empathy and practicality (not "mythic"ally). His advice is pertinent to young wives and husbands now.

In our first weeks in Brookline I spread a map of the town on top of our son's stroller to navigate the winding streets. As I was walking on a bright autumn day, I heard someone say in a friendly tone, "It will be easier if you look where you're going as well as looking at the map." It was the Rav, who was about to mail a letter. He asked what address I was looking for. When he heard Colbourne Crescent, he explained to me that the street was shaped as the name indicated, and gave me directions to the number I needed. My son Binyamin smiled in response to the Rav's friendliness, and I, overwhelmed at who was helping us, said, "Thank you."

In the next two years the kindnesses that he and his wife, Dr. Tonya Soloveitchik, showed to my husband and me persuaded me

Dr. Rivkah Blau has worked in Torah education from her high school years on. Her biography of her father, Rav Mordechai Pinchas Teitz, *Learn Torah, Love Torah, Live Torah* (Ktav, 2001) has been translated and published in Israel with the title *V'Samahta B'Hayekha* (Urim, 2006). She has created a website for Rav Teitz's *shiurim*, dafhashovua.org, where listeners can download his radio broadcasts.

to be a bit less tense, although I was still aware that I was in the presence of greatness. When Dr. Soloveitchik became ill, we called ahead and brought over a chiffon cake that she had liked when they had dinner with my parents at our home. It was a Sunday afternoon and Rav Soloveitchik invited us in for my husband to report to his wife on what was doing at school. I said I would take Binyamin, who was already two and a half years old, to the park. He said, "Please come in. Seeing your son will lift my wife's spirits." He took Binyamin's hand and said, "What would a little boy like? To see what's upstairs?" Binyamin said yes and the Rav took him on a tour of the house. When they returned to the living-room he said he was thinking what a child this age would want; would it be alright to give my son some candy? Of course I agreed, and Binyamin, very happy, thanked him. Dr. Soloveitchik said that for her Binyamin's smile was the best medicine, and I took him to the park so that my husband could continue the discussion of school business.

Over the next months my husband realized that it would be wise for him to leave Maimonides. In January 1967 he met with Rav Soloveitchik who urged him to stay, particularly in light of how difficult the year was with the loss of his brother and mother and the serious illness of Dr. Soloveitchik. But when my husband explained his reasons, the Rav understood. He wished him well when my husband told him a few weeks later that his new position would be working for Rav Aharon Soloveichik, the Rav's brother, in Skokie, Illinois.

Our son Yitzchak was born on the last *Shabbos* in July, just before we moved to Chicago. On Thursday before the *bris* we had not yet discussed who should be *sandak* [the one who holds the baby on his lap during the circumcision]. My father had been *sandak* for Binyamin, and my father-in-law did not want this role. It was obvious that the honor should go to Rav Soloveitchik, the *rav* of the city and my husband's teacher. I understood this, but knew how much it meant to my father to be the *sandak* at a grandson's *bris*. At nine o'clock that night we heard a knock at our door. To our surprise it was Rav Soloveitchik, accompanied by Abe Wintman, a faithful *ba'al ha-bayis* who often drove for his *rav*.

The Rav told us that after all his losses his would not be a happy face. A *Shabbos bris* should be a time of complete joy, and he did not want there to be a touch of sadness. He was going to spend *Shabbos* with his daughter and her family in Onset, but did not want us to think it was in anger at my husband's moving to another yeshiva. He had come to give a *brakhah* [blessing] to the baby, to bring a gift—a check for "Baby Boy Blau"—and to wish us well. After a few minutes of conversation he left with Mr. Wintman.

He solved a problem for a young couple before we had even come to it. We were moved by his understanding, his concern that a student should not think that his teacher was upset with him, his assurance of peace between a husband and wife.

The final example is from 1981 when I became educational director of the YU high school for girls in Manhattan, which had been named in memory of Dr. Tonya Soloveitchik. My husband arranged for us to meet with Rav Soloveitchik in his apartment at Yeshiva. I asked the Rav what he would like to see in a school for young women that carried his wife's name, especially in considering the pull between motherhood and career.

He said the urge to raise one's children and the attraction of accomplishing in a field of one's own were two texts that contradict each other *"ad she'yavo hakasuv hashlishi v'yakhria beineihem."* What was the third text that would resolve the contradiction? The woman herself, he said.

He explained that to be at home and resent the baby for cutting one off from being out in the world is no favor to the baby. But to be a lawyer or a doctor and to be thinking "While I'm solving other people's problems, what problems am I creating for my child at home?" is also not beneficial. He suggested that each woman has to find the proportion of hours in and out of the home that works for her and her family. The proportions can vary according to the different stages of life; one decision does not have to govern all time. But at each point she should decide with full awareness of the welfare of everyone involved. He added with a smile, "She has to decide—not her husband, not her mother and not her mother-in-law."

He recommended pointing out to students that with the improvement in life expectancy even at age forty or fifty one could enjoy decades of intellectual or professional activity. When you are in your twenties it seems the repetitive tasks involved in raising children will go on forever, but suddenly those babies are adults and there are still many valuable years remaining.

When I have repeated these insights to young women, especially those who may feel torn between conflicting responsibilities or overwhelmed by the needs of small children, they are relieved to learn that Rav Soloveitchik understood the reality of their lives and did not castigate them for their feelings. Young men who pay attention to these insights will understand the challenges their wives face; if the wife is at peace with her choices, the family is on its way to peace in the home, *shalom bayis*.

Learning from the Rav: Preparing for *Shiur*

Shmuel Boylan

After my first week in the Rav's *shiur*, I was asked to leave ("thrown out") by the administration of the yeshiva. At the time, the yeshiva had a rule that college students (i.e., pre-*semikhah)* were not allowed in the Rav's *shiur*. With the encouragement and cooperation of Rav Gorelik *zt"l*, my previous year's *rebbe*, my *chavrusa* [study partner] and I attempted to test this rule by attending the *shiur* without official permission.

I remember one of the early *shiurim* very well. The Rav was learning *Kiddushin*, but this *shiur* was with regard to a *machlokes* [dispute] between the Rambam and the *Geonim* concerning *neta revay* in *chutz la-aretz*. This *machlokes* was elucidated in *Chidushé Rabbénu Chaim Halevi*, but the Rav took Reb Chaim's *yesod* [foundation] and made it come alive in a dynamic and unforgettable manner.

After the *shiur*, my *chavrusa* and I approached the Rav, and told him that we were attending without the approval of the yeshiva. The Rav told us that he didn't care whether we were on the roster or not, as long as we came prepared.

I tell this story more than forty years later not only because it typifies the desire and drive we *talmidim* had to learn from the Rav, not only because it speaks to the Rav as both *rosh yeshiva* and yet apart from (and greater than) the yeshiva, but also because it addresses an essential aspect of learning from the Rav, namely "preparing for *shiur*." The excellent presentations of the notes of the Rav's *shiurim* actually play a vital role in my own learning process.

The Rav, in the past forty years, has been transformed from a prime explicator of texts to a text himself. His family tradition, following the *Bais HaRav*, was not to publish: "Not everything that one

---

Dr. Shmuel Boylan is Vice President of Undergraduate Education and Dean of Faculties at Touro College.

thinks should one say; not everything that one says should one write; and not everything that one writes should one publish!" The Rav's reluctance to publish under his own direction and discretion has led to an ever-growing canon of works authored by, or ascribed, to the Rav; these works are issued instead by those who loved him, to meet the thirst for his words and ideas.

These works of the Rav in elegant prose come to us somewhat cut off from the texts and contexts from which they derive—and without the requisite demand to "prepare for *shiur*," to feel the struggle for truth, for *amito shel Torah*, which played such a large role in the Rav's *shiurim*, the exploration of approaches rather than the mere expression of authority. For example, the recent *Yom Kippur machzor*, incorporating comments of the Rav, is true to the Rav's special spiritual sensitivity, but seems strangely disembodied from the Rav's commitment to text and halakhic analysis. It contains answers without questions, solutions without well-posed problems, with citations from books that the Rav never quite authored. If the Rav remains, indeed, the primary *rebbe* for our time, we must learn how to better prepare to understand that which he is teaching.

By the following year, the yeshiva had changed its policy and allowed the pre-*semikhah* students to learn in the Rav's *shiur*. The Rav had established a fearsome reputation as one who could, indeed, be very hard on *talmidim* who had not truly "prepared for *shiur*" to his satisfaction. During my years with the Rav, he adopted a somewhat milder approach to students (I am told). He also experienced several tragedies during the sixties—the loss of his mother, his brother Shmuel, and his wife. We traveled as a class by bus to Boston to share in the Rav's sorrow, and learned *Moed Katan* as a *shiur* with him as the Rav recovered from his loss. We saw the Rav in his genius and his humanity, and learned from him throughout. Later, as mature men, we gathered together in Boston for our *rebbe*'s *levayah* [funeral].

It is interesting that many of those considered the greatest *talmidim* of the Rav were with him during this "mellower" period, and shared in his travail. Participating in the Rav's *shiur*, one was, of course, deeply affected by the Rav's Torah, by his great knowledge and unique mastery of the Brisker *derekh*. Yet, ultimately, it was the force of the personality of the Rav that impressed itself on the *talmid*: the search for comprehension at the deepest level, the rejection of the superficial and the glib, the integration of Torah into a total world-view. The Rav would generally start a *shiur* as if with no previous assumptions save one—that any *sugya* could be understood if one applied one's total intellectual efforts toward its explication. The Rav would not leave a problem, even after many hours, examining suggestions of his own or those of *talmidim* until he was fully satisfied.

I have written elsewhere that the Rav did not espouse modernity, but, rather, transcended it. There was, of course, a tension within the Rav between his intellectual openness to new approaches and his personal *mesorah*. It was the Rav, ultimately, who set the limits for his students, vehemently rejecting ecumenical discussions and "scientific Talmud," focusing intellectual efforts on halakhic norms, and energizing efforts to foster *teshuvah*. The struggle between *hiddush* and *mesorah* lent an ongoing sense of drama and profundity to the Rav's personality and teachings. His "loneliness" and singularity derived, indeed, from his faithfulness to his special vision.

Two personal incidents may be of general interest. The Rav had recommended me to Dr. Bernard Lander, president of Touro College, as a budding mathematician. A few years later, I visited the Rav with Dr. Lander, who was then under attack for opening a branch of Touro College in Brooklyn. The Rav gave us *chizuk* [encouragement] but was somewhat surprised to see his student the "mathematician" as a dean. "So what do you offer in this college of yours?" the Rav asked me. When I said that many students were studying such subjects as accounting and computer sciences, the Rav responded, "Accounting and computing aren't college—the humanities, that's college!"

To the extent that the Rav saw the college experience as a positive one for leadership in the Jewish community, it was in the Western intellectual tradition that his interests lay. Yet, despite the Rav's knowledge of much of modern and Western thought, the *shiurim*, which constituted the core of his intellectual commitment and passion, never deviated from the traditional format of Talmudic dialectic with classical commentaries. (A *talmid*, who will remain nameless, once violated that norm by suggesting in *shiur* that various opinions of *Rishonim* resembled a scientific dispute between Einstein and Dirac; the Rav responded with an icy stare that was well-deserved.) The Rav modeled his *shiur* on that of his grandfather in Volozhin, and he never deviated from that model.

I last spoke to the Rav after he had retired from the yeshiva and was living in relative seclusion in Boston with his daughter and son-in-law. Once again, access to the Rav was restricted, due to his illness and infirmity. But this time I was successful, and was granted entry. The Rav was frailer than I remembered him. I first asked him about an opinion he had quoted from his father *zt"l*, that a nation (such as the Nazis) could be transformed into Amalek. I asked whether such a halakhic designation would then have implications with regard to innocent wives and children, as well. The Rav strongly rejected such a concept, reminding me that the Rambam required an approach for *shalom* [peace] prior to *milchemet Amalek* [war with Amalek], and that such a requirement made action against innocent parties impossible. I then asked the Rav for a *brakhah* for my son (now a *sh'oel u'meishiv* [resource scholar] in the Brisker Kollel), which he graciously granted. Such was my effort, on a personal level, to ensure that the Rav's blessing would be carried over to the next generation.

The question of the Rav's legacy for the *dor asher lo yada es Yosef*, the generation that never knew Yosef, those who never experienced first-hand the force of his Torah-personality and *yiras shomayim* [fear of heaven], now looms larger than ever. While the Rav often addressed societal concerns in the language of modernity, his solutions were always those of eternity, of adherence to the halakhic process and preservation of the norms of Jewish societal life. The Rav was modern in the sense that he understood only too well the superficiality and lack of meaning in much of contemporary existence, the alienation of the individual from a society without values and, ultimately, from his own inner being.

Those seeking to emulate the Rav must follow fully in his merging with the masters of *mesorah* of *Yiddishkeit*, with the struggle to comprehend the teachings of Rambam and Ravad, Rashi and Tosefot. The *D'rashot HaRan* maintains that all our learning in this world is mere preparation for the *shiur* to come in *olam habah* [the next world]. In this, as in so many things, the Rav, through his Torah, can be our lifelong *rebbe* as he helps us in preparing for *shiur*.

Rabbi Joseph B. Soloveitchik ("the Rav") as Pedagogue

Michael Chernick

R. Joseph B. Soloveitchik, known in Yeshiva University circles and sometimes beyond as "the Rav," was a master pedagogue. Evaluations of a teacher's pedagogy generally include a description of the thought patterns and modes of expression that the teacher usually uses, the teaching methods which the teacher employs, and the educational goals the teacher sets for those he or she teaches. In religious settings, in our case an Orthodox Jewish one, teaching at its best also has to do with the formation of a religious personality. The teacher's goal in forming an Orthodox Jew is that those who define themselves as such take an intellectual stance regarding issues of faith and ethics consonant with Orthodox Jewish belief and commit to serving their Creator through the practical observance of ritual *mitzvot*. This essay focuses on the Rav as the teacher par excellence of the Talmud. This means that the issue of Jewish spiritual formation—a matter of immense significance to the Rav—will be shortchanged in this essay.

Thought Patterns

From this observer's vantage point, the thought pattern that characterized so much of the Rav's teaching methods was the search for the rationale behind disputes found in the Talmud or among its commentators. There was no satisfaction for the Rav in mere translation of the Talmudic *sugya* or even the more advanced stage of successfully unraveling the Talmudic argument or arriving at a surface understanding of the words of a *Rishon*. Those were merely the first two necessary steps to the real work of Talmudic learning. That activity consisted of explaining why those who argued on the Tal-

---

Michael Chernick is the Deutsch Family Professor of Jewish Jurisprudence and Social Justice at HUC—JIR/New York.

mudic page did so, and why the commentators so often disagreed about the meaning of the very same Talmudic sources.

Thus, for example, in the classical *shiurim* the Rav gave on *Avodat Yom Ha-Kippurim*, he analyzes the views of R. Yohanan and Resh Laqish in the first *sugya* of *Yoma*. The discourse begins with the *Mishnah*'s rule that seven days before *Yom Kippur* the *Kohen Gadol* [High Priest] was to be separated from contact with the public, and another priest was to be appointed to take his place should that become necessary. In the *shiur*, the Rav urges the student to see the *Gemara* that discusses this matter and the related matter of the preparation of the priest designated to burn the *parah adumah* [red heifer] in order to create its ashes. He notes that that R. Yohanan derives the separation of these *kohanim* from the public from the seven-day separation of Aaron and his sons from the rest of Israel during the period of their education and dedication (*yemei ha-milu'im*, see Lev. 8:34). Resh Laqish derives this from Mosheh's six-day separation from the people and his call to receive the Torah on the seventh day (Ex. 24:16). Thus, according to R. Yohanan, the conceptual underpinning of the separation of the High Priest seven days before *Yom Kippur* has to do with his preparations for properly carrying out the *avodat Yom ha-Kippurim*, just as Aaron and his sons were trained in the proper performance of the sacrificial rites during the *milu'im* period. The concept that undergirds Resh Laqish's view is related to preparation for entering the *Miqdash* [Sanctuary]. The Rav documents this by a reference to *Niddah* 42a, where the *sugya* suggests an equivalency between Sinai and the *Miqdash*, and the situation "standing before God" that occurs in each of these situations. Thus, Mosheh's separation from the people seven days prior to the Revelation is the template for standing before God in the *Miqdash*.

The difference between the two opinions is not only their conceptual moorings, but their different halakhic implications. According to R. Yohanan, the separation of the *Kohen Gadol* and the priest designated to burn the *parah* has to do with their special position as priests. After all, only priests participated in the rites if the *milu'im*. According to Resh Laqish, the separation rule would apply to anyone, whether a *kohen* or not, who must stand before God in the *Miqdash*. After all, Mosheh was not a priest at the Revelation even though he served as one temporarily during the *milu`im*. Nevertheless, he was required to separate himself from the people for seven days.

Modes of Expression

The above example may now serve as an example for the analysis of the Rav's modes of expression. To review, the basic task the Rav set for himself and ultimately for his students was to find the reason for Talmudic and its commentators' disputes. The expression of this process of rationalization occurred when he lifted the dispute from its concrete formulation, in this case R. Yohanan's or Resh Laqish's midrashic support of the *Mishnah*'s rule, to its conceptual foundation. The fact that one *derashah* was drawn from *Parashat ha-Milu'im* and the other from Mosheh's role in *mattan Torah* [the giving of the Torah] recreated conceptual frameworks that transcended the actual formulation of these two rabbis' views.

The Rav was never satisfied with assertion. A *sevara* required documentation if it was to hold. Since the conceptual frameworks that the Rav uncovered were not always obvious on the surface of the Talmudic or *Rishonic* texts he analyzed, he validated them by creating what was essentially a legal brief for them. When it came to R. Yohanan's view, the connection between the *milu'im* and the separation of the *Kohen ha-Gadol* and *ha-Kohen ha-soref et ha-parah* [the priest who burned the heifer] was fairly obvious. R. Yohanan's *derashah* made that connection very directly. Therefore, the Rav did not feel constrained to document his position.

The connection between Sinai and *Miqdash* was, however, more tenuous and, therefore, in need of more support. That is why the Rav directed our attention to *Niddah* 42a. From his perspective, the *sugya* there indicated that Sinai and the *Miqdash* were equivalent since both were places where God's presence resided. The preparations God demanded of the people for standing before Him at the Revelation thus became the template for all other occasions of standing in the place where God's presence resided.

The Rav also felt that he had to demonstrate how a conceptual difference made a halakhic difference. The requirement of separation of the High Priest and the priest designated to burn the *parah* was different in nature depending on whose position one accepted. If one accepted R. Yohanan's view, then the *halakhah* of separation applied only to priests. If one accepted Resh Laqish's position, then the law of separation would apply to anyone who had to stand before God. In this case, that person turned out to be the High Priest. Since the priest who had to burn the *parah* performed his actions outside of the *Miqdash*, his separation would be classified as *mi-de-*

rabban [rabbinic] rather than *mi-deoraita* [from the Torah]. Here, too, the Rav provided documentation for this position based on the views of several *Rishonim*.

Though the above example does not demonstrate it, there was also something of the scientific method in the Rav's expression of his thoughts. The scientific method is characterized by the presentation of a hypothesis that has the possibility of both its substantiation and refutation. This allows for narrowing down possibly reasonable explanations of phenomena by rejecting the refuted ones and preserving the substantiated ones. This process continues until one arrives at the hypothesis with the highest degree of substantiation. Often enough the Rav would test a *sevara* in regard to its ability to explain other Talmudic passages and disputes as well as the various opinions of the *Rishonim*. If a *sevara* could account for a high degree of *mahloqot* [disputes], the Rav considered it a bona fide explanation of the material under analysis. If, however, he conceived of a more comprehensive *sevara*, that one supplanted the original one.

Teaching Method

The Rav's primary teaching method was demonstration. That is, he generally showed his students how to deal with the texts he taught by using the frontal lecture as his teaching method. His expectation was that the student had already mastered the assigned text and its most basic commentators. For him this did not mean only Rashi and Tosafot. Like his Brisker forebears, he used RaM-BaM's *Mishneh Torah* as a commentary rather than as a code. This also meant that *Hassagot ha-RAbaD* could not be ignored or viewed as less significant than Maimonides' words. As with Talmudic disputes, one had to consider why these two giants among the *Rishonim* stood in disagreement with each other. This extended to the different views commentators had of the same Talmudic material.

Often enough, the Rav made it clear that he intended to deal with specific medieval commentators, which meant that he provided his students with guidance as to what the focus of a *shiur* would be. It was then the students' task to use their teacher's method and to come to *shiur* with a hypothesis about where the Rav would lead them. If no prior instructions were provided regarding the focus of the upcoming *shiur*, the student's task was to prepare the Talmudic *sugya*, its basic *mefareshim* [commentators], the RaMbaM, and the widest swath of *Rishonic* literature, as he could.

This, too, was the hallmark of the Rav's method: the center of his attention beyond the Talmudic text itself was the *Rishonim*. Since the Rav eschewed *pilpul* [embroidered arguments] and searched for the simplest and most comprehensive guiding principles behind a Talmudic *mahloqet*, his concentration on *Rishonim* was methodologically the most natural choice. After all, the *Rishonim* were oriented directly to the Talmud's text. In contrast, the *Aharonim* often took up issues that were ancillary or tangential to the task of elucidating the Talmudic text itself. Even in his analysis of the *Rishonim* the aim was to understand each commentator on his own merits. He did not use one as a *kushya* [question] or *teruz* [answer] in relation to another, let alone in relationship to later authorities. The revolution in Talmudic learning that began in Brisk occurred in order to more directly engage the *Gemara* and its commentators, and the Rav continued that tradition.

From time to time the Rav used the Socratic method to encourage his students to join him in the quest for the conceptual understanding of a *sugya*. He was a sharp and incisive questioner who had little patience for less than sharp and incisive responses. Often enough he fulfilled the words of *Qohelet* (12:11), "The words of the wise are like goads, like nails fixed in prodding sticks...," and woe to anyone in the *shiur* who found himself having to be prodded by that goad. But he was as demanding with himself as with his students. His honesty as a teacher exhibited itself in his willingness to admit that a satisfactory *peshat* eluded him and that more research and thinking was necessary. But one had the sense that a *zarikh `iyyun* [requires deliberation or contemplation] remained on the Rav's mind. This wrestling with the unfinished often led to a resolution days or weeks later.

Finally, and perhaps most importantly, he was one of the most organized teachers under whose tutelage his students had the privilege to study. The Rav might set forth a number of questions at the beginning of a *shiur* that would create the framework of the ensuing lesson. Assuming one came properly prepared, this would facilitate following his discourse, even if the material was difficult. In other instances, the Rav's clarity of thought and precision of expression helped to put a complicated lesson more within the range of the student's comprehension. I believe that none of this would have been possible without his native genius and innate teaching ability accompanied by self-conscious consideration about how to present material. His Talmud was a Talmud *Arukh* [set in order].

Educational Goals

When discussing what the Rav's educational goals were, one enters the realm of conjecture. This is a rather uncomfortable territory because I believe it is *huzpah* [impertinence] to assign positions to another that he or she never espoused. Therefore, I admit that what the Rav's educational goals were for his students cannot really be known except by his confidants, and I certainly was not one of them. Therefore, what follows is what I and others with whom I remain in contact say they received from being in "the Rav's *shiur*." We assume—perhaps wrongly—that this is what he hoped we would "get" from studying with him.

Many of us received from this master the courage to be *mehadeshim*. Once one had spent any time with him and had come to understand his approach to *Shas*, one could never again be satisfied to know only the basic facts of a *sugya*. One felt under obligation to develop a theory that would account for these facts. Then one had to test one's theory against other *sugyot* and the views of the *Rishonim* in order to see whether it held firm.

Given the nature of such theorization and the initial guesswork involved, if one took the endeavor seriously, one had the sensation of doing an intellectual "bungee jump." There was both a "rush" and some fear involved, because there was always the awareness of presenting one's *hiddush* before all the generations who had worked so assiduously on the comprehension of a *sugya*. Would they approve of what one said? Did it make sense? Did it ring true? Would the Rav have approved of it were he alive to judge? Those who studied with him, however, had come to a point where we really had no choice but to "learn" in this way, and his encouragement of this kind of thinking by personal example was the support that made the leap possible. Consequently, I would infer that one of the Rav's educational goals was to make us courageous enough to use the best of our creative intellectual abilities in the service of Torah study.

The Rav was also fiercely independent. More than once he said, somewhat piqued, "I am not a *hamor ta`un sefarim*" [donkey laden with books]. This occurred especially when someone pointed out that his views differed from those of his grandfather, R. Hayyim Soloveitchik of Brisk. No matter how brilliant and respected another *talmid hakham* might be, when the Rav had a certain understanding of a *sugya* that was opposed to a colleague's or to an earlier authority, he was respectful but not imprisoned by that colleague's or authority's reputation or reading of the material.

In his "Socratic mode" what he sought from a student was not servile acquiescence or agreement, but rather an independent stance. A student had the right to disagree with or question a *sevara* proposed by the Rav, but then he had to support his critique with *r'eayot* [proofs] just as the Rav had. Even if there was a meeting of the minds between a student and this master teacher, the student was pressed for his own reasons for agreement. He, too, was expected not to be a *hamor ta`un sefarim*. These interchanges imply that the Rav's goal for his students was intellectual independence. They also indicate that he wished to inculcate the value of taking responsibility for one's opinions and their implications.

The Rav was also a perfectionist when it came to thought. He was clearly uncomfortable with intellectual loose strings lying about. By his example he tried to teach us not to accept mediocrity in our thinking. It seems in retrospect that he was expending his best efforts toward making his students intellectually rigorous, thorough, and tough. One would have to interview those who studied with him to find out whether he succeeded. But even if one found that few or many had not turned out that way, one could not say that the Rav had failed to model those traits.

Concluding Thoughts

In life the Rav was revered in YU circles, but he was a controversial figure outside the halls of Yeshivat Rabbenu Yitzchak Elchanan. His clear willingness to "think out of the box" did not always win him admirers in other sectors of the "yeshiva world." Not a few reversed a Talmudic notion. They "embraced with the left and pushed away with the right" when it came to ha-Rav Yosef Dov Soloveitchik *zt"l*. Nevertheless, many if not most of them admitted, not always gracefully, that he was the pre-eminent *Rosh Yeshiva* and *maggid shiur* of his time. Their judgment was based on the brilliance of his thought and the clarity of his expression.

What is held against him in these "circles of the ambivalent" is exactly what those of us who studied with him prized and stood in awe of: his breadth of learning in *Shas*, *Rishonim* and *Aharonim* matched by his obvious familiarity with philosophy, literature, and the sciences. He used all that had been bequeathed to him by "the One who gives humanity wisdom" *le-ha`amid talmidim harbeh ule-hagdil Torah ule-hadirah* [to produce many disciples and to increase Torah and to make it glorious]. *Yehi zikhro barukh.*

My First Year in the Rav's *Shiur*

Menachem Genack

I often think back on the experience of being a *talmid* in Rav Yosef Dov Soloveitchik's, the Rav, *zt'l*, *shiur*.

There was always the palpable sense of being part of a *mesorah*. The *Rishonim* and *Achronim* who were so much a part of the Rav's life, and when he talked about them, when he introduced their ideas into the *shiur*, it was almost as though—and this is no exaggeration—he was welcoming them in the room. He said it himself on several occasions—Abaye and Rava, Rashi and Rabbenu Tam, Rashba and the Ramban, and then the Shach and Rav Akiva Eger—they were there with us during the *shiur*. The *mesorah*, and especially of Brisk, was alive. It was an enormous privilege to feel part of that stream of history, though ancient, very much contemporary and vibrant.

Despite the Rav's outstanding brilliance, he was a humble person. This too was manifest in his *shiur*—he was never one to dictate or sway others because of his stature. But probably the best illustration of his humility took place outside the classroom. In 1969 Yeshiva University had invited Lord Caradon, the British Ambassador to the United Nations and, that month, the head of the U.N. Security Council, to speak to the College. There was, among the students, considerable resistance to the idea; they thought that the United Nations was not sympathetic, or not sufficiently sympathetic, to the position of Israel. They organized a protest to Lord Caradon's speech.

The Rav thought that a protest would hurt, rather than help, the cause of Israel, and therefore, in advance of Lord Caradon's arrival,

---

Rabbi Menachem Genack is a *Rosh Yeshiva* at the Rabbi Isaac Elchanan Theological Seminary and serves as Rabbinical Administrator and CEO of the Orthodox Union's Kashrut Division.

he spoke to the student body in Rubin Hall about why he thought protesting was not a good idea. But before he offered his opinion he discussed at some length different forms of Jewish logic—about how there are different ways of seeing an issue. And then finally he said he thought the students shouldn't protest.

Later I asked the Rav—why did he give a whole prolegomena about different forms of Jewish logic? Why didn't he just tell the students not to protest—and finished? They would have respected his opinion and backed off. He said that he wouldn't do that. He thought his opinion was just his opinion, and didn't see himself as a dictator telling others what to do. That humility was also manifest in his *shiur*; although he offered strikingly compelling arguments, he didn't dictate what had to be the case.

I entered the *shiur* in the fall of 1966. It was a magnificent, mind-opening, exhilarating experience. The Rav was teaching us how to think through a *sugya,* how to categorize ideas properly, how to "exhaust all logical possibilities in interpreting the *Gemara*" as he himself put it. But in the course of that year I observed the Rav and how he responded to the death of his Rebbetzin, which occurred during that year. His *aveilus* (mourning) was itself a lesson—the profound loss that he felt, and how he expressed it, and it brought out elements of his Torah that he himself felt he had not adequately communicated through his *shiurim.*

He had been giving *shiur* twice a week, flying to Boston and back each day he said *shiur* in order to be near his wife, who was suffering from Hodgkin's disease. As his wife's condition became more critical, the Rav stopped saying *shiurim* in February to be at her bedside without interruption. During the preceding months, both his mother and his brother Dr. Shmuel Soloveitchik passed away. On *Tannis Esther* his Rebbetzin passed away. The Rav said that were it not for the Torah, he would have been shattered during the triple *aveilus*: "If it were not for your Torah, my delight, I would have been lost in my affliction (Psalms 119. 92)."

Although he was with her so much of the time, at the moment of her death he was not, sadly, there. He had gone to New York at her insistence to make final an enormous gift from Joseph Gruss; she wanted to be sure that arrangements were complete since the gift was so important for Jewish educators.

In his euology for his wife the Rav said that he felt like Jeremiah, who left Jerusalem to go to Annatot on God's command and returned to see the black smoke of the destruction hovering over the holy city.

I went to be *menachem avel* [console the mourner] at his home on Hancock Road in Brookline on *Shushan Purim*. His *aveilus* on *Shushan Purim* itself was something of a *chiddush*: although the Mechaber writes that one should sit *shivah* on *Shushan Purim*, the Remah rules that one should not. And Rav Soloveitchik said that, should he be asked to *pasken* the question, he would follow the opinion of the Remah. But he himself could not do otherwise than sit *shivah* on that day. Sitting *shivah* was the only way he could express himself that day—psychologically he could not do otherwise.

When I got there Rabbi Teitz and Rabbi Hutner were being *menachem avel*. I sat and listened to their conversation. They spoke about why it is that for a parent the mourning period extends for twelve months, but for a spouse the period is only thirty days. Some suggested the obvious reason that for a parent, there is an additional *mitzvah* of *kibbud av v'eim* (honoring one's parents), which extends for twelve months. The Rav said that the loss is so devastating that it does not need the external halachic requirements of mourning needed to evince the pain of loss and mourning.

Although the Rav returned to give *shiur* for two weeks prior to *Pesach*, he continued to wear a torn jacket. Although, of course, such *aveilus* was not halachically required, he was not wearing the jacket as a halachic mandate. It was simply an outward expression of an inner pain.

The theme of outward, halachic requirement and internal feeling runs throughout the Rav's writings, but in the spring of that year we saw how the Rav lived it. After *Pesach* we learned tractate *Moed Katan*, which deals with the laws of mourning. One of the Rav's most important themes was that while *aveilus* consists of regimented behavior, the essence is the internal emotional feeling of loss and sadness. The *ma'aseh mitzvah*, the *mitzvah* act, consists of the performance of a commandment, but the *kiyum ha-mitzvah* [fulfillment] is a *kiyum she'balev*, an internal emotion.

The Rav's inexorable search for *emess* (truth) was another characteristic of his *shiur*, and we were enthralled and inspired by it. That search for *emess* manifested itself outside of the *shiur* as well and is illustrated by the selfless devotion that he had for Orthodox Judaism captured by the recent illuminating book of letters, *Community, Covenant, and Commitment*, edited by Rabbi Helfgot.

Indeed the Rav was the greatest theologian of his time, yet when he spoke for students at The University of Pennsylvania, and was heralded as a Jewish theologian, he felt it misinterpreted who he was and insisted that the statement be changed.

Indeed, the Rav was enormously well read and committed to Wissenschaft, but in my almost twenty years in the Rav's *shiur*, he never mentioned synthesis in *Torah U'Madah*.

The Rav was the Honorary President of Mizrachi, yet when after the Six Day war, Israel had a triumphant parade in Jerusalem, the Rav was furious. He was very concerned about what he considered extreme religious nationalism.

The Rav had a doctorate in philosophy, and Kierkegaard and Otto influenced his writings, yet he stated that the Ramban on the Torah represented a more authoritative Jewish philosophy than Maimonides' *Guide to the Perplexed*. He felt that the *Guide* was too tainted by Aristotelian logic and categories. The Rav said that any Jewish philosophy must be rooted in the *Halakhah* and based on halakhic constructs.

Ironically, the *Yad Hachazakah*, therefore, represents a more important Jewish philosophical work than the *Guide to the Perplexed*.

Dr. Shmuel Soloveitchik's funeral took place at Lamport Auditorium. He was a much loved professor of chemistry at the college, though he had suffered many personal setbacks during his life. The Rav's eulogy for his brother was both poignant and instructive. He related that when Rabbi Yaakov Gesuntheit, the author of the classic work on *Gitin, Tifereth Yaakov*, died, the Beis Halevi, the Rav's namesake and great-grandfather came to deliver the eulogy. Rabbi Yaakov had been the rav of Warsaw, but had been deposed by the intrigue of a group of *hasidim* and died a broken man.

The Beis Halevi began his eulogy by quoting the prophecy of Jeremiah to Zedekiah the king of Judah. "Thou shalt die in peace; and with the burnings of thy fathers, the former kings that were before thee, so shall they make a burning for thee; and they shall lament thee: 'Ah lord!' The Beis Halevi asked that the prophecy is in fact completely contrary to the reality of Zedekiah's ultimate death. Zedekiah died in a Babylonian prison, far from his realm. His sons were murdered in front of him and then he was blinded. Where is the peaceful scene that Jeremiah predicted? Where are the burnings, referring to the burning of the personal effects of the king in honor of the king, and the elaborate royal funeral?

The Beis Halevi answered that what Jeremiah was telling Zedekiah was that despite the bitter reality of his death, when he enters the *Olam HaEmess* (the next world) he enters not as a commoner but as a king, as part of *Malchus beis Dovid* (the royal Davidic line). And so it is with Rabbi Yaakov Gesuntheit, said the Beis Halevi, when he enters the next world he enters as rav of Warsaw. The Rav then continued, "When my brother Shmuel goes to the *Olam HaEmess,* he doesn't go as a scientist, but as a *lamdan* [a Torah scholar], as part of the Beis Harav."

Learning Torah and the teaching of Torah were the Rav's essence. The Rav clearly thought that his contribution to others was as an expositor of Torah. To portray the Rav otherwise is to distort who he was. He believed in the power of Torah to inspire and captivate anyone who would come into its orbit. I remember vividly how, after *shiur,* the Rav would be surrounded by talmidim as he made his way back to Morgenstern Dorm. We were spellbound by the Rav's words and they transformed us.

The Rav felt that the transformational power of Torah should not be limited to his *talmidim,* or *talmidei chachamim,* but also to *ba'al ha'batim* (laymen), scientists, professionals, men and women.

The core of his being, the center of his thought, was the Torah— that was the substance of his daily routine, and that was the focus of his life. The fact that the towering figure of Rav Chaim Brisker was a constant presence and model for the Rav was well known to us, and further deepened our sense of the purity of the Rav's Torah. The Rav once commented in a lecture, "My grandfather Rav Chaim was the greatest mind of his time. And I don't mean only the greatest Jewish mind."

Once I heard from the Rav that Rav Yerucham Levovitz, the renowned *mashgiach* [spiritual overseer] of the Mirrer Yeshiva, told him that Rav Chaim was unique, for he grasped the *neshamah* [soul] of the Torah. The genesis of Rav Chaim's new analytical method was his extraordinary Torah intuition. And so it was with the Rav.

The Rav's mission was to disseminate Torah, preserve the *mesorah,* establish high standards both in intellectual rigor and religious observance, and engage the mind and heart of American Jewry. To this endeavor the Rav brought his stunning intellect, his eloquence, erudition, integrity and sensitive soul.

In the 1940s and '50s most observers were writing the obituary of American Orthodox Jewry. The vibrant Orthodoxy we see today is in no small measure to the Rav's credit.

The Rav's profound connection to the *mesorah*, the emotional content of his life of *mitzvos*, and his principled search for truth are central to his legacy.

Ma'aseh Rav – V'dok

Daniel Greer

I was privileged to attend the Rav's *Shiur* the year following my graduation from Princeton College. Subsequently, while at law school, I structured my class schedule such that I was again able to participate in his *Shiur*. During those years, and until his Rebbetzin, Dr. Tonya Soloveitchik's *petirah* in 5727 (1967), I was fortunate to be invited from time to time to spend *Shabbosim* and *Yom Tovim* at their home at 10 Hancock Road in Brookline and summer cottage in Onset, Massachusetts. In later years, I continued to visit with the Rav periodically and when my family began spending summers in Onset, my wife, children and I went each year to see the Rav at the Twersky home in Brookline.

In the language of *Chazal*, "*ma'aseh rav*"—the deed is the teacher, namely, the action of a great *Torah* personality is dispositive, serving as guiding precedent. The *ma'aseh* is the *rav*, the hallmark of that authority's view in practice[1]. Five *ma'aseh Rav*, double entendre intended, and two encounters with the Rav are presented. *V'Hameivin Yovin*.

In my senior year at School I was awarded a Woodrow Wilson Fellowship for a year of graduate studies. I was most interested in attending the Rav's *Shiur* before entering Yale Law. To meet the Fellowship's requirements, I applied to Bernard Revel Graduate School and was assured, upon acceptance by the School's administration, that appropriate arrangements would be made regarding the *Shiur*. Accordingly, on the first day of the *Z'man* in Elul 5720 (1960), I seated myself in the Rav's class, then held in Room 103 in the Yeshiva's main building. Apparently, though, the Rav had not been

---

Rabbi Greer is the principal of the Yeshiva of New Haven.

[1] See e.g. *Shabbos* 21a, also *Rashi loc. cit.*

consulted and shortly before beginning the *Shiur*, the Rav looked at me quizzically, and asked, "I mean, who are you and what are you doing here?" I replied, indicating that I wanted his permission to join the class for the year but mentioned that I was not conversant in *Yiddish*—the language of the *Shiur*. The Rav replied, "Please come and see me afterwards." I did so, and the Rav again renewed his inquiry regarding my education, reasons for attending his *Shiur*, and plans for the future. He asked me to accompany him as he exited Room 103, proceeded to pace the hall, up the stairs, past the Registrar's Office, opposite Lamport Auditorium and back. He retraced these steps several times, deep in thought, pausing every once in a while with a further question. Finally, after several minutes, he declared, "There will be no problem," and left the building. The next day, I went to *Shiur*, and lo and behold, to the amazement of all the *talmidim* and my own, the Rav, without further ado, began teaching in English. And so the Rav continued to do thereafter, in erudite and scholarly English, punctuated at times with Latin expressions, in his classroom *Shiurim*.

A postscriptum. Some two years later, in the winter of 5722 (1962/63) a *Yavneh*—Religious College Students convention—was held in Boston. Rabbi Israel Wohlgelernter and I went to the Rav's home, then in Roxbury, after *Shabbos*. We asked him if, that night, he would deliver, his *Motzo'ai Shabbos Maimonides* School *Shiur* in English instead of *Yiddish*, so that the college students attending the convention could meaningfully participate. After carefully considering the matter, the Rav agreed. *V'Kach havei*, not only that *Motzo'ai Shabbos*, but from then on, much to the consternation of the old timers and to the delight of the college and graduate students, and many other young people. Through the years, hundreds flocked to that class and learned *Torah*—it was <u>the</u> place to go on *Motzo'ai Shabbos*.

Shortly after the *Yomim Tovim* in 5724 (1963), the Rav and the Rebbetzin accompanied their son R' Haym to Idlewild Airport (JFK), on his departure for an extended stay in Eretz Yisrael. I joined them at the El Al Terminal. The flight was delayed. The Rav's back was troubling him and he was in considerable pain. As there was no seating near the first floor ticketing counter, I offered to look for a place where the Rav could wait with a measure of comfort. On the third floor of the Terminal, I located a well-lit lounge area with suitable armchairs. Hastening, I happily reported to the Rav and we promptly rode the elevator upstairs. As he emerged, a look of shock crossed his face and he quickly stepped back into the elevator, ex-claiming, "Danny, this is a *beis marze'ach shel akum*[2] (non-Jew's tav-ern). How could you imagine that I would ever set foot there?" Somewhat bewildered, since the area did not have the appearance of a liquor serving bar, nor was it attended by anyone inappropri-ately dressed, I, nonetheless, quickly apologized to the Rav. We re-turned to the first floor waiting area where he remained standing in discomfort for the next several hours until his son's flight de-parted.

At my brother's wedding in Boston in 5726 (1966), I was near the Rav as he filled in the *kesubah* at the *chosson's tisch*. Before writing the name of that City, he took out the invitation from his jacket pocket and scribbled on the back a dozen or more possible ways of expressing Boston, Massachusetts, including a variety of spellings. I was quite surprised and inquired: "Rebbe with all due respect, the Rav has been in Boston for over thirty years and surely, by now, has been *mesader kiddushin* at hundreds of weddings here and written 'Boston' on all those many *kesubos*." The Rav smiled at me know-ingly and replied, "Still, one must always review."

Some time before my *chasunah* late in Tishrei 5732 (1971), I went with my prospective *Kallah*, Sarah, to introduce her to the Rav in his first floor apartment at Y.U.'s Rubin College Dormitory We asked the Rav to be our *mesader kiddushin* and he readily agreed. We had been considering various sites, among other locations the replica of the Mill Street *Shul* at the Spanish/Portuguese Synagogue. The Rav objected and said emphatically, "What you need is a hotel—a hotel. *Kedushas Beis HaKeneses* does not allow a *Shul* to be used for private events. You need a hotel." Of course, we complied. At the *chasunah*, the Rav presided, with his usual *hekpedim*, rigorously questioning the *eidim* and the like. After the final *brocho*, as he placed ashes on my forehead, the *ba'al menagen*, a well known *chazzan*, started to sing "*Im eshkochech Yerusholayim.*" No sooner had he done so, than the Rav abruptly declared "We will have none of that." The *chazzan* sheepishly but immediately stopped in mid-note. I broke the glass to the traditional calls of *Mazel Tov*.

In the Spring of 5735 (1975), after spending two years in *Eretz Yis-roel*, working and studying for *Semicha*, I came to the States with my

---

[2] See generally *Shulchan Arukh, Yoreh Deah*, ch. 114

wife and infant son, Dov. Upon my return, I was shocked to learn that during my absence, a *Shul* in Manhattan's West Side, which I helped establish, had instituted *hakofos* for women on *Simchas Torah*.

When I expressed my concern at this development, the Synagogue Rabbi informed me that he had cleared the innovation with the Rav. Together with my family, I went to visit the Rav at his Y.U. apartment. The Rav took my son on his knee and, with the tot tugging at his beard, duly informed the child that his own middle name was Dov, as well. I then broached the question to the Rav whether he, indeed, recommended *hakofos* for women. The Rav became agitated and exclaimed "This is a breach of our time-honored tradition. A *Sefer Torah* is not a toy or plaything. Our sacred heritage does not tolerate this kind of inappropriate behavior, whether or not in *Shul*." I might add, that on that occasion, I also raised with him the issue of the Manhattan *Eruv*, which a number of West Side Rabbis were advocating, claiming it had the Rav's imprimateur. The Rav definitively rejected the *Halachic* possibility of such an *Eruv* stating "Manhattan is a *reshus horabim d'Orayso*. There can be no *Eruv* here."

And, finally. While vacationing in Onset, in the summer of 5744 (1984), we traveled, with our children, to see the Rav in Brookline. My eldest daughter Esther, then eight, had just finished learning *Mishna Yoma, ba'al peh.*. She recited these *Mishnoyos* to the Rav. After she had completed six of the eight *Perokim*, he stopped her and mused, saying "You know if the *kohen gadol* on *Yom Kippur* were to get stuck in the middle of the *Avodah*, I am sure I could fill in for him." To which I commented, "Rebbe—rav lochem b'nei Levi." The Rav laughed wholeheartedly and, clasping both his hands around those of the little girl, said to her softly, "Keep learning—*Chumash, Tanach, Mishnayos, Gemora, and even Rishonim and Acharonim,* and don't be intimidated."

V'dok.

The Rav and Rav Ahron

David Luchins

I approach this assignment with considerable trepidation. Unlike the other contributors to this series, who must only worry that they are possibly misrepresenting the views of one revered Torah scholar, I face the unique danger of doing injustice to the memories of two giant figures, whose intellectual breadth, communal influence and lasting legacy utterly transcend my capacity for analysis and interpretation.

When I was originally asked to write about the relationship between the Rav *zt"l* and his brother Rav Ahron Soloveichik *zt"l* (and, yes, they spelled their last name differently) my first reaction was one of shocked inadequacy. Yes, I had spent four years in the Rav's *shiur*, but I was hardly among his most distinguished *talmidim*. And, yes, I was honored by Rav Ahron's kindness to me for the 35 years that we remained in close contact after a wonderful year in his *shiur* during my sophomore year at Yeshiva College. But, how could anyone dare to try to capture in words the remarkable fraternal bond between two extraordinary brothers who, as one family member told me, "were in awe of each other."

It was only after Rav Ahron's *b'chor* [oldest son], Rav Moshe Soloveichik, and my classmate and friend Rav Mordechai Willig, both urged me to accept this assignment that I agreed to do so, with the caveat that I do not, and cannot, claim any particular insights into the nuances of a seventy-five year relationship between two very guarded individuals. (One seeking a glimpse of this relationship need look no further than the very first item in the posthu-

Dr. David Luchins is the Chair of the Political Science Department at Touro College and a former National Vice President of the Orthodox Union. He also served as a Senior Advisor to Senator Daniel Patrick Moynihan of New York.

mously published collection of the Rav's lifetime correspondence, a near poetic response to his barely teenaged brother's letter).

The Rav used to refer to his fifteen year younger "kid brother" as the "conscience of our family." He was protective of Rav Ahron, as only a doting older brother can be, and, with the death of their father, Rav Moshe, in 1941, felt a special *achrayut* [responsibility] towards Rav Ahron.

My esteemed *mechutan* [father-in-law of one's child] Rabbi Dovid Twersky of Seattle told me a story that well reflects the Rav's attitude towards Rav Ahron:

We were learning a *diyuk* Rav Chaim had in a Rambam by which *tzitzis b'zman hazeh* (without *techeiles*) was not a full *kiyum* in the *mitzvah* and, therefore, the white threads on the *beged* might be considered a *massui* on *Shabbos*. Rav Chaim allegedly did not wear *tzitzis* on *Shabbos* outside of an area enclosed by an *eruv*.

The Rav commented. "My brother Reb Ahron does not wear *tzitzis* on *Shabbos*. You have to be a *tzadik yesod olam* [extraordinarily righteous] to not wear *tzitzis* on *Shabbos*. I'm not such a *tzadik*. I do wear *tztzis* on *Shabbos*."

Rav Ahron used to say (most notably at the Rav's funeral in Boston, where he was the sole *Chol ha-Mo'ed maspid* [eulogist during the Intermediate Days of a holiday]) that he "envied" the Rav's close relationship with their father, who was, in so many ways, the primary hashkafic and pedagogic influence on both men.

When Rav Ahron succeeded the Rav as *Morah D'Atra* [rabbi] of Congregation Moriah in 1960, the Rav declared that he (the Rav) reflected the influence of Rav Moshe's early years, while Rav Ahron reflected Rav Moshe's *derekh* in his later years. This may help explain why the Rav's *shiurim* were always so challenging, with dozens of possibilities presented and every imaginable *svara* considered, while Rav Ahron's were so much more settled and orderly, with a hypothesis, topic sentences, and clearly enunciated conclusions.

Interestingly, Rav Ahron's son Rav Moshe suggests that the Rav's *ptirah* [passing away] on *Pesach*, when *klal Yisrael* is in its "youth," and Rav Ahron's on Sukkoth, the *chag ha'asif b'acharit ha-shana* [the holiday of gathering in at the end of the year], are eerily reflective of this difference.

Both men were fiercely protective of each other. When Rav Ahron had problems in Chicago, the Rav worked the phones tire-

lessly on his behalf and was, he once told me, "unable to sleep" because of his concern for his brother. When Rav Ahron had a serious
stroke in 1983, the Rav took an extraordinary interest in every aspect of his recovery and rehabilitation. When a noted rabbinic figure
appeared to malign the Rav in an article, Rav Ahron urged his
talmidim to remove their names from the Board of his Yeshiva. When
the Rav's long final illness precluded continuing his decades-long
commute from Boston, Rav Ahron undertook to (in his words) "fill
in for my brother, just like he filled in for my father."

This is not to suggest that these two *gedolim* were clones of each
other. The differences between the two of them may best be sum-
marized by their choice of secular degrees. The Rav was a philosopher par excellence with a PhD in the discipline from the University
of Berlin. Rav Ahron was an honors graduate of NYU Law School.
The Rav grappled with issues from the seamless, timeless perspective of a philosopher. Rav Ahron provided concise legal advice. The
Rav delivered spellbinding public talks on *agaddic* topics, while Rav
Ahron was always ready with a precise, referenced *p'sak halakhah*.
And yet the same Rav would often give short shrift to *agaddita* in
his daily *shiur* and spend loving hours on the halakhic portions of
the text, while his brother, the lawyer, was the master of *agaddita*
and *hashkafah*.

This, of course, is a tad simplistic. The Rav worried about the
great issues of the *k'lal* [community], of human and communal destiny and Jewish survival. Rav Ahron celebrated the individual and
suffered fools wonderfully with boundless kindness and endearing
compassion.

The Rav rarely spoke at public affairs and, even more rarely,
touched directly on contemporary issues. Rav Ahron relished speaking out and getting involved. During my four years in the Rav's
shiur I only recall three or four times that he closed the *Gemara*, said
Kaddish d'Rabbanan, and then spoke to us about a contemporary
issue. Rav Ahron gave a weekly *shiur*, for almost half a century, directed solely to *hashkafic* issues, usually with a pronounced public
policy flavor.

They agreed about interfaith dialogue and capital punishment
(both against) and religious Zionism and civil rights of African-
Americans (both for). They disagreed about the Vietnam war (Rav
Ahron was an outspoken dove, his brother a fierce hawk) and the
question of Israel's withdrawal from the territories captured in 1967

(here the Rav was a dove and Rav Ahron a hawk). I once suggested to Rav Ahron that "your brother would have Israel armed to the teeth and give back all the territories, while you'd have them abolish their army and keep all the territories." "No," Rav Ahron said, "my brother would let Israel keep the Jewish parts of East Jerusalem."

While Rav Ahron was passionate and outspoken on these issues, as he was on every social justice question from Biafra to the Cambodian genocide, the Rav was more reserved and rarely made his views public. One notable exception took place at Yeshiva University in the fall of 1965 after Rav Ahron was quoted in *The Commentator* as calling the Vietnam War "organized murder" and advising draft evasion. The Rav, after *Ma'ariv* in the dorm that evening, told a group of students that the war in Vietnam was a *"milchemet mitzvah."* I was the chair of SOY's *Shalosh Seudot* [Student Organization of Yeshiva's third meal of the Sabbath] program at that time, and decided it might be helpful to hear what the third Soloveichik brother had to say on this subject. I accordingly scheduled Dr. Shmuel Soloveichik, Rav Moshe's middle son and a professor of chemistry at Yeshiva College, to discuss his brothers' disagreement on this issue. Dr. Shmuel was wonderful, explaining both brothers' views as products of their upbringing and environment ("My brother, the Rav, went to college in Berlin as Hitler was coming to power; he sees this as a continuation of the war against totalitarianism. My brother Ahron went to law school in peaceful post-war America; he sees this war as illegal").

What happened next is illustrative both of the exceptional relationship between the brothers Solovei(t)chik and my trepidation about undertaking this assignment. Within twenty-four hours of my *Shalosh Seudot* coup I was informed in no uncertain terms by both Rebbetzin Ella Soloveichik (Rav Ahron's wife) and Rebbetzin Tovah Lichtenstein (the Rav's daughter) that my choice of topic and speaker had not been appreciated by either the Rav or Rav Ahron. They were, I was told, perfectly capable of discussing their disagreement between themselves; they hardly needed anyone else's outside commentary (much less their own brother, whom they admired quite as much as they loved each other).

The Rov as Rov in Boston

Seth Mandel

Many people have already written about Rabbi Yosef Dov Soloveitchik. I can add a few comments on facets of him that were more evident in Boston. I merited watching and hearing the Rov not only in Maimonides School, but when he was interacting with members of the Boston community. This came about when I decided at about the age of eighteen to accompany the Rov from the *shul* in Maimonides to his daughter Mrs. Atarah Twerski's home, where he lived after Rebbetzin Soloveitchik passed away. It was a little over a mile, and after *shul* various members of the community would greet him, ask him short questions, or engage in longer discussions, usually after the *Shabbos* morning *davening*, although occasionally at other times as well. Before the Rov moved to live with his daughter, his house was quite close to Maimonides and people talked to him until he reached his door. The Twerskys' home was further away (his son-in-law davened with his father, the Talner Rebbe of Boston, in the latter's *shtiebel*, and led it after his father passed away), and no one accompanied him all the way home. Nor would the Rov, who was exceedingly modest, have allowed it, if anyone had proposed it to him, but he did not chase me away when I started. However, he would not agree that I come and pick him up at his house to walk him to *shul*. On these walks I spoke little, but heard the entire discussions that the Rov had with people of the community and visitors.

Rabbi Seth Mandel is Rabbinic Coordinator and in charge of Meat Kashrut at the Orthodox Union. He is a graduate of Rabbi Isaac Elchanan Theological Seminary and earned his PhD at Harvard in linguistics and Semitic languages.

I must give a brief account of the Boston (Brookline) Jewish community in the '60s and '70s. There were many Jews who were *shomrei Torah* Torah observant], ranging from the right-wing to left-wing,
from *chassidim* to *misnagdim*, from Europeans to those who had
Americanized. In those days, in Boston as in most communities,
there were few *talmidei chachomim*, except for some community rabbis and some teachers in the day school. I cannot let this opportunity
pass without mentioning two individuals who helped the Rov
through good and bad times, and might not be thanked publicly:
Rabbi Abelow, who ran a business, but was a graduate of Radin and
was one of the people involved in originally bringing the Rov to
Boston in the 30's and remained very close to the Rov until the end
of his life, and is buried near him; Abraham Levovitz, who passed
away in 5767 [2007], and always tried to find out what the Rov
would like and quietly go off and arrange it, without ever asking
for public recognition.

Most of the people talking to the Rov were laymen, and the questions ranged from quite good to very simple. But the level of the
question did not matter to the Rov. He treated every question as if
it were a good one, and responded in terms that the questioner
would understand. Rarely did he just say yes or no to any questioner; mostly he utilized the question as an opportunity to teach
some Torah. Even when non-religious Jews would come to discuss
matters with him (as happened quite often, when officials of the Israeli government and of various American Jewish institutions
would need to get his opinion or help on something), he would in-
sert into the conversation something from the *T'NaKh* [Torah] or
Chazal [our sages], and the questioner would come away knowing
some Torah. This was part of the Rov's view, expressed many times
in public and private in Boston (and based on the *Nefesh haChaim*),
that inside every Jew, no matter how removed from Torah, was a
"pintele Yid" [a 'dot' of a Jew] that was connected unconsciously to
Torah, and the Torah would inevitably grow inside the person and
God willing transform him.

Of course, these conversations would not have taken place had
the Rov borne a forbidding mien. But the Rov, outside of the public spotlight, was not only exceedingly modest, he also treated
everyone, including non-religious Jews, Jews with an agenda, and
Gentiles, with dignity and honor. The story has been told several
times about how he made sure that his Irish housekeeper had

money to live on after she retired, or how he would make sure that R. Aharon Kotler's sister had people to visit her when she was old. But these were not extraordinary tales of the *chesed* of a *godol*. Even the clerk in the drug store where the Rov picked up a prescription would be impressed with how the Rov treated him with honor. When watching and listening to the Rov interact with people, I would always see the Rambam in *Hilkhos De'os* 5:7 in front of me.

Unfortunately, in Boston we would see the Rambam in 5:13 as well—that a *talmid chochom* accepts insults and does not insult others. Even if we knew that one of the Rov's enemies had publicly insulted him, even when he listened to their calumnies on the phone, most people would have no idea that anything untoward had happened. He never talked about the insults; he never let on if he were upset. Nor, in all the years that I knew him, did he ever insult or criticize one of his critics, whether from the right-wing Orthdox, whether from Conservative or Reform Jews, whether from Gentiles. He would criticize the *hashkofoh* or the idea, and often we in Boston would try to guess to whom he was referring, but usually we did not know. I don't think I ever knew a man who controlled his temper so well. His anger was only in evidence during a *shiur* when he felt, in the heat of pursuing the argument, that a *talmid* had not prepared adequately (he usually apologized after the *shiur*). But outside the *shiur*, he always remained dignified and calm even when baited. The amount of internecine warfare among Orthodox Jews was an embarrassment to many of us, but the Rov was a living example of how to ignore it and work for the good of all Jews.

I have been privileged to see and hear many *gedolim* during my life, but none who kept his eye on the ultimate goal, the good of *Klal Yisroel* [all Jews], as the Rov did. It is only human nature to care first for one's friends and partners. But that is all too evident in most Rabbis, especially in our times, who feel that their responsibility lies to *anshei sh'lomenu*, people in their own group, and not to Jews aligned with other groups or not aligned with Torah. In his class on *Motzaei Shabbos* in Boston, he would repeatedly talk about the obligation of Jews, especially rabbis, to focus on the good of *Klal Yisroel*. He would tell story after story of how R. Chaim Brisker would do so, even if he upset people in his own circle by not putting their interests first. But it was not the Rov's words that hammered in his message; it was seeing him work for causes where he would get no credit when he felt it would improve conditions for *Klal Yisroel*. I have never met a more selfless person.

The Rov preached that the highest level of observance of *mitzvos*, the one toward which all Jews must strive, is to combine the practice with the understanding of the Torah behind the practice. Usually one could not see it, but sometimes it was evident that as the Rov was performing a *mitzvah*, whether it be putting on *tefillin*, taking the *lulav* and *esrog*, or observing *Shabbos*, he was going over the different issues in the *halokhos* of the *mitzvah*, reviewing the disagreements among *Rishonim* about how to conceptualize the *mitzvah*. One might ask an innocent question about this or another aspect of the *mitzvah*, and from the Rov's response, it was evident that the issue was fresh in his mind. Once after davening in the morning, Rabbi Yitzchak Simon (a *rebbe* in Maimonides who had learned in Slabodka and with the yeshiva in Shanghai) approached him with me in tow after I had shown Rabbi Simon how one of the *tzitzis* [fringe] of my *talis koton* had turned color in the wash. The Rov immediately launched into a survey of the *machlokes Rishonim* about the issue of colored *tzitzis* (I was lost after the first minute). Rabbi Simon then reviewed the mini-*shiur* for me so that I would understand it, and commented that the Rov was unique in his experience in the way that every question, no matter how minor, brought forth a review of the *machlokes tano'im* and *amoro'im*, the *machlokes Rishonim*, and different *shittos* [opinions] in how to understand an issue, rather than a quote of how one of the *Acharonim paskened*. And this was true even of *piskei halakhah* from the Rov's grandfather Reb Chaim Brisker. Never did I hear him respond to a question simply "Reb Chaim held that it was *osur/muttar*" [forbidden/permitted]. Always the response would be what the *Gemara* says and the *shittos* of the *Rishonim*.

Listening to the Rov give a eulogy was also a lesson. The Rov was famed, among the right-wing community as well, for his ability to speak brilliantly. But I wish to point out another facet of his ability. Once it happened that a simple Jew in Boston passed away, someone who was not learned and did not understand theoretical concepts easily, but was a loyal supporter of Maimonides and the Rov. The family asked the Rov to dedicate a *Motzaei Shabbos shiur* in honor of the man. Listening to the eulogy, I experienced bewilderment. It seemed as if the Rov was talking about one of the greatest Jews of the generation. But as I paid attention, I saw that the Rov was carefully adhering to the truth. The Rov spoke about the person's good qualities, stressing the importance in the Torah of those qualities and extolling the *niftar* for living up to the standards that the Torah demands. Never did he attribute to the *niftar* a quality that he did not possess. It was one of the most beautiful and inspiring eulogies I heard, without exaggerated claims that darken the words of lesser speakers.

A friend of mine, who is wiser than I but never met the Rov, once remarked that the Rov was a brilliant light that shone with thousands of facets (similar words were said by R. Aharon Soloveitchik at the Rov's funeral). The issue causing disagreements among people who are followers of the Rov is that all his followers are strong in only one or another facet, and try to explain what the Rov said in light of the facet that they focus on. Another follower, focusing on a different aspect, understands the Rov differently. Each *talmid* thinks that he is correctly representing the Rov's position and the other is mistaken. The reality is that the Rov understood things on several levels and from several points of view at once, and we lesser mortals try to remake him into the image of a *gadol* that we can relate to. The Rov's son-in-law R. Yitzchak Twersky, whose field was Jewish history, said to me during the *shivah* that the Rov was the type of extraordinary *gadol* who appears in history only once in several generations. It is a blessing to *Klal Yisroel* that we experienced in our generation a person who could show us the level that a person imbued with Torah can reach.

Reflections on The Rav

Menahem Meier

More than thirteen years have passed since the death of the great teacher of the Jewish people, Rav Yosef Dov Soloveitchik, *zt"l*, and we continue to miss his sage guidance on a host of contemporary issues. Even as I reflect on the life of that majestic but shy individual who was the *rebbe* of thousands, I feel a void. Although the Rav, *zt"l*, was shielded from public appearances for the last eight or nine years of his life, we always included him in our *tefillot*, hoping that God would miraculously intervene. However, after serving as the *Rosh Yeshiva* at Yeshiva University since 5701, he was summoned to the heavenly yeshiva on 17th Nisan 5753.

The Rav, *zt"l*, as his disciples reverentially referred to him, had a profound influence throughout his life. He was a creative Torah personality and his passionate engagement with Torah study remains vividly etched in my memory. Torah study was not simply an academic pursuit through which he captured the minds of his students. The *shiur* was charged with excitement and energy; we felt his (and our) encounter with *Hazal* [our sages], and knew that *Talmud Torah* [the study of Torah] was ultimately a religious experience. While calling for clear analysis, *Talmud Torah* was, in truth, an ongoing revelation, bonding the Jew and the God of Israel. It was our opportunity to find God in the world around us, and to serve Him with our minds.

I vividly recall during the years 5726–5727 the Rav, *zt"l*, suffered the death of his mother, his brother Dr. Shmuel Soloveitchik, and his wife within less than fifteen months. In moments of confession

Rabbi Menahem Meier served as Associate Principal, Maimonides School, Brookline, MA and was the founding Principal of The Frisch School, Paramus, NJ. He teaches at the Drisha Institute, New York, NY.

about his inner life, he revealed that these losses weighed heavily upon him; he often felt inconsolable and despondent. It was Torah study that saved him from despair. When he studied, and certainly when he taught, he felt the *Shechinah* [Divine Presence] hovering over him. Frequently citing the verse, "Were not Your teaching my delight, I would have perished in my affliction" (Psalms 119:92), the Rav was living proof of the spiritually uplifting nature of Torah study.

The Rav, *zt"l*, never referred to himself as a *Rosh Yeshiva* but rather as a teacher (*melamed*). He prided himself on that title, noting that God too was described as "the teacher of Torah to Israel." He knew that a teacher has awesome responsibility. As was evident from both his public lectures and *shiurim*, he devoted hours of preparation to every teaching occasion, his erudition and creativity notwithstanding. Beyond his extensive preparation for each class, he was able to reduce complex issues to very basic elements, to the extent that uninitiated students occasionally would be so struck by the clarity of the presentation that they would fail to see the complexity of the topic.

Both in the Brookline and New York communities he had profound spiritual authority without any means of enforcement. He never sought power or control over others. He respected people and they reciprocated exponentially—in the words of Zechariah, "Not by might nor by power but by the divine spirit."

His greatest pedagogic skill was his capacity to take his students on an exciting intellectual odyssey with him. As he presented the problem, it became the thorny problem of his students, who were occasionally tempted to offer solutions. As he developed several theories (of *Rishonim*) to account for certain halakhic phenomena, his students would explore with him—generally inwardly, although occasionally some brave souls would venture their thoughts—the strengths of each theory or the different conceptual orientation of the various approaches to a problem. The *shiur* or public lecture was never simply a sharing of information. It was an exciting journey in methodology and the *halakhic* thinking of a brilliant mind who found an authentic philosophy of Judaism in *Halakhah*.

The Rav, *zt"l*, was a gifted orator, who engaged his audiences for hours. His genius made his halakhic discourses extraordinary experiences even for the learned. However, he had another gift. He was able to speak to the learned as well as to the novice; he was able to communicate to both old and young. I recall one of the precious experiences of living in Brookline for four years (5728–5731)—the *motzei Shabbos* lecture at Maimonides School. *Motzei Shabbos* (Saturday night) became a weekly occasion for an encounter with the Rav, who would study the *parasha* or sections of the *Mishneh Torah*. This *shiur* attracted residents of greater Boston, college and graduate students from Harvard, MIT, Brandeis, Boston University, students and faculty of Maimonides School, and others who happened to be in Boston for *Shabbos*. Every week throughout the academic year the Rav attracted a wide range of men and women, with whom he explored Torah concepts and their implications for modern man. The audience never diminished throughout the four years of my sojourn in Brookline. It was an extraordinary way of spending Saturday nights.

The Rav, *zt"l*, may have been a shy individual with adults but never with children, to whom he was drawn. He generally came to visit Maimonides School on Mondays and Fridays. One Friday, as he entered the school, he noticed a young boy sitting at a table in the dining hall. He asked the boy why he was sitting in the hall and not in class. The fourth grader said that he was asked to leave class but was worried that he would miss the review session for a test in the book of *Joshua*. The Rav, *zt"l*, sat down next to the worried young student and began to study the *Navi* [Prophet] with the boy. While the fourth grader did not grasp his unique privilege that morning, he certainly was prepared for his test in *Joshua*.

While he was an extremely rigorous teacher in the classroom or lecture hall, he never failed to teach compassion and concern for others by his personal example. After *Kabbalas Shabbos* and *Ma'ariv* at Maimonides School, an entourage was always ready to escort the Rav home. Even when the entourage was eager to leave Maimonides School and begin the walk home, the Rav always waited for the last individual who had to lock the door. He would never allow that individual to walk home alone.

In the Brookline community the Rav was recognized as a man of great humility, who would identify with the pain of others. He would visit those in pain and provide them with hope and strength in his unique way. This emphasis on kindness already appears in the early writings of this intellectual giant. The Rav quotes his uncle Rabbi Meir Berlin {Bar Ilan} who told him that once R. Hayyim Soloveitchik (the Rav's grandfather) was asked to describe the function of a rabbi. He responded, "To redress the grievances of those who are abandoned and alone, to protect the dignity of the poor, and to save the oppressed from the hands of his oppressor." The Rav added, "Neither ritual decisions nor political leadership constitutes the main task of *halakhic* man. The actualization of the ideals of justice and righteousness is the pillar of fire which *halakhic* man follows when he ... serves his community." (*Halakhic Man*, Philadelphia, 5743, page 91)

He was passionately committed to Torah education for women. When Stern College opened a new program in Talmud for women, the Rav delivered the inaugural *shiur*. It should be noted that Maimonides School was coeducational for all subjects, *kodesh* and *hol* [sacred and secular], from kindergarten through high school. He visited the school frequently, saw his grandchildren study and develop there, and took an active role in defining and promoting the mission of the school.

The coeducational nature of Maimonides School leaves individuals, even some of his avowed disciples, uncomfortable. He was neither an advocate for nor an opponent of coeducational classes. His son, Dr. Haym Soloveitchik once told me that the Rav, *zt"l*, viewed coeducation not as a halakhic issue but rather as an educational question, one to be examined through the prism of sound educational theory and tested in the laboratory of life. One had to design a program to be educationally effective for each individual community.

While Torah was primary for the Rav, *zt"l*, he recognized the validity and benefits of the study of math, science, philosophy and the humanities. The latter offers us a window into human creativity and into the history of the human experience. Disciplines such as literature, history, and philosophy provide us with a means for greater understanding of ourselves, others and the complexities of our society. Following in the tradition of Maimonides, he saw *Talmud Torah* in the broadest sense to include both Torah and wisdom.

While the loss for the Jewish people is great, we must continue to celebrate the life and accomplishments of the Rav, *zt"l*, who was a divine gift to world Jewry of the twentieth century. We must make an effort to study his writings. In fact, several years ago I taught a course at Drisha Institute in New York on the Religious Thought of Rav Joseph B. Soloveitchik. We read and discussed some of the Rav's major essays, such as "Halakhic Man," "The Lonely Man of

Faith" and "Kol Dodi Dofek," as well as some of his shorter essays. The class consisted of a wide range of women—young college graduates and accomplished women approaching retirement. There were even two men who enrolled for the second semester. All of those enrolled knew of the Rav as a giant of the twentieth century but few had read his writings. The essays we studied provide poignant glimpses into the Rav's inner religious life that he sought to transmit to his students.

At the end of the year, I asked the students to respond in writing to several questions about the Rav's religious thought. They recognized that his religious thought does not deal with the issues of classical theology or metaphysics. They appreciated that the Rav's religious thought is fundamentally an exploration of man and his inner life. The focus of the Rav's religious philosophy is the human being. As the Rav deals with the inner struggles of the human soul, his philosophy, in a very real sense, transcends time. While some of the essays were written over half a century ago, they ring as true today as they did at the time of their composition. Many things change over time but man's inner life does not. As such, the fears and aspirations of man, the emotional life of man and his relationship to others and to God remain constants in a changing world.

In his writings, the Rav, zt"l, movingly shares his own inner religious life with his readers. He describes his approach to God as his wife was near death. He laments his failure to communicate the experiential dimension of Judaism to his students. He describes his feelings as a young boy as his father delivered a shiur, defending the position of Maimonides. One of my students, Dr. Gabriella Antinoph wrote, "I felt that this great thinker was sharing his own intellectual, religious and personal life struggles in such an honest and unadorned way. Rarely have I found such 'a baring of the soul' as in The Lonely Man of Faith."

The Rav and the Jewish Holidays Throughout the Year
Shlomo H. Pick

Introduction

In the fall of 1967, after three years of public high school, I arrived at Yeshiva College on the early admissions program with a burning desire to learn Torah. My first year was in the JSS program, but everyone in Yeshiva knew and felt that the personality with the most influence over the students and faculty was the Rav, who taught at RIETS. Although I did not attend his daily *shiur* in my years at Yeshiva, his *talmidim* were my *rebbei'im*, and through them, my colleagues and I began to absorb the Rav's teachings and methodology of learning. Moreover, throughout the year, we would meet the Rav before each holiday as he taught the laws, customs, and the essence of each festival to his *talmidim* as well as to the general students and alumni of the Yeshiva.

The High Holidays and *Sukkot*

One of the major contributions, if not the major one, to my preparations for the High Holidays were and still are the *shiurim* that the Rav gave before *Rosh Hashanah* and *Yom Kippur*. The Rav analyzed the various laws and customs of the Days of Awe to derive the underlying themes that lie at the heart of the *Yamim Nora'im* (High Holidays). The ideas expressed by the Rav have become a significant part of my experiences of the High Holidays.

In a series of summer *shiurim* (*yarchei kalla*) given in Boston, the Rav would analyze the laws and structure of the *Rosh Hashanah* serv-

---

Rabbi Shlomo H. Pick teaches at the Ludwig and Erica Jesselson Institute for Advanced Torah Studies at Bar-Ilan University and edited *Moadei HaRav: Public Lectures on the Festivals by the Late Rabbi Joseph B. Soloveitchik (Based upon Students' Notes)*, Ramat-Gan, Israel, 2003 (Hebrew).

ice. What is the essence of the commandment of the *shofar*? Why was it included in the *shemonah esreh*, while other commandments such as *matzah* have no connection to prayer whatsoever? The Rav analyzed the various *sugyot* in tractate *Rosh Hashanah* dealing with the sounding of the *shofar*, its shape, and the sounds that were to be made. The commandment of *shofar* may be a simple commandment of making the proper sounds from it, but with its sounding there is a further fulfillment of prayer (*kiyyum tefilah*). Just as there are different types of verbal prayers, so too, the *shofar* offers different prayers. When in danger man offers a primeval prayer, like the howl of the animal, begging God to save him. The *shofar* with its primitive sounds represents this type of primal prayer. On the other hand, the *shofar* also constitutes a song of praise, of *hallel*, a song that man, on the High Holidays, cannot offer with his voice because the Book of Life and Death is open.

What is the essence of the three *brakhot* (blessings) in the *Rosh Hashanah Mussaf* service? What is the theme of *shoferot*, the third of these *brakhot*? During one *yarchei kallah*, the Rav noted that the first three verses mentioned in this *brakhah* reflect God's revelation at Sinai. The last three refer to God's revelation in the Messianic Age. The middle three verses are from the Hagiographa (*Ketuvim*): "God ascended amid the blowing of the horn; the Lord revealed Himself amid the sound of the *shofar*." When, asked the Rav? On *Rosh Hashanah*! "With trumpets and the sound of the *shofar*, shout praise before the King, the Lord." When? On *Rosh Hashanah*! "Sound the *shofar* at the new moon, when the new moon is hidden for our festival day." When? When there is a revelation of the *Shekhinah* (Divine Presence) on *Rosh Hashanah*! The sounding of the *shofar* on this day heralds the revelation of the *Shekhinah* on *Rosh Hashanah*, each and every year. Needless to say, upon hearing the Rav that year, my *Rosh Hashanah* was (and has been) different, for upon hearing the *shofar*, and especially during the blessing of *shoferot*, I can imagine myself standing before the Almighty, as I attempt to feel the revelation of the *Shekhinah*.

During these *shiurim* the Rav would also analyze the *selichot* (penitential prayers) recited during the days preceding the High Holidays, as well as the relationship between *Rosh Chodesh* (new month) and *Rosh Hashanah*.

In the interim days between *Rosh Hashanah* and *Yom Kippur* the Rav would give his *kenes teshuvah drasha*. People from all over the world would attend. I remember the late Pinchas Peli attending from Israel. This would prove a boon for me when, after completing my studies at Yeshiva College and making *aliyah*, I would be able to continue to enjoy these *drashot* through Peli's transcriptions. Many of these were later published in his *Al HaTeshuvah* (*On Repentance*).

In these *shiurim* the Rav would analyze the types of penitence that man could encounter. These were then related to the very essence of *Rosh Hashanah*, the interim days, and *Yom Kippur*. Penitence was related to the various prayers of the day, from *Kol Nidrei* to the *Avodah* recounted in the *Mussaf* service, to the Book of Jonah, to the *Ne'ilah* service. I remember that in one of these *drashot*, the Rav analyzed two types of *teshuvah* (penitence) for more than two hours. After finishing his analysis, the Rav paused and said "Now I will discuss the philosophy of it" (this part was not included in Peli's presentation). At that point I found myself on the edge of my seat, for I had been drawn in by the drama of the Rav's presentation of his *shiur*. Now I sat back in my seat to listen to the philosophical part. Needless to say, I noticed that all my neighbors on my right and left were doing the same. The Rav's delivery and analysis had us all enthralled, at the edge of our seats, caught up by the Rav's brilliance, oratorical delivery, and the very Torah itself.

I was brought up in a synagogue with German customs. When I eventually participated in *shul*s with eastern European practices, which constitute a majority in the United States and in Israel, I would sometimes mention the venerable customs remembered from my youth and was at times ridiculed for them. One custom was the singing of the *al chet* with a joyous melody by the entire congregation, a custom considered strange in light of the weeping, muted voices confessing their sins found in most congregations. Imagine my joy when, in a *teshuvah drashah*, the Rav referred to this custom. In the above-mentioned *drashah* he differentiated between the *teshuvah* of the individual (*yachid*) and the community (*tzibbur*). The former confesses his sins after the *amidah*, with no promise of salvation, for indeed he may be even eradicated for his sins. However, the *chazzan* (cantor) representing the community, confesses in the middle of the fourth blessing of the *amidah*, the blessing containing the essence and sanctification of *Yom Kippur*. The blessing concludes with "Blessed art Thou...who does pardon and forgive our iniquities and the iniquities (*avonot*) of Thy people Israel, does

remove our ill deeds (*ashmoteinu*) year by year..." The Rav asked:
Why don't we also say "the ill deeds of Thy people Israel" as mentioned with the iniquities. The Rav explained that *asham* means a
transgression that may lead to *shmama*, utter destruction. An individual's transgressions may necessitate utter destruction of that individual, but *Klal Yisrael*, the entire community of Israel, can never
be destroyed, no matter what their sin is. With this background,
the Rav recounted the German custom he himself had encountered
while studying in Germany. The community would sing the entire
al chet with a joyous melody, for this reflected their trust in God
Who would certainly forgive the entire community their transgressions. Here is an example where the Rav elucidated the structure of the *Yom Kippur* prayer service, the differences in the text of
the blessings, and the very customs that reflect significant themes
of this Holy Day.

When one thinks of the High Holidays, one tends to think of *Rosh
Hashanah* and *Yom Kippur*, while ignoring *Sukkot* and *Simchat Torah*.
In many ways they can be included in the High Holiday season.
Nevertheless, what the students of Yeshiva usually missed were
those *shiurim* in which the Rav would prepare us for this joyous holiday. The Jews of Boston had the privilege to hear the Rav after *Yom
Kippur* and during *Chol HaMoed*, and that indeed contributed to their
holiday preparations and experiences. However, as students at the
Yeshiva, we generally went home on our own, without any halachic,
philosophical, or emotional preparation by the Rav. What I have
discovered is that with the publication of the Rav's *shiurim* and
drashot in the last twenty years, I can learn the Rav's *torot* concerning these holidays and at times actually feel the Rav saying them.
The taking of the *lulav* on Sukkot is not just a mechanical lifting of
the four species, but expresses one's praise of God in the *hallel*, and
therefore is joined with the recitation of the *hallel*.

Concerning the *sukkah*, one should see the light of the stars, the
light of the moon, and the light of the sun through the s'khakh of the
sukkah. Why? A Jew must be able to see beyond his surrounding, he
should be able to perceive the infinite universe above and the Creator. From here the Rav continued to society at large as well as the
individual Jew—Man must be able to see beyond himself, beyond
Nature, beyond a perceived random course of history. Man, and especially the Jew, must see God beyond the *levush*, the obscuring gar-

ments of nature and history. Man must experience God and his Divine Providence.

Chanukah

The Rav would often tie *Chanukah* and the *Chashmona'im* [Hasmoneans] with the weekly Torah readings, especially with the story of Joseph and his brothers. A main theme combining the two was the element of *teshuvah*, penitence. Reconciliation between the brothers and Joseph, the *teshuvah* that the brothers did, is symptomatic of the redemption, for *teshuvah* is a prerequisite for the ultimate redemption. Similarly, the *Gemara* (*Shabbat* 22b) states that *Chanukah* was established as a holiday only after a year had passed. The Rav explained that it was insufficient just to remove the physical *tumah* [impurity] from the Temple, but the spiritual *tumah* had to removed, and Israel had to do *teshuvah*. This penitence by the *Chashmona'im* led to reconciliation with the Hellenists, with their return to Judaism. Thus, *Chanukah* was the culmination of this *teshuvah*, similar to the weekly portions recounting the story of Joseph and his brothers.

In an important *shiur* given in 1971 before members of the RCA, and which I attended together with friends, the Rav tied in all the elements of the *sugya* in tractate *Shabbat* which served as the basis for the laws of the *Chanukah* lights—the oil, the wicks, and whether they must be rekindled if they go out. The Rav also added an important explanation to the nature of publicizing the Chanukah miracle (*pirsumei nissah*). The Rav taught in that *shiur*, that the goal of the *Chanukah* lights was to make known to the non-Jew the reason for the *Chanukah* holiday—the Jew would stand up and fight for his belief in one God. Hence, the means to broadcast this message is by lighting candles. However, on *Purim* and *Pesach*, the publicizing of the miracle is by means of reading the Scroll of Esther which constitutes the Written Law, or the reciting of the Passover Haggadah which is comprised of the Oral Law. The non-Jew has no relationship to Torah, and consequently, one must conclude that this announcing of the miracle is not directed to the non-Jew but to the Jew alone. The Rav explained: *Purim* and Passover celebrate the victory of life over death and this is a message that the non-Jew does not need to learn, for he naturally knows this. However, the novel message of *Chanukah* that the Jew will stand up and fight for his religion—this is a *chiddush* (a new insight), one that the non-Jew is not cognizant of, and this is the message of *Chanukah* that must be broadcast to him.

Purim

Meshenichnas Adar Marbim be-Simcha! There were many humorous anecdotes concerning the Rav and his tendency to become involved in deep thoughts, concentrating for long periods on problems and issues that bothered him, especially Talmudic ones. A famous anecdote/joke recounted how the Rav was once driving his car with his *Rebbezin*, and he ran into a tree. The *Rebbezin* turned to him and asked: "Berel, what do you think you are doing?" The Rav answered: "Oh, I thought you were driving!"

I also remember during one of the *Purim Chagigot*, a student came in impersonating the Rav. How was that done? He simply walked in dressed like the Rav as I remember him during weekdays—dressed in a dark green blazer in a hat stylish for the late sixties, with a *New York Times* under his arm. In that *Chagiga*, the "*Purim* Rav" quipped in reference to the Rav's son who had started giving *shiurim* in the Yeshiva: "*MeReb Haym ad Reb Haym, lo kam keHaym!*" With these stories, I do not mean to disparage the Rav, G-d forbid, but to show a human side of this great man. Besides being an *Ish Ha-lakha*, the Rav was also a Man of this World, aware of world affairs, Israeli affairs, Jewish affairs, and affairs in Boston and at Yeshiva. Reading the *New York Times* was symptomatic to this awareness, just as the Rav's reading of Greek or modern philosophy.

In conjunction with these stories, I always remember my first *Purim* in the Yeshiva. It was winter and snowy. The Rav was supposed to go back to Boston to his family and community but couldn't because Boston was snowed in and it was impossible to get there. As a result the Rav remained in New York at Yeshiva for *Purim*. My first encounter with this situation was after the reading of the *Megillah*. We all began to sing and dance to *Shoshanat Ya'akov*, as is customary in *yeshivot*. Suddenly and almost immediately, the Rav stopped us, and began to continue the *ma'ariv* service to its end. It is almost certain that the Rav was putting into practice the position of his grandfather (Reb Haym) and father and uncle, of being stringent in the laws of danger (*pikuach nefesh*), and any extension of the fast would constitute such a situation. (I don't recall if he actually mentioned the necessity of eating to break the fast.)

One more thing I recall from that *Purim*. As soon as sunset arrived and *ma'ariv* had been prayed, I heard that the Rav had called in his students and gave them a *shiur*. There is only so long that he could be separated from his beloved *shiurim*.

Pesach

Earlier, I described the Rav's contribution to my preparations for the High Holidays, essentially those *shiurim* that the Rav gave before *Rosh Hashanah* and *Yom Kippur*. The same can be said about *Pesach*, for the Rav analyzed the various themes, laws and customs of *Pesach*, especially *Seder* night. As with the Days of Awe, the ideas expressed by the Rav have become a significant part of my *Pesach* experience, especially the night of the *Seder*.

During the period when I was studying at Yeshiva, the Rav would give the Tonya B. Soloveitchik Lecture which presented philosophical issues of *Pesach*, often contrasting these with themes from *Purim*. These lectures were usually academic in nature. In one of these lectures, the Rav contrasted Greek views of shunning the animalistic consumption of food and the Western view of turning the meal into an aesthetic experience, to Judaism's view of elevating the meal by means of *chessed* (loving-kindness). From this point the Rav would go on to describe the *Seder* meal, continuing to the very essence of the Jewish people as being the covenantal community, which is a *chessed* community and a teaching community. The Rav began this lecture with a personal note remembering the *Seder* night at his Grandfather's house. How privileged we were to hear a *shiur* from a person who had heard Torah from the eminent Reb Haym Brisker. We felt part of the links in that great chain of tradition, *mesorah*, starting from Sinai and carrying on through the generations to *talmidei ha*Rav and even the *talmidim* of the *talmidim* of the Rav.

In the weeks preceding *Pesach*, the Rav gave even more *shiurim* on the holiday. At his weekly *Gemara shiur* in Moriah Synagogue in mid-Manhattan, the Rav stopped his regular *shiurim* on the tractate that was being learned and began to deliver *shiurim* on *Pesach* topics. In the spring of 1975 I was visiting from Israel when the Rav gave a series of *shiurim* dealing with the laws concerning *Seder* night falling on Saturday night (*motzei Shabbat*), something that hadn't happened in over twenty years. The Rav took singular stands both in his explanation of the Maimonidean position and then adopting it as actual law (*halakhah le'ma'aseh*).

In the final days before vacation and as Pesach drew closer, the Rav would give more *shiurim* on Pesach topics within the Yeshiva, teaching various halakhic themes of *Pesach* in his daily *shiur*. Usually he also gave a *shiur* to members of the RCA which was attended by students of the Yeshiva.

A major theme throughout this period was the commandment of *sippur yetziat Mitzrayim* (recounting of the Exodus) and the reciting of the *Haggadah* as a *kiyyum* (fulfillment) of the commandment to study Torah. The Rav delved into all aspects of this topic, based on Rambam's *Hilkhot Chametz uMatzah*. Of great import was the pedagogical rule given by Maimonides: according to the child's ability does the father teach his son the story of the Exodus. The very recounting of the Exodus was an exercise in the study of the Oral Law, for one does not just read the first fifteen chapters of Exodus, but instead one recites the chapter of *Bikkurim* (the bringing of the first fruits to the Temple) which only highlights the Exodus. However, we study the Oral Law concerning these verses, the *Midrash Halakhah* on this chapter. The reason of course—the whole purpose of the Exodus was to receive the Torah on Sinai.

Another important subject was that *sippur yetziat Mitzrayim* was just not the verbal recounting of the Exodus, or the Torah study of the laws of *Pesach*. It involved much more. One must not only study the Exodus, but teach it. One must not only study and teach it, he must offer praise and thanksgiving to G-d for taking us out of Egypt. One must not only do this verbally, but on *Seder* night one must invest the very meal itself as a fulfillment of *sippur yetziat Mizrayim* by mentioning the reasons for the various commandments such as *matzah, marror* [the bitter herbs] and the *Pesach* sacrifice. Finally, one cannot just be satisfied with all this, but must actually emotionally relive the Exodus on *Seder* night. Here the Rav not only taught us how to think, but how to feel, how to experience the festivals, *Halakhah*, and Judaism itself.

Sefirat HaOmer [counting of the 49 days between Pesach] and Shavu'ot

A significant theme in the Rav's approach to some of the holidays was the aspect of the *tzibbur*, the community of Israel, with each congregation representing that covenantal community. This was noted with the nature of the atonement of *Yom Kippur*, and the Rav presented it in a novel form concerning the counting of the

Omer. Besides the individual's counting of the *Omer*, the community must also count. The personal counting is to fulfill one's commandment, whether it is *d'oraitah* as held by Maimonides or *d'rabbanan* as held by most *Rishonim*. The Rav's novel insight was that according to Rashi and the *Sefer haChinnukh*, there was an obligation incumbent upon the community, the *tzibbur*, to count the days of the *Omer* as well. Since there was no calendar date for the festival of *Shavu'ot*, it was the community's counting of the *Omer* that established the holiday. The Rav further added that in some instances, for example if someone missed a specific night and counted the next morning, or according to Rashi, one who counts the evening's *Omer* too early, i.e., before sundown on long summer days, does not lose his ability to continue counting the *Omer*, The non-nighttime counting was still effective in determining the date of the *Shavu'ot* festival, and thus the next time he could continue to count with a *brakhah*. Again, the whole idea of *Sefirat haOmer* takes on new meaning in light of one's relationship to all of *klal Yisrael*.

The Rav also noted specific themes of *Shavu'ot*. These included laws and concepts of conversion as derived from Ruth, laws of *kinyanim* [acquisition of a possession through a symbolic act], also derived from the Book of Ruth, themes found in the Ten Commandments, especially the nature of "Thou shalt not covet...". The Rav dealt with the very establishment of the sanctity of this festival, whether through the *Omer* counting or the use of a *midrash halakhah* that stated that although there is no *Omer* sacrifice, and thus the counting may no longer be effective on a *d'oraita* level, there is still a biblical command to make the *Shavu'ot* festival. The Rav considered all aspects of this holiday and imparted the various topics to his students to enrich their appreciation of this *yom tov* and the days preceding it.

Israel Independence Day (*Yom haAtzmaut*)

Although the Rav opposed reciting *hallel* on this day (for purely technical *halakkic* reasons), it is clear that he had an unambiguous and positive outlook on this significant day in modern Jewish history. Not only is this portrayed in his seminal essay *Kol Dodi Dofek* (which was originally an Israel Independence Day *drashah*), but in many other *drashot* and *shiurim* the Rav emphasized the importance of the establishment of the State of Israel to modern Jewry. Most of these were given in the 1950s, and provided vital elements in fashioning his students' *hashkafah*. The Rav also noted that the State of Israel had become crucial in re-establishing Jewish identity in America. Another theme recurrent in his lectures was that of suffering and the State of Israel—how the State came about, how it continues to exist, and even the anxiety that the American Jew has concerning any news coming out of the State of Israel.

Tisha b'Av

Because the Rav was in the Boston area during the summer, most of the Yeshiva students missed his *shiurim* on *Tisha b'Av*. Through tapes and notes, and with the recent publication of *The Lord is Righteous in all His Ways: Reflections on the Tish'ah be-Av Kinot* (ed. J.J. Schachter), one can join the Rav as he explained the meaning of the *kinot*, explored the *halakhic* issues and themes of this saddest of days, experienced the sorrow of the day, and mourned the destruction of the Temple. Thus, nowadays anyone can sense that he is mourning the destruction of the Temple, Jerusalem, and all the tragedies of the Exile together with the Rav.

Conclusion

Although I never attended the Rav's daily *shiur*, his influence upon me is everlasting, for the *shiurim* and lectures that I did attend have given me a greater understanding of the festivals and holidays, and have ignited my desire to learn the Rav's torah whether through his own publications, tapes of his *shiurim* and lectures, or through the notes taken by students. This point is most significant, for every person searching for the meaning of the holidays, the intricate points of the various *halakhot*, the major themes of the High Holidays and festivals, the value of the customs practiced during these special occasions, can still learn from the Rav. Moreover, one can graduate to using the Rav's *shiurim* and students' notes to continue learning tractate after tractate, to grow in learning, to eventually become a student of the Rav, as his teachings mold one's methodology of learning and *hashkafah*.

In a sense, it was Divine Providence that in the mid-20th century, a Torah luminary of the stature of the Rav came to teach and influence the students of Yeshiva and the Jews of the entire world. I reiterate: the Rav's influence was not only on the students who studied directly with him; he inspires their children and students together with *talmidei chakhamim* and Jews throughout the world who read, learn and study his torah, essays, and philosophy. It is especially felt with the Rav's *shiurim* on tractates *Yoma*, *Pesachim*, and *Sukkah*, his *shiurim* that have been published from the Boston *yarchei kallah*, and his *teshuvah drashot* found in *Al HaTeshuva* (*On Repentance*) and *Before Hashem You Shall be Purified*, the *Pesach Haggadah Si'ach HaGrid* published by his grandson, as well as recent publications on *Purim*, *Chanukah*, and *Tisha b'Av*.

The Rav: My *Rebbe*
An Essay on the *Derekh Halimud* of
Rabbi Joseph B. Soloveitchik

Hershel Reichman

In the twenty-four years I studied under the tutelage of Rabbi Joseph B. Soloveitchik, he had the greatest impact on my life. During those years he spoke to me perhaps more than anyone else. These words were never trite; they were always as if the Almighty's words were coming from the mouth of my *rebbe*, the Rav. It was in this way of Torah transmission, as a *rebbe* to *talmid*, that I felt as close to the Rav as is possible for any human relationship on Earth.

Whether at his regular lectures at Yeshiva or in his various annual public addresses, the Rav became the centerpiece of a majestic Torah experience. Sometimes these *shiurim* were held in hot, crowded locations and the lengthy lectures could feature very technical or esoteric topics. Still, many people would come, and more important—they stayed. This was largely due to the fact that the Rav was a master teacher who could explain the most difficult material of Torah to a child or novice. In fact, the Rav told us many times in the name of his grandfather, Rav Chaim Soloveitchik of Brisk, that if you could not explain a *s'vara* (a methodical train of thought) to a child, then you did not truly understand the idea yourself. For the Rav, this was the definition of his own knowledge: to be able to explain and clarify a point to any listener.

As a student of his father, Rav Moshe Soloveitchik, and his grandfather, Rav Chaim, the Rav was of course a classic Brisker *lam-*

Rabbi Dr. Hershel Reichman is a Rosh Yeshiva in RIETS. He has authored five volumes of *R'shimot HaRav*, notes on the Talmud lectures of Rabbi Joseph B. Soloveitchik.

dan. The primary hallmark of the Brisker approach is the focus on the *yesodot* (basic principles of a Talmudic discourse or *halakhah*). In this way, the Rav always described his *derekh halimud* in the following terms: "Some people know each line in the Talmud, but Rav Chaim taught how to know between the lines of the Talmud." Thus, to the Rav, *shakla v'tarya* (Talmudic give and take) became less critical in his approach to studying the Oral Law. Instead, what became important were clarity, consistency and universal concepts. As a result, even relatively uneducated people could understand and enjoy the systematic discussion of ideas which the Rav discovered and developed.

This, I believe, is the reason for the Rav's focus on Rambam's *Mishneh Torah*. The Rambam is short and to the point in his halakhic rulings. There is no Talmudic discourse to contend with abstract concepts—the foundations of the Brisker approach. The Rav would always say jokingly that the reason he and Rav Chaim chased after the Rambam was because the Rambam usually gives no explanation and one could thereby allow for free thinking without creative restraints. In fact, he often quoted Rav Chaim as saying that, generally, the *Teshuvot HaRambam*—where he defends some of his *halakhot* from critics—did not help the Rambam's rulings but usually made them more difficult to defend.

One of the Rav's personal favorites among the *Rishonim* was the Ramban—especially his work, the *Milchamot Hashem*. The Ramban's *Milchamot* is extremely difficult and abstract and is replete with convoluted *shakla v'tarya*. Nevertheless, this was always one of the Rav's favorite texts—perhaps even more than his beloved Rambam and Raavad. He would say that the ability to read two *Rishonim* was the true test of a *lamdan*; the two are the Ramban and the Rabeinu Tam. Full mastery of learning required command of the textual dexterity of the *Milchamot*, as well as any Tosafot. In the Ramban, the Rav always searched for the *chiddush* that was usually found in one line that followed two dozen lines of complex discourse. When he discovered this, it would be with the utmost pleasure and illustrated by the widest smile one has ever seen.

Among our great *Rishonim*, in the Rav's mind, the most honored was the Rabeinu Tam. "The Rambam was the greatest individual scholar among the *Rishonim*. But the Rabeinu Tam's contribution to the Torah tradition was greater. Without him, the Tosafists—their whole approach to study of question and answer and abstract con-

ceptualization—would not exist. Rabeinu Tam was responsible for
the Ramban and for Rav Chaim."

By focusing on principles and on concepts rather than textual in-
tricacies, the Rav was able to broaden his audience in the widest
sense. But this intellectual stance was also accompanied by parallel
pedagogical techniques. These techniques were geared unconsciously to arousing student curiosity, interest and involvement.

To start with, the approach of question and answer was crucial
in the Rav's Brisker pedagogy. Indeed, Rav Chaim's Brisker method
always presents a problem to its Torah audience. Of course, man is
primarily a problem solver. Therefore, the problem challenges. It
goads and arouses. Once discovered, the solution is never to be
lightly forgotten. The Rav was brilliant at arousing curiosity with
the problem of the Talmudic issue or *halakhah*.

Secondly, the technique of vividly displaying the drama and creative process to the students was pivotal to the Rav. Each *shiur* was
an act of discovery. The Rav would rarely present packaged answers
or solutions. As he would return to the same point again and again
over the years, he would attempt new approaches to old problems
in order to be fresh and open-minded.

Many times he would pause in the *shiur*, lower his head and pon-
der. When the answer came, there was tremendous energy, enthusiasm, and power. The ultimate discovery—the *p'shat*—was
accompanied by the smile and the love of the *chiddush*. I remember
Rabbi Aharon Lichtenstein telling me once that the Rav often spent
two hours on a problem trying approach after approach. While
arousing our involvement and excitement when finally coming to a
resolution which we all thought was brilliant, it still might have
been the same conclusion that he had decided upon three times earlier over the years. How could the Rav be stumped—how could he
again go through the creative process when he had achieved the answers before? Rav Aharon explained to me that, "The Rav is not
only the greatest *lamdan* in the world. He is also the greatest actor on
Earth." While I agree with this, I also contend that the Rav was able
to suppress memory—to ignore preconceptions or old conclusions.
He could start the intellectual process from the beginning!

Consciously, he would try out answer after answer in front of the
class or audience—again and again either accepting or rejecting
them. Sometimes I or another person would say during these moments, "But the Rav said such and such last time we learned this

topic." Invariably, he would respond, "This time is not last time. We have to think through the question today and now. If we consider old problems then there may be new solutions."

This would lead him to assert many times that he was not a *posek* (halakhic decider) and continue, "I don't come to conclusions. I only discuss logical possibilities." Of course, this was perhaps a weakness of his approach. Many critics of Brisk and the Rav focused on the lack of absolute certainty. But the Rav was more concerned with honesty, reflection and creativity than with simple-minded didactics.

As the Rav focused "between the lines" rather than "on the lines" he moved into the world of induction. We are given certain *halakhot*. What can we induce from them? Induction rests upon intuition. Thus, the learning approach became intuitive since logical creativity is predicated on intuition. This was a critical notion to the Rav. Many times he would leave problems unresolved and return the next day and present a beautiful solution with the comment "When I woke up I thought of this" or "The answer came to me during *shmoneh esreh* this morning." The Rav's intuition would not permit him to say a logical absurdity. He would not allow it.

Another virtue of the Rav's method of learning was his persistence. If a basic problem was not solved, he would come back to it. In the year that the Rav taught Tractate *Yevamot*, one of the most difficult in the Talmud, he lectured for more than three hours on Tuesday, Wednesday and Thursday mornings; eventually the students became exhausted. At one point in the year, the Rav suggested that we meet on Wednesday nights "to review and to think again." After a while the majority of the students became lost and mentally drained. A petition was drawn up asking the Rav to change to a less rigorous and technical tractate. Once submitted to him, the Rav retaliated, "Where's your commitment to learning! How can you abandon any part of Torah once you start?" That was the last such request in the Rav's *shiur*.

This stress on persistence fueled a highly motivated, competitive spirit in the Rav. Indeed, if Rambam and Rabeinu Tam were the Rav's friends, they were also his competition. The Rav would quote the Talmudic adage that a person should try to achieve the level of previous generations. "First," he announced. "Become the greatest *talmid chakham* in your town—then in your country—then in your generation. Then work from generation to generation back to become the greatest *talmid chakham* in history." It sounds grandiose and certainly presumptuous, but this dream did not fail him. For the Rav, this was a reality.

One point that was crucial to the Rav in his studies was that his *emunat chachamim* [trust in the sages] was absolute. His colleagues—the *chakhmei hamesorah*—would not deceive him. They were totally reliable and dedicated to accuracy and truth. Therefore, he was very critical of newly surfaced variant texts and manuscripts. I heard him often say, "If the *chakhmei hamoesorah* did not have this text, then it's probably wrong."

This was the basis for his well-known rejection of the works of the Meiri, a 13th-century scholar whose manuscripts were first published recently. "If the Vilna Gaon and Rav Chaim did not know of the new Meiri, then the new Meiri could only be a curiosity—not a member of the exclusive club that includes the Rambam, Ramban, and Rabeinu Tam." In the same way, I remember him rejecting the newly published *Otzar haGeonim*. "Any responsa of the *Gaonim* not known to our *Rishonim* are only side factors. They cannot now become part of our *mesorah*."

Some may claim that this exclusivity was narrow-minded, but it displayed the Rav's absolute dedication and loyalty to all of the Torah scholars who have been part of the *mesorah*.

Finally, the Rav's intellectual honesty was the quality that, in effect, radiated through all of the aforementioned dimensions of his Torah study. Moreover, this was typified by his fondness for the story he would often relate about Rav Chaim's first *shiur* taught in Volozhin:

All the *gedolim* of Yeshivas Volozhin were gathered to hear the *shiur* of the famous young prodigy who, with his new *derekh halimud*, was already somewhat controversial. Rav Chaim rose to the occasion. His *shiur* was a masterpiece as it resolved difficult and enigmatic *halakhot* found in the pages of the Rambam. Even Rav Chaim's great critics were overwhelmed by the brilliance and might he displayed. As the lecture came to a close, the crowd began to call out its congratulations when Rav Chaim banged at the table and asked for silence. He sat down and started speaking again. "What I have just said, I realize, is incorrect. I recall now a *Perush Hamishnayot* of the Rambam which undermines my very premise." Deathly silence fell upon the entire room. Rav Chaim sat for a few minutes—his brain knitted in deep thought and tension. He rose and concluded, "I have no answer, but surely, cross out whatever I said before." He quickly left the stunned listeners and the room.

This intellectual honestly is what always served as the Rav's model.

Perhaps the greatest impact left on students by the Rav's *derekh halimud* was his display of the crown of Torah with all its majesty. For his students, as we listened to his *shiur*, there was no doubt that we were involved in the most important process and experience on Earth. We were studying Torah—and we could be doing nothing more worthwhile.

Our teacher was king and we were his princes.

The Rav and *Torah u-Madda*

David Shatz

The Rav *zt"l* had a proclivity for portraiture. Numerous personality types walk through his writings: halakhic man, the lonely man of faith, even "Rosh Hodesh man." In addition to these abstract types, he depicts real life, flesh-and-blood individuals, especially in brilliant eulogies. The Brisker Rav, the Talner Rebbe and Rebbetzin, R. Chaim Heller, *zikhronam li-verakhah*, to name just a few—all are captured magnificently. And not only could he paint others, but he had a propensity, to a certain extent, for self-portraiture. He speaks about his loneliness as a man of faith; his emotions during his bout with cancer; his feelings of helplessness and his need to pray when his wife was ill; and his own fears for his future. In short, his pages are full of personality types and dotted, as well, with a measure of self-description.

Yet nowhere in those writings, which span so many varieties of the human personality, do we find a character, real or abstract, who fits exactly what the Rav was: a giant of Torah whose unbounded love for it was central to his existence, the defining essence of his life, but who also pursued a Ph.D. in philosophy at a major European university and developed a magisterial command of works by scientists, psychologists, philosophers, theologians (many of them Christian), and literary artists. There are few major figures in Western thought, especially of the past three hundred years, who go unmentioned in his footnotes. And bear in mind that when you listen to a tape of the Rav, or when you get hold of a manuscript he used

Dr. David Shatz, YC `69, RIETS `72, is Professor of Philosophy at Yeshiva University, editor of *The Torah u-Madda Journal*, and editor of the series *Me-Otzar HoRav*, which is devoted to publishing previously unpublished writings and discourses of the Rav.

for oral presentation, there are no footnotes. If those blanks were filled in as in a published work, the number of figures he draws upon from outside the fold, and the number of their ideas that he invoked and reshaped, would be still more staggering. "*Rosh yeshiva* and philosopher": we don't find him addressing this conception, not a word; neither in the third person nor in the first person. This man who captured people so well never provided—so it seems—a theoretical model for living simultaneously in both the Torah world and the universe of general culture.

As I sat through the Rav's exhilarating, often electrifying *shiurim* in the late `60s and early `70s, *shiurim* that were all about *gemara* and *rishonim* and *aharonim* and were unadulterated with philosophy, my *shiur* mates and I couldn't put it all together. Then as always, YU students were struggling with the concept of "synthesis" (the predecessor term to "Torah u-Madda"). We knew the Rav was a master of both worlds, and we took this as a *"ma`aseh rav"* that validated the YU ideal. But we did not understand why he was that way. We felt like asking, *"Rebbi,* what value do you see in general culture, *ad kedei kakh,* so much so, that you endure slings and arrows, even ostracism, because you embrace it?" None of us dared pose the question. He was in this regard a mystery. At that time, to my shame, I really knew little about his philosophic writings—my interest was in analytic philosophy, a polar opposite to European-style philosophy—and there were few published writings to know. But I knew enough to know, to some degree, what he had read. As the years went on, as more and more works appeared and I became passionately involved in understanding his thought, the mystery in some ways deepened. But in some ways it inched toward resolution.

Some question *whether* the Rav had a positive attitude towards secular studies. I think it is clear from what he studied that his attitude was positive. Furthermore, his grandson R. Mosheh Lichtenstein trenchantly remarked that the question about the Rav's attitude to secular studies could easily be settled by putting his library on display. The Rav's speeches also include some very strong statements about the importance of secular culture generally. For example, in an address delivered to parents of Maimonides School in 1971, published by the school in a compilation called "Legacy," he stated,

What do we at the Maimonides school believe?. . . . We believe that the Jewish child is capable of carrying a double load, the universal secular and the specific Judaic. We believe. . . . that the child is able to study and comprehend two systems of knowledge and to excel in both. Some people deny it.

The Jewish child, they say, has to choose between being a literate Jew and a literate human being. Literacy in both realms [they say] is an absurdity. We reject this philosophy of doom. We say the Jewish child is teachable and educationable in both fields and at the same time. Not only literacy, but even scholarship in both is attainable.

Here, however, we have only an assertion that Torah u-Madda (or Synthesis) is doable—not an explanation of why the doable should be done.

In a *shiur* delivered for YU Rabbinic Alumni on February 19, 1955, the Rav invokes the image of Elkanah, the father of Shemuel, who came from Ramatayim Tzofim—two peaks facing each other, separated by an abyss. The Rav suggests that these two *ramot* represent Torah and general knowledge. Many have refused to build a bridge between these two peaks, lest they plummet into the abyss below. Yet efforts should continue. "We must build both—we have no other etzah...no other solution." Yahadut must reach the broad sectors of American Jewry. Refusal to live on both peaks will turn us into a sect and lock us into *"daled amot of batlanus."* (I thank Dr. Arnold Lustiger and Rabbi Dr. Aharon Rakeffet-Rothkoff for elucidating the contents of the Yiddish tape. A Hebrew version of the *shiur* appears in the compilation *Ha-Adam ve-Olamo*).

Here we are again. Apart from appealing to the damage of sectarianism, the Ramatayim Tzofim *shiur* does not explain *why* it is so important to be on both peaks.

The *whether* is clear, then; the *why* is so far murky. Indeed: R. Dr. Yitzhak Twersky, *zt"l*, a son-in-law of the Rav, remarked—in a memorial tribute of great beauty that appeared in *Tradition* in 1996—that in the Rav's writing, "there is no attempt to argue and demonstrate the importance of general learning as an abstract proposition just as there is no attempt to defend or glorify western culture." The Rav draws on general culture (R. Twersky focuses on philosophy) without giving a rationale for his use of it; he draws freely upon it without apology, without justification. The eminent

Professor Gerald Blidstein (in *Tradition* 1989) puts the point in the form of a paradox:

> The Rav is a paradigm of the synthesis of Jewish and Western Culture, but he nowhere prescribes this move or urges its legitimacy. The Rav constructs his thought within the categories of Western culture, but nowhere explicitly assigns a specific role to this culture.

R. Twersky's and Prof. Blidstein's words ring true, especially with regard to philosophy and literature. Still, aided, as we shall see, by R. Twersky himself, I will try to piece together some rationales for the Rav's assessment of *madda*.

The relatively easy cases are science, economics, political science, psychology and sociology. Let me here mix together "Lonely Man of Faith," "Confrontation," and *Five Addresses*. The Jew has a dual role: *ger* and *toshav*—a stranger and yet a citizen. As human beings, as part of the human community, as *toshavim*, we face certain problems in common with everyone else—problems that confront us regardless of our religious or ethnic identity, problems that arise not because of our identity as Jews, but because of our identity as humans. There are problems of disease, problems of poverty, problems of social disorder. Adam the First is not a Jew, and he has no religion yet. But his work of harnessing nature to try to satisfy human needs and solve everyday problems of living is for the Rav a *melekhet ha-kodesh* (whatever Adam the First's motives) because Adam the First is promoting human dignity. Here is an elegant paraphrase of the Rav's view by R. Shubert Spero:

> Since man is a moral agent, has been given responsibility to help others, to conserve value, to preserve life, to eradicate evil, he is morally obliged to seek the power and the knowledge, the means and instrumentation to achieve all this. If new sources of energy can eradicate poverty, if knowledge of genetic engineering promises to prevent certain diseases, then man is obligated to seek out this knowledge. As God is creative, so man is creative. (*Modern Judaism* 1986)

And it is not simply the physical sciences that enable people to live with dignity, but also economics, political science, and social

science generally. We are obligated to better this world by mar-
shalling all the secular resources at our disposal. The value of secular culture in these areas is not a *hora'at sha'ah*. It is built into the very
nature of the world, a place that is full of suffering, full of evil, full
of need. Technology, economics, political science, and social science
are not accommodations to the times. They are warriors in a battle
that Halakhah mandates and are part and parcel of the human condition since Creation. The mandate is in the Bible itself: "*ve-
khivshuha*, conquer it [the earth]" (Gen. 1:28). This doesn't mean that
every Jew has to be a doctor, psychologist, economist, or public ser-
vant. It does mean that every Jew must appreciate those who toil in
these fields, and must understand that without general knowledge
there would be no society. "I hardly believe that any responsible
man of faith, who is verily interested in the destiny of his community and wants to see it thriving and vibrant, would recommend
now the philosophy of *contemptus saeculi*."

Some call this a *be-diavad* justification, or characterize it as
"merely pragmatic." I say in reply that you may as well proclaim
that doctors who become doctors so they can save lives have but a
be-diavad rationale and a "merely pragmatic" justification. The problems that Adam the First strives to conquer are built into the fabric
of existence. The imperative that we deal with them is therefore a *le-
khatehilah*; and it is profoundly moral, not pragmatic.

To this we may add the obvious—that the study of sciences, especially the natural sciences, impresses us with the greatness of the
creator, enabling us to fulfill the *mitzvot* of *yediat Hashem* and *ahavat
Hashem*.

Now we come to the hard cases—philosophy and literature. What
value did the Rav see in these? In the *Tradition* tribute, R. Twersky
captures one possible line of thought:

> One utilizes contemporary philosophical terminology and phenom-
> enology. . . but one's goal is the same as that of the great thinkers of
> previous generations: to penetrate to the inner core of Torah, to ex-
> pound its essential beliefs. . . to understand the dynamics of Torah
> *she-be'al peh* and hence to deepen one's comprehension and intensify
> one's experience. This endeavor is not extraneous to Torah, not in-
> dependent of halacha, but is an integral, indispensable part of it.

What is said here is that the Rav was unapologetic because he thought that *madda* sources are ways of understanding and elucidating what lies in Torah itself. They are tools—not only for, say, understanding the laws of *Kil`ayim* (as he states in *Halakhic Man*), but for formulating a world view. So, if Martin Buber's philosophy of "I and Thou" would create a framework within which the Rav could explicate the notion of community, then he applied it. If in *Halakhic Man* he credits some of his discussions about *teshuvah* and time to the philosopher Max Scheler, it is because he thought Max Scheler could help him understand *gemarot* and the Rambam. If in his *teshuvah derashot* he quoted William James, it was because he felt that the sublime experience of sensing God's presence, the "reality of the unseen" in James's words, was a critical element missing in the religious experience of contemporary Orthodoxy. There is nothing to say beyond that—study of general culture requires no (further) justification because it provides a deeper grasp of Torah.

If you disagree that integrating general culture into *mahashavah* has this effect, try the following experiment. Take an essay by the Rav. Expunge all of the places where he is drawing upon general culture. Slice out mercilessly the parts that reflect Scheler, Brunner, Kierkegaard, Buber, Barth, Cohen—the whole lot of them. Then see what is left. No notion of dialectic, no comparison between halakhic man and scientific man, no "I-Thou" vs. "I-It," no sense of "the absurd," no relation between *teshuvah* and time. Compare this expunged version to the original. Which is better, more powerful, more incisive? Would the Rav have stood out to the same degree as a major thinker were he to have buried these ideas? The questions are of course rhetorical. Secular studies enhance *mahashavah*, and this is justification enough. Further—and admittedly this is my own speculative construction of an argument he might have endorsed— it is a very short step from saying that secular studies have value to him because they enhance our understanding of the Torah's world view, to saying that they have value in themselves. For truth and insight are good things to have, things God would want people to own no matter what their religious orientation.

The Rav also believed that philosophy is part of religious experience. A complaint that he launches against some of his students (in a very valuable talk that R. Rakeffet has produced in his book *The Rav*), is that they are religiously immature. Why? Because they are lacking in religious experience. Experience and philosophy go hand in hand in the Rav's thought. Philosophy is a means of deepening one's own understanding of what one is doing as a *ma'amin*, what one is doing as a *shomer mitzvot*, what one is doing as an *osek ba-Torah*, whether as teacher or disciple. The Rav's emphasis in doing philosophy was phenomenological, which is to say that he focused on explaining the inner person and not on discovering an outer, in truth unknowable metaphysical world. For this reason, if one studies philosophy (it is crucial to add: whether Jewish or general), one's religious experience and sensitivity to religion's inner core are heightened. The Rav always held that Yahadut has two components—intellectual and experiential. Philosophy was not only—and in some sense not even primarily—part of the intellectual component; it was also part of the experiential one.

What is important, furthermore, is not just having experience, but communicating it. It is critical to convey one's experiences to secular people in language that they understand. "Since Majestic Man is in need of a transcendental experience in order to strengthen his cultural edifice, it is the duty of the Man of Faith to provide him with some component parts of this experience." The Rav may have very well seen that, too, as part of his mandate when he took on the substantial commitment to translate "faith" into what he calls the cultural vernacular. If nothing else, the act of translation will aid the translator in the act of self-understanding.

I close with a description from the Rav's writings that perhaps is—after all—a description of himself. It is not put forth autobiographically, but it occurs to me that it is a fine depiction of the man.

In "Majesty and Humility," the Rav deals with the *pasuk*, "*Va-yitzer Hashem Elokim et ha-Adam afar min ha-adamah*, God created Adam from the dust of the earth" (Gen. 2:7). Rashi has two explanations of where this *adamah* came from. The first *lashon* in Rashi is "*tzavar afaro mi-kol ha-adamah, me-arba ruhos*," he took the dust from all over the Universe. "*Davar Aher, natal afaro mi-makom she-ne`emar 'mizbah adamah ta'aseh li'*"—the other *lashon* is that he took the dust from a specific place, namely the place of the *mizbeah*.

The Rav says that these two *leshonot* in Rashi, the *lashon* of *arba ruhot* and the *lashon* of *mizbah adamah*, represent two aspects of the human being. On the one hand, the human being is cosmic, *me-arba ruhot*. He is cosmic not only through his emotional or experiential involvement with the universe, but also through his intellectual involvement. His intellectual curiosity is of cosmic, universal dimensions. He wants to know about things both near and far.

Thus, man wants to roam across the cosmos. And yet, the Rav says, the traveler out to conquer infinity will surely return home. Each person is created from and attached to a single spot of origin, a spot that works as a powerful magnet to bring him home no matter how far he has traveled. The Rav quotes Robert Louis Stevenson: "Home is the sailor, home from the sea, and the hunter home from the hill."

In "Lonely Man of Faith," the Rav takes human nature, which is after all created by God, to in some way validate activities of human beings that express that nature. Perhaps we should say, therefore, that man's cosmic interests to a degree validate the Rav's own search for broad horizons. More importantly, though, it strikes me that this image of the man who is cosmic, who roams all over the universe because of his intellectual and experiential curiosity, but then returns to his spot of origin—to the world of Brisk, the world of Torah, the world of *emunah*, the world of *berit*, the world of all the fundamentals—is an apt description of this extraordinary figure.

Yehi zikhro barukh.

The Rav and the Chief Rabbinate of Israel

Charles Weinberg

I have been invited to write about a specific chapter in the life of our revered and beloved *rebbe*, the Rav. I do so with a great deal of humility and I ask, before I begin, that he will forgive me if something I say may be offensive. I will write only what I heard directly from him and not through a third party. This is a chapter that deals with the Rav, and the invitation from Israel that he make himself available for the chief rabbinate of Israel.

Before I begin with the subject material, I would like, in a few words, to describe the Rav's personal attitude and profound feelings about Eretz Yisrael.

In an address of the Rav to the Rabbinical Alumni of Yeshiva he said:

There is a great difference between historical dynamics and covenantal destiny. In historical dynamics, one event follows another. History is viewed as mechanical. The past is responsible for the present. However, the covenantal event is sustained by the covenantal promise. The future is responsible for the present. For example, the experience of the land of Israel is a covenantal one. It cannot be explained in terms of historical dynamics. The cause of Eretz Yisrael is a fulfillment of a promise. The covenant has created a new concept—destiny. What determines the historical experience of the Jew is not the point of departure, but rather, the destination of Klal Yisrael.

I was blessed by God to have served in the rabbinate for twenty-six years in the Boston area, allowing me to develop a very close

Rabbi Charles Weinberg served as spiritual leader of Congregation Beth Israel in Malden, MA from 1949–1976. He is a past national president of the Rabbinical Council of America.

and exciting relationship with the Rav. Thousands of his students will remember him as a participant in their lives. His love inspired my personal and public life, his courage and wisdom became the destiny of my family and my community activities.

The Rav and his dear wife, Tonya, had a summer home in Cape Cod. I visited with them a few times every summer. In 1960, the subject of the chief rabbinate of Israel was discussed. The Rav was encouraged by numerous leaders in Israel to make himself available as a candidate.

There were two psychological blocks that made him hesitate. One was the fact that he was a candidate for the chief rabbinate of Tel Aviv in the 1930s. However, the Mizrachi political leadership did not support him. The fact that the chief rabbinate was tied into politics was abhorred by him and discouraged him from any further consideration.

But in a number of discussions that summer, I got the impression that perhaps if he would not be just another candidate, he might consider it. I asked him, "If I would go to Israel and meet with numerous leaders, and find that there would not be another candidate, would you consider it?" He responded with a shy smile, at which time I indicated my readiness to fly to Israel.

Within ten days I was on my way, having telephoned a friend and asked him to prepare meetings for me with certain rabbinic and political leaders. Amongst them I met with Prime Minister David Ben Gurion, Foreign Minister Golda Meir, Yakov Herzog— advisor to Ben Gurion, Minister of the Interior Moshe Shapiro, Yitzchak Rafael, HaRav Maimon, Sephardic Chief Rabbi Yitzchak Nissim, HaRav Pesach Zvi Frank and others. Most of those I spoke to were very excited about the possibility of the Rav becoming Chief Rabbi.

David Ben Gurion, who met with the Rav twice, once in New York and once in Boston, had a very high regard for the Rav. He said, "I see in Rabbi Soloveitchik a great force that could also reach out to the secular Jews."

While Golda Meir questioned whether there was a need for the chief rabbinate, HaRav Maimon, one of the eminent leaders of Mizrachi said, "Even though I was opposed to him when he was a candidate in Tel Aviv, now I am for him." Similarly, HaRav Pesach Zvi Frank said, "Tell the Rav that my hand holds and supports his hand."

On the other side, there were a few who simply encouraged an unknown individual from Petach Tikvah to seek a court order to postpone elections for a year.

Yakov Herzog, who was senior advisor to Ben Gurion and who was a *talmid chakham* reacted with excitement about the Rav and said, "He is the only one who could possibly give a spiritual impulse to the entire community, even the secular."

Chief Rabbi Yitzchak Nissim said, "If the Gaon HaRav Soloveitchik will become Chief Rabbi of Israel, there will be only one Chief Rabbi, for he is head and shoulders above everyone else." He repeated his statement to HaRav Zvi Yehuda Kook, head of Yeshivat Mercaz HaRav, in the presence of a large number of yeshiva students. A number of *rabbanim* and media people sought me out and expressed excitement at the possibility of Rabbi Soloveitchik becoming Chief Rabbi.

Encouraged by what the majority said, I presented to the Rav a document that I wrote on how to set up the structure of the chief rabbi's office. This I did in order free him from spending too much time with visiting delegations, both from Israel and the Diaspora. I wanted to free him to impact the country with his brilliance in learning Torah and secular subjects.

The day following my return to Boston I drove out to the Cape so that the Rav and his wife could hear my impressions. The Rav was getting more excited as I went on, but every once in a while his wife said, "What do you want, Rabbi Weinberg—do you want him to suffer aggravation that may shorten his life? You know what they will do to him there."

She was, of course, alluding to certain elements in the *haredi* community, including some family members.

The Rav himself, as excited as he was, expressed some reservations because of the politics that imposes itself on the rabbinate. He said that the official garments of the *kohanim* were without cuffs, so that the priests will not collect any dust or dirt. The *rabbanim* of Israel should be careful not to allow a collection of political dust or dirt to destroy the sanctity they should embody.

A few weeks later the Rav showed me an article that appeared in *Hatzofeh*. The headline was that Rabbi Velvel Soloveitchik left a will in which he told his nephew not to accept the post of Chief Rabbi of Israel.

The Rav smiled and said, "There is no such will."

"How do you know?" I asked.

The Rav answered, "The Brisker family does not write wills." He proceeded to tell me that when R. Chaim traveled and saw a cemetery, he ordered his group to distance itself a few blocks from the cemetery. In fact the philosophic position of the Rav was that death is the defeat of man.

I wish to conclude as I started: underscoring the Rav's profound love for Eretz Yisrael. In a major address at a Mizrachi convention in Atlantic City, the Rav said, "Ours is the only religion that is rooted in land." In letters that he sent to me after our *aliyah*, he wrote the street address followed by "EretzYisrael." In order that the postal service in the USA should know to what country the letter is going, he wrote on the side of the envelope: "Israel."

I am firmly convinced that he felt that Eretz Yisrael would indicate a stronger historic and religious connection. It would indicate the fulfillment of a covenantal promise underscoring the concept of destiny.

The '70s:
A Legacy of Many Perspectives

Seated next to Rabbi Soloveitchik is Rabbi Dr. Norman Lamm, President of Yeshiva University and Joseph Gruss, a major benefactor of the University. (Photo courtesy Yeshiva University.)

A Special *Zechut*: Serving as the Rav's *Shamosh*

Yosef Adler

Having been in the Rav's *shiur* for six years in the early '70s, at-tended his Tuesday night *shiur* at Moriah, *yahrzeit shiurim, kinus teshuva,* and Boston *yarchei kallah* for 12 years, and listened to tapes of hundreds of *shiurim* from the '50s, I join many of the Rav's *talmidim* in recognizing that the Rav was the greatest influence in my life. I thank G-d that I had the privilege of being a student of the Rav and I will forever be indebted to my father for my early expo-sure to him. I was a sophomore in high school when he brought me to the Mizrachi convention at the Lido Beach Hotel and I sat on a ra-diator to hear a *drashah* that was eventually published in *Chamesh Drashot.* Unless one personally attended the Rav's *shiur* one can not really appreciate his true brilliance and mastery as a *maggid shiur.* As *mara d'atra* of Congregation Rinat Yisrael in Teaneck and a teacher in yeshiva high schools for three decades I have delivered thousands of *shiurim* and invariably have found some *chiddush* of the Rav to share with my congregants and *talmidim* to illuminate the *sugya.*

However, I also had the good fortune of serving as the Rav's *shamosh* [attendant] for two years, 1975–76. Much of the time was occupied tending to the Rav's personal needs. He had a bad ulcer and could not eat the cafeteria food. Mrs. Feuerstein, a devoted friend in Boston, lovingly prepared meals which were shipped to me to prepare for the Rav. Drivers had to be arranged to bring him to and from LaGuardia Airport. One had to keep his appointment schedule and, most importantly, make sure that he had time to rest. Unfortunately, this meant saying 'no' to certain individuals who were always looking to spend time with the Rav. In this essay I will share with you an aspect of the Rav not recognized or appreciated

Rabbi Yosef Adler is Principal of the Torah Academy of Bergen County and Rabbi of Congregation Rinat Yisrael of Teaneck, NJ.

by all. That he was the greatest *maggid shiur* of our generation is acknowledged by all. But not everyone believes that the Rav was a *posek* as well. The Rav answered everyone's questions. I and hundreds of others who came to the Rav's apartment in the Morgenstern dormitory asked the Rav questions concerning *hilkhot Shabbat*, *aveilut* [mourning], *kashrut*, birth control, women saying *kaddish*, required height of *shul mechitzot* [partitions] and countless other areas of Jewish law and practice. He listened patiently and then offered his opinion. As chairman of the *halakhah* commission of the Rabbinical Council of America, the Rav helped formulate public policy on numerous issues.

But it was not only distinguished *rabbanim* or *talmidim* to whom the Rav gave of his time. A young girl from Bergen County had become motivated to live in accordance with Torah *u-mitzvot*. Her parents, however, were vehemently against her decision, and refused to *kasher* their kitchen or to adhere to any standards of *kashrut*. This girl was in a dilemma. I broached the subject with the Rav, who said that he wanted to speak with her. The time he gave and the sensitivity he exhibited were remarkable. The young girl, whose previous contact with the Rav had been limited to hearing his name being mentioned at an NCSY [National Conference of Synagogue Youth] convention, was awe-struck that this elderly scholar would be willing to listen to her personal problem.

There were numerous such episodes when, after delivering a three-hour *shiur* on Tuesday morning and having to prepare for his Moriah *shiur* that night, he spent hours in the afternoon with people in distress who sought his guidance.

There were some humorous episodes as well. On a Tuesday evening in October of 1975 I returned with the Rav to his apartment after his *shiur* in Moriah. As I was about to say good night he asked me to turn on the television. Quite surprised, I asked him what he would like to watch. He answered, "The World Series." As the Boston Red Sox were competing that year in baseball's championship series, the Rav felt the need to keep abreast so that he could engage his young grandchildren.

Meetings with Mr. Gruss were remarkable. The Rav had developed a wonderful relationship with Mr. Joseph S. Gruss, perhaps the greatest contributor to Jewish education in our history. The relationship was developed and cultivated by Dr. Tonya Soloveitchik, the Rav's wife. She was instrumental in convincing Mr. Gruss that supporting Jewish education is the most important philanthropic area he could enter. Whenever the Rav and Mr. Gruss were to meet, Mr. Gruss offered to come to the Rav's apartment. However, the Rav always declined, preferring to meet in Mr. Gruss' office instead. When I asked him why, he said, "If Mr. Gruss comes to me, I have to be a perfect gentleman as his host. If I go to him I can be far more aggressive in asking him to broaden his support for yeshiva education."

Acting as the perfect gentleman was a trait that always characterized the Rav. Every *Rosh Hashanah* and *Pesach*, it was the Rav who went to the fifth floor of Yeshiva's Furst Hall to wish Yeshiva President Dr. Samuel Belkin a *ketivah v'chatimah tovah* and a *chag kasher v'sameach* before Dr. Belkin would have a chance to come to him. He always called Rav Moshe Feinstein, Rav Shneur Kotler (and prior to that Rav Aharon Kotler) before a *Yom Tov* as well. He sent a handwritten *shanah tovah* card to anyone who took the trouble of sending him the standard printed greeting for the Jewish New Year.

On the few occasions when he ate in the cafeteria, the Rav would stand in line like everyone else despite the fact that most students thought he should be served first. During my years at Yeshiva, Rav Lessin was the *Mashgiach Ruchani* of RIETS. He was from Slobodka and preached to YU students as if he were still in Slobodka. Occasionally, he would come into *shiurim* to give an old-fashioned *schmuess* [a chat on ethics]. The *derekh eretz* [respect] that the Rav demonstrated for him was clear. Then, after Rav Lessin finished, the Rav translated and interpreted his words to make them more meaningful for students who did not understand the Yiddish.

I am certain other *talmidim* feel as I do that the Rav helped shape the person I have become, the career I have chosen, and the *hashkafat olam* I now embrace. For that, there are no adequate words to describe my appreciation. Instead, one episode will capture it all. On a Tuesday evening at Moriah a few weeks before *Pesach*, the Rav delivered a *shiur* on a Mordechai concerning the occasion when the day before *Pesach* is *Shabbat*. After raising several questions on the standard explanation of the Mordechai and proposing an original approach to alleviate those difficulties, the Rav concluded the *shiur* by saying, "For this I deserve a *l'chaim*."

The joy and ecstasy of sharing Torah with his *talmidim*—what a model for all to follow.

The Rav as a *Melamed*

Azarya Berzon

I was privileged to learn under Rabbi Joseph B. Soloveitchik for close to five years. Those were the five most special years of my life. During that period, the Rav was the focal point of my life. The preparation for *shiur*, the participation in the *shiur* itself, the reviewing of the *shiur*—all this took up more than just time—it was also a psychological and emotionally profound experience. During that time, I was trying to understand the Rav's way of thinking, how he would analyze a *sugya*, his *hashkafah* about the Jewish world and the world of Torah study. In general, my dream was to create a relationship with my *rebbe* that would sustain me throughout my life.

I would like to focus on three aspects of the Rav as a teacher, a *melamed*.

First, his clarity.

The Rav was and always viewed himself as a *melamed*. This role represented his very essence. Without doubt, he was a *melamed* par excellence. When I think about the many teachers that I had in both Jewish and secular studies, I can think of only one other professor who was in the same league as a pedagogue, but the Rav far exceeded him.

We the *talmidim* would prepare for the *shiur*, sometimes for long hours. Nevertheless, we would often walk into class confused about the *sugya*. A new *sugya* would baffle us; we were overwhelmed by new phenomena, new terms and concepts that were unfamiliar. It

Rabbi Azarya Berzon is the founder and head of Yeshivat Sha'arei Mevaseret Zion and its women's division, Michlelet Mevaseret Yerushalaim. He served on the rabbinic faculty at Yeshivat Ma'aleh Adumim for three years and on the staff of Yeshivat Shaalvim for 10 years.

was difficult to put the pieces of the *sugya* into perspective. The Rav was amazing at taking the *Gemara* and clarifying it. It was a powerful experience to watch the Master reveal the deeper meaning of the *sugya* in front of one's very eyes.

When I first joined the *shiur*, the Rav was teaching tractate *Hulin*. It was very difficult for me. The *sugya* was about *melika b'chatos ha'of*, a complex topic from the world of *kadshim*. I had just returned from three years of learning in Israel. My English was not up to par as far as the Rav's was concerned. I also had trouble understanding his German accent. The style and approach were unlike anything I had been exposed to. I had never been in a *shiur* where the *rebbe* expected his students to analyze the various opinions of the *Tannaim* in a *Mishnah* or a dispute amongst the *Amoraim* in the *Gemara* conceptually, i.e. to come up with the underlying *lomdus* that would explain the root of the halakhic issue. The Rav would sometimes use words that were five syllables long. A close friend of mine was eager to ask a question, and the Rav responded, "Would you quell your curiosity for just one moment!" These were the elegant statements that used to come out of his mouth just in passing. It was difficult for me to be in a *shiur* made up of more than a hundred brilliant students who were far more used to the Rav's *derekh* than I was; I was used to being amongst the top *talmidim*, but all of a sudden I was almost a nonentity. It took me some six months to adjust to the *shiur*, but as a result my learning changed for the rest of my life.

By the time I had completed my third year in the *shiur* I had achieved seniority rights and was able to sit literally next to the Rav at his table. It was exciting to watch the Rav. I would watch his forehead, his hands, and his legs while he was teaching; his legs used to move under the table in sync with the rest of his body. Every ounce of energy and every part of his intellect and his body was involved in the learning. It was *khol atzmosei tomarna* ["all my bones shall say," Psalm 35.10], the physical and intellectual aspects of the Rav's teaching integrated to form one harmonious entity which was alive and vibrant. Often I wondered what the Rav's performance in *shiur* would look like if played back on a video screen with background musical attachment.

My father *zt"l* attended the Rav's Tuesday night *shiur* in the Moriah synagogue on the West Side of Manhattan. He tried not to miss the *shiur* as he always enjoyed it immensely. Once my father approached the Rav at the end of the *shiur* and said,

"*Rebbe*, I am afraid I might not get *s'khar* (Divine reward) for attending your *shiur*."

The Rav looked at him and said with surprise, "What do you mean, Rabbi Berzon?"

My father explained, "*Rebbe*, there are many things that I enjoy doing. I could go to a movie or theater or the opera. But I want to attend your *shiur* because I get physical pleasure from your *shiur*."

The Rav responded in Yiddish, "That's exactly what it means to study Torah *li'shmah*!" [for its own sake].

I learned from this episode that there is a level of Torah *li'shmah* in which even the physical body becomes part of the experience of Torah learning and derives pleasure from the study of Torah. This was something we felt as his *talmidim*. The Rav's ability to put the pieces of the puzzle together and to make a *sugya* suddenly radiate light was a most uplifting experience.

The second aspect I want to discuss is the Rav's originality and creativity.

The Rav could not tolerate anything that was old or stale, even if he himself had said it. When a brilliant student once commented while the Rav was trying to work out *p'shat*, "*Rebbe*, this is what you said when we learned this *sugya* five years ago…," the Rav didn't allow the *talmid* to conclude his sentence. Instead he slammed his hand on his desk and exclaimed, "Forget about what I said five years ago! Pay attention to what I am saying now!"

The Rav always taught us that just as God is unique as the Creator, man too must be unique. He must be original. In his writings and essays the Rav went to great lengths to emphasize the centrality and significance of being original, especially in Torah learning.

Rabbi Dovid Dunner, who attended the Rav's *shiur*, had previously studied for seven years at the Brisk Yeshiva in Israel with Rabbi Berel Soloveitchik, *zt"l*. We once asked him after *shiur* to compare the Rav to his first cousin, Rav Berel of Yerushalayim. He responded, "Your *rebbe*, the Rav, is like a *ma'ayan* (spring), whereas my *rebbe*, Rav Berel, is like a *nahar* (river). The role of the *nahar* is to carry what it heard from previous generations to the next generation. My *rebbe* transmitted the Torah of Reb Chaim and Reb Velvel. Your *rebbe*, however, is the *ma'ayan*; he is truly an original thinker. All his Torah is his own."

The third element I would like to mention is what our sages call *mora rabbo*.

Oursages tell us, *z'rok mora ba'talmidim*, a *rebbe* should instill in his students a certain measure of fear and awe. Sitting at the Rav's feet as a *talmid* was quite a challenge. One could not participate in the *shiur* with a laid-back attitude. The students felt pressured and tense, and the Rav generated that tension. First and foremost, he was such an intellectual giant, and one had to match up to his standards; secondly, one was well aware of the fact that he was sitting amongst the finest minds of the yeshiva at that time, and had to measure up to them.

The Rav would call on students to read the *Gemara*; since you never knew whose name the Rav would call, you always had to be on your toes. If you did not read properly, the Rav would assume you were not prepared and would lace into you. If you did not review the previous *shiur*, or prepare for the next one, the Rav might call on you and he could tell that you did not prepare properly, so the pressure was constant.

As a *talmid* in the *shiur*, you had to learn when and how to ask a question. A student who was new and did not yet know the ropes was well advised not to ask a question. You had to achieve a certain level of Torah knowledge and master the Rav's *derekh ha'limud* to a serious degree before you could expect that your question would enhance the process of Torah learning. For most of us, it would take years of learning in the *shiur* before we were ready to ask a question or offer an answer to the Rav's question which would advance the goal of the *shiur*. The Rav's *derekh* was based on critical analysis, on precise categorizations, and on defining the underlying fundamental concepts of the *Halakhah*. The Rav demanded of his students that they read every word on the *daf* [page of] *Gemara* and in the *Rishonim* carefully, always wondering "What's the *chiddush*?" The Rav once borrowed a *Gemara* from a student, and when he noticed that certain words on the page were underlined, he exclaimed, "If it was my *Gemara*, I'd have to underline every word on the page!"

When I was in Boston for the Rav's summer *shiurim* (groups of students rented apartments in or around Brookline to participate in the Rav's daily *shiur* at the Maimonides School), we were studying a complex *sugya* in *Taharot*. I asked a question and the Rav cut me off in the middle and said, "Berzon, you just listen. Don't ask any questions."

The summer *shiurim* were very special, and the ambiance was much different from that in New York. While the Rav was in New

York—during the three days that he delivered his *shiurim* to us as well as the *shiur* in Moriah—he was extremely busy. People used to pounce upon him with all sorts of questions, personal or communal. But some of us were blessed with the opportunity to be with the Rav in Boston in the summer and to hear *shiur* from the Rav four times a week outside on the porch of the Maimonides School. The Rav did not wear a tie; the collar button of his shirt was open; he put on a straw hat when he left. He was calm. It was a different atmosphere from the one we were used to at Yeshiva. For us as students, to have those few rare occasions to get to know the Rav on a personal level was a special experience. For many of us, the most memorable part of the summer in Boston was *Tishah B'av*, when we would listen to the Rav's reading and explanations of the *Kinot* for eight consecutive hours.

On more than one occasion I had the privilege to be the Rav's driver. On Thursday afternoon after a busy work week the Rav returned to Boston on the shuttle from LaGuardia Airport. My claim to this honor of driving the Rav was based on the fact that I was going to Queens anyway (I was taking courses at Queens College). Once the Rav asked me what I was studying in college. When I told him I was taking philosophy, he responded, "The science of *chakiros* [investigations; searching]." As a student of the *derekh ha'chakiros* I appreciated the Rav's precise definition of the discipline of philosophy. When we got off the Harlem River Drive and approached the bridge, the Rav insisted on paying the seventy-five cent toll over the Tri-Borough Bridge despite my objections that I was driving to Queens anyway.

When I got engaged, I brought my fiancée to meet the Rav. Despite the fact that the Chief Rabbi of Israel was waiting outside, the Rav spent time with us. He was charming. When we left, my wife commented that the Rav was like a *zady* [grandfather]. She couldn't believe that this was the man whom I feared so much.

When the time for our wedding came, I asked the Rav to officiate. He agreed to come in for the wedding. Afterward, my father sent two checks to the Rav as a thank-you for officiating, one for the Rav and one as a contribution to the Maimonides School in Boston. When the checks were returned from the bank, both were cashed in the name of Maimonides. The Rav did not take any of the money for himself.

This is an aspect of the Rav that is not well known. The Rav was a great *ba'al tzedakah* [giver of charity]. On a bus trip from Boston to New York, I met two students from the Lakewood Yeshiva. To start a conversation I asked them, "What brought you to Boston?" They told me that they volunteered to go on a fundraising trip between school terms. When I asked them, "How did it go?" they responded, "Not too well, except for one nice check that we received." I asked if they would share with me the details behind that one success story.

They began telling me that they went to the Twersky home to see the Rav. Rabbi Twersky *zt"l* answered the door and told them that the Rav was resting and that he couldn't be disturbed. But as they were leaving, a voice from upstairs called, "Who's there?" Rabbi Twersky answered, "Two students from Lakewood Yeshiva." The Rav said, "Let them stay!" He came downstairs to ask how his friend Rabbi Shneur Kotler was doing. The *talmidim* left the house with the best check they picked up in the city of Boston.

How the Rav Changed My Spiritual Life

Aharon Bina

In August 1970, my wife Malke and I were married in Baltimore. Shortly thereafter, we set off for New York to allow her to pursue her studies in Yeshiva University's Bernard Revel Graduate School. We moved to the Washington Heights neighborhood where I felt stranded. I had learned in Ponovez for over a decade and was looking for a *beit midrash* to continue my studies. I began by learning in the Rabbi Moshe Feinstein *zt"l Kollel*, headed by Rav David Feinstein.

A short while later I decided to try Rabbi Yosef Dov Soloveitchik's *zt"l shiur* and *Kollel*. The problem was that in order to be accepted one had to either have been enrolled in Yeshiva College or possess an accredited undergraduate degree. I was very fortunate that Yeshiva's president at the time, Rabbi Dr. Shmuel Belkin *zt"l*, was a student of my grandfather in Slonim before the Holocaust. Dr. Belkin arranged for me to meet with one of the university's vice-presidents. When he refused to allow me to learn at Yeshiva, an argument ensued between the two administrators in my presence. As president, Rabbi Dr. Belkin *zt"l* pulled rank and sent me to the Rav's apartment for an interview. The Rav knew my father and had tremendous respect for him. Yet, more importantly, he also was a close friend of my uncle, Rabbi Moshe Cohen, the principal of the Maimonides School in Boston. After a successful interview, the Rav accepted me into the RIETS *Kollel* headed by his son-in-law, Rabbi Aharon Lichtenstein *shlit"a*.

It took me a while to get my bearings in the Rav's *shiur*. Even after I became acclimated to the Rav's high level of English, I was very disheartened. The Rav's style differed greatly from what I had been accustomed to in Ponovez. I had heard that the Rav delivered a

---

Rabbi Aharon Bina is *Rosh HaYeshiva* of Yeshivat Netiv Aryeh in the Old City of Jerusalem.

p'shat shiur focusing on the fundamental points of the Talmud and incorporating primary *Rishonim* like Rashi, Tosafot, and the Rambam. I had spent more than a decade learning at what the Rav himself described as the best yeshiva in the world. I had therefore expected that once I was able to overcome the hurdle of understanding the Rav's English, the *shiur* would be rudimentary. Instead, I was surprised. With unmatched analyses, the Rav, on a daily basis, showed me how little I understood. With my *chavruta* [study partner] I prepared for the *shiur* for hours, hoping that maybe this time we would be able to anticipate what the Rav would say in the following day's *shiur*. We were rarely successful. To this day, I still regret the years spent learning complicated *Acharonim* instead of focusing on what was truly important: the core principles and relevant details of the Talmud. In a word, clarity of *sugyot* was where the genius of the Rav lay. All of the fancy *seforim* are meaningless unless one has a firm grasp on the language of the *Gemara*.

Although the learning was different from his style, the Rav *zt"l* had great respect for the Ponovez Yeshiva. On several occasions the Rav *zt"l* told me how privileged I was to have learned under Rav Shmuel Rozovsky *zt"l*, the great *Rosh Yeshiva* of Ponovez. It is true that Rav Shmuel *zt"l*, the greatest *Rosh Yeshiva* of my generation, had a greater command of *Gemara* and *Rishonim* than the Rav. As great a *lamdan* as Rav Shmuel was, the Rav's ability to analyze and convey was unparalleled. In addition, the Rav's *shiur* brought the Torah to life. We were able to feel the distress of a complex question on the *Gemara*, as well as the tension of an argument between the Rambam, the Ravad, and Rashi. I cannot describe the excitement we felt upon hearing the Rav's explanations which brought clarity to the entire *sugya*. The three-hour *shiur* felt like five minutes. Rav Shmuel's *shiur* was known as the "best show in town" but the Rav's was the greatest on Earth.

Moreover, I have no doubt that the Rav's teaching ability surpassed that of his illustrious grandfather, Rav Chaim *zt"l*. Although Rav Chaim *zt"l* created the Brisker method of Talmudic learning, the Rav *zt"l* developed and expanded upon it. The Rav's brilliant use of *Halakhah* and *Aggadah* during his famous *yahrtzeit drashot* in memory of his father and his great contributions to areas of *machshavah* [thought; philosophy] prove without a doubt that his ability to convey teachings was unrivaled by anyone before him and unmatched ever since.

During my stay at Yeshiva, eighty students attended the Rav's *shiur*. I would venture to say that about half of them truly understood the *shiur* while the others were onlookers content to boast that they had the *zechut* to attend the *shiur* of such a giant. The most dedicated students in the *shiur* become some of today's greatest scholars and leaders. The list includes Rabbis Hershel Billet, Menachem Genack, Aharon Kahn, Aharon Lichtenstein, Heshy Reichman, Hershel Schachter, Michel Zalman Shurkin, and Mordechai Willig. What I believe separates this group from the rest of the Rav's cadre of students is their ability to implement the most crucial element of the Rav's learning: his diligence. I recall watching these students completely immersed in their learning during *seder*. Listening to the Rav's *shiur* and being part of this incredible *Kollel* changed my life forever.

Although the Rav was known to raise his voice during *shiur*, it is important to point out how caring and warmhearted he was. He was often stopped on his way to the cafeteria by poor people seeking his counsel. No matter how unkempt they may have appeared, the Rav spoke to them with great warmth and love.

The greatest compassion and affection, however, was reserved for his family. The Rav's grandchildren learned in Yeshivat Netiv Meir, established by my father, at a time when overseas phone calls were a rarity. Nevertheless, wishing to keep his grandchildren up-to-date on the sports news, he would frequently send them telegrams with the latest scores. In this way, the Rav *zt"l* was a regular grandfather, always looking to spoil his grandchildren. Furthermore, he personified the Litvaks of the pre-Holocaust era whose essence was to make a *mitzvah* of being a *mentsch* and showing appreciation to others. In a letter to my father, the Rav wrote that since my father was educating his grandchildren, he wanted to help support my father's yeshiva. The Rav therefore directed members of the Boston community to send donations to my father's yeshiva.

I must admit that I am troubled by the fact that the Rav *zt"l* is considered one of the leaders of Religious Zionism yet chose to live in America. Of course, as President of Mizrachi he gave stature to Religious Zionism as a Torah movement, and his *Kol Dodi Dofek*, which for many years was required reading in Religious Zionist schools in Israel, inspired many to understand the religious significance of the establishment of the State. Although I subscribe to Ben Gurion's definition—a Zionist is one who lives in Israel, not one who talks about Israel—the Rav felt he was sorely needed in America.

With regard to American Jewry, the Rav was a realist. He was involved in aiding all sections of the Jewish community, financially and spiritually, while fully realizing that certain groups would never accept him. It hurts me greatly to see that while many within the *haredi* world are beginning to accept the Rav's Torah, they still refer to him in less than respectful terms. I recall visiting a relative whom my wife and I frequently went to for *Shabbat* and whose apartment was owned by a famous *Rebbe* who lived upstairs. One Friday night, after *Maariv*, the *Rebbe* asked me in Yiddish where I was learning. When I answered proudly that I attended the Rav's *shiur*, he began to curse the Rav in front of the large crowd which surrounded the *Rebbe*. Soon after, however, he called me over and quietly asked me if I could get him notes of the Rav's *shiurim*. I was so incensed by the way he publicly ridiculed the Rav that I refused. Whether due to jealousy or a number of other factors, this person continues to launch assaults on one of the last generation's greatest Jewish leaders.

There is no question that today's American Jewish community owes its *Yiddishkeit* and its institutions to Rav Aharon Kotler *zt"l*, Rav Moshe Feinstein *zt"l* and, of course, the Rav *zt"l*. Yeshiva University is one of the largest Torah centers today. This is greatly due to the Rav's impact there. Without Yeshiva, the concept of a professional who could also be a *talmid chacham* and *yarei shamayim* [G-d fearing] would still be a whimsical dream. As this model continues to become more common even among the *haredi* circles in America, it becomes more evident that the Rav *zt"l* had a powerful influence on their communities, despite their resistance. Rav Shlomo Zalman Auerbach *zt"l* once said to me that he does not understand why in Jerusalem so many learn in *kollel* and do not follow the teachings found in Tractate *Kidushin* (29a) that require a Jew to teach his son a trade. The Rav was the first to provide a solution for this in America. Through his leadership at Yeshiva and in his various other capacities as leader, Orthodoxy in America continues to grow to this day.

Understanding the Rav's "Philosophy"

Eugene B. Borowitz

Ever since the famous—notorious?—article by David Singer and Moshe Sokol about the Rav's thinking and the radical difference between his first substantial article, *Ish Hahalakhah*, and his last, lengthy paper, *Uvikashtem Misham*, there has been a substantial difference of opinion of how to understand the integrity of thought behind two such radically different papers. In method, tone and concern they seem quite contrary to one another and the perplexity can be extended to certain aspects of his other major writings.

I should like to suggest, as a working hypothesis for further research, a solution to this issue. Of course, the easiest way to see if my ideas or those of any other student of the Rav's thought are faithful to his thinking would be to compare them with all the Rav's writings. Unfortunately for those qualified to examine such an archive (and for all those who might be influenced by what was found there), we do not have a full bibliography of the manuscripts he left behind him. Until access to all of his as yet unpublished writing is made available, one cannot hope to be even reasonably sure that one properly understands so capacious a mind as his.

In my own case, there is a further difficulty in my daring to offer even a tentative resolution of so substantial a problem: I was not a student of the Rav and therefore cannot claim that in the course of my discipleship, I gained some special insight into his thinking which now prompts this proposal. While my "bona-fides" for writ-

Dr. Eugene B. Borowitz is Distinguished University Professor, Sigmund L. Falk Distinguished Professor of Education and Jewish Religious Thought, Hebrew Union College-Jewish Institute of Religion, New York. His most recent academic book is *The Talmud's Theological Language-Game, a Philosophical Discourse Analysis* (SUNY Press, 2006).

ing on this topic are not substantial, please allow me to give some idea of why I believe that my doing so would have been acceptable to the Rav, which is certainly not to suggest that he would agree with the substance of my suggestion.

Here is a brief account of my encounters with the Rav. While visiting my friend Steven S. Schwarzschild, *zt"l*, in Lynn, MA, in the latter part of '50s, I went with him to a meeting of the Massachusetts Board of Rabbis and heard a lecture to that group by the Rav. A few years later, when I heard that the Rav was giving a Federation sponsored course to a small group of New York area rabbis, I tried to discover what its content was. However the rabbis had been asked not to discuss that so I could only get a few hints about his thinking. Putting these in the context of the theological discussions of that time, I suggested in an article in *Commentary* that the Rav was a Barthian. When, a few years later, I was named as the Reform representative to a Jewish Education Committee of New York supervisory committee for a generous gift of Joseph Gruss, I had the joy of serving with the Rav at the committee's quarterly meeting for a number of years. At the first session, when I introduced myself to him, he teased me and with a smile said, "So you think I am a Barthian." Having by that time learned more about his thinking, I was properly embarrassed by my early error and muttered something about not having had more than a few hints to go on. In 1966 *Judaism* published my article "The Typological Theology of Rabbi Joseph Baer Soloveitchik," the first full-scale treatment in English of his thought. The Rav never commented on that one and I simply note that when we occasionally crossed paths, he was unfailingly cordial to me. All that somehow convinced me that, though I was not an intellectual *ben bayit*, I was somehow an acceptable student of his thought. And it is in that spirit that I venture this speculation about what fundamentally drives his major essays in all their diversity.

Let us begin with what I think is the fundamental misunderstanding of his purpose in writing "*Halakhic Man*." I do not mean by that to deny in any way that the Rav was fully committed to the classical *halakhah*. Any suggestion that something like that might be the case completely falsifies the Rav's wholehearted dedication to the centrality of the Law in Judaism. Nonetheless, many of his interpreters and students besieged by the way non-Orthodox interpretations of Judaism seemed to be convincing people that full-scale halakhic observance was not mandated in the modern world, were thrilled that the Rav had mounted a major defense of the *halakhah*. The essay appeared to make an irrefutable case that the *halakhah* needed to be central to one's existence if one seriously wanted to call oneself a pious Jew. It was therefore a major counter-argument to the appeal of the modernist shrinkers of Jewish obligation, the Reform, Conservative, and other Americanizing Jews.

It is this reading of "*Halakhic Man*" that makes "*Uvikashtem Misham*" so troubling an aspect of the Rav's thought. This last, lengthy, searching, highly personal, emotionally oriented statement hardly seems like the kind of religious statement a halakhic man could make. While it has some references to law and obligation, its major concern is the human situation, particularly in times of deep personal anguish. Where halakhic man continually has reference to what the Law requires and what might be driving that obedience, the passionate believer of the later essay is more concerned with feelings and what one's belief leads one to in times of stress and suffering. In short, if you take "*Halakhic Man*" to be a major defense of Orthodoxy and its central affirmation, then you do not know what to do with "*Uvikashtem Misham*." And I shall be so bold as to hypothesize that this perception is probably the reason why, though it is one of the few searching, lengthy statements of the Rav's in print, it remains, nearly 30 years after its publication, untranslated.

I do not think it is forcing the issue to suggest that the Rav surely had a sense of the unity behind his works and, though he certainly operated on an intellectual level well beyond ours, it is an act of faithfulness to his teaching to seek to elucidate that integrity as best we can. For myself that begins with reading "*Halakhic Man*" somewhat differently from has been done heretofore, but not in any way to minimize its glorification of the *halakhah*. Rather, I wish to call attention to the means by which the *halakhah* is adulated. The Rav is at pains to show how one whose life is built on the Law and legal thinking, is extraordinarily rationalistic. That is, following the Law requires the cognitive discrimination of what ruling specifically applies to a given situation; should there be no exact law covering the case, an analogical rule must be educed to yield the relevant *halakhah*; should a case arise for which no analogy suggests itself, Halakhic Man must exercise his rational creativity in order to determine his duty in this previously unanticipated situation; and, in general, when the Law suffuses one's life, one has a matrix for responding to the universe in all its wonder. What the Rav is subtly but effectively pointing out in the sub-text of his great essay is that one doesn't need to abandon the Law to be that modern ideal, a rationalist. (Note, please, that the specific sense of that term is the one given it by Hermann Cohen, whose epistemology was the subject of the Rav's doctoral dissertation, and whose usage supplied the rationale for most non-Orthodox Jews.)

I am suggesting that the Rav had a double purpose in writing *Halakhic Man*. He not only wanted to glorify the life of the Law but to quietly write a polemic against those who thought they needed to desert traditional Judaism in order to be fully rational. And years later, when the intellectual climate changed and the passion for rationalism gave way to the intense personalism of existentialism, he did the same thing. A caring Jew does not need to give up the demands and guidance of traditional Judaism in order to face the uncertainties and challenges of being human. *"Uvikashtem Misham,"* while religiously exploring the seismic events of life, also carries on a subtle polemic against existentialist personalism as a reason for abandoning Judaism and its vision of the inner human life.

The Rav, I am arguing, was a faithful watchman, aware of whatever new movements seriously sought to displace traditional Judaism and ready to demonstrate that they had nothing to offer that Torah had not already anticipated. And that is why it seems to me that the Rav's scope should not be limited to the role of champion of the *halakhah* but expanded to the more inclusive one *Ish Hatorah*. He was the great expositor and defender of Torah with all its infinite dimensions.

One other consideration persuades me that this analysis has much to commend it. The philosophical problem of validating one's religious stance by means of a current form of intellectuality—rationalism, existentialism, or what have you—is that these ways of thinking first commend themselves as means of bolstering your position but in due course become its arbiter. What you believe has to accommodate itself to the outside philosophy and Torah then becomes only what your external philosophy will allow it to be. The Rav, I am convinced, understood that intellectual trap and was happy to forego the benefit for fear of the ensuing loss. This explains his extraordinary insistence in his essay "Confrontation" that we not only should not/cannot honestly discuss matters of belief with people of other faiths but that *we cannot do so even with people of our*

own religious community! I believe the Rav was warning us against
the perils of utilizing some intellectual system other than Torah to
explain what we believe lest in translating our innermost beliefs into
a commonly available language we subject them to that language's
sense of admissible truth. The Rav might one day sound like he was
justifying Judaism as a higher rationalism and another day as a
higher existentialism, or, when it came to inter-faith discussion, as
a believer in incommunicable religious experience. He was not committed to any of these or other such modish forms of thinking. For
the Rav there was only one adequate source of truth, Torah.

Teacher Not A Spokesman

Shalom Carmy

Serious reading takes time: especially reading work that presupposes real familiarity with Torah and with a range of secular disciplines. In the opinion of many influential people, time devoted to studying the major writings of maran haRav *zt"l* is better spent proclaiming what the Rav really thought. Another cause for discomfort with the written word is that it often contradicts what the influential speakers want him to have thought. A third reason to avoid the written record is that sometimes the relevant texts are not easily available, and inertia overcomes the Rav pundit who, in principle, does not object to reading the primary material.

The wildly divergent positions trumpeted by Rav revisionists to the right and to the left have become an embarrassment to those who care about his legacy and a source of confusion for all who care about truth. I have met spokesmen for the theologically liberal side of our community who, treating religion as politics by other means, concede an indifference to accuracy, as long as they can advance their objectives. One suspects that some traditionalist expositors share with them the conviction that they are doing the Rav or the community a favor by fabricating or suppressing information.

Against these tendencies the best defense is faithfulness to the public record, the writings that the Rav chose to publish in his lifetime or left in the hands of his executors, and the views he expressed repeatedly in public discourses. When a pundit blatantly misreads or ignores the public record I am immediately prejudiced against anything he or she says.

Rabbi Shalom Carmy teaches Jewish Studies and Philosophy at Yeshiva University and is the Editor of *Tradition: A Journal of Orthodox Jewish Thought*. He edited *Worship of the Heart: Essays on Jewish Prayer* (Ktav 2003) based on the manuscripts of Rabbi Joseph B. Soloveitchik.

In what follows I will ground myself in the public record of writing and action. I will allude to personal knowledge only in conjunction with what is in the public domain. My personal connection with the Rav was limited. Beginning in 1976, when he asked me to assist in editing *ketavim* [manuscripts], I was privileged to enjoy, in addition to my previous exposure to the Rav in the *shiur* and at public lectures, an extraordinary amount of "face time." It would be difficult to exaggerate the value of this experience for my growth as a *ben Torah* and as an intellectual personality: my revered mentor R. Walter Wurzburger *zt"l*, in urging me to take advantage of my good fortune, often reminded me that *shimmush talmidei hakhamim* [caring for scholars] is greater, in significant respects, than learning itself. When appropriate I have spoken and written about my "apartment hours."

You, who never encountered the Rav in his lifetime, are right to envy me the opportunity. Through the luck of being at the right place at the right time, or due to the Rav's perception of my receptiveness on certain subjects, it is probable that I gained insights not vouchsafed to others. Yet several hundred hours over nine years revealed to me only a fraction of the Rav's varied activity even during that prolonged period. By contrast, R. Wurzburger's intimate relationship extended over half a century, including his first decade in the Boston pulpit, and he received regular guidance from the Rav not only in intellectual matters but in rabbinic practicum and a wide variety of public policy issues as well. Hence, it is incredible to think that I have genuinely earthshaking knowledge about the Rav completely concealed from his family or from other attentive *talmidim*. In that respect, my situation is different from yours in degree but not in kind. The advice I give you—test what you hear by what you can ascertain independently—is a policy I follow myself.

Here are three areas where the Rav's views are hotly contested despite obtainable evidence.

Secular Studies

The Rav's son-in-law, R. Yitzhak Twersky, stated the obvious: nobody who examines the first page of *Halakhic Man* can deny the importance and thoroughness of the Rav's engagement with the history of philosophy and cognate disciplines. Students of *U-Vikkashtem miSham* will have no difficulty grasping the plain underlying religious motive behind the Rav's pursuit of general knowledge. In

Torah God uniquely seeks us out, and reveals His will to us by commanding us with *mitzvot*. The divine imperative is "democratic" inasmuch as it applies equally to all Jews regardless of temperament or intelligence: the Gaon of Vilna and the shoemaker of Vilna hear the same *shofar* and lift up the same *lulav*. However, God has also given us the task to seek Him out. Each individual searches for God in accordance with his or her own capacities, employing all means at our disposal—science and the humanities; logic and religious experience.

R. Abba Bronspiegel, while recognizing that in the debate about the legitimacy and value of secular studies the Rav's position was unambiguous, has made the important observation that the Rav did not use the term *Torah uMadda*. This phrase, the motto of Yeshiva University, is a political slogan: like all slogans it can mean many things, or it can mean nothing. R. Lamm, having inherited the phrase as President of YU, produced an insightful volume that attempted to give *Torah uMadda* substantial intellectual meaning: he distinguished several possible legitimate roles that general studies could play in the education of an individual for whom Torah is primary. The Rav was no more obligated to define his outlook in terms of an institutional mantra than a Harvard professor is compelled to *darshen* [explicate] Harvard's seal. Since he was averse to the herd mentality in religion and in education, it is not surprising that he chose not to do so.

One point should be clear. Though a *frum* [observant] individual who has chosen not to enter seriously into the study of Western culture cannot accompany the Rav all the way, and may forfeit other spiritual and intellectual benefits too, the same is true, even more so, of the modernist who lacks interest in the Rav's passionate commitment to *Talmud Torah* [study of Torah] as well. Thus the Rav cannot legitimately be made into the paladin of a Modern Orthodox "*Torah uMadda* sect" divided from the rest of Orthodoxy by virtue of its attachment to higher professional education and other middle class status symbols.

Hallel on *Yom haAtzmaut*

As Chairman of the RCA Halakha Commission, the Rav, in 1953 penned a responsum regarding the reading of *Hallel* on *Yom haAtzmaut* [Israel Independence Day]. He endorsed reading the *mizmorei Tehillim* [chapters of Psalms] that comprise *Hallel* if the community wanted to on the morning of *Yom haAtzmaut*. He strictly prohibited reciting a *berakha* [blessing] on the *Hallel*. He also expressed reservations about reading these chapters at night, but did not advocate risking controversy over this practice. Subsequently, in several *shiurim*, he reiterated his objection to the *berakha*. At YU he was observed participating in *minyanim* that recited *Hallel*.

It has recently been alleged that on these occasions the Rav did not recite *Hallel*, but only pretended so as not to give offense. Offhand this contradicts the written record. There is no evidence that the Rav changed his mind on the subject. The argument that he had second thoughts about the religious significance of the State of Israel does not hold water, since the Rav's Zionism was not rooted in messianic speculation or in illusory expectations for the religious transformation of the governing elites, but rather in the success of Israel in defending Jewish lives and facilitating vibrant religious institutions.

It is possible to resolve this contradiction. Perhaps the Rav held a *siddur* in front of his face and pretended to go along with the *Hallel* at night. Perhaps he was even present where the *berakha* was recited and chose not to protest. In 1978 he was asked his opinion during morning *minyan* in the dormitory, and when the *hazzan* prefaced *Hallel* with the *berakha*, he walked out. However, this open show of displeasure may have resulted from the fact that his ruling had been solicited and then flouted. (The person responsible later insisted there had been a misunderstanding.)

Territorial Compromise in Israel:

During the first *Teshuva Derasha* I attended, with prominent journalists and diplomats among the overflow audience, the Rav stated in no uncertain terms that security needs should govern any negotiation about the land conquered in the Six Day War. The decisions should be made, not by rabbis, but by experts in the field, just as regarding mortal questions of health we rely on physicians. Genuine peace should override all the halakhic considerations in favor of continued Jewish sovereignty. During the Begin years he told journalists that "the Jewish people were a wise and intelligent nation (*am hakham ve-navon*)" and that they would, he prayed, act accordingly. When he met with Begin in the summer of 1977, the newly elected Prime Minister was sagacious enough not to raise the subject, and the Rav did not respond to questions that had not been posed to him.

Since the Rav so rarely intervened in Israeli affairs, and generally deferred to local rabbinic authority, I am convinced that he spoke out in this case only because he feared serious harm, either to Israel or to the repute of Judaism in Israel, from the uncompromising pronouncements by Israeli rabbis, without a dissenting voice. The only similar involvement I recall was in *Tishre* of 1982. The Lebanon war that summer enabled the Christian militia allied with Israel to control the southern part of the country. Christians perpetrated a massacre in the Palestinian camps of Sabra and Shatilla. At that time the Rav stepped in forcefully, insisting on a commission of inquiry to investigate what various members of the government knew about the situation and what they had done with this information. (The report of the ensuing Kahan Commission led to the removal of Ariel Sharon as *Sar ha-Bittahon* [Minister for Security].)

Then, and often during those years, the Rav expressed, both in public and in private, a fear that Israel might become too reliant on its military might. The fundamental concern is as old as the Torah's warning against the heresy of believing in *Kohi ve-otsem yadi*—in the absolute power of force, even if in the Rav's case it was fortified by knowledge of history and philosophically informed insight into human nature. Listening to tapes of that period, I am surprised by the frequent pained comments in this vein.

Let me emphasize that the Rav did not endorse any particular peace plan then and would not have presumed to judge later proposals. The entire point of his ruling was to assign the life and death decision to responsible secular experts. In 1978 a group of American Jewish leaders proposed to visit the Middle East to add their wisdom to the protracted negotiations between Egypt and Israel. There can be little doubt that many of these leaders, unschooled in the nerve-racking art of diplomacy and greedy for photo ops and sound bites, would have ended up as instruments of pressure on "intransigent" Israel. The Rav told the Orthodox representatives to stay home, and through this veto torpedoed the entire junket.

Currently there is, of course, no consensus among military experts. Therefore R. Schachter has argued that the Rav's view cannot serve as a practical guide for Israeli citizens and must be supplemented by other halakhic ideas: when doctors disagree, the decision devolves upon the patient, i.e. the Israeli public. This is a plausible emendation of the Rav's position. Yet it would be quite possible for the Rav to hold that, since the Israeli political system does not provide for referenda, the only poll that counts is on election day and the government must be regarded as representative. I don't think anyone can know for sure.

It is even more important to recognize that the Rav's theoretical willingness to trade land for peace was not grounded in optimism about human nature or the imminence of the messianic age. Several times I heard him remark, with resignation mixed with a kind of moral satisfaction, that the people of Israel were so hungry for peace that if the Arabs proposed a truce, even one not worth the paper it was written on, Israelis would display mass enthusiasm for it.

One difference between a spokesman and a leader is that the former tells people what they want to hear; the latter, what they need to think about. More often than not, the Rav did not echo the slogans popular in the community. Even when he affirmed common judgment, he provoked serious reflection and soul-searching. Thus he was not afraid to challenge the glib certainties of religious Zionists, just as he had insisted that yeshivot and intensive Torah study were not mere relics of the past. When Jews were afraid to be labeled soft on Communism, the Rav ruled halakhically that a teacher should not testify about a colleague's political commitments in the remote past, since Judaism believes in repentance and what had happened twenty years before had no bearing on the present; yet in the 1970's, when it was fashionable to oppose the Vietnam War, the Rav came out as a hawk, while nevertheless counseling antiwar students to stand their ground and not hide their views lest the Nixon administration punish Israel. Thus in the 1940's and '50s, when American Jews looked upon Franklin Roosevelt as a god, the Rav publicly criticized him, and decades later, when some American Jews found the courage to habitually condemn American policy in the Middle East, he reminded us that failure to understand the mysterious relationship of the Jew to *Erets Yisrael* does not automatically brand a Gentile anti-Semitic.

Serious thinking is harder than serious reading, though less time-consuming. I must apologize for devoting my remarks to the public Rav, largely omitting the unique characteristics that many of you crave to hear about, precisely because they can only be experienced and elude description. In the end the essential teaching of the Rav was the high adventure of Torah study; we remember the man who, having confronted a Rambam hundreds of times, could yet fasten on it afresh, and put his finger on a phrase whose significance had previously gone undetected. We remember the struggle yet again to define precisely a dispute of the Ramban and the Baal haMaor, and the attempt to once again bring to life the personalities of the great Biblical figures and the drama of their destiny. It was the insight into the human condition informed by Torah and by mastery of human thought and culture. By addressing a few FAQs I hope to clear away the gossipy topics and make room for the more essential themes of life and death and Torah.

As Kierkegaard has taught us, existential truth is best conveyed by indirect modes. Whenever one of the Rav's students, or the students of his students, succeed in reduplicating the passion and the intelligence, in making human creativity a vehicle and domicile for a life of *yirat Shamayim* [awe before God], that is where the Rav's teaching vocation remains alive.

The Rov *zt"l*: The *Nigleh* and the *Nistar* The Revealed and the Concealed

Mordecai E. Feuerstein*

I almost didn't write these words. I did not jump at the opportunity to contribute to this volume. The impact and legacy of Maran HaRav Yosef Dov Halevi Soloveitchik on the study of Torah is so profound, so ground-breaking and wide-ranging that there are many more qualified than I to describe it and to convey it to future generations. To repeat that which is said is unnecessary while to reveal what has not been revealed might not be my right. Nonetheless, with some trepidation I put to paper a few recollections and thoughts, in the hope and belief that the events I witnessed will help give a fuller picture of the unique giant I was privileged to know and to serve.

My life was enhanced by the Rov in two distinct realms. On the one hand I, like so many others, sat for many years in his *shiur* as a *talmid* straining to absorb as much as possible of the intellectual radiance that he put forward. And, like so many of these students, I went on to serve in the North American rabbinate as one of his *musmachim* and as a continued beneficiary of his advice and guidance. However, it was in another realm that I was impacted perhaps even more profoundly. My family, going back to my grandfather and continuing with both of my parents, enjoyed close relationships with the Rov, working with him as partners and as his emissaries in

Rabbi Mordecai Feuerstein is Rabbi of the Synagogue of the Suburban Torah Center in Livingston, NJ.

*Special thanks to my son-in-law, Rabbi Daniel Z. Feldman, for his suggestions, input, and careful review of this essay.

a wide array of communal and national responsibilities, ranging
from the needs of our shared local community of Brookline, to the
national (sometimes international) activities of the Orthodox Union
and Torah Umesorah. I was born into this connection, and was privileged to continue as the Rov's personal assistant in the years shortly
following the passing of the Rebbetzin o"h. In this capacity, I witnessed a Rav Soloveitchik not visible to the public eye, not always
fully grasped by the legions of admirers of his intellectual, academic
and Talmudic mastery.

Upon reflection, I have come to realize that the two realms—that
of the personal and devotional and that of the great public *marbitz
Torah*—in which we interacted, should not be compartmentalized;
each was fully dependent upon the other. The great feats of genius
that the world saw were, in reality, products of a saintly lifestyle
that the world rarely saw. And that religious stature, in turn, was
wholly defined and nourished by the efforts of the mind. It was a
synergy that could be appreciated only by witnessing these parts
together.

Unlike the *shiurim* that were heard by so many, relatively few
talmidim ever got to see the personal side of the Rov. He wrote much
about *yiras shomayim* as it interfaced with *talmud Torah* and with
tefilla, transforming both of them into genuine *avoda shebalev*. But the
Rov by nature was a shy person with respect to his personal life;
what the *talmidim* witnessed in *shiurim* was the *iyyun*, the *amkus*, the
rigor and that's what they seek to emulate. They never had the
chance to experience the *gadlus* of the Rov in *avodas hashem*, his *davening*, and his reactions to encounters of everyday life.

We had a *rebbe* who wrote and spoke profoundly about *ruchniyus*.
While so many who studied under him in his *Gemara shiur* relegate
these articulations to his exceptional capacity to poetically verbalize
the sublime, in truth, they are much more than that. Feeling "the hot
breath of infinity on one's tired face" is not just a poetic expression
used by a master *baal masbir* to articulate the nuances of the religious
prayer experience. It is an actual reality of the Rov's passionate experience of *tefilla* and *talmud Torah*. The benefit of the stories that are
told is in conveying to those who did not have a personal relationship with the Rov a sense of his spirituality, his piety, and his *yiras
shomayim*.

Some people had the opportunity to stand beside the Rov during
the *avodas Yom HaKippurim*—to see him, even physically assist him,

as he bowed for *noflim al pnaihem*, with a look of awe and intensity on his face that was as frightening as it was unforgettable. Those who had the opportunity to stand beside him when he *davened* *Neilah* sometimes couldn't see the face underneath the *talis*. But just watching his hands—open in pleading, clenched in determination, as he struggled and fought with *Hakadosh Borukh Hu* for *selicha*, *mechila, v'kappara* for *Klal Yisroel*—was profoundly inspiring. Those who saw and experienced these things have an obligation to bring this anecdotal testimony to the fore, so that people can have some grasp of a living picture, not just an intellectual impression.

One summer, we were learning *Masseches Nazir* in Boston. At the end of the summer, as *Elul* approached, the Rov decided that there should be an additional *limmud* at the end of the *shiur*. Accordingly, he came in with the *Likutei Torah* of the *Baal ha'Tanya* and began to teach it. Afterwards, at the conclusion of the *shiur*, this was the subject of much conversation among the *talmidim*, a discussion which continued at the local synagogues during *Mincha* and *Maariv*.

The next day the Rov chose not to continue teaching *Likutei Torah*, and never returned to it again with us in the *shiur*. Subsequently, he was asked by one of the lay people in the Brookline community who had heard about this, why he had stopped. He said he sensed 're-sistance' in the air. "Unfortunately, my *talmidim* are interested only in my mind, not in my heart."

The Rov was clearly disappointed in us. I have often thought about that incident which caused him *agmas nefesh*. As his *talmidim*, we were not living up to what he sought to cultivate. The Rov sometimes bemoaned this in his writings. The Rov wanted to cultivate people who were not only intellectual *talmidei chachamim* and *yodei Torah*; he wanted *talmidim* who also passionately struggled to experience *kirvas Elokim* in every aspect of their lives.

I agreed to participate in this endeavor, not so that I could repeat stories that are known or even add stories that are not known. It is because of the responsibility that I feel to the legacy of the Rov to help complete the picture, to illustrate how the intellectual was informed, and in fact defined by the emotional, the spiritual, and the deeply personal. It is my fervent hope that with these recollections, I can do my part to contribute to the message that the Rov wished so dearly to impart.

We have mentioned the Rov's complete immersion in the prayer experience. The Rov's relation to prayer was a direct outgrowth of the intensely real feeling he had of interacting directly and communicating with the *Ribbono shel Olam*. There was no question in his mind that at those moments he was in direct commune with the Divine. When he taught the halakhic prohibition of eating before *davening*, he presented it as if it were obvious and unnecessary. "How could one eat before *davening*?" he asked. "You think you need food to live? You need the *Ribbono shel Olam* to live!" The Rov believed not only that he communicated with G-d through his prayers, but that G-d communicated with him through the events of life.

An incident occurred on a Tuesday morning. The Rov flew in from Boston and before giving the *shiur*, which often extended from 11 a.m. to 2 p.m., he went to his apartment for a cup of tea and a piece of pastry. We were talking when, somehow, the cup tipped off the table and scalding hot tea spilled all over him. There was a tremendous commotion; as he jumped, I ran to help. I was very fearful that he had sustained some injury or perhaps he was in pain. But he didn't talk about any of that. Standing there with his soaked trousers, he said, "You know why this happened to me? It happened because I'm wearing my *Shabbos* suit during the week." I said, "What do you mean?" He replied, "This is my *Shabbos* suit. I was rushing this morning and took it by accident. Before I left the house, I realized I had taken it, but I was too lazy to go back and change into a weekday suit."

I will never forget that. It was a very clear indicator of what I had seen many times before—that the Rov related to all the adversities and frustrations of life in a spiritual way. The *Gemara* in *Arachin* (16b) asks *"ad haychon tachlis yissurim"*—up to what minimus or point of insignificance can we attribute *yissurim* (suffering—whether physical, spiritual, or emotional) as being heaven-sent. Several examples are provided—such as inadvertently putting one's right arm into the left sleeve or pulling the wrong number of coins from one's pocket. Even these minor frustrations, the *Gemara* tells us, are not accidental. They're a form of communication from above—they're sent *mi'lema'ala*—and have instructional significance.

In fact, the Rov, in my experience, was always feeling that *Hakadosh Barukh Hu* was tapping him on the shoulder and was in touch with him through the events of his day. He had a religious interpretation of that which occurred to him. This was the sense from the things he said to me and the stories he told—that the relationship was always on his consciousness. Whereas others would be frustrated or angered by what happened, or would resent it, there was no anger, there was no resentment about the spilled tea or about other mishaps. Rather, there was *hachna'ah*. The Rov acquiesced—and accepted what he perceived to be a Divine message.

He once told me that during *Kol Nidre* of 1966 when the *aron kodesh* was open in the Maimonides School in Brookline, a mishap occurred, and the Torah in the *aron* fell sideways. The Rav became very upset. Rabbi Yosef Blau, who is now the *mashgiach ruchani* at Yeshiva University, tried to comfort him. Years later, when I was sitting alone with the Rav, he reflected on this mishap and said, "Rabbi Blau didn't understand why I was upset. I knew when that happened that my Rebbetzin would not survive the year." And, alas, that was the year she passed away, in the spring of 1967. The fact that the Torah fell (it didn't fall out; it fell in the confines of the *aron*), was a message. It was somehow a communication; the Almighty was speaking to him through the various events that were happening.

Despite his great stature and acclaim, the Rov was completely without any pretension of any sort. He never had a personal secretary. He would open the door himself. He answered the phone himself. He never let me take out the garbage (when he was aware I was doing so), never let me make his bed, never saw me washing dishes in the apartment without coming to stand beside me and converse with me until the chore was done. As I reflect upon those occasions, I am overwhelmed to realize the picture of humility they paint. At the time, the thrill of talking with him overshadowed the incredible lesson he was wordlessly imparting by example. I didn't put it together, that he was not willing to have me do his dishes while he sat and did something else.

Chazal tell us: "*kol hagadol mechaveiro, yitzro gadol heimenu.*" Whoever is greater than his friend, that person's inclination, his impulses and inner drives are also greater than those of his friend. We often imagine that the righteous and the great of the Torah world somehow have an easier time resisting the *yetzer hara*; that if we were as spiritually inclined as they were, we would also sit and study Torah day and night. But it is not that way at all. It's not true. The greater a person becomes in Torah, the more powerful the temptations to use the special gift with which G-d endows him for personal aggrandizement, rather than for the purpose of being *mekadesh Hashem*.

It follows, therefore, that the Rov, in his immense Torah greatness, was someone who had to deal with the kinds of pressures of the *yetzer* which drew greatness of character and heart from him. Rav Aharon Soloveichik, *zt"l*, in his *hesped* at the Rov's funeral in Boston, said that the Rov worked on himself and galvanized all of his talents and his abilities with strenuous discipline and perseverance. In several conversations, the Rov made it clear to me that he fought an ongoing battle with himself all his life to reach *shleimus* on a spiritual and pietistic level—to be the *eved Hashem* that he understood the Almighty wanted him to be.

The Rov stood firm in the face of any kind of pressure. When it was a matter of his principles or convictions, no one could sway him for any reason—even though he would lose friends, even though he would lose supporters, even though interest groups would come out against him. He was fearless; he would stand alone in the face of pressure to safeguard his principles. Not even from the 'religious right' in the 'name of Torah' could he be swayed, if he felt that his approach was the approach of Torah.

I once heard the Rov humming a tune and asked him what it was. He replied, "A *schlager*." At first I was nonplussed, but then realized it was a "hit" tune from the Rov's university days in Berlin. The Rov's departure from Warsaw in 1926 to attend the University of Berlin raised quite a wave of 'comment' in certain quarters. I remember a conversation in which the Rov described an aspect of his stay in Berlin which, in his day, was one of the great centers in Europe for the treatment of diseases and disorders of the eye. Many *talmidei chachamim* came to Berlin for treatment and some of them were hosted by the Rov. On one occasion, he had a deep discussion about some *lomdishe sugya* with one of his guests. After an extended give and take, the guest, highly impressed with his host's obvious erudition, asked the Rov: you are so immersed in Torah learning, how do you have time for the university? To which the Rov replied, "When you put time into learning, I, too, put time into learning. And during the time you devote to discussing my going to university, I am busy attending classes."

There was a certain integrity and nobility to the way he held his positions, and the way he related to people who differed from him. The ideology—he wouldn't countenance; but the individual—he respected. He knew the etiquette and *derech haTorah* of *machlokes*.

He never allowed disagreement to become personal. He never descended to the rudeness, psychological abuse, disdain, and disrespect, the ugliness, which one sometimes encounters, whether from the right wing of Orthodoxy or elsewhere. He respected the human being, with whom he may have ideologically differed. The Rov always emulated the famous precept articulated by Bruria (*Berakhos* 10a): *Yitamu chataim min ha 'aretz—chataim v 'lo chotim.* "Let the sin be removed from the land, not the sinner."

In terms of his relationship with the "*yeshiva-velt*" he was not only the consummate gentleman, but he was, in the accolade of the *Gemara* (*Yoma* 23a), a true *ohaiv Hashem*. We are told: *Hane'elovim ve'einam olvim*—those who are insulted and do not insult in return; *shom'in cherpasan ve'einan meishivin*—who hear themselves humiliated and do not retort; *osin me'ahava usmeichin bi 'yisurin*—who serve out of love and happiness in spite of affliction; *aleihen hakasuv omer*—regarding such individuals the verse proclaims (*Shoftim* 5:31): *Ve'ohavav ketzeis hashemesh bigvuraso*—"Those that love Him (i.e. the *ohavai HaShem*) are like the sun rising in its power."

If you think about the image, what does the sun 'rising' have to do with its power? Perhaps the image is of a dark cloud obscuring the sun. When the cloud passes, the sun re-emerges undiminished in its power. *K'tzeis hashemesh* does not refer to the sun rising but, rather, to the sun re-emerging, going out from behind the cloud. At that moment it is clear that the sun is just as strong, that the sun never changed. So it is with the true *ohaiv Hashem*.

The Rov was that way. He never allowed himself to be changed by whatever unpleasantness or insult was directed at him from the "*yeshiva-velt*." The Rov would have *never* tolerated *any* of his *talmidim* referring to other *Roshei Yeshiva* by their initials, in a *derech zilzul*. I spoke to him about it many times and he never expressed bitterness about the fact that this was happening to him.

I was in the Rov's apartment when the phone rang and a prominent *Rosh Yeshiva*, one of the distinguished *Gedolei HaTorah*, requested to speak to the Rov. An extended conversation began over a difficult Rambam. At one point, the Rov was speaking, and suddenly, he put the phone down. He looked at me and said, "He hung up." I asked, "Why?" The Rov said, "I heard voices of people entering the room, and he hung up." The next day, this *Rosh Yeshiva* called back to apologize and explained that he abruptly terminated the call because some *talmidim* had entered his office, and he was afraid that they might find out that he was consulting with Rabbi Soloveitchik! The Rov responded graciously; there was not a hint of anger. All he revealed was that the episode mystified him in a way. Even afterwards, he never spoke disrespectfully of this *Rosh Yeshiva*. This, I believe, is a true measure of his greatness.

In Boston, in the early 1940's, the Rov undertook to protect the *shochtim* who were being worked at a pace (some toiling 24 hours at a stretch, for very meager wages) which made it impossible to really be performing *shechita* properly. As a result, a major confrontation occurred between the powers that held sway in the meat business and this new rabbi in town, Rabbi Soloveitchik, who was taking the side of the *shochtim*. In 1941 the attorney general of Massachusetts launched an investigation in response to information that had been "provided" to him, alleging that the Rov was reaping monetary gain at the expense of the Jewish community and not declaring it as income on his tax returns. A fourteen-month process ensued, at the conclusion of which, Judge Abraham K. Cohen declared that the charges against Rabbi Soloveitchik were "sheer fabrications." Furthermore, he said, "Those who originated [the charges] knew that they were unfounded. The evil rumors were spread with malice and the Rabbi was dreadfully abused and baselessly accused." (Cf. Rakeffet-Rothkoff, *The Rav: The World of Rabbi Joseph B. Soloveitchik*, vol 1., pp. 30–32)

Rabbi Dr. Haym Soloveitchik mentioned to me that shortly after this happened, on Yom Kippur evening, the Rov was walking home from *shul* and passed one of the rabbis who was known to have instigated the investigation against him. To the amazement of Rebbetzin Soloveitchik, who had suffered along with him through the baseless accusations, the Rov immediately was *makdim shalom* to this person. He wished him a *Gut Yahr* and a *G'mar Chasima Tova*.

Years later, in the early 1970's, the Rov helped another one of the rabbis who had instigated this libel against him, who had now, himself, come under legal investigation. A request was made from his family for the Rov's intervention to help his cause and save him from a possible sentence of incarceration. The Rov was ready without a moment's hesitation. Amazed, I remarked, "Look what these people did to you! They dragged your name through the papers." (In fact, when the Rov was ready to come to Yeshiva University after his father had passed away, *The Commentator* came out saying it was not appropriate that a person who had been under criminal investigation should be chosen as *Rosh Yeshiva*.) "No *nekima*, no *netira*" (no revenge, no holding of grudges) was the essence of the Rov's response. Here, again, one saw his *gadlus*.

These things, I believe, are very instructive for our contemporary climate. Things are so polarized today that there are very few people in the Torah-world who would talk to adversaries in a respectful and deferential manner. It is a rarity.

What those of us who were *zocheh* to hear *shiurim* from Rabbi Soloveitchik have is the love of *talmidim* for the *rebbe* who opened up the world of *lomdus* for us. But those who got to know him had a reverence of a different kind, in a sense, because they saw inner greatness—true inner greatness in this towering ethical personality.

The Rov's greatness was also evident in the genuine care and sensitivity that he showed for his students. Some of the stories are well known such as the fact that he changed the time of *shiur* to accommodate the treatments of a seriously ill student, and did so without explanation so the student would suffer no embarrassment. Similarly well-known is the time he tracked down a student during lunch hour to apologize for his harsh response to the student's suggestion during *shiur*, and to acknowledge that the student had been right.

In his later years the Rov's demanding approach in the context of the *shiur* (which often consisted of ninety students or more) was tempered by his sensitivity to the needs of an individual student. There was one student who was so intimidated by the rigors of the interactive *shiur* that he maintained a pseudonym while in class, apparently not willing to expose his real identity to possible criticism. Several months into the year, I was walking with the Rov when I heard another student attempting to inform him of this ongoing subterfuge. The Rov declined to respond to the informer. When I asked him about it, the Rov said, "I've known it since the first day, but he's frightened, so leave him alone."

Similarly, the Rov allowed his classroom criticisms to be expressed with humor and to be responded to in kind. To a student whose response was close but not enough, the Rov said, "You hear bells ringing, but you don't know where." Following the reading of a difficult text and being peppered with questions along the way, the Rov offered me a back-handed compliment: "Your *ivreh* (Yiddish for Hebrew diction) wasn't bad." To which I replied, "What does the *Rebbe* expect? I learned Hebrew at Maimonides." The Rov smiled.

The Rov's concern for his students continued after they left the classroom and went out into the rabbinic trenches. When I served as a Rov in Vancouver, the local Orthodox *rabbonim* formed a *Beis Din* for a *mesiras haget* (delivery of a *get*). On one occasion there was a very bitter and contentious divorce between a husband who lived in Calgary and his estranged wife who had relocated to Vancouver. The *get*, written by a *sofer* in Winnipeg and sent by registered mail to our *Beis Din* in Vancouver, arrived on a Thursday. The wife was under a court order (connected to the effectuation of her civil divorce) to accept the *get*. This court order was due to expire on the following Monday. We quickly convened the *Beis Din* on Friday morning to carry out the *mesirah*. The wife arrived in a state of extreme tension. Barely cooperative, she immediately warned us that she had only a few minutes to spare.

The proceedings began. The *get* was read and checked against the list of *simanim* that the Winnipeg *sofer* had sent under separate cover to confirm that this was indeed the authentic *get* which he had written. Three of the four *simanim* "checked out," but to our dismay one did not. The *sofer* indicated that lines seven and eight in the *get* were *shuros bilti meuros* (contained no "entangling letters" which descended downwards from line seven—like a *kuf*—or ascended upwards from line eight—like a *lamed*). This was not correct. In our version of the *get*, lines six and seven were *bilti meuros*, not lines seven and eight. We called a recess of the proceedings. The woman threatened to walk out if the matter wasn't resolved within fifteen minutes.

I went into the adjoining room with another of the *dayanim* and called the *sofer* in Winnipeg only to discover he had left for Israel and could not be reached. Thereupon, I called Rabbi Soloveitchik, explained our predicament and the fact that we were operating under a court-imposed Monday deadline for delivery of the *get* and could not possibly have a new *get* written in time. Once the court order expired, there was no hope this woman would accept a *get*. The Rov asked a few questions and then there was silence. After two or three minutes, I asked "*Rebbe*, are you there?" He replied, "I'm thinking." Another few minutes passed in silence. "*Rebbe*, she's threatening to leave in fifteen minutes." "All right, call me back in half an hour." At first I couldn't believe what I was hearing, until it suddenly dawned on me. The Rov was not prepared to permit the delivery of the *get* but he didn't want to say so, thereby tying my hands and precluding my seeking a *psak* elsewhere. I thanked the

Rov and wished him a good *Shabbos*. We called the Beis Din of Montreal and Rav Hirshprung *zt"l* and R. Hendel were *matir* for us to proceed and deliver the *get*.

This episode was indicative of the Rov's attitude in responding to *sheilos*, and reflects the Rov's concern for the predicament of the community rabbi. What we miss so much is the grasp which the Rov had of the total situation. It is not easy to find *poskim* who are able to intuit things about a rabbi's setting and about the results which might emerge from a course of action (one policy or another) which, often, the rabbi himself hadn't considered.

I remember when we were learning *Masseches Eruvin*. There was an unusual air of tension around the Rov during the *shiurim*. The numerous details and measurements the subject entailed constituted a particular challenge in terms of defining the conceptual issues underlying the *chilukei deos* in the *Gemara*. One day, as I was crossing Amsterdam Avenue, the Rov was about to step off the curb and go to Furst Hall. He said to me, "Are you following the *shiurim*?" "I'm trying," I replied. He shook his fist and said, "Have courage!" and strode across the street. He seemed to me like a general in the midst of a campaign, rallying the troops; as if we were engaged in an arduous struggle for understanding, and we needed his encouragement to fight on and not give up.

To the Rov, not only was *limmud haTorah* a profound and serious undertaking, but the precise and accurate teaching of Torah was a tremendous *achrayus*. It was as if he felt a personal responsibility to the generations that preceded him and that would follow, to make sure that *emes* was arrived at through his teaching. I believe that is why he wasn't interested in hearing how he had explained a *sugya* the previous time he had learned it. *Ein beis midrash b'lo chiddush*. The purpose was to reach the *emes* today, to be *mechadeish* in this session of *ameilus baTorah*, not to recapitulate what had been said before.

The Rov would often tell the story of the appointment of R. Chaim of Brisk to be *Rosh Yeshiva* of Volozhin.

I have already told you that when Reb Chaim was appointed a rosh yeshiva in Volozhin, he was very young. There was opposition because of his youth (he was in his 20's) and particularly to his new method of analysis... Charges were brought before the board of trustees [*gabbaim*] of the Yeshiva. The Kletzker Rav claimed that Reb Chaim did not teach Torah properly and that his method was strange... So they came to Volozhin to investigate the matter... Reb

Chaim said a *shiur* on *Yevamos*…and the visiting rabbis were just enchanted. Toward the end of the *shiur*, Reb Chaim [suddenly] recalled a passage from Rambam which he felt refuted his analysis and declared: "*Rabbosai*, whatever I said is wrong. I made a mistake. The Rambam says just the opposite!" Then he sat down… Reb Chaim remained the Rosh Yeshiva. He did not lose his job. This is seeking the truth of Torah. I remember as a child that my father trained me in a similar fashion. Whenever there is a mistake, admit it immediately. Do not try to defend errors.

(Rakeffet-Rothkoff, vol. I, pp 182-183)

As with his grandfather and father, the Rov was always rethinking … perhaps there was a better, sharper way to say it. A dramatic expression of this occurred in the fall of 1972 (5733), when we were learning *Masseches Chulin*. I remember we were studying a text on *daf hey, amud beis*. The Rav gave a rather intensive *shiur* on Thursday, and, as was his practice, he flew back to Boston later that afternoon. On the following Tuesday morning he returned to New York, and gave a 2–3 hour *shiur* on the very same *sugya* he had covered Thursday, from a completely different perspective. After the *shiur*, while I was preparing lunch for him, I asked him: Why did you repeat? What made you go back?

He said that right after the *Shabbos*-noon meal, he went to sit in the living-room (in the Twersky residence at 122 Addington Road, Brookline). Across from him sat his daughter Dr. Atarah Twersky. Having eaten, he was a bit drowsy, and soon fell asleep. Suddenly he saw the image of his father, Rav Moshe Soloveitchik *zt"l* walking towards him holding an open *Gemara*. He greeted and called out to his father. Rav Moshe kept approaching closer and then turned the *Gemara* around so it was facing the Rov. It was open to *Chulin, daf hey, amud beis*. His father said just one thing to him: "You can do better." Then Rav Moshe turned around, walked away, and disappeared.

The Rov woke up with a start. He told me that Dr. Atarah Twersky was alarmed and feared that something had seemingly seized him. But the Rov said nothing. He walked to his room and he worked on the *Gemara*, for two and a half days, from *Shabbos* afternoon until Monday night, when the insight upon which he based Tuesday's *shiur* came to him.

In explaining the statement of Resh Lakish (*Chagiga* 16a) that "One who gazes upon the Nasi … his eyes grow dim," the Rov wrote:

When one sees the Nasi (the head of the High Court)... and he is a genius of Torah, possessing great intellectual force, a creative mind, deeply penetrating intuition as though attuned to divine knowledge (*ruach hakodesh*) ... When one encounters a wondrous example of a great and powerful mind, he inevitably realizes that human thought is dependent upon the Almighty Himself... When a Jew encounters such genius he blesses G-d, 'Who apportions something of His wisdom to those who stand in awe of Him' ...over the fact that the wise man has been given a share of the Supreme Wisdom (*hachokhma haelyona*). And it is thus that we should understand the statement of the Talmud: 'He who gazes upon the Nasi'—and fails to discern the Master of the Universe projecting intelligence and wisdom upon him—'his eyes are dim.'

(*On Repentance*, pp. 135–7 / *Al HaTeshuva*, pp.202–3)

He told me about the Malbim, the great Torah commentator, who in 1834 paid a visit to the Chasam Sofer in Pressburg. The Malbim was a younger person, about twenty-five years old at that time, while the Chasam Sofer was at the zenith of his career, one of the greatest *rabbanim* of the 19th century and of the whole period of the *Acharonim*. The Chasam Sofer accorded much honor to the Malbim, seating him on his right side at the *Shabbos* table, enabling them to speak together at greater length.

Apparently, after the *Shabbos*-day meal, the Malbim was so engrossed in what he had heard from the Chasam Sofer that he wandered back to the *shul*, lost in thought. It was quite dark inside the empty *shul*, and the Malbim found a place to stand near what seemed to be a wall, and remained there in profound contemplation.

Later when the congregants began returning to *shul* for Mincha, they were stunned to see the Malbim standing near the *aron*, still deep in thought, right in the *makom kavua* of the Chasam Sofer! An angry murmur swept through the crowd; people were about to step forward to rebuke the Malbim when the Chasam Sofer walked in. Quickly sizing up the situation, he stopped them and said: *Zol ehr blaiben shtayn* ("Let him remain standing there"). The Malbim awoke from his trance and, horror-struck to discover that he had inadvertently been standing in the Chasam Sofer's place, offered the Chasam Sofer profuse apologies, which were accepted.

For the rest of his life, the Rov told me, the Malbim used to sequester himself in a room for a period of time, right after *Shabbos*

Mincha. Afterwards, he would emerge red-eyed from weeping. With the passage of years, he gradually came to interpret the Chasam Sofer's words, *Zol ehr blaiben shtayn* as a punitive decree: Let him remain standing where he is now—his qualitative advance in Torah knowledge is over. Where he is now is where he will stay. The Malbim sensed that the divine gift of creative inspiration which he had experienced before his inadvertent slight to the honor of the Chasam Sofer, had been irrevocably taken away.

I understood from the way the Rov told me this story and the conversational setting in which he presented it, how much he realized that his learning, his insight, and his great mental powers were a trust given to him by *HaKadosh Barukh Hu*—a gift that could be taken away. He struggled all his life to be *zocheh* to what he recognized was the *Yad Hashem* that was allowing him to be *mechadeish* and to be *marbitz Torah* in the extraordinary fashion that he did.

There were a variety of expressions he used which reflected his absolute determination—sometimes a grim resolve—to fight for intellectual understanding at whatever cost. I remember the striking way he described a particularly difficult piece of *Gemara*: "This is a cold-compress *sugya*." The mental strain in deciphering it might bring on a crushing headache, necessitating the application of cold compresses for relief, but the battle would be waged until a breakthrough was achieved. The *milchamtah shel Torah* was not for the faint-hearted or the weak-willed. Perseverance was essential and indispensable.

In *shiur*, he rarely said, "That's enough for today; we'll continue tomorrow." He either solved the problem at hand or we sat there and worked at it with him for hours. I remember the day when John Lindsay, the mayor of New York, came up to YU as part of his re-election campaign. He was expected around 2:00 p.m. and many of those attending the *shiur* expected it would be over in time for them to hear Lindsay speak. The Rov started his *shiur* around 10:30 a.m. The focus of the *shiur* was a problematic Rambam in *Hilchos Eruvin*. The Rov suggested several answers but after much discussion, rejected them one by one. As the *shiur* entered its fourth hour in search of an acceptable solution, one of the *talmidim* suggested an entirely different approach to the Rambam which would alleviate the difficulty. The Rov responded that he remembered, as a youth, being in the room when his father and uncle were discussing this very Rambam with Reb Chaim of Brisk. R. Moshe pointed out the very same difficulty we were discussing in the Rambam but R. Velvel, taking the same approach as we had, maintained there was a simple answer. And, said the Rov, if R. Velvel held there was a simple answer, we were going to find it, and there was no need for the different approach which was now being suggested. (He paused for a moment of humor by recalling the *baal-habayis* who woke up in the middle of the night to find a thief running around in his bedroom. He cried out, "*Ganev, ganev,* how did you get in here?" To which the thief replied, "Never mind how I got <u>in</u> here. Just tell me how to get <u>out</u> of here!" Turning to the *talmid* who had suggested the different approach to the Rambam, the Rov said: Never mind how we got <u>into</u> the problem. Just help us find a way to get <u>out</u> of it.) Ultimately, the Rov came up with a workable resolution just minutes before Lindsay and his entourage arrived.

I remember after difficult three-to four-hour *shiurim,* the Rov would often come back to his apartment, go straight to the table, open his *Gemara* and continue working on the problems of the *sugya* for several hours more. There was no thought of stopping to eat lunch. My attempts to provide him with lunch were futile and I would eventually be forced to leave the food on the table.

One evening during my college years, I accompanied my father who had some documents to deliver to the Rov at his 10 Hancock Road address in Brookline. As prearranged, at 10 p.m. we rang the bell, and Rebbetzin Soloveitchik answered the door. My father explained that the Rov had requested the documents we had brought. Mrs. Soloveitchik seemed very subdued and serious; her eyes were red. She expressed her regrets and plaintively explained, "He hasn't left his desk all day. Not even to eat or drink. He came home from the *minyan* this morning and said he was troubled by a difficult Rashi. He went into his study fourteen hours ago and still hasn't come out." The envelope was left in her keeping and we walked back to the car in utter silence, with a heightened conception of *ameilus baTorah.*

The Rov told me that when Reb Chaim Brisker was sitting in a room with people who were *yodei sefer,* he would often suddenly turn to someone and inquire, "What are you thinking about?" I wondered aloud if people weren't caught speechless in the privacy of their thoughts. The Rov explained that R. Chaim was sure that people were thinking about Torah. For what else would a person delight in thinking about? His only question was which *sugya* were they delving into, what intriguing problem they were wrestling with.

Indeed, the Rov was constantly preoccupied with *"trachten in lernen."* Everywhere he went, he was *hogeh baTorah*—walking in the street, sitting on a plane waiting for takeoff, in a cab, and, at times, even when someone was talking to him. I came to realize that—in a manner described by the Ramban, whereby a person can be *davuk b'Shekhinah* at the same time that he is going about his everyday affairs—the Rov was often in two different worlds at once. He could be ostensibly involved in a conversation on an overt level, but his deeper consciousness was elsewhere. A discerning observer could notice how, in a muted and reserved way, his right hand would gently begin to move, the index finger inscribing arcs of writing on the arm of the chair. It was always a sure sign that the meeting needed to come to an end, quickly.

The Rov used to talk about being "faithful" to Torah, being "loyal" to Torah. Loyal and faithful towards one's spouse mean that on a mental level, at least subliminally, one is constantly aware of or preoccupied with the other. The Rov had a total involvement with Torah, all the time.

Once the Rov worked with such riveting focus on one of his famed *yahrzeit derashos*, sitting hunched over a writing desk for long hours, that he severely bruised his rib cage from the pressure of the position. He had been oblivious to the pain throughout.

In the Rov's view, quite often errors in learning and failure to comprehend were the result of a moral flaw—not just an intellectual one. They occurred because we didn't care enough or weren't committed enough to have reviewed the *sugya* as many times as necessary to achieve clarity of understanding. It reflected a lack of seriousness. This was the perspective from which he would at times react with an acerbic comment (especially in earlier years). His goal as a *rebbe* was not just to get the idea across. It was to get the *emes* across! Achieving the correct interpretation or understanding was, in a spiritual and theological sense, a matter of life and death.

The Rov left us with an awareness of the majesty of learning Torah—it was so much more than just an intellectual exercise. It was an implementation of the awesome mandate given at Sinai. It was an encounter with the Torah giants of Jewish history who had a stake in our discussions (*shakla v'tarya*). It had the potential to be such a powerful spiritual experience that it was capable of constituting a veritable *kiyyum tefilla* in its own right. It was the ongoing revelation of Sinai right before our very eyes. Rav Hershel Shachter has said, "With the Rov, Monday and Thursday was *kriyas haTorah*; Tuesday and Wednesday was *kabolas haTorah.*"

I was once present in my parents' home when the Rov reminisced about his early childhood years studying with his father, R. Moshe *zt"l*, who, he said, was a very strict teacher. If R. Moshe asked a question that required an answer of five words, he was not satisfied with an answer of four or six words. The Rov was asked how, as a youngster, he could tolerate that kind of pressure. He reflected for a moment and said, "To me, as a child, learning was a colorful landscape." Torah was full of exciting vistas and colorful perspectives. It was too fascinating for anything or anyone to push him away. From his earliest youth, learning was not just studying; it was not just an intellectual pursuit. It was an overwhelming, all-embracing experience of the heart, mind, and imagination. Even as a child there was color, excitement, and fascination—which made it possible to handle the pressure of being taught in such a demanding fashion.

At times, the Rov couldn't understand how we were so blasé about "thrilling" concepts in the *Gemara*. He once told us that when he was a youngster and first heard the concept of *ksusei mechtas shiurai*, he found the notion so riveting that he couldn't sleep for two weeks. We were learning *Masseches Eruvin* at the time (whether a *lechi* used in *avoda zara* had measurement and dimension) and he was amazed that we could respond to such a concept with complete equanimity. In other words, learning, for him, was not merely intellectual. It was also a very emotional, thrilling and exciting experience.

I remember, in particular, during the summer *shiurim* in Brookline (I believe we were learning *Masseches Horayos*) the Rov was analyzing a "*shvereh* (complicated) Rambam" and remained dissatisfied with some of the resolutions suggested by the classic commentaries on *Mishne Torah*. (He found the *Maggid Mishne* on this point especially problematic.) There were about 25 to 30 *talmidim* sitting out on the sunlit lawn behind the Maimonides School building. (*Shiurim* were given in the afternoon, that year, and often went on for three or four hours.) Suddenly the skies darkened and we moved our chairs under the roof of the outdoor portico. The Rov resumed the *shiur*. It began to rain very heavily, and a violent thunder and lightning storm broke out. The Rov continued with his analysis, all the while paying no attention whatsoever to the torrential downpour and the almost deafening thunder claps which were breaking overhead. There was a surreal gloom and darkness around us. Suddenly, after what seemed like a protracted period of intensive struggle, the Rov formulated an alternative answer to the *Maggid Mishne*'s suggested resolution. I remember it was a "break-through" idea—imaginative, creative, and elegant, as only the Rov was capable of formulating. A commotion of questions and explanations broke out as we strained to get a better grasp of what the Rov was saying. For a few minutes we were lost—first, in total concentration and then in the delight of understanding the *chiddush*. Just at that very moment—one couldn't help noticing it—the rain stopped, the gloom lifted, the dark-grey skies began retreating, and a ray of sunlight broke through. We were stunned. I remember looking around and making eye contact with Rabbis Menahem Genack, Heshie Billet, Bezalel Safran, and others among the *talmidim* there. Nature's timing was so symbolic, so uncanny, that we all broke out in smiles of amazed wonder. The Rov's clarification and the return of light coincided. Afterwards, when the *shiur* ended, we milled around on the drying patio and the thought was expressed that the puzzle presented by the "*shvereh* Rambam" and the *Maggid Mishne* for seven centuries, had just received a beautiful resolution in our presence. We felt we had been witness to a historic moment.

Ashrei she'zachinu.

Personal Glimpses and Lessons Derived

Zev Friedman

"Join the army—or get out!"

I remember the day very well. I was a senior in high school, and after hearing repeatedly about the Rav's greatness from my *rebbe*, Rabbi Chait, I decided to experience the Rav's *shiur* myself. I entered Furst Hall, found the classroom and took a seat. Little did I know that it was adjacent to the "infamous column."

The Rav entered and we all stood up; the *shiur* began. The Rav pointed in the direction of the column and said, "Alright, you in the blue shirt, read." I looked down and realized—I was wearing the blue shirt that caught the Rav's attention. I said, "*Rebbe*, I'm just a visitor here," to which the Rav retorted, "There are no visitors here; either join the army—or get out!"

While I was temporarily shaken, I stayed for the *shiur* and realized that he was conveying a valuable lesson to me and the others: *limmud haTorah* is not a spectator sport; one has to dedicate oneself wholeheartedly to the task; *yagaata-matzata* [if you work hard you will find, a play on *Megillah* 6b].

"Who is he?"

After I graduated from high school I spent a *Shabbos* in Boston with Robert Young, the *shammos* to the Rav *zt"l* at that time. A number of friends made me an emissary to ask the Rav a wide spectrum of questions dealing with *halakhah le'ma'aseh* and clarification of a *sugya*. I dutifully memorized nineteen questions which spanned the four divisions of *Shulchan Arukh* and many *mesekhtos*. I arranged

---

Rabbi Zev Friedman is the *Rosh Yeshiva* of Machon HaTorah, an educational cooperative in Lawrence, NY, including HAFTR, Rambam Mesivta and Shalhevet, which will open in September 2008.

with Robert to join him as he walked the Rav home from Maimonides on Friday night. I asked the Rav if I could ask him some *shailos*. He agreed, and I proceeded to list them all. To my amazement, he answered each question immediately with tremendous clarity and profundity. I walked home reveling in the beauty of his answers. When Robert returned, he told me the Rav had asked about me, inquiring, "Who is he? What is he learning—*Shas*?" Despite the Rav's unanswered questions about me, he did not let on that he found our encounter strange in the slightest way. Initially I found the incident humorous, but later realized how instructive it was. He taught me how one must respond with sensitivity to the question of a *talmid*.

"We were wrong. I think about the *shiur*."

It was a sunny and cool summer week in Boston, perfect weather for my *chevrusa* and me to go biking and enjoy the outdoors. We had just finished a complex *sugya* and felt both relieved and fulfilled in what we had learned. The next day the Rav walked into *shiur* and announced that the *sevara* he had worked out to answer the difficult questions was wrong and proceeded to show why. He then offered the *shiur* some *mussar*, saying, "The difference between me and you is that after the *shiur* is over I think about it, and you go on with your normal routine." The incident opened my eyes to the brutal intellectual honesty one must employ in learning, and the challenge to revisit and perfect one's conclusions.

"Have a good trip"

It was the summer of 1971, my first summer learning with the Rav in Brookline. A mother, accompanied by her teenaged son, approached the Rav and said, "Rabbi Soloveitchik, my son is leaving to learn in Israel; can you give him a *brakhah*?" With a smile the Rav quickly responded, "Alright, have a good trip!" The lesson here is obvious.

"I believe I have the answer"

The Rav often shared anecdotes of his grandfather, Rav Chaim zt"l with us. One day we were learning a particularly difficult Rambam, on which the Rav commented, "Rav Chaim asked the following question and simply didn't have an answer." He paused, smiled, and said, "But I believe I have the answer." I derived from this the need for intellectual courage to explore difficult and seemingly unanswerable questions.

"So what's the answer?"

We were in the middle of learning when the Rav stopped and posed a fundamental eye-opening question. A student blurted out, "I was just about to ask that question," to which the Rav responded with his inimitable smile, "Alright, so what's the answer?" The implicit message to me as a 20-year old was that *shiur* was not about scoring points or impressing the *rebbe*, but about pursuing the truth. A healthy dose of humility is needed in learning.

"Put away the Brisker dictionary"

We were learning on the outdoor patio of Maimonides, and were analyzing a *machloket* in the *Gemara*. After a number of suggestions were offered by *talmidim* and rejected, one student proclaimed, "Oh, it's *cheftza gavra*." The Rav said, "Put away your Brisker dictionary and explain it to me in your own words." Thinking for yourself was the lesson of the day.

"Put away your sociology"

On another occasion, while analyzing a *sugya*, a student read from an English translation of the *Gemara* a sociological explanation for Rava's position, based on the time and place where he lived. The Rav rejected this approach and said, "Put away your sociology, put away your psychology." It was clear that Talmudic analysis has its own methodology based upon strict logic.

"We don't tamper with the Jewish calendar"

In the Rav's explanations on *Tisha b'Av* one felt the *kinot* come alive. He dissected each *kinah* [lament] and showed the obscure quotation from our sages on which it was based. I was sitting on the floor next to the Rav when the question of saying a *kinah* in memory of the *k'doshei haShoah* was raised. The Rav demurred and by association explained that all Jewish tragedy is to be commemorated on *Tisha b'Av*. The Crusades, the Chmelnitzky massacre, the Shoah, and even Israelis being murdered in Athens because they are Jews—all result from the *churban haBayis* [the destruction of the Temple] and are part of our *golus* [exile] experience. For this reason he said there should be no day other than *Tisha b'Av* to commemorate the Shoah.

When pressed about the establishment of *Yom haShoah*, the Rav said, "We don't tamper with the Jewish calendar—and I don't just mean the Holocaust."

The idea that *halakhah* is to be viewed and determined by its own framework regardless of one's personal or political views rang clear from this statement.

Note: I do not want to suggest that one can divine what the Rav was thinking when these events happened. I want only to share with the reader what I took away, and hope that these lessons can enhance one's growth as a *ben* or *bat Torah*.

Hineni He'Ani Mi'ma'as

Itzhak D. Goldberg

Dedicated to the memory of Mr. Abraham Levovitz zt"l, a close friend of the Rav and a communal leader whose advice, kindness and warm friendship we will always cherish.

(Editor's note: The meaning of this title will become clear with the translation of the prayer on the penultimate page of this essay.)

When attempting to describe personal interactions with the Rav one risks a shift in narrative focus from an effort to describe the Rav to the *dor asher lo yada et Yosef* [the generation that did not know Yosef] to an emphasis on a perceived "unique" relationship the writer may have had with the Rav. Therefore I believe it is critical to emphasize at the outset that I am humbled by the undertaking to portray **any** aspects of the Rav's personality and find myself inadequate to the task.

I was privileged to become acquainted with the Rav as a member of the Maimonides community in Brookline, Massachusetts. In 1977 I became a post-doctoral fellow in vascular biology at Harvard Medical School. I, my wife, Rina, and our children moved into a home on Colbourne Crescent in Brookline just a few houses from the Rav. While we left the Boston area in 1985 we still consider ourselves active members of the community and maintain close contact with our Boston friends. The synagogue of the Rav's Maimonides School is where most of my interactions with the Rav took place.

Rav Moshe Lichtenstein, the Rav's grandson who visited the Rav in Boston, writes: "The Rav was a very modest person. His concern

---

Dr. Itzhak D. Goldberg, MD, FACR is the CEO of Angion Biomedica Corporation and Clinical Professor of Radiation Oncology at the Albert Einstein College of Medicine.

for the people and his attachment to them brought him to serve as a shul and school rabbi, a position which he undertook with the fullest spiritual and emotional involvement rather than remaining in the confines of the *bet midrash*. He lived amongst his people and loved them. Anyone who wanted to know the Rav fully had to see him at home, within his community, in Boston. There, he and the members of the community developed a warm relationship of mutual love and care as the *Gadol Hador* was transformed into the local rabbi, relaxed and at home amongst his *ba'alei batim*." (Memories of a Giant)

The Rav was indeed involved with his congregants in Brookline in a uniquely personal way. When I inquired about the *lehi akuma* in our *sukkah* the Rav did not merely inform me of the *halakhic* standards but elected to accompany me to our home to personally assess the dimensions of the *sukkah*. When my wife was due to give birth on *Yom Kippur* the Rav advised me that if I didn't remain home with her then he himself would. Occasionally, on *Shabbat*, the Rav would join the participants of the *Kiddush* Club in their homes and often inquired after their children. When our daughter was involved in a car accident, the Rav, while teaching in New York, conveyed a message to us that he was including her in his prayers. In turn, our young children were easily engaged with the Rav as well. Our family would gather by the window facing the path the Rav would traverse so that we could accompany him on the twenty-minute walk to the synagogue. After services, our children would line up to shake the Rav's hand, ask him questions, and volunteer personal anecdotes. One Sunday morning our oldest daughter whispered to the Rav that it was her brother's birthday. The Rav immediately asked that I purchase a gift for which he insisted on paying. On another occasion our son inquired whether one should recite *Sheheheyanu* at the start of a new season and our daughter asked about her obligation to answer *Amen* after the *berakha* of *shelo asani isha* [the blessing for men]. The Rav truly enjoyed these interactions with young children and welcomed them with a broad warm smile. Between *Minha* and *Maariv* on *Shabbat* afternoons about 10–15 congregants would gather around the Rav and pose questions about the *parasha* or any other topic. This open question forum followed by the Saturday night *parasha shiur* and the Sunday morning *Gemara shiur* afforded a small community of mostly professionals, businessmen and academicians the unique privilege of about five hours of learning and personal interaction with the *Gadol Hador* every weekend.

There are more appropriate congregants who can more ably portray the Rav and his community in the Boston area. The Abelow, Edelman, Feuerstein, Gopin, and Levovitz families among many others lived and worked with the Rav for many decades and together built the Maimonides community and school. They have a much broader view of life with the Rav. I would like however to make several personal observations regarding the *Yamim Noraim* [High Holidays] prayers.

I grew up in a home where the emotional component of the *Yamim Noraim* experience was paramount. As Holocaust survivors, followers of the Gur dynasty and of Rabbi Elimelech of Lezhentz, *Yom Kippur* was a day of trepidation and yearning for atonement expressed by agonized outpouring of emotion and tears. As a child I vividly remember visiting my grandparents on *Erev Kol Nidre* [before the first prayer] and embracing them while they openly wept. This childhood memory was seared into my religious persona and dominated my experience during the *Yamim Noraim* for years to come.

In stark contrast, the Rav recounts in *Halakhic Man* his father's reaction to observing the *baal tokea* [one who would blow the *shofar*], a *Habad Hasid*, crying before sounding the *shofar* on *Rosh Hashana*. "Do you weep when you take the *lulav*? Why then do you weep when you sound the *shofar*? Are not both commandments of God?" his father asked. To the Rav's father's thinking, the technical performance of the *mitzvah* of *shofar* and the technical performance of the *mitzvah* of *lulav* were to be equally executed without inserting subjective emotional input. The Rav continues: "The mystics cleave asunder the barriers of the objectivity and the concreteness of the commandment. On a wondrous craft they navigate the waves of a mysterious subjectivity that surges and flows, that is constantly changing its shape and form, that is always metamorphosing, assuming new images, different guises; and the waves come and sweep the craft and carry them unto paradisiacal realms. **Not so ha-lakhic man!**" In *Halakhic Mind* The Rav carries this viewpoint even further: "Mystical trends which dominated Bergson's biologism and intutionism, phenomenological emotionalism, the so-called humanistic hermeneutics, and the modern existential philosophy have played an important role in the confusion that pervaded European thought…When reason surrenders its supremacy to dark, equivocal emotions, no dam is able to stem the rising tide of the affective stream."

In *Worship of the Heart, Essays on Jewish Prayer* by Rabbi Joseph B. Soloveitchik (edited by Rabbi Shalom Carmy) the Rav dissects the *mitzvot* into the two well-known components: *"maase ha-mitzvah"* (the piecemeal process of actual execution) and *"kiyyum ha-mitzvah"* (compliance with the norm). He describes *maaseh ha-mitzvah* as a religious technique, a series of concrete media through which the execution of the *mitzvah* is made possible. For prayer *maaseh ha-mitzvah* is expressed by the standard text template. The Rav then proposes the following analogy: "There is technique in painting, the proper selection and use of colors, the expert strokes of the brush, and so on. Yet the painting as a piece of art is something different from all these details. It can never be integrated through a piecemeal, additive process, combining the various phases of the execution of the details of the artistic work. It is the personal element, the talent of the artist, the instantaneous creative spark that makes the work worthwhile from an artistic viewpoint." Whether the artist is focused on a realistic depiction of his subject or creating paintings utilizing color, shape and texture with no representative subject matter, mastery of technique is a prerequisite.

Working in a biomedical research laboratory the concept of the technical "piecemeal process of actual execution of a project" resonates with me. Whether the scientific approach is by a hypothesis-driven paradigm or by data-driven inductive methodology, the technical requirements are exacting and demand meticulous experimentation. Development of scientific tools or discoveries of new phenomena typically require multi-step, complex protocols that entail timely introduction of various components and conditions. Often these experiments must be repeated due to a narrow tolerance for errors. This critical role of technique in developing a platform for scientific discovery was clearly demonstrated by the parallel assembly-line type processing in the Human Genome Project. Similarly, in the field of bioinformatics, the development of a molecular modeling computer platform based on complex algorithms seems distant from its application for the discovery of drugs for life-threatening diseases. And while the tedious technical execution of these tasks seems extremely disconnected from the overall goal, they are critical and clearly indispensable. These rigorous technical scientific executions are akin to the artist's "brush and color techniques" and the "piecemeal, additive process" described by the Rav.

If an artist is required to employ a meticulous technique to express an idea and the scientist must follow an exhaustive process, shouldn't a similarly exacting standard apply to the technique of prayer?

For the Rav the prayer technique was rooted in careful *halakhic* interpretation of text and liturgical *nusach* [version, style] as well as an adherence to demanding standards. One example of the Rav's approach to prayer can be demonstrated by his perspective on the public repetition of the *amida*, especially on *Yamim Noraim*.

The Rav posited that *tefillat hatzibur*, communal prayer, is defined and expressed by the repetition of the *amida* by the *shaliah tsibbur* [the emissary of the congregation, the *hazzan*]. The Rav always stood at attention during the entire repetition. The Rav was so persistent in following this *minhag* [custom] that one *Shabbat* when he was already quite frail, the Rav collapsed during the repetition and was rushed to the hospital. The Rav insisted on standing at attention even during the repetition of the long *amidot* on *Rosh Hashana* and *Yom Kippur*. Since all prayers on *Yom Kippur* included additional *selihot* and were quite lengthy, the Rav was standing at attention virtually the entire day. Every year, just prior to *Kol Nidre*, the Rav would gather three men and using his own language (rather than the standard *machzor* text) ask for *hatarat nedarim* [annulment of vows]. The Rav would then specifically request nullification for his custom of standing at attention, lest his strength fail him during the coming *Yom Kippur*.

The Rav was vigilant in listening to every word of *hazarat hashatz* [repetition by the *hazzan*]. In spite of the fact that the Maimonides Synagogue was filled during the *Yamim Noraim* there was total silence during the *amida* repetition. Occasionally the Rav would ask the *shaliach tsibbur* to repeat words that were not clearly heard. During the *Avodah* [the portion of the prayer recreating what was done in the Temple], for example, the *shaliah tsibbur*, flanked by two assistants, would slowly recite aloud the entire text while the Rav and the congregation were repeating every word quietly. It was indeed a beautiful example of *u'neshalma parim sefateinu* [our prayers will be in place of the sacrifices]. There was almost no communal singing. The emphasis was entirely on meticulous recitation of the text with proper grammar and punctuation using the traditional liturgy rather than engaging the congregants in aesthetic popular singing.

The Rav was very familiar with the long-established Ashkenaz liturgical *nusach* of the *Yamim Noraim* and was the *shaliah tsibbur* for *Neilah* [the closing prayer] for many years prior to my arrival in Brookline. In one of the *Yarhei Kalla* summer sessions when the Rav covered topics related to the *Yamim Noraim* he discussed the role of the *shofar* in transforming *din* [judgment] to *rachamim* [mercy]. At one point he turned to one of the attendees and asked him to recite the statement in the *Rosh Hashana* morning prayer repetition using the liturgical *nusach*: "With the *shofar* I will persuade Him, and with bended knee; in the company of friends in His garden I will enjoy His friendship." The Rav then proceeded to point out how well the change in the musical notes reflected the transition from *din* to *rahamim*, from tension to relief.

The Rav implemented certain modifications to the standard prayerbook text of the *amida* repetition. Many of these changes were based on *Nusach Hagra* [the version of the Vilna *Gaon*]. He required the *shaliah tsibbur* to deliberately pause between certain words and refrain from taking a breath between others to separate or connect specific phrases. These changes were based on logical and careful analyses of the sources and at times reflected seminal concepts related to the prayer service. This emphasis on form was especially prominent during *Malkhuyot, Zikhronot* and *Shofarot* on *Rosh Hashana* and the *Avoda* on *Yom Kippur*. The Rav's emphasis on sentence structure and its impact on the textual meaning are demonstrated by the pause he introduced in the middle of the following sentence in the *Avoda* service:

Anna **(pause)** ///// *bashem kaper na la-hataim etc…*

This pause highlights the idea that the *Kohen Gadol* asks the Almighty to atone for our sins on Yom Kippur **through** the medium of His Name. This concept of atonement through the medium of His Name parallels the idea expressed later in the same prayer: *ki bayom ha-zeh yekhaper aleikhem* to be interpreted not as **on** this day but **through** this day, by the unique power of the sanctity of *Yom Kippur, itsumo shel yom mekhapper*. The parallel structure of **ba-yom** and **ba-shem** (through the *Yom Kippur* day and through His Name) was developed by the Rav in a 1979 lecture during which he made the following comment: "If the Name of *Hashem* provides *kappara* [atonement; forgiveness] and the day of *Yom Kippur* also provides *kappara*, then it would therefore seem that the two are equivalent. The *Benei Yissashar* points out that as opposed to other holidays where the holiday's name appears in the beginning of the respective Torah narrative, the appellation of *Yom Kippur* appears only after the description of the *Yom Kippur avoda*. He suggests that this narrative sequence reveals to us that the *kedusha* [sanctity] of Yom Kippur is derived from a hidden world. This concealed *kedusha* is the reason why the *Talmud* tractate is named *Yoma* and not *Yom Kippurim* (as opposed to *Shabbat, Pesachim, Rosh Hashana*). It is interesting to note that the *gedolei Hasidim* never used the appellation "Yom Kippur"; they referred to the day as *Yom Hakadosh* (see Before *Hashem* and *Benei Yissaschar, Tishrei Mamar* 8). While the Rav did not elaborate on this idea one might explain the parallelism between the *kappara* through the power of the hidden *kedusha* of *Yom Kippur* and the *kappara* through the medium of the *kedusha* of the Name of *Hashem* is related to the fact that both may represent *rachamim*. The Ramban in describing the difference between *Rosh Hashana* and *Yom Kippur* maintains that *Rosh Hashana* is a day of judgment that is tempered with mercy (*din berachamim*) while the essence of *Yom Kippur* is a day of mercy tempered with judgment (*rachamin badin*) (*Vayikra*, 23.24). Similarly, the *Shem Hameforash* [G-d's name] reflects *Hashem's* relation to the Jewish people based on lovingkindness and mercy. Perhaps the critical role of *kappara* through the quality of mercy (represented by *Yom Kippur* and *Shem Hashem*) is highlighted in the final crescendo of the *Neila* prayer: *midat harachamin aleynu hitgalgeli* (attribute of Mercy, overflow upon us)."

In 1983 two weeks prior to *Rosh Hashana* the Rav's brother-in-law, Mr. Simmy Gerber *zt"l*, the *shaliah tsibbur* for *Yamim Noraim* for many years, took ill. Mr Abraham Levovitz *zt"l*, a close friend of the Rav and President of the Maimonides School, asked me to temporarily serve as the *shaliah tsibbur* for *Rosh Hashana*. Although I had served as a *shaliah tsibbur* for many years in various venues I could not see myself in this role in the presence of the Rav. It was only after the Rav specifically agreed to my appointment that I anxiously and reluctantly accepted Mr. Levovitz's *zt"l* request (see *Kesef Mishna, Veharav*, Maimonides, *Hilchot Tefila* 5, 12). I spent the following two weeks meeting with Mr Gerber and the Rav and learn-

ing the Rav's *minhagim* and *nusach*. As Mr. Gerber's condition did
not improve after *Rosh Hashana*, I served as *shaliah tsibbur* for *Yom
Kippur* as well (*Maariv, Musaf & Neila*). I have had the privilege to
serve in this role each year ever since.

While it is difficult for me to openly describe the spectra of emotions I experienced as a *shaliah tsibbur* at Maimonides on *Yamim Noraim*, it is not surprising that a dominant component, particularly
during the years the Rav attended the prayer services, was a feeling
of inadequacy. For many years just before the *Musaf* service of *Rosh
Hashana* I would meet Mr. Henry Feuerstein, the *baal tokea*, in the
coat room where we were both preparing for our respective roles
during *Musaf*. Looking into in his eyes one could clearly perceive
his inner emotion of *nirash venifhad* (trembling and frightened). I assume my eyes mirrored the same expression. A few minutes later
the *tefilla* of *Hineni He'ani Mima'as* transferred me into the role of
shaliah tsibbur:

> Here I am, impoverished of deeds, trembling and frightened from
> the dread of Him Who is enthroned upon the praises of Israel, I have
> come to stand and supplicate before You for Your people Israel, who
> have sent me, although I am unworthy and unqualified to do so ...
> Let them not feel humiliated by my willful sins and do not find them
> guilty for my inadequacies for I am a careless and willful sinner. Let
> them not be ashamed of me and let me not be ashamed of them. Ac-
> cept my prayer like the prayers of an experienced elder whose life-
> time has been well spent, whose beard is fully grown, whose voice
> is sweet and who is genial with other people.

The perception of inadequacy and acute responsibility persists
today as the congregants of the Maimonides *Minyan* endeavor to
perpetuate the traditions of the *Gadol Hador* who molded their community for so many decades. For the remaining members of the
community who were privileged to pray with the Rav the following
paragraph from the *Neila* service has unique relevance:

> The needs of Your people are many, but their intellect is inadequate;
> They can not express their needs and desires.
> Please understand our thoughts before we call out
> O great, mighty and awesome G-d.
> Gone and vanished are those who know entreaty,
> Who can eloquently express the order of prayers.

In June 2007, thirty years after our family first moved into the Maimonides community, one of our daughters commenced a radiology residency at the Massachusetts General Hospital in Boston and moved back to Brookline with her husband and their two children. Prior to my own move in 1977, my *chavruta* in medical school, Dr. Yaacov Tendler, advised me to find a residence close to the Rav *zt"l*. "You have a once in a lifetime opportunity to live close to a *Torah* Giant," he stated. If only I could give the same sage advice to my children in Brookline today.

In closing this fractional and flawed narrative I would like to echo the prayer the Rav offers after completing the magnificent description of Halakhic Man:

"This essay is but a patchwork of scattered reflections, a haphazard collection of fragmentary observations, an incomplete sketch of but a few of halakhic man's features. It is devoid of scientific precision, of substantive and stylistic clarity. Indeed, it is an indifferent piece of work." The Rav concludes: "And if I have erred, may God, in His Goodness, forgive me."

Initial Encounters

Shmuel Goldin

I cannot lay claim to the title "*Talmid* of the Rav" in the way that so many others quoted in this volume clearly can. During my two years in Rav Soloveitchik's *shiur*, I did not grow personally close to him; and, in the years which followed, I spoke with him personally less than five times.

I wondered, therefore, when asked to contribute to this work, what my contribution could possibly be.

Then I realized that perhaps I am in the position to represent the countless "others"—those of us whose personal contact with the Rav was limited but who, nonetheless, feel his presence in our thoughts and lives every day. If I can somehow capture the way the Rav so profoundly touched us, an additional layer of his greatness and power will be revealed.

The best way to share my personal perspective is to describe my first encounter with the Rav.

During the months preceding my entry into the Rav's *shiur*, I found myself growing increasingly nervous, even frightened. I was not, however, most concerned about what you might expect. Certainly, I was terrified of the Rav's fabled temper and his unwillingness to countenance fools. I felt, however, that I could safely protect myself from his possible wrath by doing what so many others had done before me: by hiding behind the pillars which were spaced around the *shiur* room. (Little did I know that such protection was

---

Rabbi Shmuel Goldin has served as spiritual leader of Congregation Ahavath Torah in Englewood, New Jersey since 1984. He is the founding director of and lecturer at the Eve Flechner Torah Institute. The author of *Unlocking the Torah Text* on *Bereishit* (Gefen Publishing, 2007), he is writing a second volume on *Shemot*.

not always available, as the seats behind the pillars were always at a premium and in great demand.)

No, what really haunted me more than anything else was the fear that I would be different, that I would fail to be impressed by the "great man"; that I would not be affected by his brilliance; that I would not find his *shiur* to be the mesmerizing experience that had been described to me by so many. After all, I had studied Talmud for years in *shiur* after *shiur*. While I found the subject matter interesting, no previous class or *rebbe* had particularly moved me. How could I be certain that the Rav would be different?

I therefore approached the first day of *shiur* with the Rav with a degree of trepidation...

To put it bluntly, I was immediately "blown away." I quickly realized my mistake: *I had never really learned Talmud before. The first time that I truly learned Gemara was with the Rav.*

Picture the scene that greeted my eyes during those first few days. Roughly 100 students surrounded their elderly mentor as he openly wrestled with the Talmudic text, Rambam and commentaries before their eyes. These students, however, did not sit in rapt attention. To the contrary: the *shiur* was a beehive of activity as, simultaneous with the Rav's teaching, students discussed, deliberated, debated and argued with each other in an often vain attempt to simply keep up with their *rebbe*'s train of thought. Even after hours of preparation (necessary if you were to have any chance of following at all), you simply could not understand the Rav unless you were actively involved in the process as the class unfolded.

The noise in the room would grow; periodically the Rav would pound on his desk and demand quiet; things would quiet down for a short while and then the noise would begin to build again.

And so it went for hours at a time; in class after class; in sessions that could each last for up to three hours. By the time each *shiur* ended we were mentally spent and physically exhausted.

What impressed us so much during those mental marathons? The list goes on and on. It wasn't just the Rav's overpowering intellect but also: his passion for the truth; the originality of his thought; his ability to perceive and categorize vast tomes of text in structured, ordered fashion; his deep intellectual honesty. I remember those rare times when, after hours of building a particular theory, the Rav was confronted with a particularly difficult question from the floor. The Rav would stop short in mid-sentence; consider quietly; close the

Gemara and dismiss the class, saying, "I was wrong and must reconsider..." More often than not, the next class would resume with a successful defense of his original position. How taken we were, however, by his unwillingness to cut intellectual corners. He simply would not continue unless he was sure that he was right.

Above all the greatest lesson that the Rav transmitted to us can be summed up as follows: whereas other teachers demand: *think like I think*, the Rav demanded: *think, like you think*. He insisted that we learn to think for ourselves. Woe to the student who simply parroted back the Rav's positions to the Rav. He demanded that we work the issues through, that we understand and assimilate the information before us, and then that we either accept his position or develop another defensible approach. He was not satisfied until his students learned to stand intellectually on their own.

The Rav's insistence upon original thought explains, in great measure, the wide range of perspective and opinion which can be found on so many issues among the Rav's *talmidim* today. If it sometimes seems difficult to pinpoint the Rav's philosophical and halakhic legacy from among the wide-ranging claims offered in his name, it is partially because he did not spoon-feed his students. Instead, he insisted that we ourselves become part of the ongoing process of *Halakhah*. He did not see himself primarily as a *posek* (decisor of Jewish law) but as a teacher; a teacher of those who, he hoped, would carry the mantle of leadership within the Jewish community for years to come.

Above all, he wanted those future leaders to struggle for themselves within the sacred parameters of their heritage. That demand for originality, creativity and continued study within realms of Jewish thought and law remains, I believe, the Rav's greatest legacy to this day. That demand transmitted to me in those first few moments in the Rav's *shiur* changed my life forever.

Reflections of Two Generations of *Shamashim*
Dovid Holzer

Introduction

My father and I were both privileged to be *shamashim* [attendants] of the Rav for many years. In that time we were able to glimpse certain facets of the Rav's character, and attempted to learn from the example he set. While it is impossible to capture such a majestic life in one little article—nor even in volumes of memoirs—we would like to focus on one of the Rav's unique traits, which my father and I both had the honor of witnessing decades apart from each other.

My Father, Rabbi Emanuel Holzer's Story

Although the legality and availability of *shechitah* in the United States is taken for granted nowadays, it was not always so. In the 1950's *shechitah* was tolerated and merely permitted, but was not recognized as an approved humane method of slaughter. Because of its weak limbo status, groups such as the ASPCA (American Society for the Prevention of Cruelty to Animals) attempted to actually have *shechitah* explicitly outlawed within the US, on the grounds that it was unnecessarily painful to animals. Had they succeeded, this would have been a grave blow to *kashrus* in America, and perhaps the entire nascent *kiruv* [bringing Jews 'close' to their Jewishness] movement (imagine if becoming *frum* [observant] meant being a vegetarian!).

In those days all the Jewish organizations worked together: the Rabbinic Council of America, the Agudath Israel, the Synagogue Council of America, the National Community Relations Advisory

---

Rabbi Dovid Holzer has taught in Michlala College for Women in Jerusalem and was the first principal of Yeshiva Elementary School in Miami Beach. He has written extensively on a wide variety of halakhic and theological works.

Council—everyone sent a joint delegation with the Rav at its head to the United States Senate to plead the case for *shechitah*.

With the Rav traveling to Washington, we wanted to be sure that the senators and congressmen appreciated who this man addressing them was, what role he played in Jewish life in America. So Rabbi Klavan of the RCA had us call all of the Rav's *talmidim* in the Washington area, and arranged for them to attend the hearing. Imagine the assembled congressmen's surprise when they got to this hearing and found over a hundred *rabbanim* in the audience! The congressmen knew these local rabbis, and they all showed up in person to honor the Rav. This no doubt had a positive impact on the outcome.

The Rav gave testimony to the Senate committee in his masterful and inimitable style. I was there as an assistant to the Rav, organizing his papers and taking notes. You can therefore imagine my surprise when, while sitting next to him at the Senate hearing, the Rav unexpectedly said, "My colleague Rabbi Holzer will now continue."

I recovered quickly and started presenting the material we had prepared for that day. Specifically, I had the privilege of tutoring such notable Senators as Hubert Humphrey in *hilchos shechitah*. We felt it was necessary to explain precisely what variations *halachah* allowed in *shechitah* techniques, so that we could work out a compromise which would minimize the animal's suffering while remaining strictly within the bounds of *halachah*.

One of the issues of concern at the time was stunning the animals before slaughter so they would not feel pain. I was asked if the animal must be conscious during *shechitah*. Wishing to defend the position that stunning should not be allowed by *halachah*, I responded that the animal must be fully conscious at the moment that the *shechitah* is performed. As soon as I said this, the Rav began tapping his pen on the table. When I looked over, he caught my eye and asked aloud, "And can you tell me, Rabbi Holzer, where is the source for that law?"

I was taken aback, but quickly realized that I did not actually have any basis for my statement. I retracted it immediately, and continued with the testimony. After the session was adjourned I approached the Rav and said, "*Rebbe*, you *shechted* me in there!"

The Rav smiled at my pun, but explained that when you give testimony, you must have complete honesty and integrity at all times.

And what if the cow was sleeping when the *shochet* approached? Would it be an invalid *shechitah*? I was trying to overemphasize certain aspects of *halachah* in order to maneuver a better position, and the Rav wouldn't have it. He would brook no misrepresentation of *halachah*, no matter what was at stake.

Rabbi Dovid Holzer's Story

To put my story in a better context, let me first tell you the *seder ha'yom* [agenda; order of the day] in the Rav's *shiur* during the 1970's. Morning *seder* began at 9:00, when the students would begin preparing the *sugya*. Somewhere between 11 and 11:30 I would go to escort the Rav from his on-campus apartment to the classroom. Typically the Rav would call roll, then glance around the room and select the person who would have the honor of reading the *sugya* aloud that day. I always felt bad for Nate Kahn, who at about 6"4 was a frequent "winner," despite his heroic efforts at slouching.

The *shiur* was never a lecture, but always interactive, questioning, back-and-forth analyzing, the Rav helping each of us find our own perspective on the *sugya*. After a series of questions and development, the Rav finally gave us a breath of fresh clarity in his own explanation of the *sugya*, and the roughly two-hour long *shiur* concluded close to 2:00. It was followed by *mincha* and then lunch. Part of my job as the *shamash* was to hand the Rav reminder notes as to the time, since his doctors had advised him not to go too late and overtax himself. On most occasions, these notes were promptly ignored.

I remember well one day in *shiur*—I can't remember the *sugya*, but the incident stands out in my mind—when the Rav had just gone through a very difficult *Tosfos*, and came out with a *p'shat* which seemed to resolve all the issues within *Tosfos*. It had been a long two hours, and we were all looking forward to the approaching lunch break. Then, just before the Rav's *gemara* closed, someone in the back raised his hand, and asked the Rav a question about his solution. The Rav thought about it for a moment, and was seemingly troubled by it. He put his head down to think for what seemed like eternity, but was probably about ten minutes. All one hundred and twenty of us sat there in hushed silence while the Rav remained sunk deep in thought.

Finally the Rav picked up his head and announced, "Forget everything I said. We have to re-analyze the *Tosfos*." He began again from scratch, building up a new *p'shat*, all because of the difficulty. By the time we finished, we were far into lunchtime, possibly past it. The hour did not bother him; time was never an issue. The fact that a student had seen a fatal flaw in his approach was of no concern to the Rav's ego; the truth was at stake! Many teachers in his position might have opted to dismiss or evade the question, especially when in such a public forum. But to the Rav, absolute intellectual honesty far outweighed any such consideration. The *Torah* demands that it be presented in the most accurate way that man can understand it.

Conclusion

These two vignettes illustrate the Rav's commitment to intellectual honesty in the face of both personal embarrassment and potential legal sanctions against an integral part of Jewish life. In our experience the events we have recounted were not isolated, but typical of the Rav. He always invited questions, and refused to allow personal pride to interfere with the search for truth. For the Rav, representing the true *halachah* overrode all political or social considerations. He was not interested in what was popular, but what was true.

The Rav often warned those seeking to represent the *Torah* to be wary of their own self-interest. If you have any personal stake in the outcome, it colors your ability to see the truth. The Rav himself was ever-cognizant of this danger, and avoided it assiduously. Clearly, presenting *Torah* and *halachah* as accurately and honestly as he could was of paramount importance to the Rav. If we could all work towards the same intellectual rigor and candidness, it would both enrich our own lives and be a lasting tribute to the ideals of our *rebbe*.

Reliving Sinai

Doniel Lander

Reflecting on the Rav *zt"l* and the *shiurim* I heard from him, is much more than an exercise in nostalgia; it is, fundamentally, an expression of self-awareness and self-definition. Although a quarter of a century has passed since I attended his class, my seven-year stint in the Rav's *shiur* remains the formative experience of my life and continues to provide the spark that ignites my passion for *Limud HaTorah* [study] and *Harbotzas HaTorah* [teaching].

The Rav often conveyed to us the concept that Torah study is essentially a reenactment of *Matan Torah* [the giving of the Torah]. Indeed, both *Bavli* and *Yerushalmi* derive *halachos* concerning Talmud Torah from revelation at Sinai. The Rav's *talmidim* understood this to be an experiential fact, for the spirit of Sinai characterized every element of the *shiur*.

The mood at revelation was defined by the paradoxical mix of trembling and jubilation. Recognition of the Rav's greatness projected a similar sense of trepidation but simultaneously, there was also profound ecstasy, as a result of the Rav leading us to the depths of the *Yam* [sea of] *HaTalmud*.

Somehow, the Rav was able to transcend his physical constraints. In ill health, afflicted with a painful back and assorted ailments, he delivered his *shiur*, oblivious to the clock and to his personal handicaps. When the *shiur* concluded, he would almost collapse in his chair, but while he taught Torah, the Rav was animated and excited, a young man with boundless energy and unlimited endurance. The picture that *Chazal* paint of Sinai, the sweeping aside of all corporeal limitations, was on vivid display.

Rabbi Doniel Lander is *Rosh HaYeshiva* of Yeshivas Ohr Hachaim and its affiliated Mesivtas, Yesodei Yeshurun and Yesodei Yisrael.

The Rav himself understood this to be his role: to retransmit the Torah to waves of generations in the same manner as the *Ribono Shel Olam* conveyed the Torah to the *Dor Hamidbar* [G-d to the generation in the wilderness]. He proudly claimed the mantle of *melamed*, explaining that this title also describes the Almighty in His relationship to the Jewish people.

This was the Rav's aspiration and he succeeded brilliantly because he followed precisely the Divine model. *Midrash Rabah* recounts that the Almighty, in a wondrous display of humility, descended from His celestial seat of glory in order to teach Torah to the multitudes. The Rav's entire essence and in particular, the manner in which he conducted the *shiur*, also bespoke greatness of modesty.

It would not have been terribly difficult for the Rav to have used the *shiur* to showcase his endless string of *chidushim*. But instead, the Rav devoted the *shiur* to his *talmidim*, to train them in the methodology of *lomdus*. The Rav taught us how to probe; he encouraged us to question and he insisted that we never remain contented with superficial analysis.

And this devotion knew no bounds. I remember the day we learned the *sugya* of *Kiddush Hashem* in *Pesachim*. It was a very long *shiur*, much longer than the average three-hour duration. After that draining *shiur*, the Rav accepted questions from those who surrounded his desk—as he often did—and continued to discuss the *sugya* with fifteen inquisitive *talmidim* for yet another two and a half hours.

When the Rav's writings were posthumously published, many students expressed surprise that much of our *rebbe*'s Torah had been hidden from us. Following the divine precedent, our revered *rebbe* descended from his own seat of glory, eschewing self-promotion, in order to focus his attention upon the growth of his students and the development of their learning skills.

Another important parallel, often overlooked: every morning we preface the *Shema* with the recognition of the love *Hakadosh Baruch Hu* [G-d] showered upon *Klal Yisroel* as He presented the Torah to them. In the gaze that the Rav affixed upon his *talmidim*, the spirit of love that characterized the original transmission of Torah was once again evident and deeply felt.

Ramban maintains that there is a special prohibition against forgetting *Ma'amad Har Sinai*. The experience of revelation is etched into our very soul. I, too, shall never forget the drama and palpable *kedusha* that permeated the *shiur*. I shall never forget the Rav's intoxication with the Torah. And I shall always treasure, with everlasting gratitude, the precious keys to the *mesorah* that I was privileged to receive from my beloved *Rebbe*.

Tuesday Evenings with the Rav*

Morris Laub

Some call him J.B. Others, Reb Yoshe Ber. Still others, the Rav. All the appellations refer to Rabbi Joseph B. Soloveitchik, the renowned Talmudist of Boston and New York. The first two cognomens are his nicknames, privy to his pupils and former pupils. The last may be used by all, including those like myself, who are not his pupils or disciples.

The *rebbe-talmid* relationship is a special one. Not only does it imply teacher and pupil, but it means master and disciple. In both meanings, the relationship is, reciprocal—a *rebbe* is not a teacher unless he recognizes his students as pupils, nor is he a master except of those he acknowledges as disciples. I, like many others, unrecognized as we are as pupils or disciples, can only regard Rabbi Soloveitchik as the Rav, the rabbi, a title he cannot deny us, for he is a rabbi, and for most of his pupils, disciples and plain admirers like myself, he is a special rabbi, a unique rabbi, ergo, the rabbi.

For some two hundred odd men and a handful of women he is the Talmudist who gives a *shiur* every Tuesday night at Moriah Synagogue, located above a supermarket and next door to a music school on Broadway and West 80th street in Manhattan. Moriah is an Orthodox synagogue, founded and frequented largely by diamond merchants, formerly of Belgium and now in New York, mainly on 47th street between 5th and 6th Avenues. These worshippers bring with them business acumen, specialized commercial

Morris Laub was director of the Joint Commission on Social Action of the Conservative movement, and was also director of the World Council of Synagogues.

Reprinted with permission from Congress Bi-Weekly Volume 38, #11. © 1971 American Jewish Congress.

knowledge, piety and love of learning. Their synagogue, modest, old-fashioned, is a very model of worship and study. A *shiur* is given several evenings a week as well as on Sabbaths, but the *shiur* is the one organized by the Chevra Shas Haklalith of New York and given by the Rav every Tuesday evening from 8 to 10.

The regular attendants at the *shiur* are rabbis, in and out of pulpits, most of them former students of the Rav at the Yeshivat Rabeinu Isaac Elchanan of Yeshiva University, rabbinic colleagues who never studied under the Rav, laymen who can follow a *shiur*, young students and professional men, and persons like myself, auditors, who delight in having our spirits refreshed and learning imbibed during our youth renewed at the well of Torah. Who the women are I can only guess; I can barely see them, for they sit modestly behind a partition, but with curtains raised, so that the Rav can be seen more clearly. Are they *rebbetzins*? Jewish day school graduates? Where did they learn enough Talmud and Yiddish—the *shiur* is in Yiddish—to be able to follow? Most are young, this much I can see from a cursory glance at them as we leave the synagogue. In any crowd, they would be indistinguishable from others. But here they are not only distinguished by their very presence, but by their obvious facility in swimming in the sea of the Talmud.

A *shiur* is not a lecture nor a seminar nor a classroom discussion. It is an exercise in participatory pedagogy. The Rav explains, analyzes, 'synthesizes,' pulls disparate strands together and weaves them into a beautifully patterned fabric. But in doing so he constantly is the classic *shiur* master, hurling challenges, stopping to ask questions, waiting for answers, inviting queries, probing into his listeners' consciousness, demanding concentration and vocal expression of differences. The listener at the *shiur* is not passive, and if he is active even to the point of interruption, he is not frowned upon by the master nor disdained by his fellows. On the contrary, a brilliant insight is commended. Even a silly question is forgiven though the questioner has uttered something inane. Can we be wise all the time? It is easy to be silent—many of us, including myself, are, but at a *shiur* interruption is not a sign of chutzpah or a breach of discipline. It is an accepted norm, almost de rigueur.

The Rav's *shiur* has been going on for many years. I have been attending for eight years, more or less regularly. When I started, the group was somewhere in the middle of tractate *Berakhoth*. Then we

went on to *Megillah,* and now we are about sixteen pages deep in
Taanith. The pace is very slow, but also very thorough. All of us are
urged to come prepared and judging from the chorus of responses,
nods of recognition and interjections referring to a passage in the
Jerusalem Talmud, Maimonides or some other great commentator,
most of us do. I sometimes spend a few hours in preparation, but
most times I merely glance over the next few lines together with the
Rashi and passing look at a Tosafot, the classic commentators. I usually make a mental note about the ease or difficulty of a passage to
come and I usually am wrong. What I think easy turns out to be an
illusion, for the Rav uncovers meaning after meaning, each increasingly complex and my head begins to swim with the revealed intri-
cacies and I look at myself in a befuddlement as a simpleton who
cannot make a judgment as to what is hard and what is easy. Of
course, all the complexities are eventually resolved and the passage
suddenly is lucid and easy again, but only in the sense that a beautiful structure, so pleasing at first glace, takes on greater beauty after
an examination of what went into it between blueprint and actual-
ity. On the other hand, I am sometimes stumped by a passage that
seems very hard to me and I try to work it out in advance, often
without success. At the *shiur* I learn that it really is very easy; all it
needed was a single reference to another passage or to a statement
in a commentary, or another meaning to a key word. And what
seemed so hard is now so simple! The Rav's *shiur* is a series of sur-
prises, topsy-turvy Talmudic terms, and delightful astonishments.

The Tuesday evening *shiur* follows an unwritten scenario. It is
announced for 8:00 and everyone is in his seat, never assigned, but
a regular seat nevertheless by dint of custom, before 8:00. We are
not only students but worshippers, so there will always be a service
or two or three before the *shiur.* The people around me converse
about the events of the day, but mostly I hear stock market talk, law
court talk, and professional rabbinic talk. The Rav rarely comes at 8,
usually ten minutes after 8. His arrival is greeted with a sudden
hush. Everyone rises and waits till he takes his seat next to the Ark.
It is pro forma to rise when a rabbi enters, but our rising is not a
mere formality; ours is so obviously a mark of respect, love and affection. The Rav strides in briskly, removes his coat, changes to a
yarmulka, ascends the *bimah* [platform] around which all of us are
seated in a flattened U pattern, waits patiently till the microphone

is affixed to his jacket and begins with his opening question, "Where are we?" waits for no answer but proceeds immediately to where we left off last week. He begins quietly, calmly, but soon he is all gestures and emphasis, using his arms, head and body in eloquent accompaniment to the rise and fall of his voice as the *shiur* leads him to greater and greater animation. He repeats a point over and over and the successive iterations add new nuances. He looks at his audience questioningly, quizzically and invites responses and ripostes. Sometimes he is impatient at an interruption and silences the interjector summarily, but at other times he says, "Now you should ask a question. Why don't you." One can almost feel the tense concentration at trying to find the question he wants.

The Rav is a man of contrasts. He is of medium height, slight of build, with a neatly rimmed, square, progressively graying beard adding dignity to his calm face. His modest style of dress is modern, as it probably has been all his life whether as a student in the yeshiva of his famous forebears or in the German universities where he took his doctorate in philosophy. He strikes me as being a shy man, a loner, but seated on the *bimah* he is gregarious, at one with the body of his listeners, working with them, at them, for them. Nothing seems to give him so much pleasure as teaching and navigating through the Talmud. His face as a teacher is aglow with the knowledge that he is a link in the long honorable tradition of his family of teachers and rabbis, while his demeanor away from the lectern is that of a retiring man, alone with his thoughts, a man to whom being aloof is most natural.

The *shiur* is usually in two parts. The major portion is devoted to the Talmudic text before us, the minor portion on an exegetical explanation of a verse in last week's Torah reading, usually as expounded by Nachmanides. It is said the Rav purposely selects last week's portion rather than next week's to insure his not being quoted in scores of pulpits the following Sabbath. I suppose he is quoted the following year for there are many who take notes. For a while, some even had tape recorders until requested by the Rav to forego this practice. I notice that all in my section have honored his request. However, in an adjoining section there is one who continues taping surreptitiously. Why? I imagine the Rav's prohibition is not directed against modern recording devices as such, for he does have his own technician who tapes his *shiurim*, but rather against the possibility of unauthorized publication of unedited tapes.

Once in a great while, the Rav will in a few words call attention to the presence of a visitor and plead his cause, usually that of a yeshiva in Israel. I am happy to say we respond quickly and, I hope, generously.

The *shiur* flies by and it's 10:00. We have covered perhaps half a dozen lines and heard a stimulating interpretation on a verse from the Pentateuch. The Rav rises and so do we. And we hurry out to car, bus, train, or taxi. I am immersed in thought and wonder as I leave and eagerly look forward to my next Tuesday evening with the Rav. May his strength increase!

On the Tuesday Night Public Shi'urim

Dear Mr. Laub:

I read your article for the Congress Bi-Weekly. Please accept my sincere thanks. I am grateful not so much for "what" you said about me—I am undeserving of the accolades and the kind words you bestowed upon me—but rather for the "how" you said it. I am impressed particularly by the emotional warmth and the affection with which you portrayed the Tuesday evening shi'urim. The portrayal of those shi'urim was done with literary finesse and dignified sentimentality.

To be frank, sensitivity in general, and religious sensitivity in particular, is a rare phenomenon in this day and age. The modern Jew is in dire need of religious experience, of a great ecstasy in living as a Jew and "being involved" in Jewishness. No matter how committed the contemporary Jew is, he is completely unaware of the emotional dimension of the religious act. The lack of warmth and joy in observing the law and practicing Judaism is appalling. He is mostly either over-intellectualized and too sophisticated or superficial and utilitarian in his relationship to the Almighty. That is why I am so appreciative of an encounter with a Jew who is not only committed and knowledgeable but also rich in emotion, beholding a vision and radiating the enthusiasm of the dreamer.

You are right that I love teaching. The latter is as far as I am concerned, a great experience, inspiring, redeeming and cleansing of body and soul. I enjoy sharing knowledge with others; I like the dialogue between teacher and student and I find fulfillment in it. I am not lonely when I teach! With the conclusion of the shi'ur or lecture, however, I return to my "lonely" abode in anticipation of another opportunity to teach.

With blessings for life, peace and all good things,

Sincerely,

Joseph Soloveitchik

My Grandfather – The Rav

Mayer Eliyahu Lichtenstein

I

The relationship between grandfather and grandson is two-fold in depth and character. On the one hand, a grandson has the option to develop a unique and intimate relationship—getting to know his grandfather from a unique angle which others don't have the possibility to experience. But on the other hand, the two-generation gap between them inevitably means that a grandson knows his grandfather at old age, after the peak of his career and rich activities, often when his health declines and his pace slows down. Therefore, in fact, a grandson can not be privileged to know his grandfather in a mode that others can. A grandson can only get to know his grandfather "from behind," as Rabi characterized the relationship between himself and Rabi Meir:

> Rabi said: The reason that I am sharper than my colleagues is that I saw Rabi Meir from behind him and if I had seen him from his front, I would be even sharper, as it is written 'And your eyes shall behold your teachers' (*Eruvin* 13b).

The above analysis of the dual nature of the relationship between grandfather and grandson is true regarding my relationship with my grandfather the Rav *zt"l*. I was born when the Rav was 61 years old. I moved to Israel with my family when I was seven, and started annual summer visits to learn with the Rav when I was fourteen years old. After I graduated from yeshiva high school, I spent one year learning with the Rav in YU, during the academic year

Rabbi Mayer Eliyahu Lichtenstein is on the rabbinic faculty of Yeshivat Otniel in Israel.

1981–1982. During these five years, 1978-1982, the Rav was in his late seventies while his physical condition was declining. He wasn't at the height of his strength. I wasn't privileged to hear one of his majestic public lectures—*tshuva kinus* or *yahrzeit shiur*. Many *talmidim* of the Rav learned from him much more Torah than I was privileged to acquire, and knew him for many more years. But on the other hand, my being his grandson did enable me during our years of acquaintanceship to form a unique relationship with him. Paradoxically, the decline in the Rav's health and the slowing down of his pace, made him less intense and less rigorous, more calm and perhaps more accessible. I heard from the Rav many stories about his early years and mentors (Reb Chaim Brisker, his father Reb Moshe, his uncle Reb Menachem Krakovsky and others), which I later learned that my parents had never heard from him. During those years, he was less independent and therefore required more *shimush*, a situation which creates a unique angle, which *Chazal* have described—"Attending to those who study Torah is greater than studying it" (*Berachot* 7b).

Even though my acquaintance with the Rav was short and I am not entitled to call him my *Rav Muvhak*, he actually made a tremendous impact upon my life, and his image keeps accompanying me till today. Since many others knew the Rav better than I, the focus of this essay will not be the Rav's image as he was, but rather I'll focus upon our relationship, describing the impact he made upon me.

II

I don't have many clear memories of the Rav from my early childhood years in New York in the late sixties. We lived in Washington Heights, and the Rav lived in Boston, spending three days in NY every week. During his stay he was very busy, and didn't spend much time with us. After the passing away of my grandmother Dr. Tonya Soloveitchik *zt"l* in 1967, the Rav immersed himself in intensive Torah study and teaching and was very active. I remember visits to his small apartment in Morgenstern Hall (Morg 101), and his weekly visit at our apartment on 11 Ft. George Hill for theWednesday night suppers he used to eat regularly with us. Even though part of the Rav's astonishing ability to excite his audience was due to his ability to share with crowds of thousands of people his private feelings and emotions, he was a very shy person and on a personal base seldom expressed emotions. He never kissed us, and would only extend a shy handshake to us. We always knew that his heart is full of love for us, and that he was shy expressing it. Contrary to the Rav's habit, my other grandfather, Dr. Yechiel Lichtenstein zt"l, would express his love through the many kisses he would shower upon us. One of my brothers commented during those years that one handshake from Zayde (that's the way we referred to the Rav) is equivalent to ten kisses from *Saba* (that's the way we referred to Dr. Lichtenstein).

This shyness of the Rav in expressing inter-personal relations didn't make it easy to keep a close and meaningful contact with him after we moved to Israel in 1971. During the seven years I didn't see him, there wasn't much contact with him. Long distance phone calls were less common in those days, and the contact was kept through infrequent letters. From time to time he would send us a present, but it wasn't on a regular basis. He didn't even call or send me a gift for my Bar Mitzvah! Even though I had little contact with him during those years I knew that I have a very special grandfather, a Torah giant, and that we were meaningful to him however he chose to express it.

III

My meaningful relationship with my Zayde was established when I spent the summer of 1978 with him. I was privileged to participate in his *shiurim*, learn with him privately at home, accompany him for his daily walks, and sit near him in *shul*. I cherished those precious moments, and felt the excitement being so close to my zayde. I still have my notebook in which I wrote the various *divrei Torah* and stories I heard from him. That doesn't mean that I understood all of the Torah I heard from him. That summer the Rav delivered *shiurim* on the eleventh chapter of Tractate *Zevahim*. Can you imagine what it means for a fourteen year old to participate in those *shiurim*? The impact they made upon me was not because I fully understood them. I particularly remember a three hour *shiur* the Rav delivered on *hechsher kelim*, referring constantly to the concept of *ta'am ke-eikar*. It was a wonderful *shiur*, but I had only one problem which prevented me from understanding it—I never heard of the concept of *ta'am ke-eikar*!

During the next five years, my understanding of the Rav's *shiurim* grew, but unfortunately his health deteriorated and together with that the forcefulness of his *shiurim*. Still, I kept learning from him eagerly, cherishing every word I heard from him.

IV

Even though I learned most of my Torah from my father, Rav Aharon Lichtenstein *shlit"a*, my acquaintanceship with the Rav made a tremendous impact upon me. This impact is less on my knowledge and training and more on my disposition and love of Torah. At the *Brit Milah* of the Rav's firstborn great-grandson, Meshulam Twersky, the Rav referred to the *Gemara* in *Kiddushin* 30a:

> Rabi Yehoshua ben Levi said: Anyone who teaches his grandson Torah, Scripture deems it as if he received it from Mount Sinai; as it is written: "You shall make them known to your sons and your grandsons," and next to this, "The day that you stood before Hashem your God at Horev."

The Rav pointed out that while Rabi Yehoshua ben Levi seems to express this merit of "As if he received it from Mount Sinai" to one teaching his grandson and apparently not to one teaching his son, the Rambam in *Hilchot Talmud Torah* states that one's son precedes one's grandson in regard to Talmud Torah. The Rav explained that the *Gemara* and the Rambam are referring to two different concepts. While the Rambam is referring to the obligation to teach the content of the Torah, the *Gemara* is referring to a different obligation—the transmission of the *Mesorah*. The Rav explained that besides the *mitzvah* of Talmud Torah, there is another obligation to make sure that our generation will transfer our heritage to the next generations, from a deep commitment to the continuity of the Oral Tradition. Regarding these two obligations, there is a different role for father and grandfather. While the father has the primary role teaching his son Torah, the grandfather has the primary role transmitting the *Mesorah* since he is closer to the revelation at Sinai, and his teaching his grandson transmits the oral tradition two generations forward. I will add that this analysis reflects the different nature of the relationships of parents and grandparents to their descendants. Since grandparents are not in charge of the actual raising of the child, they form a different relationship from parents.

The Rav emphasized many times that the *rebbe-talmid* relationship is two-fold. It combines an intellectual encounter together with an emotional, experiential and existential relationship. I suggest, combining together these two statements of the Rav, that the father's obligation to teach his son Torah is rooted more in the intellectual sphere while the grandfather is more qualified to attach his grandson emotionally to Torah.

The above analysis describes my debt towards my two great teachers—my father and my zayde. While most of my training and my knowledge was acquired from my father *shlit"a*, my Zayde, the Rav, gave me my passion for Torah and a commitment, a sense of joining a chain of *Ba'alei Mesorah*. Since I was a young boy, my father devoted major effort to teach me Torah. As children relate to learning, I had my difficulties enjoying this learning. The turning point in my attitude towards learning was the summer of 1978, when I truly met my Zayde. The blessing of the *Gemara* to the grandfather "As if he received it from Mount Sinai" is true regarding the grandson as well. Being near my Zayde's was like being near Mount Sinai. That summer opened my heart and soul and enabled me to dive into the world of Talmud Torah.

V

When I first met the Rav, I was so overwhelmed by his wisdom that I thought it must be that everything he said was true. I tended to agree with all his views and ideas. When I matured and developed my own world view, I started to design my own independent views. As of today, I have different views from the Rav regarding fundamental issues.

Many people mistakenly think that a true *talmid* has to accept the views of his master. I think that the contrary is true. The historian Jacob Katz was asked when he turned ninety if he had studied anything from the works of Karl Marx. He responded: "Of course; all historians have learned from Marx except for the Marxists, since they are *hassidim*." Here, Katz has defined a deep truth. A true *talmid* learns from his master how to think and not what to think. A true *talmid* doesn't duplicate his master while a *hassid* imitates his master but doesn't learn from him.

When I first met the Rav I was a *hassid*. When I matured and started thinking independently, I developed into a *talmid*, and then and only then did I begin trúly to learn from the Rav. I sense today that I have a deeper understanding of the Rav. I'm inspired by him daily, even when I conclude and act differently from the way he would have. I speak with him constantly, and I'm sure that he would have been proud of my independence. It was a great privilege to know him, and I'm committed to continue his legacy, as understood by me, his loving grandson and *talmid*.

The Rav and the Tisha B'Av *Kinot*

Jacob J. Schacter

Rabbi Joseph B. Soloveitchik had a great and lasting impact on Jewish life and learning in the twentieth century as a teacher of Torah (he often referred to himself as a *"melamed"*) in various formal and informal settings, as a philosopher and as a communal leader.

One of his many contributions was to illuminate the book of *Kinot* recited on Tisha B'Av. The Rav was a master of the Bible and had the wide-ranging knowledge of rabbinic literature (Talmud and Midrash), medieval Hebrew poetry, and Jewish history necessary to understand and fully appreciate the *kinot*, using his prodigious knowledge in all these areas to unlock that which had previously been closed for generations. He opened up the book of *Kinot* for us and revolutionized our thinking about Tisha B'Av, the *hurban* and Jewish national tragedy in general. For this reason, as well as for so many others, our generation owes him a tremendous debt of gratitude.

From the late 1960s until the mid 1980s, the Rav would spend all or much of the day of Tisha B'Av teaching. Shaharit would begin at 8:00am in the Maimonides School, the yeshiva day school founded by the Rav and his wife in Boston. At about 9:00 am, the Rav would deliver a *shiur* on issues relevant to Tisha B'Av for about an hour and, after about a five-minute break, would begin the recital of the *Kinot*. After reading a few words or phrases, he would stop and comment, sometimes for a moment or two and sometimes for more extended periods of time. Those assembled would regularly interrupt with questions and insights and the Rav would stop and ad-

Jacob J. Schacter is University Professor of Jewish History and Jewish Thought and Senior Scholar, Center for the Jewish Future, Yeshiva University.

dress their points. This mixture of reciting and learning, reading and studying, the traditional plaintive sweet sing-song of the *Kinot* interspersed with the traditional robust sounds of Torah teaching, would continue for many hours. It was my privilege to be personally present from 1973–1981 and that experience still deeply resonates with me.

Each year, the Rav opened the *Kinot* book and studied it as if he was doing so for the first time, and the results were never predictable. Sometimes he repeated the basic interpretations he had suggested in previous years or presented them in a slightly different way, sometimes he suggested new interpretations and sometimes he explicitly took issue with interpretations he had given in years past. Very often, until the early 1980s, this combination of a spiritual and intellectual experience would last until late in the afternoon.

The Toras Horav Foundation published much of the Rav's teachings on Tisha B'Av under my editorship in *The Lord Is Righteous in All His Ways: Reflections on the Tish'ah Be-Av Kinot by Rabbi Joseph B. Soloveitchik* (Jersey City: Ktav Publishing House, Inc., 2006). But there is still more to share. Some of his comments on the first few passages of the *kinot* follow.

Shavat Suru Meni

Shavat suru meni. This phrase invokes a verse in Eikhah (5:15), "The joy in our hearts has stopped (*shavat mesos libenu*)." This, of course, does not mean that, until then, during the entire time the *bet ha-mikdash* was standing, all Jews rejoiced every day, every hour. Of course, Jews mourned, Jews suffered, Jews wept, and Jews cried. Surely Jews were not continually happy before the *hurban bet ha-mikdash*. But there were moments during which they rejoiced. And then came *Shavat mesos libenu*. Suddenly the joy in our hearts stopped. We cannot find joy anymore. Yes, after the *hurban bet ha-mikdash*, sometimes one suffers and sometimes one does not suffer. One leads a normal life, does business, studies, lectures, travels, quarrels, fights. Merchants are busy selling and buying, scholars are busy studying Torah, and workers are busy with their manual labor. But inwardly, deep down in his heart, the Jew cries. There is not any joy left in his life.

Shima'uni okhrai. The word *okhrai* refers to someone who does not gain anything from a particular act. He simply enjoys the suffering and misery of others without deriving any benefit from it. Many peoples rejoiced when Jerusalem was destroyed. In fact, even now they still rejoice. They have no conflict now between themselves and the Jewish people, they gain no benefit from the downfall of Jerusalem, but they still rejoice over its suffering.

Ad pil'ei Gilgol havuyah. Gilgol refers here not only to the geographic place by that name but to all the miracles that transpired during the fourteen years during which Joshua conquered and partitioned the land.

When Joshua entered Eretz Yisrael, Rahav the Harlot told the spies, "I know . . . that the fear of you has fallen upon us and all the inhabitants of the land have dissolved because of you. We heard and our hearts melted" (Yehoshua 2:9, 11). There was respect and fear for the Jew. The inhabitants of the land stood in awe before the Jew, before the camp of the Jewish people.

Gilgol hearkened back to a period of great vigor and might, the time of the conquest of Eretz Yisrael and its partition among the tribes. Gilgol, the period of conquest and partition, is characteristic of the period of "the resting place and the heritage" (Devarim 12:9). So, says Rabbi Elazar Hakalir: "I had been expecting the miracles of Gilgol, just the opposite of what occurred with the *hurban*." He is saying that we would never have believed that the initial sanctity of the land, the *kedushah rishonah* established by Joshua, would come to an end. We believed that the land would never be conquered again by someone else. We expected that the same miracles that had transpired during the invasion of Eretz Yisrael by the Jewish people led by Joshua would repeat themselves again. But, instead, the period of Gilgol is *havuyah*. It is covered up, hidden, concealed and gone. In fact, when Nevukhadnezzar came, that sanctity did *not* continue, in keeping with what the Rambam said (*Hilkhot Bet ha-Behirah* 6:15-16) with regard to the Land of Israel as a whole, "*Kedushah rishonah kidshah le-sha'atah ve-lo kidshah le-atid lavo*."

Nuptzu hasidehah. What is *nipetz*? What is the difference between *nipetz* and *shiver*? *Nipetz* means to break into very small particles. In other words, reconstruction is impossible. In the case of *shiver*, however, reconstruction is sometimes possible. Hazal (*Sanhedrin* 52b) talk about some vessels that can be reconstructed and some that cannot. Certain objects you can reconstruct, reform or refashion. But *nuptzu hasidehah* means that her pious ones were utterly destroyed, converted into dust.

When it came to the *hurban bet ha-mikdash*, regardless of how tragic it was, it is something that could be reconstructed. Although the *bayit rishon* was destroyed, the *bayit sheini* was built. Although the *bayit sheini* was destroyed, the *bayit shlishi* will be built, even more glorious, beautiful, and magnificent. Yes, we weep and we mourn over the destruction of the *bayit rishon* and the *bayit sheni*, but all is not lost, all is not hopeless.

But the loss of "her pious ones" is different. Hazal say (*Shir Hashirim Rabbah* 6:12; *Kohelet Rabbah* 5:16) that if a scholar dies, a great Jewish leader, there is none that can take his place, his loss cannot be reconstructed. Here there is no return, there is no substitute. This is impossible to restore.

Ayeih hasidehah. This is blasphemy, *hiruf ve-giduf.* Our enemies ask: "Where are your great, pious, powerful men who should be protecting you from being completely destroyed?" Here Kalir is emphasizing the blasphemy that took place as a result of the *hurban.*

We also know that during the time of the Ten Martyrs the *Hakhmei Hazal* had to face an executioner who uttered words of blasphemy before they were executed (*Midrash Eileh Ezkerah* in *Ozar Midrashim* [Eisenstein], 443). And, in fact, our enemies also engaged in blasphemy during the Holocaust as well. "Let your God help you, let Him save you," they said.

Patzu ma'aseh ervah li-nidehah. This is a reference to the *keruvim* that were in each other's embrace. Hazal tell us (*Eikhah Rabbah,* Pesihta 9) that when the *bayit rishon* was destroyed and desecrated, all the nations entered it looking for gold. But the Amonites and Moabites came into the Holy of Holies not interested in the loot. They were interested in something else, to show that the Jew never acknowledged monotheism, that he was an idol worshipper and guilty of paganism just like the other peoples of the world. Instead of focusing on the booty, they came into the *bet ha-mikdash,* took the *keruvim* out into the streets of Jerusalem and showed them to the Gentile multitudes who had invaded the city. "Look at the *keruvim,*" they said. "The Jews are just like every other people. They too worship idols. The nation that said that one should not worship idols is itself worshipping them. In their most sacred place they are worshipping the *keruvim*." This *hillul shem Yisrael* is the most tragic expression of exile. One has not only to be a liar to accuse Yisrael of paganism or idolatry, one has to be a *hatzuf u-mehuzaf*.

Atah kalim hikhbadita u-mei'edyi eirmuni. This refers to the rabbinic statement (*Shabbat* 88a) that at the moment the Jews said "we will do (*na'aseh*)" before "we will hear (*ve-nishma*)" (Shemot 24:7), six hundred thousand angels came and presented each Jew with two crowns. One had *na'aseh* on it and the other had *nishma*. And when they sinned by worshipping the Golden Calf, down came wicked angels and stripped each one of the two crowns from their heads. This, too, we remember on Tisha B'Av.

Koli le-hashmi'a ba-Arav higrimuni. This refers to the story in the Midrash (*Eikhah Rabbah* 2:4) about how the Arabs of Arav, the *Benei Yishmael*, treated those refugees, exiles and fugitives who came to their land. According to this passage, many exiles came to Arabia and, because they were very thirsty, they asked the Arabs for some water to drink. But instead of giving them water, they gave them very sharp, salty, spicy foods. This stimulated their thirst even more but the Arabs again denied them water. They gave them empty pitchers in order to torture them and the Jews died from thirst. The people had expected help and, once again, they were betrayed. This, too, we remember on Tisha B'Av.

Siftei meshorirei devir damimu le-hadbi'ani. *Devir* is the *bet ha-mikdash*. This refers to the Gemara in *Ta'anit* (29a) that, on Motzaei Shabbat, when the *bet ha-mikdash* was destroyed, the Levites were in the midst of singing their song while standing on the platform there. The song they were singing was "He turned upon them their own violence, and with their own evil He will cut them off" (Tehilim 94:23). But they did not have the opportunity to complete the verse and say, "The Lord our God will cut them off" when their enemies entered and captured them. The enemy thought that when they would enter the precincts of the Temple, the Levites would stop singing. But they continued to sing because the halakhah is that during a time of a governmental decree (*gezerat ha-malkhut*) one must insist upon performing even a so-called "minor *mitzvah*" (*Sanhedrin*

74b). They wanted to spite the enemy, to show them that, regardless of their temporary successes, the song in the *bet ha-mikdash* will go on. They did not stop singing, even for a fraction of a second. But, while they were singing, they were killed.

There is also another interpretation. *Devir* could also refer to the Holy of Holies. We say in *Amitz Koah*, the part of the Musaf service on Yom Kippur describing the Temple service, "... and he [the High Priest] entered into the *devir*." In that case, the *meshorerei devir* could not possibly refer to the Levites because they sang in the *azarah*, on the platform, and not in the Holy of Holies. To what, then, could it be referring?

In one of his sermons, Rabbi Menachem Krakovsky [the Rav's uncle] quotes the *Zohar* (or *Tikkunei Zohar*) in Aharei Mot that states that during the *bayit rishon* when the High Priest completed his service in the Temple on Yom Kippur, he first waited for the smoke of the incense to fill up the Holy of Holies and then would not leave until he heard the ministering angels singing songs with words from Tehillim. Maybe this is the reference here, that now this song was silenced. This is not the literal meaning of this passage, and it is also uncertain that Rabbi Elazer Hakalir had the *Zohar*, but maybe this is the meaning of *meshorerei devir*. In that case, it refers not to the Levites but to the song of the angels.

Tikra li-shakram kos kamus bi-finekha. Kalir is asking for compensation, for revenge. He asks that *Hakadosh Barukh Hu* should repay them and give them the cup of bitterness that is hidden.

Tavo kol ra'atam lefanekha. My faith in the eternal covenant reached between God and Abraham, Isaac, and Jacob encourages me to believe that all the crimes against us will be punished and that Zion and Jerusalem will be restored.

Tavo el tzar asher kilanu. Did the enemy actually destroy all of us? He was not successful, God forbid. But it means that his *intention* was to destroy us. Did he not say earlier that they wanted to destroy us as a people? Their intention certainly was to do that.

Ram habeit na amkha kulanu. Almighty God, in spite of everything, in spite of the fact that we have sinned, that we have been alienated from You for a long time, that we have suffered so much, still we have not given up on our relationship with You. Take a look! We are Your nation, even now. True, we are scattered over the entire world. We comprise many tribes, each with its own community, language and mores. We look differently from one another. A Jew from Halah and Havor and an American or Canadian Jew do not look alike. But, in spite of all the differences within the Jewish people, despite the differences of ability and the incommensurability of historical destinies, we are dedicated to You. We will never desert You. We will never feel alienated from You, no matter how distant we may be from You. There is something that unites all of us and, of course, that is the Torah. And since we belong to You, You cannot rid Yourself of us. We belong to You and You belong to us.

Zekhor Adoshem meh hayah lanu. Why is *zekhirah* or memory necessary here? Why need we speak of memory or remembrance? There is no need for *us* to say: "Remember." Is it not a reality for us that Nevukhadnezzar and his cohorts invaded Eretz Yisrael, destroyed the *bet ha-mikdash*, and killed hundreds of thousands of Jews? We know very well about the *hurban* and its impact. But the reference here is not to us, it is to *Hakadosh Barukh Hu*. We ask that *He* should remember what He promised us and end our *galut*.

Eikhah Atzta ve-Apkha. We mention here all the covenants that were established from the days of Abraham on down that were ignored during the time of the *hurban*. In spite of the promises that *Hakadosh Barukh Hu* made to Abraham, Jacob and Moses, the *hurban* took place. And, like many other *kinot*, this one too is an alphabetical acrostic.

Ve-lo zakharta berit ben ha-betarim asher berarta li-vhunekha. You did not remember the *berit* that You clarified or explained to those who were tested by You, like Abraham. That *berit* featured the promise of Eretz Yisrael, and we simply do not understand why that promise is not being implemented as yet. We simply do not understand why Eretz Yisrael does not yet belong to us.

The *berit ben ha-betarim* also clarified that, from now on, *Hakadosh Barukh Hu* and *Kenesset Yisrael* are partners. Whatever is done to the Jew is considered as if it was done to *Hakadosh Barukh Hu*. The *pasuk* states (Bamidbar 10:35), "Arise, O Lord, and let Your foes be scattered, let those who hate You flee from before You." The Midrash

(*Sifrei*, Beha'alotkha, Piska 26; see also Rashi, *ad. loc.* s.v. *mis'anekha*) asks, "Does the *Ribbono shel Olam* have enemies?" And it answers, "Yes. Whoever hates the Jewish people is as if they hate *Hakadosh Barukh Hu*." And that was established by what act? By the act of the *berit ben ha-betarim*.

But there is still more significance to the relevance here of the *berit ben ha-betarim*. There is a deeper connection between this covenant, Edom and the *hurban*. The Torah says (Bereishit 21:12), "Through Isaac (*ki bi-Yizhak*) will offspring be considered yours" and Hazal (*Nedarim* 31a; *Sanhedrin* 59b) emphasize that this applies to only some of the descendants of Isaac, but not all of them ("*bi-Yizhak, ve-lo kol Yizhak*"). Edom and Esau were left out of the *berit ben ha-betarim* and do not belong there even though Esau was a son of Isaac. There was a specific promise made, an agreement, a contract, a covenant established, that asserted that Esau will not share in this *berit* nor in any of the prophecies and revelations in which Abraham encountered *Hakadosh Barukh Hu*. He is to be excluded from and have no share in this great partnership between Him and Abraham's children. And now, we claim, the *bet ha-mikdash* was destroyed by this very same Esau (Edom). This same Esau whom He *excluded* from this covenant is the one who walked into the Holy of Holies and desecrated the *beit ha-mikdash*. How can this be?

Li-vhunekha. To those who were tested by You and passed the test. This is a reference to a statement in Hazal (*Midrash Zuta Shir Hashirim* [Buber] 1:15) that Esau had a choice, an option. If he had not sold the birthright, he would have been entitled to the same destiny that God bestowed upon Jacob. Abraham was tested and he passed the test; Esau was tested and he failed the test.

Laglot be-yad ge'im ge'ulekha. You have exiled the people whom You have redeemed from Egypt into the hands of those who are vain and proud, the wicked ones, a reference to the Romans. That Eretz Yisrael does not belong to us is number one. Number two is *galut* or exile, not only from Eretz Yisrael but from other lands as well.

Ve-lo zakharta deligut dilug derekh asher dalagta li-degalekha. You did not remember what You planned for Your people had the sin of the spies not taken place. They would have entered Eretz Yisrael quickly, as it says, "It is eleven days from Horev by way of Mount Seir to Kadesh-Barnea" (Devarim 1:2; and see Rashi, *ad. loc.*). In colloquial Hebrew we call it *kefizat ha-derekh*. *Kefizat ha-derekh* and *dilug derekh* mean the same thing, to leap, to make a jump, to shorten the distance. We say to *Hakadosh Barukh Hu*: "After the people left Egypt, You were in a haste to bring them into Eretz Yisrael. Yes, they sinned and, as a result, their arrival was postponed for many years, but You had originally been eager to bring them into Eretz Yisrael as soon as possible. Why? Because it was important that Eretz Yisrael be populated by the Jew. This combination of Eretz Yisrael and the Jew is very important. Eretz Yisrael is the land of the Jew. And what did You do now? You exiled Your people."

First we ask why the land was devastated; this is "*Ve-lo zakharta berit ben ha-betarim.*" And then we ask why was there a separation between the land and the people; this is "*Ve-lo zakharta deligat dilug derekh asher dalagta li-degalekha.*"

Ve-lo zakharta deligut dilug derekh asher dalagta li-degalekha u-vechen dibarnu zekhor Adoshem meh hayah lanu. What is the link here? The verse says in Jeremiah (2:2), "I recall for you the kindness of your youth, the love of your nuptials, your following Me into the wilderness, into an unsown land." When the Jewish people left Egypt and went into the desert, their leaving was an expression of faith in God and in Moses. The redemption from Egypt was not only a miracle on the part of *Hakadosh Barukh Hu*; it also spoke well of the faith of the Jews who were prepared to "follow Me into the wilderness, into an unsown land." In that verse, *Hakadosh Barukh Hu* said to Jeremiah prior to the *hurban* that He will always remember that act of faith and the complete trust which the Jewish people demonstrated in Him when He told them to leave Egypt, a civilized country, and go into the desert. And, therefore, we now take the liberty to say: "Recall, O Lord, what has befallen us." That faith of the Jewish people during the time of the exodus should have protected her from the Babylonian as well as from the Roman exile.

Eikhah hagta be-hegyonkha lahadof be-yad holilim hamonekha. How could You deliver Your multitudes into the hands of the known blasphemers who reject You?

The main characteristic of *holilim* is that they have no code of behavior. A *holel* is someone who has no moral law, who cannot discipline himself, who does whatever his mind tells him, whatever gives him pleasure. Sometimes one reads in the press or hears on the radio about many crimes committed by teenagers. From the description of the kind of life they lead, one can see that they are the typical *holel*, without the rule of law, with no ability to discipline themselves.

Hamonekha. The *hamon* referred to here is not a wild, undisciplined, reckless crowd but rather the *Kenesset Yisrael*. And, the larger the crowd, the more conspicuous is the presence of the *Shekhinah*. We find this idea in the context of *Birkat ha-Mazon*. The Mishnah (*Berakhot* 49b) says in the name of Rabbi Yosi Ha-Glili that ten men reciting the Grace After Meals together say, "Let us bless our God," a hundred say "Let us bless the Lord, our God," a thousand say "Let us bless the Lord, our God, the God of Israel," and ten thousand say "Let us bless the Lord, our God, the God of Israel, Lord of Hosts Who dwells in the cherubs." The basic principle is: "They recite the blessing in accordance with the size of the assemblage." The bigger the crowd, the more numerous the multitude, the higher is the level on which the Jew finds himself.

This is very strange. Usually, a crowd *lowers* the intelligence of the people. When people get together, they influence one another and *lower* the common level of intelligence. In Yahadut, however, it is different. The Torah wants a gathering or an assemblage to *raise* the level of its participants and enable activities that an individual cannot do alone like *Kaddish*, *Kedushah*, or *Barkhu*. The Jew somehow becomes exalted, his mind is enhanced, by the fact that he joins the multitude. "He became king over Yeshurun when the numbers of the nation gathered (*be-hit'asef rashei am*)" (Devarim 33:5). That is why many things that cannot be done in private can be accomplished if a multitude is present.

La-hamulekha. To those upon whom You had mercy. *Hemlah* is pity, sympathy, compassion. On the Yamim Noraim we say, "Have compassion on Your handiwork (*hamol al ma'asekha*)."

What is the difference between *rahamim* and *hemlah*? *Rahamim* means love, not just pity. On the verse of "And you shall love the

Lord, your God," (Devarim 6:5), Targum Onkelos says "*Ve-tirham.*"
Rahamim means not only that *Hakadosh Barukh Hu* has pity on us, or
feels compassion for us, but He *loves* us. Many times the Targum
translated *ve-ahavta* as *rahmanuta* (see, for example, to Bereshit 22:21,
25:28, Shemot 20:5, 21:5). *Rahmanuta* means that I love a person because I have good reason to love him, because he deserves it; I consider him worthy of my love. There is a value judgment involved in
the love. It is not that I love you because I cannot help myself but
love you. No. It is a conscious act.

Hemlah, by contrast, is a natural, almost compulsive, reaction on
the part of a human being. In *hemlah*, there is no value judgment. If
one will walk on the street and see somebody in pain, one will feel
compassion for that person whether one knows him or not, whether
he is "worthy" of one's compassion or not. One cannot help but
have pity on him. This is *hemlah*.

This is what we say to *Hakadosh Barukh Hu*. "You don't remember the closeness of Horev that You established *la-hamulekha*," to the
people whom You must love even if You want to reject them. Even
if You resent them, even if they are sinful, You must love them. You
cannot help Yourself, as it were, but to love them. It is *hamulekha*,
not *rihumekha*. You *must* have compassion for them. You are *impelled*
to love Yisrael, as it were. So, if this is the case, why do You punish
us so much?

U-ve-khein hivinu. I understand some of the earlier words like
bitinu or *dibarnu* or *konanu*. But what is *hivinu*? In Hebrew, *hivinu* is
like *havat da'at.* We have a commentary on *Yoreh De'ah* called *Havat
Da'at*. It means the formulation or the expression of an opinion like
that of a judge. It carries authority; it means something. A judge will
say, "My *havat da'at* is such and such" and since the litigants submitted their case to him, they are bound to carry out what he says.
The *havat da'at* of a judge, therefore, is more than just the expression
of an opinion. It carries significant weight.

So here we say to *Hakadosh Barukh Hu* that we are expressing our
opinion *as judges* that He owes us "food, clothing and a marital relationship" (Shemot 21:10) and He has not yet paid up His debt. We
are now arguing a legal point. You are *obligated* to redeem us! You
are *obligated* to send the *mashiah* because You are our husband, and
a husband is obligated to redeem his wife from captivity. "*U-ve-
khen*," and that is why we have the hutzpah to "*hivinu*," to express

our *havat da'at*, our authoritative opinion, that *"Zekhor Adoshem meh hayah lanu,"* that You should remember what happened to us.

Eikhah tarahta be-tarhakha litrof be-yad teme'im tela'ekha. Until now we spoke about the *hurban bet ha-mikdash*. Now we are speaking about "devouring by the unclean," referring to the pogroms and massacres to which we have been subjected through-out the nineteen hundred years of our exile.

"Litrof be-yad teme'im tela'ekha" is a reference to the law of *ma'aser behemah*. If I have ten animals, I am obligated to bring one as a sac-rifice. How does one determine which animal is to be brought? The Mishnah (*Bekhorot* 58b) says that their owner gathers all his animals into an area with a narrow passageway. He has a whip with red dye and as the animals enter the barn, he counts one by one—one, two, three, four, and so on—and after each one says to himself *"hulin,"* profane. When the tenth comes in, he swings the whip on it, marks it red and says, "This one is *ma'aser.*" This tenth animal that becomes sanctified is taken to Jerusalem to be offered as a sacrifice and its blood is sprinkled on the altar.

Only the tenth is *kodesh*, sanctified. But what about the nine that were not marked as sanctified? Have they no part in the sanctifica-tion at all? Of course the first nine are not holy. Those nine are them-selves profane. But if not for the fact that one could count the first nine, there would not have been a tenth, one that would be *kodesh*. The first nine are responsible for the *kedushah* of the tenth. Only be-cause there were nine *hulin* is the tenth one considered *kodesh*. They themselves may not be *kadosh*, but they are responsible for and share in the *kedushah* of the tenth.

So too here. The *paytan* is saying that even the disregarded ones are also "Your lambs." They also belong to You. Every Jew has in-herent *kedushah*. All the members of the Jewish community are "Your lambs." The entire *Kelal Yisrael*, good or bad, sinners or not sinners, is holy. Even those who are not counted as the tenth still have a share in the holiness. Every Jew has a share in *Hakadosh Barukh Hu*.

The Rav: A Boston Memoir

Jeffrey R. Woolf

Thirty-three years ago this past summer [1973], I entered the Rav's shiur for the first time, and my life was transformed. The place was not Furst Hall, but the *Bais Medrash* of the Maimonides School in Brookline. Every summer, for six weeks, the Rav would say *shiur* on a given *massekhta* to a group of forty-fifty people. The *shiur* took place from Monday–Thursday and lasted from two to three hours, between 4 p.m. and 7 p.m. It was intense, intensive, inspiring, awe-inspiring and often very daring. Most of the *talmidim* were from YU, a few were not.

I was in the latter group.

When I came to study with the Rav, something that I was privileged to do for almost ten years, I had never previously been in a formal yeshiva setting, although I had heard *shiurim*. I was pretty much an intense auto-didact when it came to learning, though I had had the benefit of an extraordinary Hebrew education at Boston Hebrew Teacher's College, which helped tremendously, and the warm encouragement of teachers who were themselves close to the Rav, such as Rabbi Dr. Isaiah Wohlgemuth and Rabbi David Shapiro (whose suggestion it was that I attend the *shiur*). It was Rabbi Wohlgemuth who approached the Rav on my behalf, to ask permission to attend the *shiur*. The Rav, graciously (and he was always gracious), agreed. I found out later that he was intrigued by the prospect of an HTC graduate attending his class. It was only seven years later, on the morning before my wedding, that I discovered that, unbeknownst to me, he had kept abreast of my progress, both in Boston and later, when I came to RIETS. That was typical of him. He did things quietly, especially when it came to acts of *hesed*.

Rabbi Dr. Jeffrey Woolf, RIETS '82, is a Senior Lecturer in the Talmud Department at Bar Ilan University.

I shall never forget those first weeks in the *shiur*. I fell in love with the Rav, and with the *Brisker derekh*. At the same time, though he had mellowed considerably over the years (as Professor Haym Soloveitchik noted in his unforgettable eulogy of his father), we still very much feared him. I knew, of course, that the Rambam in *Hilkhot Yesode ha-Torah*, describes the dialectical tension between Love and Awe, *Ahavah ve-Yir'ah*, in our relationship to God. In the *shiur*, and later as I was privileged to develop a more personal relationship with him, I learned that in the *rebbe-talmid* relationship, the two co-existed simultaneously.

It's important for me to emphasize that I came to the Rav in the interest of growing in *lehrnen*. However, I was (and remain) a person who firmly believes in the value of the broadest education possible. At the time that I started in the *shiur*, as a university student majoring in history, I was already caught in the clutches of the Heraclitean struggle between, what I later learned were, 'Torah' and '*Hokhma*.' Here, too, the Rav quickly became the preeminent influence upon my life. By personal example, and by direct instruction, I learned how Torah and *Hokhma* 'in the widest sense of the term' (as he, himself put it) were mutually fructifying, though the absolute autonomy of *Halakhah* was non-negotiable. It was the Rav who gave me the tools to struggle with, and negotiate, the intellectual, cultural and psychological challenges that Judaism faced (and faces) in an already then Post-Modern world. In a very real sense, he became the *rebbe* of both my mind and my soul.

How did he do that? After all, in the years when I first reflected on these issues, he had published very little. In fact, *Ish ha-Halakhah*, *The Lonely Man of Faith*, and *Confrontation* were pretty much it. To begin with, as Professor Yitzhak Twersky wrote, the Rav didn't need to preach the desirability of a general education. He just did it. One sees that from the footnotes of all of his writings, right up to his retirement.

There was, however, more. Every *Motzai Shabbos*, the Rav would give a *shiur* in "Thought" at Maimonides. Sometimes it was the *parsha*. On other occasions we studied Rambam. Before the various holidays we always concentrated on *inyyana de-yoma* [current matters]. The Rav would hold forth, reading from his hand-written notes, and frequently departing therefrom. The room was almost always packed to the gills, even in the worst weather. Men and women, rabbis and professors, Harvard undergraduates and MIT graduate stu-

dents, artists and poets, business people and professionals, came together to hear the Rav. I distinctly recall one woman who drove
ninety minutes from New Hampshire in order to attend. I was often
struck by the very dissonance of the *shiur*. After all, Boston is a college town. Saturday night is party night. Yet here were up to two
hundred people who, week after week, came to learn from the Rav.
On the other hand, here was a very busy man who, despite his tax-
ing schedule, wanted to teach on Saturday night and often had to be
reminded that the hour was late, so that he could go home to rest.

The Rav's delivery, in an incredibly elegant but accessible English, riveted us to our chairs. I remember that he gave us a special
treat when he would comment on world affairs and local Jewish im-
broglios. These were the years of Watergate, Vietnam, the Counter-
culture, the Six Day War and the Yom Kippur War. We thirsted for
insight into a world gone mad, and the Rav obliged. Sitting now in
my home in Eretz Yisrael, I recall with special fondness his lyrical
odes of love to Eretz Yisrael. I try to re-read my notes on *Lekh Lekha*
every year. The *shiur* went on from 8:15 PM until close to midnight
(and sometimes, later than that). Despite the long hours, we were always hungry for more.

It was in those lectures, that I was able to see the Rav 'do it.' In
those *shiurim*, in front of people from his beloved community, he let
himself go. Descartes mixed with Maimonides and Kirkegaard hov-
ered over a discussion of the *Akedah* [binding of the sacrifice, Isaac,
to the altar]. What stunned me from the first time I went was the
way that he seamlessly segued from one to the other. I had never
seen before, and never seen since, such sovereign mastery of both
Torah and general culture. No one present had any doubt that the
Rav's position was 'mimeni re'u ve-khen ta'asu' [see from {my ac-
tions} and do the same].

Again, and this must be emphasized, while there is absolutely no
doubt that the Rav never retreated from his intense engagement
with *Hokhma* (and his ongoing involvement in the Maimonides cur-
riculum is proof), his absolute priority was always Talmud Torah,
in the more restricted sense. The former had absolutely no value
without the latter. I remember that in the spring of 1976 I faced a
dilemma. I had been accepted to both Harvard Graduate School and
directly into the *Semikha* program at RIETS. I wanted to go to learn,
but the offer from Harvard could not be deferred. I called up the
Rav and asked for an appointment.

We met at the Twersky home, which was a bit awkward since it was Professor Twersky who was pressuring me to choose Harvard. I laid out my quandary to the Rav. Without divulging the exact content of the conversation and since he never told me to do anything, he made it very clear that graduate school was a better option, on one condition. That condition was that I must keep up with my learning, and preferably in his Sunday morning *shiur* at Maimonides.

It was, as they say, a 'no brainer.' The Sunday morning *shiur* for the Boston Hevrah Shas (that had brought him to Boston forty years earlier) was an incredible experience. It was the embodiment of *qol demamah daqah* [sound of fine silence]. In the years that I attended, there were never more than twenty people there. Five or six were elderly members of the Boston Orthodox community. The rest were local rabbis and students. Qualitatively, the *shiur* did not lag behind that which the Rav gave at RIETS (as I discovered when I came to Yeshiva in 1978). In a sense, it was better. Rabbi Mordechai Feuerstein used to say that if you really want to learn the Rav's *derekh*, you should come to Boston, go to graduate school and prepare all week for the Sunday *shiur*. He was so right. The Rav was part *maggid shiur* and part tutor. Since he was on his home turf, and the crowd was small, you could ask questions easily and not stop until you (and he) were satisfied that you understood.

To return to my original point, from our conversation in March of 1976, I certainly understood that Talmud Torah comes first. However, I also understood that, in the absence of that, there is no reason not to maximize the breadth of one's knowledge. This approach is, in a sense, a profound and very difficult *humra* [rigorous interpretation]. However, as the Rav said so many times, a Jew is commanded to live heroically. The easy path is not his path. Dialectic struggle is the dominant characteristic of Jewish life, as it is the leitmotif of the Rav's writings and the formal cast of Brisker *lomdus*.

Of one thing, however, I am sure. The transformative moment in the Maimonides *Bes Medrash*, when I first encountered Rav Soloveitchik, and the many other moments that came afterwards, changed my life, enriched it and continue to inspire it, every day.

The '80s:
An Aging Giant

The Rav at Kenneth Brander's wedding. Rabbi Brander is currently Dean of the Center for Jewish Future at Yeshiva University. (Photo courtesy Kenneth Brander.)

Transformation

Binyamin Blau

"The Rav is coming." Those four words rang out and seized my attention. Not only was it my first year in the Rav's *shiur*, but it was my first day in Yeshiva and I was not sure of how the system worked. We had simply been learning *b'chavrusa* [with a study partner]; it was unclear when *shiur* would begin and when it would be appropriate to engage in the practical matter of eating lunch. Hearing the announcement that the Rav was on his way, I assumed it meant that we needed to get ready for the upcoming experience. I was excited and nervous, having heard so much about the daily *shiur* from my father and having had the privilege of learning with the Rav during a summer in Boston.

To my great surprise the classroom began to empty out. Noticing my confusion, my *chavrusa*, a veteran of the *shiur*, explained to me that due to Rav Solovietchik's frail health the trip from his apartment over to the classroom would take a while; during that time students typically ran and caught a quick bite to eat. I was puzzled: the walk from his apartment in Morgenstern to our room in Furst Hall was only two blocks; how could it take the Rav so long? I leaned out the window and saw him bent over and walking slowly, and began to understand.

While I now appreciated how the system worked, a new query presented itself. The Rav was well known for his marathon *shiurim*,

Rabbi Binyamin Blau is Upper School Principal of the Fuchs Mizrachi School in Cleveland and *Rosh Kollel* of the Torah Tzion *Kollel*. He previously served as a member of the rabbinate in Elizabeth, New Jersey where he taught at the Rabbi Teitz Mesivta Academy and Bruriah High School. He also taught at Yeshivat Mevasseret Tzion in Israel.

but in his present condition that seemed impossible. How would someone who appeared so physically broken be able to give *shiur* for even thirty minutes? I was a bit despondent. He then shuffled into the classroom and the *shiur* began.

The transformation seemed magical. As the Rav taught he grew younger and stronger before our very eyes. His voice became more audible, his gestures more animated. Teaching Torah literally gave him life. It was an amazing experience that would be repeated daily. The Rav would teach for over two hours and his *shamashim* would have the unpleasant task of reminding him that the doctors did not want him overextending himself. When he acquiesced and ended his class, his true health would be revealed once more. The Rav would often revert back to his frail condition, and there were days when we refrained from even asking questions so as not to task him.

Incredible as the life-giving force of Torah was, it was made even more remarkable by the manner in which the Rav delivered his *shiur*. Despite having taught these subjects numerous times, he approached each topic without any preconceived notions. His thirst for authentic *limud Torah*, combined with his impeccable intellectual honesty, led him to analyze each *sugya* with the freshness that our sages described when they stated the Torah should constantly appear new in our eyes. While men half the Rav's age were teaching finely honed, but sterile lectures, he was engaging in a vibrant, creative process.

An incident during *Aseres Y'mei Teshuvah* was my introduction to what I later realized was a daily occurrence. Attendance at the *shiur* increased before *Yom Kippur* as numerous guests joined us to hear the Rav examine the Rambam's *Hilchos Teshuvah*. The Rav posed a penetrating question, noting an apparent contradiction in the words of the Rambam, and he asked his *talmidim* to offer an explanation. Various suggestions were introduced until one individual gave a brilliant exposition—one that the Rav himself had once taught, and that had later been transcribed in his work *Al HaTeshuvah*. The Rav thought about the response and stated, "That is a good answer. Who said that?" The young man quickly replied, "You did, *Rebbe*." The Rav smiled and said softly, "Yes, yes," and then proceeded to propose an entirely new elucidation of the conflicting texts.

I learned a great deal of *lomdut* during my years in the Rav's *shiur*, and it was an honor (albeit a poignant one due to his decline) to be a member of the class during the final years that he taught at Yeshiva. However, more than any specific piece of Torah that he taught us, it is the image of a person being transformed through the transmitting of Torah that remains imprinted on my soul.

The Rov as a Personal Rebbe

Kenneth Brander*

When most people think of Rov Joseph B. Soloveitchik, they tend to focus on his brilliance. I do not have the ability to expound on the Rov's intellectual greatness. However, as someone who, from age nineteen through twenty-three, was not only in the Rov's *shiur* but also was one of his *shamashim* (assistants), I was blessed to be able to observe the Rov closely, spending more time with him than I did with my own parents.

I got the position of *shamash* because my *chavruta*, who was one of the Rov's *shamashim*, was leaving Yeshiva University for medical school. He suggested me as someone who could take his place; soon after, the Rov's son, Dr. Haym Soloveitchik, asked me to serve. Initially, I turned down the position. The thought of being in the Rov's presence on a daily basis for long periods of time, was too intimidating. However, Rabbi Yosef Blau, the *mashgiach* of YU, encouraged me to reconsider; listening to Rabbi Blau was one of the best decisions of my life.

Rov Moshe Feinstein was fond of saying that the Rov was the *melamed* of our time. In *shiur* the Rov was at home with any *sugya* in *Shas*, any issue in *halachah* and any philosophical idea. His philosophy of Judaism was often articulated with language found in Kant, Hegel, Kierkegaard and Cohen, but his ideas were predicated on the ideals found in Rambam and Ramban. He used all of his knowledge to be an effective teacher, and every *shiur* introduced us to another color in the tapestry of Torah. I remember the Rov once explaining

Rabbi Kenneth Brander is Dean of Yeshiva University's Center for the Jewish Future and Rabbi Emeritus of the Boca Raton Synagogue, FL.

*This essay was adapted from a lecture delivered by Rabbi Brander at the 2002 OU National Convention.

why *hotza'ah* (carrying on Shabbat) was categorized by Tosafot (*Shabbat* 2a, s.v. *y'ziot ha'shabbat*) as a *melachah geruah* (an inferior creative act Biblically forbidden on *Shabbat*). *Melachot* forbidden on Shabbat are normally creative in their nature; *hotza'ah* lacks a creative aspect. To explain the difficulty the rabbis had in classifying *hotza'ah*, the Rov drew an analogy to the Communist party. He described how the Communist leaders tried to show how every type of workers' union was "productive," but they had difficulty articulating the productivity of the transportation union. Unlike every other union that created a product, the transportation union simply moved goods from one location to another. Just as the union did not easily classify the transportation workers as being "productive," *hotza'ah*, said the Rov, did not easily classify as a forbidden category of work.

The Rov's clarity, charisma and intellectual integrity made *shiur* exciting, and his classroom became a gathering place for all types of people—from young *semichah* students to veteran *roshei yeshivah*. Immediately after *Sukkot* or during the first week of *Nisan*, when YU was in session and other yeshivot were on vacation, the Rov's *shiur* would be attended by many guests who just wanted to see and hear the Rov.

Often at the end of the *shiur* there would be questions on what was taught, and the Rov would answer them all. One time, a younger student asked a question. The Rov answered the question and ended *shiur*. As I was leaving, the Rov asked me if I knew where that particular student ate lunch. I told him I thought at a restaurant called McDovids (where the Center for the Jewish Future storefront is now). The Rov indicated that he wanted to go there. As we entered the place, the MTA high school students, who were playing pinball, recognized the Rov and froze. Even the non-Jewish man flipping hamburgers behind the counter knew who the Rov was and froze as well. The Rov went over to the student, who was trying to digest his hamburger, and indicated that he would base the following day's *shiur* on the young man's question.

At one point, due to the Rov's health, his *shiur* had to be limited to two hours. During *shiur* I typically sat next to the Rov. I devised a technique to deal with the time limit. I would slip pieces of paper to him depicting the passage of time. On the first day, the system worked like a charm. I handed the Rov the sheet indicating that two hours had passed, and he ended *shiur*. Everyone in the room was shocked. The next day, however, after signaling the Rov, he continued to teach. How does a twenty-year-old deal with the fact that the *gadol hador* is not following his medically prescribed time limit? All the students had their eyes fixed on me to see how the situation would unfold. After another forty-five minutes passed, I rose, closed the Rov's *Gemara* and announced that *shiur* was over. The entire room was quiet. The Rov turned to his students and said, "Even the Satan doesn't have as good an assistant as I do." All the students laughed, and *shiur* was over. Rather than engage in conversation, I walked silently with the Rov to his apartment in Morgenstern Dormitory (Morg 101). He asked me what was wrong. I told him that I had not ended the *shiur* of my own accord. I was just following instructions. I would have loved to sit in *shiur* for an extra hour. The Rov responded, "Kenny, you know that when I wake up in the morning, I am in pain, and in the afternoon many times I am in pain. But when I deliver a *shiur*, I am pain-free. You know better than the doctors. You know that when I am teaching I have no pain." How true that statement was. Often the Rov entered *shiur* with blurred vision, yet he would read the *Gemara*, Rambam and Rashi as if his sight was fine. Sometimes he would ask me to open the *Gemara* to the *daf* he was teaching. He would point to the *Gemara* as if he was reading from inside the text, but I knew that he wasn't; he was reciting it by heart.

The next day I decided I was not going to remind the Rov when to stop. However, an hour-and-a-half into the *shiur*, the Rov turned to me and asked me how much time he had left.

The Rov had a reputation for being tough in *shiur*. The demands he made on his *talmidim* were due to the love he had for them and his commitment to being the best *melamed* he could be. However, outside of *shiur*, his demeanor was welcoming and gentle. I remember many times people left the Rov's apartment comforted, either because the Rov had a solution to their problems or simply because he had listened so intently. Hearing the pain of another Jew had an effect on the Rov. His meetings with people—whether it was with Menachem Begin or with a simple Jew—never became routine. After meeting with someone in distress, it would become harder for the Rov to walk, sleep and eat. Recognizing how the Rov internalized the pain of others, we made sure not to schedule consecutive appointments to ensure that he would not be emotionally taxed. The Rov cared about everyone, including Mrs. O'Shea, the Irish woman who cleaned his apartment, and the security guard in the Morgenstern hallway. He was a regal person and treated everyone with a tremendous amount of respect.

Toward the end of his tenure at YU, one of us would sleep in the Rov's apartment. The Rov would always wake up early, but I remember once waking up around three o'clock in the morning and realizing that the Rov was not in his bed. He was sitting in his chair in the living room. I asked him what was wrong. Apparently, that afternoon, some individuals had asked him a halachic question. He told them to return the next day for the answer. The Rov said that he knew what the halachah was but that it would be heartbreaking for them. Therefore, he could not sleep.

There was a special camaraderie that the Rov shared with Rov Moshe Feinstein, Rov Yaakov Ruderman and the Lubavitcher Rebbe. Whenever Chabad came out with a new *sefer*, the Rebbe would send *shelichim* [messengers] to the Rov to give him a copy. Rov Moshe, Rov Ruderman and the Rov would call one another before every *chag*.

On *Ta'anit Esther* of 1986, when Rov Moshe passed away, the Rov was not feeling well. His family was concerned and asked us *shamashim* not to inform the Rov of the *petirah* (death). That morning the *New York Times* that was normally delivered to the Rov's apartment was somehow not received, and the radio next to his chair that was always tuned to News Radio 88, was broken. We thought we had done a great job of shielding the Rov from the news.

I rarely spent time in the afternoon in the Rov's apartment. I was in Rov Hershel Schachter's *kollel*, and therefore I was only in the apartment late at night and early in the morning. However, the week before *Pesach*, the Rov had one of the other *shamashim* call the third-floor *beit midrash* and ask that I drive him to the airport. This was clearly not the norm. Until this day, every time I trovel on that stretch of the Grand Central Parkway, I have a hard time steering because I remember the Rov turning to me and saying, "Kenny, why didn't you tell me that Rov Moshe Feinstein was *niftar*?" At the time, I did not know what to say. Eventually as we got closer to the Eastern Airlines shuttle, I turned to him and said, "Rebbetzin Twersky [his daughter] told us not to tell you."

I thought we had done an incredible job of keeping this secret and wanted to understand where we had failed. "*Rebbe*, how did you find out?" I asked. He replied, "It was Rov Moshe's turn to call me to wish me a good *Yom Tov* and there could only be one reason that he didn't call."

The President of the Yeshiva, Rabbi Lamm, and the Rov used to meet on a regular basis. Initially there was a disagreement between them about where they should meet. Rabbi Lamm felt he should go to his *rebbe*; the meetings should take place in the Rov's apartment. However, the Rov felt that Rabbi Lamm was the president of Yeshiva University and that he should come to Rabbi Lamm's office, to show the position the proper respect. This argument was not settled by these two great minds, but by the president's administrative assistant Gladys Cherney and me. We would rotate; Rabbi Lamm would go to the Rov's apartment and the next meeting the Rov would walk to Rabbi Lamm's office.

When my wife and I got engaged, I wanted her to meet with the Rov; I asked his permission to bring her to the apartment. He immediately said yes. Parkinson's disease especially affected the Rov at night, and it was hard for him to walk. But when he heard that my *kallah* [bride] was at the door, he got out of his chair, walked on his own, opened the door and escorted her to the couch. Only after she sat did he take a seat.

It was a tremendous *berachah* that the Rov attended our wedding. Under the *chuppah* [wedding canopy] he had several memorable exchanges with us. Tragically, it was his last public event.

I think that most people think that the Rov inherited Rov Chaim's mind. The truth is that he also inherited Rov Chaim's heart. I would like to conclude with the idea Rov Ahron Soloveichik *zt"l* stated at his brother's funeral. When the *Beit Hamikdash* was burning, the *pirchei kehunah* (younger priests) went to the rooftop to surrender the Temple keys to heaven. Rov Ahron explained that this was not an act of greatness but rather one of cowardice. Even when the *Beit Hamikdash* was burning, no one had the right to surrender. And it was that surrender that doomed the Jewish people to a long and difficult *galut* [exile].

Over the past fifty years or so, many of us have had the privilege of being students of the Rov. His passing is not a time to surrender or abandon his calling but to recommit ourselves to be both the students and teachers of his tradition. We must recommit ourselves to embrace not a Torah shaped by modernity but a modernity that is shaped by Torah. May *Hakadosh Baruch Hu* strengthen us and give us the capacity to move from being students of the *mesorah*, students of *moreinu verabbeinu* haRov Yosef Dov Soloveitchik to being teachers of his *mesorah*.

Yehi zichro baruch.

The Rav as an Aging Giant (1983–1985)

Howard Jachter

What would you do if you were eighty years old, highly accomplished in your field and suffering from a debilitating illness? If you would be like most people, you would not dedicate yourself to hard work and a demanding schedule, since you have already accomplished your life's mission. Rav Yosef Dov Soloveitchik, despite having already established his fame and special place in Jewish history, strove vigorously to maximize his contribution to the Jewish people even at age eighty and beyond, despite the profound challenges and limitations imposed on him by serious illness.

Many high quality books and essays have been printed that explore the many facets of this legendary figure. However, I have yet to see a discussion of the heroism and courage displayed by the Rav during his last years of serving as a *rebbe* at Yeshiva University. I was privileged to witness this heroism having studied in the Rav's *shiur* from 1983–1985 and serving as a *shamash* to the Rav during this period of time, the last two and a half years that he graced the halls and neighborhood of the YU community. I hope our discussion will call attention to yet another aspect of the Rav's legacy to YU specifically and to the Jewish people in general.

In a public *shiur* delivered at YU in 1981, the Rav (aged seventy-eight at the time) cited *Tehillim* chapter ninety which proclaims "The days of our years are seventy years, and if with courage, eighty years." The Rav explained that the challenge facing an eighty year old is whether he can muster the courage to believe that he remains a worthwhile human being who still can contribute. It was obvious

---

Rabbi Howard Jachter is a teacher at the Torah Academy of Bergen County and has authored two volumes of *Gray Matter, Discourses in Contemporary Halachah.*

to anyone who was close to the Rav during his last years at YU that he met this challenge with a dignified but fierce determination.

It was heartbreaking to watch Rav Soloveitchik struggle to board an airplane, enter and leave a car and it was painfully obvious that it would have been so much more comfortable for the Rav to forego his weekly commute from Boston to New York to deliver *shiur* at Yeshiva. The Rav, though, was determined to continue contributing to *Am Yisrael*. I asked the senior *shamash* why the Rav, who needed two students to help him walk across Amsterdam Avenue from his first-floor apartment in the Morgenstern dormitory to his *shiur* room in Furst Hall, did not prefer to have a professional nurse assist him through his daily routines instead of the cadre of YU *talmidim* who served as his assistants. Wouldn't he receive a superior level of care, not to mention a greater measure of privacy? I was told that the Rav strongly preferred *talmidim* since he very much wanted the company of those with whom he could learn and discuss Torah. In retrospect, seeing each of the Rav's assistants emerging as an important rabbi and/or Jewish educator, I realize that the Rav also wanted to have the opportunity to develop a relationship with his *talmidim* that would inspire them to reach great heights within *Am Yisrael*. Indeed, every one of the *shamashim* took a bit of the Rav's personality and greatness and was propelled spiritually by the close encounter with this great man, whose dedication to Torah and *Am Yisrael* radiated from every fiber of his being.

The Rav's modesty was astounding. His apartment in the Morgenstern dorm was the height of simplicity and he treated every visitor young and old with the utmost respect. There was not a trace of arrogance in his personality, in accordance with the Rambam's teaching in *Hilchot Dei'ot* that even a bit of haughtiness is intolerable. I recall one Thursday in the fall of 1983 when Rav Ovadia Yosef visited YU and was driven by members of the Sephardic community in a beautiful black limousine, as is appropriate for a Torah giant. The Rav, on the other hand, was more than content to be driven to LaGuardia Airport in a *talmid*'s battered fifteen year old car. The Rav's assistants were deeply moved by his breathtaking humility to the extent that each finds arrogance distasteful. We think if the Rav exhibited no arrogance, what right has anyone to be arrogant. This is not to say that the Rav did not dress in a dignified, albeit modest, fashion. On the contrary, the Rav once gently chided me that I should dress in a more formal and dignified manner.

Despite the infirmities of old age, the Rav indefatigably pursued King David's challenge to "sing to Hashem a new song." I was astonished when the Rav announced a few weeks before *Pesach* of 1984 that he would devote his *shiur* to topics relating to *korban Pesach*, a topic on which he had not yet delivered *shiurim*. Surely the students would have been satisfied to hear Rav Soloveitchik deliver thoughts on *Pesach* that he had delivered in the prior forty years of lecturing at Yeshiva. The Rav, on the other hand, had different plans. There were new trails to blaze and frontiers to conquer even at age eighty. One day in November 1984 one of the *talmidim* pointed out to the Rav that in yesterday's *shiur* he had explained a passage in the Rambam in a different manner than he had explained that day. The Rav without batting an eyelash responded, "Never mind what I said yesterday." For the Rav, the Torah was ever fresh, as if it was presented by *Hashem* to His people anew every single day (see Rashi to *Devarim* 6.6).

In the midst of privately discussing the propriety of purchasing a German-manufactured automobile, the Rav displayed one of the facets of his greatness. He said to me that perhaps he had erred when he strongly urged Israeli Prime Minister David Ben-Gurion to desist from accepting reparations from the West German government. Israel's politicians and citizens were embroiled in a searing debate in the 1950's about whether to accept reparations from the German government in compensation for the Nazi atrocities. In a relatively rare public expression of his views regarding matters of public policy, the Rav at that time expressed his forceful opposition to the State of Israel accepting the proposed reparations. Astonishingly, thirty years later, the Rav said to me that maybe history proved him wrong, as the State of Israel would not have developed economically as it had done in the past three decades, had she not accepted money from the West Germans. How many older people have the courage and integrity to state upon reflection that they regard a major position that they fought for in years gone by as mistaken?

The Rav did not simply repeat assertions he had made in his earlier years. For example, in the course of preparing an article for *Hamevaser*, I asked the Rav in September 1985 to confirm the report that he believes that one does not recite *Birkat HaGomel* [blessing to thank G-d for bringing one to safety] upon the completion of a plane ride. The Rav confirmed that this had been his position. However, he told me that he had just modified his position and believed that one should recite this *bracha* upon safely returning from a very long-distance airplane trip such as from Israel to the United States. The Rav explained that in the wake of the *Achille Lauro* hijacking (in the Rav's words) "We had returned to the age of the pirates."

The Rav was a consummate gentleman. Once, a *shamash* had unwittingly granted an interview with the Rav to a Christian missionary. The *shamash* told that the Rav avoided debate and instead calmly and politely told the missionary that he did not share his views. When the *shamash* realized his error, he quickly escorted the missionary out of the Rav's apartment. On another occasion, a group of rabbis from Long Island met with the Rav regarding a quandary they had regarding an *eruv* they were trying to establish. When a halachic solution could not be found, one of the younger *rabbanim* in the group asked if it would be appropriate to place a *lechi* (portion of the *eruv*) on someone's property without permission. The Rav emphatically insisted that the *eruv* not be created in such a manner.

Interactions with the Rav were an encounter with history in the making. Although the Rav was famous for his long-held reluctance to publish his *shiurim* and lectures, towards the end of his career he relented and oversaw the publication of the *Yahrtzeit Shiurim* he delivered in memory of his father, Rav Moshe. He published with the assistance of many of his leading *talmidim* the two-volume *Shiurim L'Zecher Abba Mori zt"l*. I witnessed my other primary *rebbe*, Rav Aharon Lichtenstein *sh"lita*, prepare the second volume of this great work together with his father-in-law, the Rav. I was also privileged to see the Rav's daughter, Dr. Tovah Lichtenstein, present the second volume to the Rav and the deep satisfaction he experienced upon seeing the publication of his great work. In conversation the Rav told me that in the *Shiurim L'Zecher Abba zt"l* he sought to create a new genre in Torah literature, halachic prose. He told me that he sought to emulate the genre of scientists who present sophisticated science to a lay audience in a manner which may be understood even by a non-scientist. In the *shiurim*, the Rav said, he tried to present sophisticated Torah ideas in a manner that can be understood even by those who are not high-level *talmidei chachamim*. The Rav added, with a charming twinkle in his eye, that he believed that he succeeded in accomplishing this goal.

Although not privileged to hear the Rav's *shiurim* in his prime years, I nevertheless benefited from being with him during his last years at Yeshiva. The Rav impacted greatly on all those he interacted with even in his last years, especially with the *shamashim* with whom he developed a deep personal connection. We were witness to a giant of indomitable will who was a role model in every aspect of life. He bestowed some of his majestic personality upon his *talmidim*, which we in turn seek to impart to our *talmidim* as well.

On Translating *Ish ha-Halakhah* with the Rav: Rabbi Joseph Soloveitchik's Supplementary Notes to Halakhic Man

Lawrence Kaplan

Sometime in the late 1970s, at the request of my teacher and doctoral supervisor, Rabbi Professor Isadore Twersky, son-in-law of mori ve-rabbi, the Rav, I undertook to translate into English the Rav's classic essay, Ish ha-Halakhah, to be published by The Jewish Publication Society. After some discussion between the Rav, Professor Twersky, Maier Deshell, the editor of JPS, and me, it was agreed that I would prepare a draft of my translation and then meet with Rav to review it.

I proceeded upon the translation in my usual dilatory manner, and only in the spring of 1981 did I complete my draft. I arranged with the Rav to meet him at the home of the Twerskys in Brookline during the course of the summer to review the translation.

We met over a period of two weeks—one at the beginning of the summer, the other at summer's end—three days each week for several hours a day. Our procedure was as follows: I would read aloud from my draft and the Rav followed along in the Hebrew original, commenting extensively on my translation. At times we would struggle over almost every word and phrase, striving to capture its precise nuance, attempting to balance precision with elegance. More relevant for this essay, the Rav, not surprisingly as the author of Ish ha-Halakhah, felt free to expand upon, qualify, or simply revise and rewrite it. Taking down the Rav's dictation was a truly breathtaking experience, as I saw how the words just flowed from him, effort-

---

Dr. Lawrence Kaplan is Associate Professor at McGill University in Montreal and translated *Halakhic Man* by Rabbi Joseph B. Soloveitchik.

lessly combining to form entire sentences and whole paragraphs: always grammatical, always perfectly balanced and precisely phrased, always eloquent. Only on one or two occasions when the Rav wished to make particularly extensive additions, did he not rely on dictation but carefully wrote out his observations.

Since my task was to translate faithfully the original Hebrew text, and not—as Professor Twersky put it—to create a revised version, I did not include any of the Rav's revisions or expansions in the published translation. However, as already indicated, I had taken extensive notes, and I carefully culled all the expansions from these notes to form a pamphlet, "Rabbi Joseph Soloveitchik's Supplementary Notes to Halakhic Man," which I hope to publish in full in another forum. Here I will cite some of these notes, providing context and briefly commenting on their significance.

I wish to make it clear that since these notes were not included in the published translation neither the Rav nor Professor Twersky ever reviewed them or authorized their release. They therefore should be taken simply as impromptu observations and reflections of the Rav on Halakhic Man [Henceforth: HM], circa summer, 1981.

* * *

In his supplementary reflections the Rav significantly expanded upon his descriptions of cognitive man, homo religiosus, and, of course, the essay's hero, halakhic man himself. As in HM itself, the Rav stresses the drive for clarity, for answers, on the part of cognitive man. A new motif, found in the following expansion, is the Rav's emphasis on the spirit of optimism with which cognitive man approaches nature.

What motivates cognitive man in his search is his desire to resolve a mystery and to find a solution to the enigma of being. He does it by watching both the grand cosmic drama and the plain everydayness of nature. Cognitive man is basically an optimist, and he believes that his efforts to chart the vast and distant lanes of the universe and the ordinary byways of our immediate surroundings will not prove futile.

As the Rav points out in HM, p.10, in contrast to cognitive man, "the consciousness of homo religiosus is overflowing with questions that will never be resolved. He scans reality and is overcome with wonder, fixes his attention on the world and is astonished. Moreover, the astonishment which overcomes homo religiosus…is not just a means to an end… but is the ultimate goal and crowing glory of the process of cognition of homo religiosus." In a brief, but striking expansion the Rav elaborates upon the religious significance of homo religiosus' astonishment.

For homo religiosus astonishment is an experience in itself. To be astonished is to experience God.

In particular, the Rav in his expansions emphasizes the uniqueness of halakhic man. What is of particular interest is that, for the Rav, the fundamental differences between halakhic man and homo religiosus are clear. The point he consistently emphasizes is that despite significant commonalities shared by halakhic man and cognitive man, halakhic man fundamentally differs from cognitive man as well.

Thus, at the beginning of section V of HM the Rav notes, "Halakhic Man's approach to reality is, at the outset, devoid of any element of transcendence. Indeed, his entire attitude to the world stands out by virtue of its originality and uniqueness" (p. 17). The following expansion was interpolated by the Rav between these two sentences.

As such it differs fundamentally from the response of homo religiosus to the cosmic drama and is similar to that of cognitive man. However, neither should halakhic man's approach be identified with that of cognitive man.

In a similar vein, in HM, p. 38, the Rav writes:

> If a Jew cognizes … the Sabbath laws and the precepts concerning the sanctity of the day in all their particulars… he will perceive the sunset of a Sabbath eve not only as a natural cosmic phenomenon, but as an unsurpassably awe-inspiring, sacred, and exalted vision— an eternal sanctity that is reflected in the setting of the sun.

The Rav added a supplementary comment, serving as a lead in to the above, in which he expands upon the similarity and difference between halakhic man's mode of cognition and that of cognitive man.

To be sure, halakhic man studies the world, explores its paths and byways as does theoretical man. However, halakhic man's cognition not only perceives the cosmic dimension of existence but also discovers a halakhic identity in all phenomena. To be more precise, the cosmic dimension and halakhic identity merge into one experience.

This approach of the Rav particularly comes to the fore in his expansions to his discussion of halakhic man's attitude towards time. In HM, p.121, the Rav writes: "The halakhah ... is not particularly concerned with the metaphysics of time. Moreover, it is not inclined to transform time into pure, flowing, evanescent quality." To this he added the following supplementary observation:

> Again we are confronted by the basic discrepancy between the outlook of homo religiosus and that of halakhic man. The former will certainly subscribe to the philosophy of the qualitative experiential time—stream, while the latter is more inclined to accept time in scientific, quantitative categories.

This expansion leads back to the continuation of the paragraph: "The fact that the concept of time in Halakhah is bound up with measurable time periods ... demonstrates that Judaism ... wishes to establish a time that is fixed and determined." Lest the reader conclude, however, that halakhic man's attitude towards time is fundamentally similar to that of cognitive man, inasmuch as both view time in quantitative terms, the Rav, in a particularly eloquent observation, introduces the following caveat:

However, although halakhic man acts in a manner characteristic of the scientist in his approach to the problem of the two conceptual alternatives of time, time as streaming quality or frozen quantity, he nevertheless insists upon total time, not fragmented time. Time, for the scientist, is composed of infinitesimal moments. Time, for halakhic man, and in this respect he resembles homo religiosus, cannot be fragmented or torn apart. Rather quantifiable, mathematical time must find its full realization in eternity. Halakhic man thus quantifies time, and, simultaneous with such quantification, he turns time into an endless stream flowing between eternity and eternity.

The Rav, however, expanded not only upon the contrast between halakhic man and both cognitive man and homo religiosus, but upon another contrast as well. In HM, p. 90, the Rav speaks of halakhic man's "zeal for the truth, granted him by the Almighty," and goes on to say "Thus, halakhic man will not be overly lenient; but, at the same time, he will not be overly strict. The truth will call to account those who dishonor it, be they extreme rigorists or extreme permissivists." In the following comment the Rav elaborates upon the nature of halakhic man's objection to both the extreme rigorists and extreme permissivists.

Halakhic man is neither a liberal nor an extremist. He dislikes the liberal who is ready to compromise, but also disapproves of the extremist who introduces superficial literalism into the system of halakhic truth.

If I might, at this point, allow myself to interpolate my own purely personal, "unscientific" comment, I believe that this incisive observation is exceptionally prescient and sheds much light on the roots of certain recent unfortunate developments taking place within the Orthodox community, both on the left and on the right. Indeed, a sage is greater than a prophet!

One of the characteristics of halakhic man that the Rav emphasizes in HM is the exoteric nature of his religious viewpoint, as expressed particularly in halakhic man's approach to prayer. In this connection, in HM, p. 43, the Rav writes:

> No person, according to the Halakhah, needs the aid of others in order to approach God. A person needs no advocates or special pleaders.... And just as the Halakhah rejects the notion of human intercessors, so, too, it rejects the notion of transcendental intercessors such as angels or seraphim.

In a supplementary observation the Rav elaborates on halakhic man's objection to addressing prayers to angels.

For this reason, many scholars omitted the recital of any kind of request or petition addressed to angels, even though such a petition, seen from a liturgical point of view, would seem in place, inasmuch as it enhances the ecstasy of the prayer community. We are confronted here by a glaring discrepancy between the custom of the average Jew who, in moments of urgency and crisis, is guided by his emotional needs to address himself not only to the Almighty but also to His ministering angels and the practice of halakhic man for whom the principle of religious exoterism, as embodied in the a priori halakhic concept of prayer, overrules all experiential needs.

However, the Rav's blanket assertion that "a person needs no advocates or special pleaders" raises the obvious objection that in fact we do ask people to pray on our behalf. In response to this objection, the Rav added the following extended supplementary comment.

This is the lengthiest of the Rav's expansions, and he carefully wrote it out in longhand.

Of course Jewish prayer is community prayer. I pray for the many; the many pray for me. We find many instances in the Bible when one individual prays for another. Moses, for instance, prayed for Aaron. However, the prayer of the community is rooted in the gesture of praying together, not in that of praying for each other. People who share distress together share also in the act of praying. Moses prayed for Aaron because he experienced the suffering and travail of Aaron. He suffered no less than Aaron the pangs of frustration. Prayer is motivated by need. To pray for each other means to live through a common passional experience which urges, which impels man to pray together.

Therefore it is permissible, moreover commendable, to ask someone to pray for me, since something very important will be manifested by praying together, viz., the unity of existential destiny, the oneness of the sufferer and fellow sufferer, even though the latter physically feels no pain.

What has been forbidden is to plead with transcendental beings such as angels and seraphim to pray on one's behalf. The angels are not exposed to suffering; they feel no need which is sufficient to stimulate prayer. They cannot join the sufferer, cannot experience his tragic destiny. They, should they happen to intercede one's behalf, would find themselves praying for, not with the individual.

It is unclear whether the Rav in drawing this sharp distinction in this supplementary observation between asking humans to pray on one's behalf and asking angels to do so is just clarifying the position he expressed in HM or perhaps tacitly modifying it.

This exoteric approach of halakhic man to prayer, for the Rav, expresses itself in another way. In the following supplementary observation the Rav expands upon the contrast he draws in HM, pp. 58–59, between halakhic man's approach to prayer and that of both homo religiosus and his more theoretical variant, the religious philosopher, as exemplified above all by Maimonides.

The halakhah rejects both the powerful subjective emotion sweeping homo religiosus off his feet as well as the elegant, abstract speculative concepts produced by the philosophical mind. When halakhic man prays, for example, it is in a quiet and controlled manner, in accordance with a certain protocol: neither dancing, nor singing, nor ecstatic gesticulations form part of the halakhic concept

of prayer. And at the same time halakhic man does not allow esoteric philosophical abstractions to determine the text of prayer.
Recital of prayers, for halakhic man, is always in accordance with
the simple logic, the sturdy common sense of the average prayerful
community.

As is well known, the Rav in HM recounts many anecdotes about
his father, R. Moshe Soloveitchik and his grandfathers, R. Hayyim
Soloveitchik and R. Elijah Pruzna [Feinstein], viewing them as ex-
emplars, par excellence, of halakhic man. One story in particular
aroused a great deal of controversy and criticism.

Once [the Rav relates] my father was standing on the synagogue
platform on Rosh Ha-Shanah, ready and prepared to guide the
order of the sounding of the shofar. The shofar-sounder, a God-fear-
ing Habad Hasid, who was very knowledgeable in the mystical doctrine of the "Alter Rebbe," R. Shneur Zalman of Lyady, began to
weep. My father turned to him and said: "Do you weep when you
take the lulav? Why then do you weep when you sound the shofar?
Are not both commandments of God?" (pp. 60–61)

The Rav goes on to explain that the shofar-sounder wept, because
according to mystical doctrine, "the sounding of the shofar protests
against reality and denies the universe itself," in contrast to "the taking of the lulav and the etrog, [which] sustains and affirms the beautiful and resplendent world." Halakhic man, however, the Rav
notes, "is completely immersed in the cosmos whether on Rosh Ha-
Shanah or Sukkot" (p. 62).

Be the Rav's explanation of the significance of this story as it may,
upon being told the story one prominent Rosh Yeshiva was heard to
exclaim: "How is it possible to criticize a pious Jew for crying when
performing a mitzvah?!" In two supplementary observations the
Rav tacitly sought to respond this criticism.

First he explains the view of the Habad shofar-sounder.

Thus, for the mystic, this esoteric distinction between the symbolic significance of the commandments of sounding the shofar and
taking the lulav and the etrog finds particular expression in the emotional aura surrounding these commandments.

Then he proceeds to explain the position of halakhic man.

Of course the halakhah was aware of the uniqueness of the holiness of Rosh Ha-Shanah and Yom Kippur as days of awe. "R. Ab-
bahu said: The ministering angels asked the Holy One, blessed be
He: Why doesn't Israel recite songs of praise [i.e., Hallel] before Thee

on Rosh Ha-Shanah and Yom Kippur? He replied: Is it possible that the King is sitting on His throne of judgment and the books of the living and the books of the dead are opened before Him and Israel should recite songs of praise?!" [Rosh Ha-Shanah 32b] Maimonides adds, "Hallel is not recited on Rosh Ha-Shanah and Yom Kippur because they are days of repentance, awe and fear, not days of especial rejoicing." [Laws of Hanukah 3:6] Yet the commandment of sounding the shofar is performed by halakhic man in a spirit similar to that of taking the lulav.

One may wonder whether the "Yet" at the paragraph's end truly counterbalances the "Of course" at its beginning; or, to state the matter differently, whether this comment satisfactorily responds to the objection of the prominent Rosh Yeshiva. Indeed, one may perhaps wonder further whether the Rav may not have been aware of the fact that his response was not entirely satisfactory.

Finally, scholars have argued regarding the extent to which HM's mode of analysis can be characterized as dialectical. While some stress the essay's dialectical quality, others, including myself, maintain that the dialectical moment in the essay just serves as a prelude to the moment of reconciliation and synthesis. Whatever one's opinion on this question, it is noteworthy that in many of the Rav's supplementary observations he strikes a distinctly dialectical pose.

Thus, at the very beginning of HM, the Rav notes:

> Halakhic man is an antinomic type for a dual reason: 1) he bears within the deep recesses of his personality the soul of homo religiosus, that soul which...suffers from the pangs of self-contradiction and self-negation; 2) at the same time halakhic man's personality also embraces the soul of cognitive man, and this soul contradicts all the desires and strivings of the religious soul. (pp. 3–4)

In his very first supplementary comment, the Rav expands upon this second reason.

In this respect, then, halakhic man suffers from an antinomic existence precisely because of the clash between the two personas abiding within him. The goals of homo religiosus differ from that of cognitive man. Their scales of value are incommensurate; they are committed to different teleologies.

This heightened dialectical approach becomes especially evident if we contrast the explanation offered by the Rav in the text of HM itself as to how to understand the religious significance of the laws of mourning as set forth by Maimonides with the explanation offered in an appended supplementary comment. In HM, pp. 76–77, the Rav writes:

In times of mourning and dejection, in moments of pain and grief…, [halakhic man] is not crushed by his burden and is not given over to despair and black depression. His affective life is characterized by a fine equilibrium, a Stoic tranquility. It exemplifies the Aristotelian golden mean and the ideal of the well balanced personality set forth by Maimonides; it is guided by the knowledge of the inevitable and the means of triumphing over it provided by the rule of the Halakhah. "He who does not mourn for his dead relative as prescribed by the Sages is cruel; but he who grieves for them more than is customary is stupid" (Laws of Mourning 13:1). This is the standard of halakhic man in the affective realm.

But in his supplementary comment the Rav offers a strikingly different understanding of this statement of the Rambam. Rather than indicating that the "affective life" of halakhic man when confronted by death "is characterized by a fine equilibrium, a Stoic tranquility… [and] exemplifies the Aristotelian golden mean and the ideal of the well balanced personality set forth by Maimonides," it rather gives voice to a sharply dialectical approach to death comprised of defiance and surrender.

The halakhah is conscious of the omnipotence of nature and the inevitable and invincible with which man is confronted. At the same time it attempts to defy the inevitable in existence. This dialectical approach is reflected in the laws of mourning which express protest against and defiance of nature as well as surrender to God, the Creator of the inevitable in the cosmic drama. The halakhah has commanded man to mourn. What is mourning if not an attempt to defy nature and change it? On the other hand, the halakhah said that excessive mourning is forbidden because it shows an immature mind and childish naiveté.

And one last example. In his famous note 114 (pp. 157–158), citing an extended excerpt from Y. L. Peretz' short story, "Travel Pictures: A Little Boy," the Rav very eloquently and movingly argues that Peretz's affecting portrait of the little orphan boy, both wailing for an extra onion and praying that the Messiah would come and the moon would become bigger, may serve as a symbol of the Jewish people as a whole.

The orphan forgets that his father will soon take for himself a new wife, a stepmother, and that he will become a stepchild who will have to cry for a piece of bread; he prays for the suffering moon, pining away on account of her sin, and he sees in her torments a cosmic injustice. Is not the image of the Jewish people reflected in such yearnings? Bitter exile and cosmic righteousness, the bleak life of the ghetto and the dream about the replenishment of the moon, the yearnings for the perfection of creation and ugly poverty—can there be a greater coincidence of opposites?

In the following expansion, the very last the Rav added to HM, he elaborates on this dialectical portrait.

Isn't the Jew, as portrayed in this short sketch of Peretz, a combination of precisely these irreconcilable opposites: pettiness bordering on the ridiculous and cosmic hopes bordering on the metaphysical? Who is the Jew if not a person who both yearns for cosmic redemption and longs for a miserable scallion and slice of bread?

* * *

As I stated above, in my attempt to carry out my mandate to translate faithfully the original Hebrew text, I did not include any of the Rav's suggested revisions of the text in the published translation. At two points in the text, however, my translation diverges in slight but perhaps significant ways from the Hebrew original. In the first instance the change was introduced inadvertently; in the second it was introduced deliberately.

The inadvertent change: After the Rav concludes his discussion of halakhic man's exoteric approach to prayer (HM, p. 44), he—at least according to my English translation—goes on to say the following: "This exoteric approach is also the reason why many great halakhic scholars disapproved of the cult of the tzaddik in the Hassidic world. These great halakhic men had no sympathy for any practice which, in their opinion, contradicts such a fundamental halakhic principle as religious exoterism."

A comparison with the Hebrew original will show that my English text is a faithful, albeit somewhat expanded, translation of the original—faithful, that is, with, in my view, one significant exception. One day, after my translation appeared, I happened to be rereading it and comparing it against the original when I noticed that the phrase "in their opinion" has no counterpart in the original and that, whether intended so or not, it serves as a way whereby the Rav subtly disassociates himself from the view expressed by these "great halakhic men." I, of course, must take ultimate responsibility for the translation, but it would seem that the Rav, under the guise of a purely stylistic expansion, succeeded in, as it were, "smuggling" this phrase, with its substantive implications, past me. Were a second edition of HM to appear, I would delete the phrase.

The deliberate change: In the very last section of HM (p.134) the Rav speaks of Judaism's "awareness of and esteem for the individual," and, in this connection, cites the famous mishnah in Sanhedrin (4:6) thusly: "Kol ha-mekayyem nefesh ahat mi-Yisrael, ke-ilu kiyyem `olam maleh," "He who preserves a single life from Israel it is as though he preserved an entire world." For a long time I was of two minds as to how to translate this mishnah. Leaving to the side my universalistic tendencies, there were three reasons why I was tempted to leave out the word "mi-Yisrael." First: As rabbinic scholars like Hanokh Albeck and Ephraim Urbach have noted, the word "mi-Yisrael" is not to be found in the best manuscripts of the Mishnah. Indeed, it is not found in the text of this mishnah in the Rambam's Perush `al ha-Mishnah. Second: The Rambam in Laws of Sanhedrin 12:3, in citing this mishnah, omits the word "mi-Yisrael," though, to be sure, in Laws of Murder and the Preservation of Life 1:16, he cites the mishnah with the word "mi-Yisrael." (A quick glance at the differing contexts of these two halakhot should suffice to enable one to account for the difference.) Third, and most important: The Rav himself in his essay, "The Community," (Tradition Spring, 1978), p. 10, cites the mishnah, omitting the word "mi-Yisrael." Despite all these considerations, mindful of my mandate I said to myself, "No hokhmes. If the Rav cited the mishnah using the word 'mi-Yisrael,' that's how I'll translate it."

As I said earlier, our procedure was that I would read aloud from my draft and the Rav followed along in the Hebrew original, commenting extensively. When I came to this passage I proceeded to read: "He who preserves a single life from Israel it is as though...." Before I could finish the Rav interrupted me. I can still hear the tone and cadence of his voice saying clearly and emphatically, "Strike out 'from Israel'." I was more than happy to comply.

* * *

I would like to end on a personal note. One day as I was coming in to meet with the Rav a former student of his was just leaving and was profusely thanking the Rav for all his help. After the student left, the Rav turned to me and said, "He was asking me for my help in finding him a position as a Maggid Shi`ur." He then continued: "The problem with my students is that they all want to be Roshei Yeshiva. Now if they wanted to become melamdim, that would be fine, because to be a melamed is an act of Hesed. But to be a Rosh Yeshiva—that's Gevurah!" I think back to the many hours I spent with the Rav on those long hot summer days in Brookline years ago, and as I recall the warmth and charm with which he put me at ease and made me feel welcome, as I recall his wit and eloquence, and especially as I recall the time and effort and, indeed, the profound intellectual energy and creativity he expended in reviewing my translation, I feel privileged to have been the recipient of so much of the Rav's Gevurah and Hesed alike.

Glossary

Acharon(im) scholar(s) of the later centuries

Aggadah (aggadita) the portions of the Talmud that are not *halakhah*

a"h (alav ha-shalom) may he rest in peace

Bavli Babylonian Talmud

bais midrash [also spelled *beit midrash, beth hamedrash*] study hall

Brisk Yiddish name for Brest-Litovsk, a city in eastern Europe that became famous in Torah study for the generations of the Soloveitchik family who taught there; their approach became known as the *Brisker derekh*

chag ha-semikhah celebration of rabbinic ordination

chavrusa [also *chevruta*] study partner

chevra shas Talmud study group

chiddush(im) new insight(s), interpretation(s) [also spelled *hiddush*]

da'as Torah knowledge of Torah (wisdom that comes from profound knowledge of Torah)

derekh approach; way

derekh halimud approach in learning

drashah, plural

drashot exposition(s), sermon(s)

eruv symbolic act or enclosure to establish a community or a continuity of space or time for Sabbath purposes

gadol (plural gedolim) great person(s)

gadol ha-dor great one of the generation

gaon genius [plural *Geonim;* also names the scholars of the 9th to 11th centuries]

Gemara the portion of the Talmud written by the *Amora'im*, scholars in the period after the *Mishnah*, which was the work of the *Tanna'im*

Halakhah (also spelled *halacha*) Jewish law

halakhah le'ma'aseh applied, as opposed to theoretcal, Jewish law

347

haredi a devout person

hashkafah outlook, philosophy

hiddush(im) new interpretation(s)

hiddushei Torah new interpretations in Torah

ilui prodigy

kollel community (in Torah study, a community of students) "learn"
    from Yiddish

lernen=study; "learn by=study with (a translation of Yiddish *lernen*
    bei)

lomdus (Torah) learning, erudition

mashgiach ruchani director of religious guidance

mesekhta (also spelled *mesechta* or *massekhta*) tractate of the Talmud

mesorah tradition (what is transmitted from generation to genera-
    tion)

musmakh(im) ordained rabbi(s)

muvhak distinguished

parshah portion; short-hand way of referring to the weekly portion
    of the Torah

pasken to judge, rule, decide

p'sak judgment; verdict; ruling

posek (im) decider(s) of Jewish law

rebbe teacher; when the 'R' is upper-case, either the teacher or a Has-
    sidic leader is being addressed

RIETS Rabbi Isaac Elchanan Theological Seminary, the rabbinic
    school of Yeshiva University

Rishonim early scholars

rosh(ei) ha-yeshiva head(s) of the yeshiva

sefer (sefarim) book(s)

sefer Torah Torah scroll

semikhah rabbinic ordination

sevara, svara speculation, logical argument, methodical train of
    thought

shailah or *she'eilah* (plural *she'eilot*) question(s) in Jewish law

Shas shisha sidrei Mishnah the six orders of the *Mishnah*

shiur lesson; an active process with the teacher and student both
    discovering and arguing in an effort to probe the full meaning of
    the text

maggid shiur one who gives the lesson

sh"lita acronym for "may he live a good, long life"

sugya (sugyot) unit(s) of halakhic discussion

talmid(im) student(s)

talmid hakham scholar, learned person

Torah uMadda Torah and secular studies, the two disciplines at
    Yeshiva University

yar[c]hei kallah a Torah study session of several days' duration, pri-
    marily for non-full time students

yehi zikhro barukh may his memory be blessed

Yerushalmi the Jerusalem Talmud, composed in Israel

zt"l (zekher tzaddik li'v'rakhah) of blessed memory